Here's why CQI is the hottest topic on today's college campuses:

"Traditional pedagogies are not compatible with the quality practices and needs of evolving contemporary industry. In fact, many corporations are suggesting that our products – students – lack necessary skills and competencies required of the modern workforce . . . the cost of training the college graduates we [business] have hired recently in both rudimentary and functional skills has almost caught up with the cost of sending them to school in the first place . . . ."

– Shulman, Luechauer

"Administrators think they do well by absorbing outside flack so that faculty can do their jobs. In fact, faculty may have been shielded so effectively that they don't know the wolf is at the door. Most don't recognize that the questions being asked by the public (about how and how much faculty work) are serious and are not likely to go away."

– Banta

"Some articles on TQM stress top-down leadership. . . . Others, particularly in education, suggest that bottom-up leadership is the key. It takes both . . . . The power motivating change must come from faculty who value learning, teaching and service enough to want to improve. . . . Top-down leadership must empower faculty to lead, encourage innovation, and provide funding and freedom to experiment."

– Mullin, Wilson, Grelle

"There is a significant difference between stating a commitment for TQM and actually incorporating the principles in day-to-day behavior. Most organizations beginning the quality journey still adhere to policies and procedures burdened with redundancies and unnecessary inspections . . . ."

– Winter, Winter

CONTINUOUS
QUALITY
IMPROVEMENT

Making the Transition to Education

EDITED BY DEAN L. HUBBARD

PRESCOTT PUBLISHING CO.

Continuous Quality Improvement:
Making the Transition to Education
Edited by Dean L. Hubbard

Copyright © 1993 by Prescott Publishing Co.
P.O. Box 713, Maryville, MO 64468

Designed by Carole Gieseke

Printed in the United States of America
First Printing: 1993
10 9 8 7 6 5 4 3 2 1

Library of Congress Cataloging in Publication Data
Continuous quality improvement: making the transition to
education / Dean L. Hubbard
    p. cm.
Includes bibliographical references and index.
ISBN 0-9633819-8-9
    1. School management and organization – United States.
2. Education – United States – Quality control.
3. Total quality management – United States.
    1. Hubbard, Dean Leon.

LB2085.C65 1993 371.2 QB193-993 CIP 93-85009
ISBN 0-9633819-8-9: $22.95 Softcover

TABLE OF CONTENTS

Editor's Preface

The perception is becoming widespread that higher education – along with elementary and secondary education – is failing to keep pace with the standards of quality required for this nation to remain competitive in a global economy. Enough books have been written pointing out the shortcomings of education to convince the average person, at least, that serious attempts are in order to ameliorate the problems which appear to plague education at all levels. Thus, there seems to be a growing need for books describing specific strategies for managing quality in an educational setting. While several recent titles address individual approaches to, or the philosophical underpinnings of, Continuous Quality Improvement (CQI), this book is one of the few collections of case studies describing successful attempts to implement quality management concepts in the variety of settings which make up a typical college or university.

Administrators, board members, faculty and other students of higher education will benefit from a thoughtful, analytical and sensitive reading of *Continuous Quality Improvement*. While every institution has its own unique features which must be taken into account when considering any innovation, the functions of most collegiate institutions overlap sufficiently so that we can learn a great deal from each other, in spite of differences in size, clientele, mission and the like. Further, while acronyms such as "TQM" – along with an excessive devotion to gurus and an obsessive focus on tools and techniques – will doubtless pass, it is inconceivable that Americans will suddenly decide that quality is no longer important. By sharply focusing on ways to improve the quality of higher education, this book demonstrates that there is, indeed, an application in higher education for the principles and techniques of Continuous Quality Improvement currently being refined in this nation's leading industries.

The thesis of the book is straightforward: *The principles and techniques for continuously improving quality, which have been demonstrated as effective in manufacturing and service environments, can be applied or adapted to educational institutions.*

More than 40 authors contributed to the book, representing the widest possible array of functions within the academy and from industry: presidents, chief academic officers, deans, faculty, directors of student and academic services, consultants, and a Fulbright Fellow. Each was asked to describe specific, first-hand examples of CQI applications in education which had worked. In fulfilling their assignment, each demonstrates a clear grasp of the nuances of the topic which will capture the attention and respect of educators in every part of the enterprise. They display a convincing sensitivity to higher education as a unique organizational type and, in that context, discuss potential applications of CQI. They avoid sweeping caricatures of administrators and faculty as recalcitrant, arrogant and unwilling to consider new approaches – the impression one frequently gets from higher education's critics. (While some academics – certainly not all – display those attitudes, adoption of that posture not only alienates the entire group, but also fails to come to grips with the complex issues associated with the topic we have set out to explore.)

Several hurdles are surmounted. For example, those wishing to use approaches which have succeeded in improving quality in industry as a template for higher education must figure out how to gain general acceptance for a definition of quality which reflects the needs and dreams of students, rather than the aspirations of those who run the enterprise. In the words of a recent AGB report, *Trustees and Troubled Times in Higher Education* (AGB, 1992), too often quality in higher education "is measured more by the kinds of students excluded and turned down than by the kinds of students included and turned out...not by how much value is added to students' knowledge, but by the size of the endowment, the range of scores and the number of doctorates produced." The report goes on to suggest that "quality, in short, has become something to stoke academic egos instead of students' dreams." Simply asserting that quality must be defined differently in different settings does not remove the problem. In practice, a hierarchy of definitions of quality for higher education must be developed, all of which are different in some respects, but, nonetheless, complementary (aligned, to use the parlance of the Malcolm Baldrige National Quality Award). Several authors give examples of how this can work in practice.

A second problem when improving the quality of education is the need to differentiate the process from the product. In spite of Deming's eschewal of Management By Objectives, most governors and legislators feel that outcomes are the only appropriate measure of quality. Yet, many of those advocating reform in elementary and secondary schools point to excessive intrusion into the realm of process as a main cause for current problems. Indeed, at least at the collegiate level, it would be considered an unacceptable transgression of academic freedom to prescribe how to teach. Thus, a strong case needs to be made to convince higher education's constituents that careful attention to the process of education is an appropriate starting point. Several of the authors in this book make that case.

Third, the temptation to focus only on what is easily manageable must be avoided. Several past reports of efforts to apply TQM in higher education contained an admission that, so far, they have been unable to apply such principles to the academic side of the enterprise. This seems equivalent to an automobile manufacturer focusing on tidying up the grounds and improving food in the cafeteria rather than making certain the cars run. At the risk of minimizing their importance, starting with internal services may send a wrong signal regarding the central mission of the organization. Would it not be better to begin with curriculum and instruction, the heart of the institution, and then hope that the concepts will spread to other parts of the institution? The second section of this book is devoted to successful examples of CQI principles being applied to the relationship between student learning and instruction.

Finally, there is the temptation to focus on what is easily measurable. In education, that often means the lower-order cognitive skills of recall and understanding, as opposed to the higher-order skills of analysis, synthesis and evaluation. In fact, since creative thinking may not blossom until several years after the student has graduated from college, test results must always be viewed somewhat tentatively. Furthermore, it is difficult to establish cause-effect relationships between particular curricula or teaching strategies and higher-order cognitive skills. Nonetheless, assessment lies at the heart of CQI. This issue is also addressed by several of our authors.

After reading this book, one comes away convinced that education can and must be improved in America. Furthermore, as those of us in education confront the challenge, it is clear that there is much we can learn from Deming, Crosby, Juran, Taguchi and others who are working systematically to improve quality in the manufacturing and service sectors of this nation.

As editor of this work, I am particularly indebted to my co-authors. Their willingness, promptness in meeting deadlines, skill in writing, and adeptness made my task easy. The editorial team, Carole Gieseke, Patti Smedley and Melody Lowe, demonstrated a mastery of the details of their profession that embodies the essence of what we are discussing: quality.

Dean L. Hubbard

AGB Higher Education Issues Panel, *Trustees and Troubled Times in Higher Education*, Washington, D.C.: Association of Governing Boards of Colleges and Universities, 1992, p. 22.

PART I:

CQI on the Campus

1

Process Improvements Using Team Environments

Scot M. Faulkner

"What we need to do is eliminate the dumb stuff we are doing."

The president of a 9,000-student university looked around the table at his provost, his vice presidents, and the dean of the Business School (who had initiated the discussion). They had all heard and read extensively about Quality Management, but had never heard it expressed in such eloquently simple terms.

That is the challenge for educational institutions — to capture the true essence of Quality Management and make it user-friendly. Philip Crosby, one of the founders of the modern quality movement, stated it best: "If you work hard enough, you can make quality management difficult."

It has been the unfortunate experience of many companies and organizations that they become swamped in the dogma, factions, techniques and terminology of quality. And they lose sight of why they tried Quality Management in the first place. Too many Quality Management implementations sink under the weight of elaborate implementation plans, involving multiple committees and subcommittees.

The University president and his executive staff faced the dilemma of bringing Quality Management to an entire campus and staying focused on what quality is really about. How should they begin?

First, the president's remark reminded everyone around the table to focus on the simple basics of quality. Quality Management is, simply put, common sense performed systematically. The idea is to understand that normal people, if properly motivated, will do the right things when allowed by management to do so. Problems can be identified, solved and ultimately prevented when management gives employees the information they need to provide quality goods and services to others.

Second, the University staff remembered that Quality Management implementations fail when they try to create artificial settings and artificial activities. People already conduct work and interact with others to make an existing organization or institution viable. The pathway to success lies in recognition of these existing arrangements and activities and making them effective.

They decided to use existing work groups as the basis of their Quality Management effort. They realized that many organizations have been able to achieve sustainable improvement through a straight-forward effort of education, and by improving the way existing groups work and the way they address their work.

The basic building block of any successful Quality Management implementation is teamwork. More basic than this is understanding what a team is and how to make the team work for the general good of the institution.

Education is full of groups which can become teams: there are faculty groupings under academic departments; there is the administrative core of the college or university; there is usually a student government or faculty/student "community council;" there is an alumni organization.

There is a difference between a group and a team. Having people meet once a week to discuss specific agenda items is a group meeting. For a team to develop out of this environment takes time and conscious effort.

IDENTIFYING TEAMS

What is a team? There have been whole books written on the subject. A group turns into a team by developing two complimentary characteristics: the ability to achieve results and the ability to sustain and renew itself. Both are needed for a team to live and thrive. There have been many examples of groups of people achieving success but never wanting to work with each other again. There are also many examples of well-meaning people enjoying each other's comraderie but never accomplishing anything.

Before anyone can identify groups for team development, you have to understand why you are embarking on this effort. The University started its implementation of team development as a part of a Quality Management effort. It decided, through a "Quality Awareness Session," that it needed to determine why it was trying Quality Management in the first place. The president and his administration recognized that they needed a better answer than "because we think we need quality." They needed a reference point, a "measure of success," to assess how things were going, and what still needed to be done next to assure and sustain success. One dean suggested using the "five whys" developed by Japanese industry (that is where one asks as many "why" questions as is needed to find the root cause of a problem or issue). For example:

"We need to start a quality effort."

"Why?"

"Because other colleges are trying it."

"Why?"

"Because they think it will reduce costs."

"Why?"

"Because it has worked in industry. Costs were killing their capabilities. Industries couldn't compete. They found that many costs were avoidable. This Quality Management stuff seems to develop an ability for people to work smarter and to find ways of making things better."

"What does that have to do with us?"

"We are being squeezed. We can't raise tuition. Yet, we must improve our services. We must also be more responsive to our students."

"Why?"

"Because our costs are out of control. . . . Also, it seems things just don't happen the way they are planned."

"Why?"

"Because people don't communicate with each other."

"Why?"

"Because everyone is more concerned about their own turf than with the mission of the school."

"Why?"

. . .and so it goes until a "change agenda" is developed.

The change agenda took more than one meeting of the president's executives. The agenda ended up looking like a wish list of what whould be different if everything worked the way everyone hoped. This agenda was then refined. Some of the vice presidents, conferring with the deans, addressed specific areas under their responsibility. Finally, the list was expressed in realistic, measurable terms.

A general brainstorming session added a rough estimate

of how long each change would take. After a month of sporadic discussion, a road map for the future was ready.

Armed with the change agenda, the president and his administration began to assess whether any groups within the University needed to be created to address their identified issues, or whether existing groups could cover the priorities on their list.

DEVELOPING TEAMS

The University decided to start with existing group formats, leaving the work of establishing ad hoc groups until later. For them, the most common group was the staff meeting. A person with line responsibility meets with his or her direct reports to hear about their past, present and future activities. Staff meetings are people's least favorite meeting (unless you include executive briefings). Information may or may not really be shared. It may be a forum for competition, and it sometimes becomes a hunt for dropped balls, cracks things fell through or scapegoats. And it may just be deadly boring. Some staff meetings die out as "weekly" becomes "monthly," as "monthly" becomes "when we have something to discuss." What to do?

The president and his administration understood that, with a focused effort, staff meetings can be successful. In one session, they thought about the meetings that had been useful and positive in their lives; some recalled community volunteer meetings. They were asked, "What made it positive?" Their list included:

❖ There was a real reason to meet
❖ The meeting had structure, an agenda
❖ The topic was of personal interest
❖ They had a vested interest in the outcome
❖ They played an active role in the proceedings
❖ Their role was valued by others

❖ Something actually got done

This was a great starting point for a lively discussion on staff meetings. They realized that their direct reports probably thought the same way. They also asked themselves, "Why meet? What is in it for me? What is in it for anybody else? Can we get something done?"

The administration realized this is where the principles of Quality Management intersected with daily routine. Take the change agenda, divide the items into those which impact specific office operations, then have those offices discuss an assigned issue at a staff meeting. Have these staffs then "flesh out" the issue, and make it real for them. Have them further divide the issue into digestible (implementable) components. Then, have them determine if some aspect of a strategic issue can be completed next month or next semester.

They understood the importance of digestibility. One vice president recalled how the United States got to the moon in the 1960s. Of course, there was the vision: President Kennedy said, "We shall place a man on the moon by the end of this decade." But how did it happen? First, the Mercury Program tested the feasibility of manned flight, then Gemini tested docking and flight longevity, then — and only then — did Apollo achieve the ultimate goal. Along the way, each piece of the larger effort was completed, celebrated and built upon.

The vice president concluded, "The staffs at our school are our Mercury Program. We showed it works there; we can launch a larger effort."

This decisive meeting of the administration also looked at another component of Quality Management. In staff meeting environments (in this case, those staff which reported to the vice presidents or deans of the individual Colleges, or who support operations at the University), the strategic or macro-level concerns, (which are important to the administration) may not be the burning issues of the day. The people around those staff tables are already facing a full desk of issues and problems. For a staff meeting to be relevant to everyone, day-to-day issues should also be discussed. Many organizations have found that this "cleaning up the landscape" of smaller, staff-oriented issues, opens the door for working on larger-scale issues. It truly could be the Mercury Program as it shows the feasibility of effort, in this case through problem solving and working together.

It was the consensus of the group to defer the assigning of strategic action items and, instead, focus first on the issues generated within the staffs. "So how do we do this?" asked one of the vice presidents around the president's table.

First, it was decided that all vice presidents and deans must understand one of the basics of quality: that people will do the right thing if allowed by management to do so. Management must send out a clear, consistent signal — backed up by consistent, sustained actions — which shows that an open, supportive environment exists in the staff meeting and in the work environment in general. To accomplish this, an executive-level seminar on quality was scheduled.

The role of manager/executive as facilitator was difficult for some of the administrators to understand, let alone adopt as a behavior. After additional discussion, the administrative team, along with the deans, decided a focused team-development effort was warranted. The administration and deans opted for a joint one-day, team-building retreat to be held off-site. The goal of the session was for everyone to leave understanding what makes for an effective team. They sought a facilitator who would not just recite someone's litany of terms and concepts. They wanted to learn from actual structured team situations.

THE TEAM RETREAT

Groups become teams through a number of predictable steps. These steps can take weeks or minutes, depending upon the circumstances. Three leading scholars on team behavior state the steps in these ways:

Schultz: Inclusion/Control/Affection
Bion: Flight/Fight/Unite
Tuckman: Form/Storm/Norm/Perform

What each is saying is that group members become members of a defined team once they have gone through various stages of getting acquainted, identifying each participant's similarities and differences from others in the group, and the group as a whole coming to terms with these issues.

The team retreat, or team-building session, drew out these issues quickly and constructively by using simulations coupled with debriefing discussions. The challenge was to have simulations that were interesting, stimulating, relevant and insightful. Thankfully, numerous resources are available to find the right selection. One of the most popular is the *Encyclopedia of Icebreakers*, produced by Pfeiffer and Company out of San Diego. This book lists 415 exercises which run from 10 minutes to an hour, can be used for elementary school pupils or corporate CEOs, and are applicable to newly formed groups or groups which have been working together for years.

Through the facilitator, three modules (including one from Pfeiffer and one from NASA) helped the group see the benefits of improved team behavior. The session also showed that each person in the group has a role (sometimes many roles) to play in making the group a team. These roles relate to the task to be performed and the renewal of the team as a viable, capable entity:

TEAM TASK ROLES:

Initiator – defines goals, proposes solutions

Information Seeker – asks for facts and information

Energizer – motivates members, stimulates productivity

Orientator – keeps group discussing issues related to goal

Information Giver – offers facts and examples pertaining to task

Opinion Giver – offers values and opinions of ideas under discussion

Coordinator – clarifies relationships between facts and ideas

Evaluator/Critic – evaluates evidence presented to group

TEAM MAINTENANCE ROLES:

Encourager – provides praise, support to others

Harmonizer – mediates disagreements by reducing tension

Compromiser – mediates disagreements by finding common ground

Standard Setter – identifies group standards/norms

Follower – passively accepts ideas and conclusions

The energy and fun of the simulations (they should be fun, even humorous) allowed participants to work on issues that echoed real-life situations, but were designed to draw out specific object lessons and insights. With the facilitator's help, the participants reflected on each exercise and saw how their role, and the role of others, contributed to the outcome of the assigned task and viability of the team. The session concluded with a set of action items for how to work together more effectively. The retreat also pointed out some collective and individual behaviors which offered both opportunities and pitfalls. Sessions designed to address these specifics are pending for a future retreat.

THE STAFF AS A TEAM

The aftermath of the team-building session started with how the president related to his staff and how the various vice presidents related to theirs. Thankfully, the president was already predisposed toward a facilitative management style, but now he has a better understanding of his role as the team leader. Other staffs also started to see immediate shifts in tone and a change in the format of the staff meetings. The vice presidents began to listen more, and they let everyone have their say before a decision was made. Some decisions began to be reached through consensus, instead of simply being announced. Others on these staffs attended mini-sessions on team building to understand their critical role in helping foster and justify this new openness. Staff members began to tentatively raise issues in nonconfrontational, constructive ways. It is hoped that as the vice presidents and deans reciprocate by respecting staff inputs, an environment of trust and openness will continue.

A key element of this new team approach was the realization that collective, cooperative effort is superior to individual effort, if one wants sustainable improvement. There was also a new way of viewing people around the table. Fellow staff members realized that there were those among them who had better and more detailed information about the work and tasks being addressed, as well as those who had greater authority to act on that knowledge. Depending on the matter under discussion, this may be the same person, or it may be different people (see Figure 1). Certainly, it becomes apparent that the higher one is in the line organization, power to act accumulates, but knowledge of intimate details recedes (See Box #2 in Figure 1). Armed with this insight and tying to other concepts germinating since the initial team-building session, each person around the table now began to see each other's worth and began to see why they were all there (the role of "information giver" relates to Box #3 in Figure 1). This process may take time, but a good manager or occasional outside facilitator can nurture this new way of thinking into ever stronger bonds of trust, respect and loyalty.

Figure 1: Participation Matrix

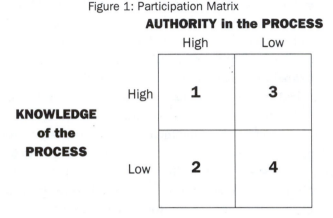

As the group begins to solidify as a team, the move to team-driven Quality Management can begin.

QUALITY MANAGEMENT IN TEAMS

One of the most frequent questions asked by attendees at the University sessions was, "What is the first thing I do to start implementing quality?" The answer was to start with the very next staff meeting and go around the room and ask what are the work-related hassles and problems that frustrate people and hurt their work effort. In the staffs that attended the mini-team development sessions (discussed earlier), there was some lively dialogue. The ground rules for these discussions were:

❖ No names or personalities discussed (you must assume absence of malice)

❖ Try to keep away from "world peace"-type strategic issues (it's too frustrating)

❖ All issues are placed on a flipchart (to capture and build upon)

❖ No criticism of other's issues (if someone says it's a problem, it is)

Under some circumstances, people did not immediately speak up. Some managers used other means to draw out information. Several went around the table so that each staff member had a turn. Another had each person write down their first round of issues on index cards (without names), hand them in, and had someone shuffle and hand them back out to be read by each other. Still another vice president had his group fill out cards anonymously, then he posted all the cards together on a large board for everyone to read. Each of these methods greatly aided the flow of information and issues.

These initial exercises netted change agendas for individual staffs. The next challenge (and key signal from management) was to never let the list disappear. After looking at these lists (some were written on the flip chart; others were on separate cards taped to a board), the vice president or dean asked some of the following questions:

❖ "Do any of these items link to any others mentioned?"

❖ "Do any of these items seem like symptoms of larger issues?"

❖ "Do any other issues come to mind after looking at the list?"

Issues and clusters were added, based on this round of discussion. Then they posed this question:

❖ "Can we, as a group, solve any of these issues without outside help?"

Some staffs were surprised at how many of the items on their lists were truly in-house issues that could be resolved. There was then a call for volunteers to meet before the next meeting and propose approaches. Most staffs felt this was a full enough agenda to work on for now. However, one staff decided to go one step further and address the remaining items:

❖ "Who can help us with the rest of the list?"

A list of the new resources (other offices, departments) were placed by each item. Once again, volunteers were asked to approach these individuals and report back at the next meeting.

One team (more knowledgeable about Quality Management concepts) asked whether additional information (like measurement data) was necessary to document and better define any of the issues. This laid the ground work for ultimately measuring success. If we ask, "How do we know it's a problem?" we can one day ask, "How do we know the problem has really been solved?"

The staff meetings went on to other routine agenda items. What was important at this stage was the role of the vice presidents and deans in accepting information on problems in a supportive way. If everyone starts to realize that the executives want to really hear from their staff, the staff will be more forthcoming.

Several weeks later, this new approach had its second set of staff meetings. The previous lists of problems and hassles were displayed and action items were reported. Staff members have been impressed at the constancy of executive commitment. The lists have now been reviewed in each subsequent meeting; they have not gone away. Today, they remain a permanent part of the staff meetings.

Thankfully, early on there were some happy milestones as some identified hassles were resolved and removed from the lists. The person or persons who raised the issue stood up and crossed the item off the list, declaring the matter solved. This was a time of rejoicing, for a dragon (hassle/frustration), which was tearing up some part of the office landscape, had been slain.

As the meetings have continued, new items have been added to the lists. The same questions asked in the initial round of meetings were revisited. Over time, patterns have occasionally emerged from these lists that point to broader issues. Once again, tasking out the actions and continuous followup has been the key. Every round that occurs shows indications of the staff's faith that the manager will not "shoot a messenger" and that many issues are within the staff's ability to address. Further down this path, the staff may decide, as have others who have implemented this approach, that their ability to identify or resolve issues needs enhancement. They may want a refresher course on problem solving or obtaining feedback, or they may want to sharpen their measurement skills. The manager now becomes a resource provider, either arranging for individual skill building or sessions for the whole staff.

The vice presidents are planning to promote having those who report directly to the deans and administrative officers start a similar team-building/staff meeting enhancement cycle with their direct reports. This cascade effect assures and validates support from the top, and it allows for pacing of the deployment to the individual capability and comfort of each manager. There is always the cautionary note that trying to push an effort faster than this may result in some shots ringing out elsewhere around the campus as a skeptical manager shows that they would rather have a dead messenger and ignore the dragon for the time being.

If all goes well (and this process is being monitored and fostered proactively), the administration plans to assign its original list of strategic issues downward to be addressed by relevant staffs. The administration has already accepted some tactical issues flowing upward for executive action from the staffs. The University is now assessing whether informality should govern this two-way system or whether a more formal written request for action would be helpful to the flow of information and action items.

The efforts to build effective teams, to enhance the effectiveness of existing staff meetings, and the linking of staffs to problem solving and process improvement is ambitious. However, as with any Quality Management effort, clear, consistent focus from the top and a methodical, realistic implementation approach tied to realistic issues and outcomes is the recipe for success.

Scot M. Faulkner is president of the Farragut Management Institute, a Washington, D.C.-based training organization. He is a former vice president of Philip Crosby Associates, Inc. (the world's largest Quality Management firm) and served as a faculty member at the Crosby Quality College in both Princeton, N.J., and Winter Park, Fla. He is a frequent guest lecturer at numerous universities in America and abroad.

Faulkner has compiled over 15 years in senior management, including positions at the White House, the General Services Administration and the Department of Education. His public service also included Peace Corps country director in Malawi, Africa, and director of congressional affairs for the Federal Aviation Administration. Prior to this, he spent four years as a congressional aide. Faulkner holds a master's degree in public administration from American University and a B.A. in government from Lawrence University. He studied at Georgetown University and London School of Economics.

2

Team Effectiveness

Robert S. Winter
Elizabeth S. Winter

The literature dealing with Total Quality Management (TQM) consistently defines the critical elements of this management philosophy within an organizational setting. Commitment from the top, customer focus and employee focus are all required to affect the cultural transformation, which is imperative to successful implementation of TQM. In most "TQM" organizations, the focus on customers and employees is actualized through the formation of teams.

This chapter will look at organizations from a team perspective, with the tenet that the success or failure of TQM in organizations hinges, in large part, on the success or failure of teams. The literature (and plain common sense, for that matter) confirms that just establishing groups of employees charged with solving problems, does not automatically lead to effective problem solving. While education and training are critical components to team success, they alone are not sufficient.

The attitudes and, consequently, the behavior of employees are clearly affected by the organizational environment. The nature of relationships among employees and with managers, which have been cultivated over the years, create a set of perceptions and expectations that can either support or hinder the implementation of new management philosophies based on trust and respect. To achieve the full potential of teams, thoughtful preparation and planning must take place. There are too many unhappy reports of TQM efforts gone awry because of ill-prepared groups of employees called "teams" or "quality circles."

WHAT MAKES A TEAM EFFECTIVE?

Team effectiveness, from a TQM perspective, is perceived as the ability of a group to function as a cohesive unit which progresses from identifying problems or issues to specifying and recommending changes needed to improve a process. Within this broad definition, one can identify different, interrelated components which enhance the effectiveness of groups.

❖ **Speed and Timeliness.** In a traditional organizational environment, where decisions are made by the few with little or no input from those performing processes or those receiving the products and services derived from those processes, decisions can be made quickly and in a timely manner. Group efforts require participation and consensus building and, necessarily, take more time. Consequently, they are often dismissed by managers as ineffective. The tradition of crisis management and a perception of immediacy, rather than a real need for quick results, are more often the reasons for rejecting the use of teams. The old adage, "If you don't have time to do it right the first time, where are you going to find time to do it again?" may come back to haunt these decision makers. Timeliness, redefined in a team setting, requires a focused effort by all team members. While spending the necessary time to meet, analyze, and discuss relevant issues, teams must avoid the common pitfalls of lengthy and unnecessary meetings, redundancy, focus on political agendas, reliance on intuition (without collecting necessary facts) and finger pointing.

❖ **Interaction Among Team Members.** Each member of a team brings his or her own attitudes, customs and traditions to the group. Diversity in organizations is a positive element, but only when individuals recognize that differences add value to discussions. Effectiveness, then, can be assessed in terms of the positive interaction among team members. In addition to advancing the group process, individuals who get to know and respect each other within the team environment start the process of reducing societal barriers throughout the workplace. This is an important step toward cultural transformation.

❖ **Marginal Improvement.** A significant debate is transpiring over whether the focus of team efforts should be on results (the "what") or the process-improvement method (the "how"). Those who favor results view effectiveness in terms of the size and impact of the identified improvement. The greater impact a team's solution has on improving a process (and the more critical the process is), the more effective the team is. On the other hand, those who value the problem-solving process itself are less concerned with the magnitude of improvements; effectiveness is measured in terms of the systematic procedure adhered to in arriving at solutions. Incremental improvements are highly valued. The discipline acquired through adherence builds more effective, efficient teams over time. Systematic, dynamic and thorough analysis minimizes the chance of overlooking a viable solution or "solving" the wrong problem.

❖ **Customer Satisfaction.** In the TQM environment, quality is defined primarily in terms of customer satisfaction; team effectiveness should be measured in the same context and by the same standard. The recommendations and actions resulting from a team's process-improvement activities should meet and/or exceed the expectations of its customers. This requires that a team clearly identify all of its customers and solicit their perceptions of quality product and/or service.

❖ **Satisfaction of Managers.** Teams do not operate in a vacuum. They are often established by managers to investigate and improve specific processes. How effective a team is can be measured, then, in terms of the sponsoring manager's level of satisfaction with the team's output. To insure success in this endeavor, sponsors must clearly communicate their requirements to the team; their expectations must be reasonable, and the communication lines must remain open throughout the problem-solving process.

HOW ARE TEAMS ESTABLISHED?

The fundamental premise for establishing teams is that, by "empowering" employees, organizations will invest their time, energy and creativity to affect positive change. Empowerment and decentralized decision-making are easier articulated than accomplished. Most individuals who have succeeded in becoming managers have done so by emulating actions and attitudes that often run counter to the concepts of participation and empowerment. Change in behavior cannot occur just by reading about a new management philosophy; a lot of internalizing and reflective thinking must take place. The organization can foster this behavior by providing appropriate settings for discussing TQM philosophy and the implications of establishing teams.

Evolution of Teams. As more American organizations adopt TQM, there will be more models to study and analyze. There is, however, some documentation to suggest that as organizations "mature" with TQM and become more "comfortable" with it, a phenomenon called self-managed teams can evolve. This occurs when employees are truly empowered to devote their time and effort to the improvement of processes as they see fit. Teams are created informally and autonomously, frequently from the bottom up.

This model is not common in higher education. Most colleges and universities are still in the early stages of adoption of TQM principles and processes; managers tend to initiate, prioritize and guide the formation of teams. Often a criteria of criticality is used, identifying processes which are most crucial to the operation (for example, processes affecting student retention rates), to rationalize the formation of teams. This selection process is generally top-down and, if the delegator is not careful, may be viewed as another autocratic imposition. It is important that managers describe the process free of pre-conceived solutions, and that they incorporate language that affirms the value placed by management on the knowledge of employees.

Team Players. Once the critical processes have been identified, it is customary for the **team sponsors** (managers responsible for those processes) to select leaders and facilitators to work with a team. **Leaders** are generally content experts and, like other team members, are familiar with the process under study. These individuals help the sponsor choose team members, help the team establish and follow its agenda, and meet its common goal. Leaders also act as team spokespeople and as liaisons between the team and its sponsor. **Facilitators** assist the team with the technical aspects of the process-improvement model and provide guidance on group dynamics. Facilitators do not need to know the process under study; they aid the team in applying tools for analysis and consensus. Each of these players affects the team's ability to successfully arrive at process improvements. The ability to listen, to have empathy, to show respect for all people and ideas, to provide encouragement, and to detect problems before they become crises are characteristics of good leaders and facilitators.

Team members are the "owners" of the process; they are the people who are affected on a daily basis by the process and they are the beneficiaries of the recommended improvements. The size of the team should fluctuate between six and 12 members. Smaller numbers do not generally provide sufficient diversity, and larger ones hinder the active participation of each individual member.

The care used to select appropriate issues and the shared understanding of the roles of each individual affecting the team's efforts is just a necessary first step.

WHAT TRAINING AND EDUCATION IS PROVIDED?

Team effectiveness is dependent upon a culture that values continued education and personal development. An investment in education and training demonstrates that management views employees as an important resource and is willing to put the time and money into preparing them to fully participate in the growth and improvement of the organization.

Content. The adoption of new management philosophies requires more than learning new concepts and applying new techniques; to be fully realized, and therefore fully utilized, employees must truly embrace, or "buy in" to the philosophy. This indicates the need for fundamental changes in attitudes, behavior and discipline; affecting these changes is the challenge of training programs. Programs designed simply to transfer knowledge or to teach new techniques are insufficient to prepare and support the members.

Training programs must allow for open dialogue between teachers and participants and among the participants themselves. This open conversation must encourage the sharing of concerns and anxieties brought about by implementation of a new management philosophy. As an example, concepts of employee participation and empowerment represent significant changes in behavior that cannot be realized quickly and easily. Training programs must encourage managers to express their views on the impact of empowerment and participation on time, power and control. A manager's knowledge of the basic principles of TQM are meaningless unless he or she can relate them to day-to-day functions.

Trainees. Although there are common threads for all educational efforts, training programs must be designed to accommodate employees with different roles and perspectives across the organization. At the **executive level,** the emphasis of the materials and dialogues must focus on the broad, organizational implications of having employees involved in teams and how to provide appropriate support and guidance to team members and sponsors.

On the **middle-management level,** sponsors need to reflect on their new role in a quality organization and how team efforts can enhance their ability to meet objectives. They also need to ascertain how they can most successfully integrate a new, methodical system of problem solving into an environment that has traditionally demanded and rewarded a fast-action, directive style of management.

Training for **individual team members** must impart the fundamental principles of TQM and must address the organizational implications of the new management philosophy. It is in the training domain that employees should become familiar with and comfortable working in an open, collaborative environment. By mastering a variety of analytical tools specifically aimed at improving processes, team members develop the skills and the confidence necessary to identify and solve complex problems incrementally.

HOW ARE MEETINGS CONDUCTED, AND WHAT PROCESS ARE THEY USING?

The question is often asked, "How do teams differ from conventional committees?" This is a legitimate question since, in higher education, there is a long tradition of establishing committees to study policies and procedures.

The contrast between the two becomes apparent when those who have participated in committees report their frustrations over lengthy, redundant, ineffective (i.e. their recommendations are not implemented) meetings which frequently have hidden, political agendas. These committees of "experts" are often given unreasonable tasks to accomplish within unrealistic time frames, and yet, this model for policy formulation and problem solving is used again and again. It is no wonder university faculty and staff have adopted the popular notion that the best way to assure that a problem will go unresolved, lost in a bureaucratic quagmire, is to "send it to committee." This is also why it is imperative that employees selected to work on teams understand the distinct differences between teams and committees so that they will not prejudge the process and minimize its potential.

Components of Meetings. Team meetings should be described and modeled in training programs. This starts by following an agreed-upon agenda which is focused on the specific stages one goes through to ultimately identify process improvements. Minutes (which record the progress of the meetings) are prepared, as a standard practice, by rotating team members. Five conditions characterize the team process:

❖ The members of the team are the practitioners and "owners" of the process under study; therefore, they are the major beneficiaries of their hard work and recommendations

❖ Teams develop a set of ground rules to guide their periodic meetings; these rules are used to insure appropriate group dynamics and to insure the efficient use of time

❖ Decisions are reached by consensus; votes are avoided and every opinion is considered important and valuable

❖ The active participation of all team members is encouraged and facilitated by techniques like brainstorming

❖ Each meeting ends with an evaluation to determine what was done right and what can be done better in future team gatherings

A critical first step, preceding any attempt to analyze processes, is the development of the team's mission statement – an exercise that results in a shared understanding of the reasons for the team's existence and develops team cohesion and direction. This step is often coupled with an exercise that allows the team to visualize an ideal set of conditions.

The Problem-Solving Model. The central activity of all teams is the improvement of processes by using a problem-solving model. This model should embody specific, deliberate steps which are compatible with the basic principles of TQM (customer focus, management by facts and continuous improvement). It must foster thoughtful and comprehensive analysis. The model guides the selection of a specific process, collection of appropriate descriptive data, identification and analysis of the root causes affecting potential improvements, and the design, testing and final recommendation of improvements. Tools and techniques, such as pareto charts, run charts, fish-bone diagrams, force-field analysis, histograms, flow charts and brainstorming, are used throughout the process to achieve the team's ends.

Team members need to understand and regularly apply the new techniques. Because the process differs significantly from past practice, it needs to be followed strictly until it becomes routine.

HOW ARE TEAM MEMBERS RECOGNIZED FOR THEIR EFFORTS?

What is in it for me? This is a legitimate question which may or may not be articulated but is certainly contemplated by employees when they are requested to perform activities that are not clearly related to their job functions. It deserves an appropriate response. The demands made of team members are significant. They are requested to add to their regular work load on the assumption that process improvements will ultimately save them time and improve their quality of work life, but they may not realize the changes or the advantages for months. They are asked to learn new disciplines that empower them to make decisions previously made by managers – but they may wonder why they are being solicited to do the work for managers. They are asked to use analytical and presentation skills that are new to them – and possibly intimidating. They are asked to develop a new relationship with their working colleagues, and they are asked to be patient at a time when business as usual is anything but usual.

The organizational response to their questions and their concerns must be honest and forthright. Leaders need to communicate that when employees are asked to be team members, they are being asked to participate in an important effort; they will be provided with extensive training which is, in itself, an indicator of the value placed on the process. Experience shows that employees are energized by the attention they receive, particularly when it comes from the top. This attention reiterates the importance leaders place on the work teams are doing. The obvious trust and confidence management accords teams sends a powerful message. Successes in moving through the problem-solving process itself is a motivational factor and keeps positive energy flowing, but all of the good feelings engendered may exist for only a limited time; more is needed. But what more can be done?

Put Your Money Where Your Mouth Is. Although monetary rewards are a clear sign of recognition, and are routinely used in industrial settings, this is an almost alien concept in higher education organizations, and many are not willing or able to initiate this tactic to support team efforts. Within colleges and universities, merit increases are traditionally granted to recognize individual efforts. This model could be utilized to reward team members as well, through the application of salary increments to the base or by providing bonuses. The difficulty in all of these schemes resides in establishing a sensible criteria for the allocation of these funds. Should teams be rewarded on the basis of the largest improvement, the most critical improvements, or just because an improvement was accomplished? Since how a team works is considered just as important as their accomplishments, it can be argued that salary adjustments should be based on both the how and the what of team efforts. Whatever the inclination of the decision makers, this is an issue which must be resolved and consistently implemented.

If the leadership can build some type of monetary reward component into their program, they will find that it is a strong motivator – not because of the intrinsic value of the award so much as the powerful, uncompromising notice it sends to participants that their endeavors are truly appreciated.

Appreciation and Celebration. There are other ways to demonstrate appreciation. Beyond the talk, organizations must create occasions for celebration. New team members must have the opportunity to meet with senior management to hear directly how their time and effort is valued. Annual events like team fairs and luncheons provide these opportunities to celebrate and highlight successes. Campus publications should be employed to feature team efforts, and special publications (reports and newsletters) can be used to share information among teams and team members.

Perhaps the most rewarding event occurs when team members make a formal presentation to their managers. This is the team's opportunity to share and showcase their hard work and their recommendations for improvements. It is when management sees the lengthy process, rendered in surveys, graphs and flow charts, and hears the team's story. This is when managers can observe and acknowledge the hard work and thoughtfulness that has gone into the process. This is truly an occasion to celebrate.

HOW IS SENIOR MANAGEMENT DEMONSTRATING ITS COMMITMENT?

The role of senior management has been alluded to throughout this discourse. Their primary function has been depicted as the providers of encouragement and as the purveyors of incentives and rewards. As employees become involved in teams and experience the impact of empowerment, they start listening with heightened sensitivity to the messages, spoken and unspoken, that are delivered by management. Formal statements from senior management in support of TQM are important, but what employees seek is a consistent, visible and persistent message through actions.

Walking the Talk. There is a significant difference between stating a commitment for TQM and actually incorporating the principles in day-to-day behavior. If teams are established based on the premise that employees are valuable, trustworthy and deserve respect, then all policies, procedures and actions must reflect these sentiments. Most organizations beginning the quality journey still adhere to policies and procedures burdened with redundancies and unnecessary inspections designed to respond to "special" causes (a dishonest employee, for example). Senior management must demonstrate its commitment by stopping the issuance of such policies and procedures and by reviewing and reversing old ones.

("Special" causes are unusual variations that take place within a process. All processes have inherent variations – in cycle time or errors, for example – but some special cases may generate unique conditions. There is a tendency to modify processes to correct "special" causes rather than dealing one-on-one with these unique problems and then improving processes to affect the common causes.)

Evidence of senior management commitment is expressed irrefutably through their agendas. It is common practice to minimize the interaction between senior managers and their employees and customers. For the sake of symbolism, appearances are made, hands are shaken and niceties are exchanged, but these occasions alone cannot impart the caring, interest and focus on employees which are crucial in the establishment and nurturing of teams. Only when employees see and experience earnest contacts with management will trust and respect be conveyed.

A TQM organization must demonstrate its reliance on employees by stopping the pervasive activity of second-guessing and by explicitly supporting risk taking. These kinds of cultural and behavioral changes can only be initiated from the top.

Two Scenarios. The need for visible and active senior management commitment is based on the assumption that their actions cascade throughout the organization, affecting in some manner all individuals. If the CEO is directive and autocratic, it is reasonable to expect that managers on the next level will act in the same manner. At some point these people will become the sponsors of teams in which employees have been empowered. It is easy to see the potential for conflict if this scenario is realized.

The flip side of this disaster-in-the-making would start with a leader who has embraced the principles of Total Quality and has already empowered the senior managers who have felt confident to empower their middle managers. The spiral continues on its positive course, in an open, supportive climate, which is undeniably suited for fostering teams and team work. This is the ideal situation. Our mission is to strive towards this model.

WHAT IS TEAM EFFECTIVENESS?

Team effectiveness must be defined within the context of the principles of TQM and, consequently, must be inexorably linked to customer satisfaction. Effectiveness is measured not only by the team's outputs, or solutions, but also by its devotion to a thoughtful, systematic process for problem identification and process improvement. Resulting changes need not be comprehensive; teams should look for incremental solutions which will become part of the organization's continuous improvement legacy. Successful teams are, by definition, focused, cohesive and disciplined.

At every level of an organization, people contribute toward a team's effectiveness and success. Manager and team members must all work together in an open forum, respecting each other's perspectives, contributions and unique roles in this dynamic process. Senior managers must articulate their support for teams and demonstrate their endorsement in concrete terms as well. While the intrinsic rewards of teamwork are substantial, extrinsic rewards and recognition are needed to convey senior managers' appreciation of employees' contributions and their advocacy for the process.

The most fundamental expression of commitment is a leader's dedication to redefining the organization to create an open, supportive environment in which teams, and all members of the organization, can thrive.

REFERENCES

Caroselli, M. *Total Quality Transformations – Optimizing Missions, Methods and Management.* Amherst, Mass.: Human Resource Development Press, Inc., 1991.

Ciampa, D. *Total Quality – A User's Guide for Implementation.* Reading, Mass.: Addison: Wesley, 1992.

Gitlow, H. S. and Gitlow S. J. *The Deming Guide to Quality and Competitive Position.* Englewood Cliffs, N.J.: Prentice-Hall, 1987.

Kennedy, L. W. *Quality Management in the Nonprofit World.* San Francisco: Jossey-Bass, 1991.

Manning, G. and Curtis K. *Group Strength.* Cincinnati, Ohio: 1988.

Senge, P. M. *The Fifth Discipline: The Art & Practice of the Learning Organization.* New York, N.Y.: Doubleday, 1990.

Wellins, R. S., Byham W. C. and Wilson J. M. *Empowered Teams –Creating Self-Directed Work Groups that Improve Quality, Productivity and Participation.* San Francisco: Jossey-Bass, 1991.

Robert S. Winter joined the University of Illinois at Chicago (UIC) in 1991. Previously, he worked at Florida International University, both as an administrator and a faculty member. Winter received two degrees in industrial engineering and a doctoral degree in business from the University of Illinois at Urbana-Champaign. Upon completion of his doctoral degree, he worked at the University of Illinois system in the planning office.

Winter's current responsibilities are to plan and facilitate the adoption of TQM at UIC.

Winter has written several articles and made numerous presentations about the application of TQM in educational settings. In Dade County, Fla., he worked closely with staff of the school district, assisting in the adoption of school-based management. Currently, his research focus is the adoption of TQM in higher education.

Winter is a member of: the American Society for Quality Control, the Association for Quality and Participation, the Chicago Quality Council, the Association for Institutional Research and the American Association for Higher Education.

Elizabeth S. Winter led the office of Instructional Television Production at Florida International University for 15 years before moving to Chicago. In addition to her administrative responsibilities, Winter conducted workshops in instructional technology and television production for the University's Teacher Education Center and for universities in South and Central America.

During her tenure at FIU, Winter enlisted colleagues from throughout the University to subscribe to a teleconference series entitled "The Quality Imperative." The monthly conferences exposed participants to some of the leaders in the quality movement and inspired the creation of a University task force on quality.

Since moving to Chicago, Winter continues to pursue her own research in Total Quality and is participating in team training at the University of Illinois at Chicago.

3

Team-based TQM: A Model for Post-Bureaucracy

Marvin E. Lane

INTRODUCTION

Total Quality Management (TQM) challenges the practitioner to shed self-imposed paradigms which limit one's perception of possibilities for organizational structure. Total Quality Management theory also challenges the practitioner to pursue perfection through continuous improvement. The result is many paths being explored in the name of continuous improvement based on the assumption that TQM is a model for perfecting an organization by removing non-value-adding steps from systems and processes. Some find TQM a vehicle for creation of new paradigms regarding the shape and function of organizations.

TEAM- AND INFORMATION-BASED MODEL

As a TQM practitioner with over four year's experience in

the day-to-day implementation of TQM, the author has formulated an organizational model based on TQM theory. The model, which is team-based, is applicable to large and small organizations. A moment of truth, which spurred the development of the model, was the author's realization that the paradigm for current organizations was based on the concept of control. The author realized that information could be the paradigm for empowering individuals and the foundation for an organization.

The author's thesis is that TQM is a team-based empowerment paradigm. The employees of the organization are empowered through the implementation of the TQM philosophy and through application of TQM tools to day-to-day decisions. Employees' decisions will only be as good as the quality of information provided. Within traditional organizations, management's role has been to control information and thus control employees by either withholding or sharing information in the decision-making process. Empowered TQM employees need information that enables them to make appropriate decisions, plus the employees need information that allows them to assess how they are doing in relation to the organization's mission and vision on a day-to-day basis. The author's organizational thesis is that information can be a primary factor for maintaining constancy of purpose for an organization, rather than control through line and staff relationships.

REFLECTION ON BUREAUCRACY

Traditional organizations are usually bureaucratic. The bureaucracy concept was created for a time when a few individuals could manage all of the organization's information. Work was divided into small, incremental steps which often required little training and limited intellectual activity on the part of the worker. The pattern in larger, more sophisticated organizations, using the services of professionals, is to divide the work into small incremental parts, with a system of checks and balances and inspections. A bureaucracy, while serving its creators well, has its share of negatives. A bureaucracy creates its own resistance because employees are treated as robots and granted minimal empowerment. Work is designed to limit opportunities for self expression, and the employee is expected to produce work per supervisor specifications. Employees' experiences cause many to believe that success is outside of their control. The employee often becomes a robot, performing routine tasks on a day-to-day basis, knowing that no one will listen or pay attention if improvements are suggested.

A bureaucracy, with its systems of controls and checks and balances, promotes approval seeking by the employee, especially one who seeks upward mobility. Promotions go to employees who work within the system and who pass positive information to the next level of the organization. This often makes workers say what they don't mean and denies the upper levels of the organization access to pertinent information that could mean the difference between success and failure.

A bureaucracy also fosters negative political behavior. Disenfranchised employees who feel they have no control over their situation engage in negative behavior and sometimes use sabotage, which may be as simple as failing to pass along information that could save embarrassment to the organization. In general, a bureaucracy causes employees to see themselves as vulnerable and helpless without any power to affect their day-to-day work activities.

AN EMPOWERMENT PARADIGM

Richard Johnson in his book, *TQM: Leadership for the Quality Transformation*, provides an excellent explanation of empowerment. He defines empowerment as a three-phase process of moving from power over others to power through others, culminating in empowerment of others. Traditional organizations have functioned for centuries with the concept of power over others. Control is the key factor in maintaining discipline and for keeping the organization focused on its goals and objectives. Control is accomplished through rules and regulations, with minimum flexibility for special circumstances. Only those with power can break the rules and respond to special circumstances. Traditional organizations often embrace the concept of customer service, but instead of being a natural outgrowth of the organizational climate, it is an add-on feature. Employees are expected to provide excellent customer service even though operational systems and processes may make the task almost impossible. Employees are held accountable for errors caused by systems and processes that lead to irritated customers. Satisfaction happens if systems chance to intersect at the point of delivery or interaction with the customer.

A bureaucracy relies on inspection to prevent mistakes. The organization is built on the premise that mistakes will happen because employees are not diligent in carrying out their day-to-day responsibilities. Therefore, administrators or supervisors are charged with identifying and correcting mistakes. The reader is challenged to obtain a copy of his or her employer's organizational chart and, after observing the line and staff relationships, to turn the chart on its side. Amazingly, there is a direct correlation between the formal organizational chart and the assembly line process. Information and work flows along a channel from the bottom to the top of the organization. Employees report to a unit, which reports to a division, which reports to a regional office, which reports to the home office. Interspersed throughout the reporting relationship are numerous contact points with information flowing from the top or the bottom of the organization. Each inspector in the process is expected to ferret out mistakes and to prevent incorrect information from flowing to the next level of the organization. It is in the best interest of each supervisor to be sure that negative information doesn't reach the next-level supervisor. Therefore, the primary purpose of a traditional organization is to provide filtered information to higher levels in an organization and then allow only need-to-know information to flow down the organization.

The power-over-others empowerment process is the traditional model for conducting day-to-day work. The model provides direction and coaching, but little participation in decisions by employees and minimal delegation. The worker is told what to do and does not need to know how his or her work fits into the overall design of the organization. As stated above, customer service and satisfaction may happen if systems of the organization by chance happen to intersect at the point of delivery of a product or service.

Organizations implementing TQM should move quickly to level two of empowerment. Level-two empowerment involves employees in day-to-day work decisions and is called empowerment through others. The work force becomes involved in shared decisions, and the decision-making process begins flowing to lower levels in the organization. The day-to-day work processes are organized around teams, a mechanism for harnessing the human potential of an organization to begin the process of continuous improvement. The workers feel better about the organization because they are given control over their work area and have input into the decision-making process. The employee is granted increasing power to make changes that do not affect systems or processes beyond the work unit.

Empowerment through others and the teaming process are motivating factors for the work force, if the organization has first addressed extrinsic motivating factors. Extrinsic factors – such as pay, benefits, working conditions and the way workers are managed – are fairness issues that need to be addressed before empowerment becomes a meaningful reality. During the empowerment-through-others phase, workers should perceive the organization as treating employees fairly, and management should focus on strategies that allow employees input into decisions through a teaming environment.

TQM organizations discover that active motivation flows from empowerment-through-others activities which address intrinsic motivators. Intrinsic motivators are information which informs the employee about the organization and how he or she fits into the overall picture, granting of control over a work area, respecting the individual for what he or she does, plus investment in training for workers which allows them to grow as human beings through life-long learning experiences. The empowering organization supports and capitalizes on the strengths of the teaming process, and begins the transition to recognizing the work-unit teams as the primary vehicle for conducting the organization's day-to-day work.

EMPOWERMENT AND CUSTOMER SERVICE

Empowered employees become aware that they may not be providing high-level customer service. Improved customer service is a natural outgrowth of the empowerment process and springs from the employees' desire to improve their working relationship with internal and external customers. It has been stated that customer service is nothing more than a reflection of the organization's climate. It then follows that an empowerment process which improves the organizational climate will improve customer service.

MOVING FROM CUSTOMER SERVICE TO SATISFACTION

Empowered employees working in teaming relationships make a startling discovery as they provide improved levels of customer service. During their discussion and interaction with customers, it is acutely brought to the employees' attention that some customers are not satisfied. The employee becomes aware that the systems and processes used to conduct their day-to-day work may not be aligned with the expectation of customer service and satisfaction.

EMPOWERMENT TO OTHERS

The stage is now set for the final step – empowerment, which is power to others. When power is granted to others, employees become empowered to act as the leader's agent, have the power to complete assigned projects without seeking approval from supervisors, and the employee is permanently granted power to change and modify systems and processes within the work area. As employees become more proficient, they are eventually granted permission to change and modify systems and processes that are cross functional. When employees improve a cross-functional issue, they join with other departments in the process of continuous improvement.

Power to others requires a formal problem-solving model, because the temptation is always present to change systems and processes without considering all the facts. Employees who have been trained in problem-solving techniques use the skills to pursue continuous improvement. Employees eventually become experts at translating data into information, using the tools of TQM.

The change agent in an empowerment model is training for each and every employee in the organization. The goal of the training process is to engage each employee in the pursuit of life-long learning. The organization's training program becomes an investment in the development of the organization's human potential. Training provides employees with the skills and knowledge base which empowers the organization to continue to grant power to others. Workers that become highly skilled are leaders empowered to act as the leader's agent.

EMPOWERED TEAMS

The empowerment process discussed above assumes that the organization will use a team-based approach to implement TQM. The process discussed below is not a project team, a group activity, a committee, or an informal work group. The most frequent error made by those implementing TQM is the assumption that renaming a committee, a task force, or a work group a team will make the group a team. A team is a special creature and can be defined. It has been said that a team is group of people working toward common goals. Others have said that a team is a joint effort by individuals in which the individual's subordinates personal interests and opinions for the unity of the team. The author believes that teamwork provides members a sense of connectedness with the larger organization through their day-to-day work activities and through the information flow within the organization. A team is also a vehicle for building consensus for effective problem solving.

WORK-UNIT TEAMS

The challenge to a TQM organization is to organize teams in an effective and efficient manner to accomplish the work of the organization. A work-unit team is comprised of individuals who share common responsibility regarding a particular work activity. The team should have at least three, but not more than eight or nine, members. The team should receive formal training in the teaming process, problem-solving skills and conflict resolution. In addition, the team should receive training in team building and be made aware that diversity is a strength to be capitalized on for the benefit of the work-unit team. For purposes of illustration, a work-unit team is identified in Figure 1. The work-unit team is represented by a circle which denotes a particular work-unit team in the author's college. The team has a facilitator who conducts meetings. The facilitator is selected by the team and sets the agenda for team meetings, with input from the team members. The facilitator serves as a conscience for the team and keeps members focused on the agenda and on the issues at hand. Meetings should have a set time to begin and end. The team supervisors meet with the team on a frequent basis but do not control the meeting or the agenda. The supervisor may suggest items for the agenda and will provide information to the team to assist them in their decision-making process. Over time, the supervisor will spend less and less time working with the team on a day-to-day basis. However, for the appropriate flow of communication and connectedness with the larger organization, the supervisor must meet with the team on a regular basis. Experience indicates that once a team is fully functional, they resolve many of the work-day problems without involving their supervisor. However, for the appropriate flow of information within the organization, the supervisor needs to be informed of decisions that may affect his or her ability to carry out other activities on the organization's behalf.

Figure 1

Pictograph of Work-Unit Team

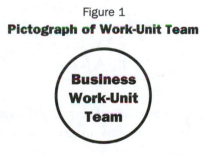

MANAGEMENT TEAMS

The author's college quickly learned about the need for connectedness between several work-unit teams that work for a major section of the campus. Figure 2 is a pictograph of the

Instructional Management Team at the author's college. The smaller circles represent the work-unit teams, which are connected by an inner circle which includes supervisors for the management team. The reader will note that the larger circle is labeled as the FACT Team. See Figure 2 below.

Figure 2
Pictograph of Instructional
Department Management Team

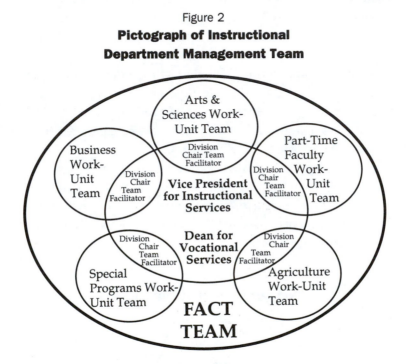

A new term was introduced above, which was the concept of management teams. The work-unit team was the first vehicle for implementation of TQM. Shortly after formation of the work-unit teams, it became obvious that a formal vehicle for information flow within, among and between the work-unit teams was needed. The supervisor needed a process for receiving and disseminating information. The organization also discovered that the relationship between the management team and the organization needed to be further defined.

Work-unit teams denote a group of individuals who work together on like work. The Departmental Management Team denotes a group of work-unit teams who work within a common area of the organization and report to a major administrator of the organization. The function of the Departmental Management Team is to facilitate the flow of information within the Departmental Management Team. The Departmental Management Team continues the process of empowerment to others by empowering individuals within the Departmental Management Team to become responsible for the day-to-day activities of their department and to engage in cross-functional problem solving. In a sense, the Departmental Management Team becomes the glue that keeps a portion of the organization working as a harmonious group on day-to-day work activities. It also becomes the link to the larger organization. Information will be shared later regarding an All Campus Management Team that is in the process of being developed to facilitate the flow of information between the work-unit teams, the departmental teams and the organization's leadership.

ALL CAMPUS MANAGEMENT TEAM

The model for implementation of TQM described above, and which is acknowledged to still be in a developmental stage, is a structure for information to flow from the top to the bottom of the organization without the traditional filters. The organization is developing an organizational structure which is depicted in Figure 3.

The pictograph represents the model for a team-based TQM organization that uses empowerment and information to keep the organization focused on the accomplishment of its vision. The Executive Leadership Team (shown in Figure 3) is comprised of the president and of three vice presidents who have been empowered by the president to operate at level three, the "power to" paradigm. The organization's vice presi-

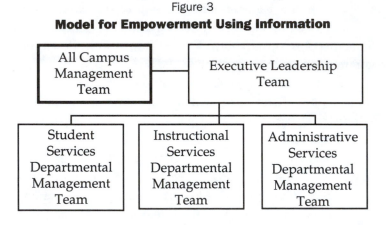

Figure 3
Model for Empowerment Using Information

All Campus Management Team	Executive Leadership Team

Student Services Departmental Management Team	Instructional Services Departmental Management Team	Administrative Services Departmental Management Team

dents function as extensions of the president and are considered equal with the president except on those items that are specifically delegated to the president by policy, statute or law. In a sense, the vice presidents serve as extensions of the president and are specialists who are assigned leadership roles with a Departmental Management Team. The vice presidents' role is to provide the appropriate information and leadership to allow a Departmental Management Team, which is comprised of work-unit teams, to accomplish their work in a manner that fosters continuous improvement.

This novel approach to organizational structure is possibly due to the creation of an All Campus Management Team. The All Campus Management Team is comprised of representatives from the Departmental Management Teams and will consist of support staff, faculty and administrators. The nine-member All Campus Management Team, plus the president, complete the membership. The All Campus Management Team is charged with providing information that has not been filtered directly to the president. They will also share information among and between the members of the Departmental Management Teams as one function of their membership on the All

Campus Management Team. The team will play a primary role in the finalization of the budget by confirming that a fair and equitable resource-allocation process has been utilized for the organizational teams. The team will make the final review of organizational policies again, with the primary role of ensuring that organizational processes have allowed appropriate input into the development of the policy. The All Campus Management Team will also have a voice in the development of new philosophical directions for the campus.

The organization proposed by the author is a different paradigm for organizational structure. The proposed organization will not be held together by the traditional concept of supervisory control over employees. Rather, the organization will be maintained on a day-to-day, long-term basis through the sharing of information between and among the work-unit teams, the Departmental Management Team, the Executive Leadership Team, and the All Campus Management Team.

THE EMPOWERMENT PROCESS – A REVIEW

Scarce resources and changing expectations for organizations challenge management striving to help employees become high performers. The author believes TQM provides a theoretical basis for empowerment of employees through the teaming process. The empowerment process moves from power over others to power through others and culminates in the granting of power to others. In the final stage, the employee is empowered to act as the leader's agent and is given freedom to improve systems and processes within their work unit and to work on cross-functional systems and processes in a teaming relationship with other work-unit teams and Departmental Management Teams. Effective teams require immediate access to information which tells the team how they are performing on a day-to-day basis. The information must be linked to the vision and mission of the organization. It must serve as a key guidepost in helping employees know that the actions they take on a day-to-day basis and their plans for continuous improvement will assist the organization in the accomplishment of its mission and vision. The TQM practitioner reaches a profound moment of truth when he or she is struck by the realization that information can be a new paradigm for empowering individuals and a foundation for developing a different organizational structure. The measure of success for an organization that is implementing TQM is the degree to which empowerment is freely and willingly given to employees, within the context of an information system that provides access to information which tells the worker how they are performing on a day-to-day basis.

SETTING THE EMPOWERED ORGANIZATION BOUNDARIES

Leaders of an organization establish boundaries within which an empowered work force conducts continuous improvement. These boundaries have to be team owned and the team has to be committed to incorporating the realities of the boundaries into their day-to-day work-unit activities. The boundaries are the vision of the organization which clearly articulate the organization's desired state. The mission of the organization broadly defines the breadth of activities that may be undertaken to turn the organization's vision to reality. The boundaries are further defined by the long-range plan which outlines specific steps that will be taken to support the mission and vision of the organization. The long-range plan is further defined through strategies that will be employed to accomplish the desired vision for the organization. And finally, all organizations have policies which further define and refine boundaries. The TQM organization continually reviews its policies to be sure employees have maximum flexibility to achieve the organization's vision.

The new paradigm empowers the individual through

information and vacates control as the primary mechanism for ensuring that the organization remains focused on the accomplishment of its vision. The author believes TQM theory supports the thesis of information, serving the role control does in the traditional organization. Traditional organizations filter and prevent negative information from reaching the top of the organization. Often, the very information executive leaders need to make appropriate decisions for the organization is not available because of the filtering process.

CONCLUSIONS

TQM organizations that empower employees cease to use inspection as a process to prevent errors. Therefore, the employees must have access to relevant information so the team will know how they are performing. Information must be organized into a logical, understandable form and be immediately accessible. Receiving feedback three days after the fact, in most cases, does not promote continuous improvement. The desired state for the TQM information system is immediate feedback controlled by the employee performing the task.

The thesis of this chapter has been that implementation of TQM can follow a logical, sequential, empowerment process in an organization. Many strive to rush the process or to focus on one particular aspect of implementation. It is tempting to use the Statistical Process Control tools to tighten management controls over employees. Such action leads to frustration and disenfranchisement of the very employees the organization depends on for the accomplishment of its vision. TQM, when implemented appropriately in conjunction with an empowerment paradigm, prepares the organization's culture for increased empowerment through training and life-long learning options. Training programs, while seemingly mechanical to some, actually are a process of continual investment in the employees of an organization. These programs ensure that the employees are appropriately equipped to respond to the ever-changing internal and external environments.

TQM is rooted in the teaching/learning philosophy. Sometimes a supervisor is the teacher and the employee is the learner. Other times the employee is the teacher and the leader is the learner. The front-line employee, if he or she has appropriate information, should be allowed to transmit information to the leaders who need the information. Often it may be top management who needs the information. The front-line employee should be allowed to move his or her information without filtering through the organization. The challenge becomes the implementation of an organizational structure which allows information to freely flow from the top or the bottom of the organization without being accosted. The leader's challenge is creation of an organizational paradigm which allows this to happen through a model such as the one proposed by the author.

REFERENCES

Covey, S. R. *Principle Centered Leadership.* New York, New York: Summit Books, 1991.

Covey, S. R. *The Seven Habits of Highly Effective People.* New York: Simon and Schuster, 1989.

Juran, J. M. *Juran on Quality by Design,* New York: The Free Press, 1992.

Gitlow, H. S. and Gitlow, S. S. *The Deming Guide to Quality and Competitive Position.* Englewood Cliffs, N. J.: Prentice Hall, 1987.

Lane, M. E. *Quality in Education.* Los Angeles: ERIC Clearinghouse for Junior Colleges, University of California, 1992.

Senge, P. M. *The Fifth Discipline: The Art & Practice of the Learning Organization.* New York: Doubleday, 1990.

Spanbauer, S. J. *A Quality System for Education.* Milwaukee, Wis.: Quality Press, 1992.

Walton, M. *The Deming Management Method.* New York: Perigee Books, The Putnam Publishing Group, 1986.

Marvin Lane, president of Lamar Community College, is a native of Iowa and holds a B.A., M.A., and Ed.D., from the University of Northern Colorado. Lane's background includes nine years in the retail grocery business; experience as a cook, janitor and truck driver; two years K-12 teaching experience; and seven years K-12 administrative experience.

Lane's exploration of quality began in collecting articles referencing quality. Lamar Community College began the development of a model for implementation and a plan to provide training for all campus staff. Student Services Teams were organized in the spring of 1989, followed by faculty teams in the fall of 1990. The Business Office formed its first team shortly thereafter. Most recently, the campus has formed an Executive Leadership Team which is comprised of the vice presidents and president and will shortly organize an All Campus Management Team to replace the president's cabinet.

Lane's accomplishments include national presentations, papers and articles. He is president-elect of the Continuous Quality Improvement Network, a national network of community colleges that have undertaken a comprehensive implementation of TQM.

Lane serves on the HRI Board and the Rotary Board of Directors. He is a member of the Colorado Alliance for Business Task Force to develop a plan for business and industry to jointly sponsor a pilot TQM program in the Jefferson County Public Schools, a member of the Task Force for Colorado School Restructuring for the Colorado Department of Education, and a member of AACC, Phi Delta Kappa and the ASQC.

4

Piecing Together the Full Power of Total Quality at a Community College

Richard D. DeCosmo
Jerome S. Parker

Delaware County Community College (DCCC) began implementing Total Quality (TQ) in 1986. At that time, the College developed a three-fold strategy: first, use the principles to improve administrative systems and processes; second, develop curricula to teach TQ; third, encourage teachers and faculty to use the principles in teaching and learning. This three- step plan was designed to take up to 10 years to implement. The plan followed an "inside-out" approach to changing the culture of the college. The leadership team sought to understand and use the rubrics of TQ first, followed by other administrators and support staff and, finally, by teachers and students. Each phase of this plan, of course, called for different strategies.

Administrative Processes: To integrate TQ into the

administrative systems and processes of the College, the first step was education of the executive staff. This was followed by several waves of short-term projects as "live ammunition" with which to train the rest of the administrative staff members. Hourly staff members were included in these projects and training sessions. Each improvement project illustrated one or more of the major sections on DCCC's continuous improvement "wheel" (Figure 1, p. 53).

DCCC soon learned that project teams could produce results easily, but infusing the TQ principles and practices into the daily work of the organization was harder. A strategy DCCC called Administrative Fundamentals was developed to achieve this infusion. The Administrative Fundamentals process will be described later in this chapter. After substantial progress with this process, a more advanced phase began. This phase included the design and redesign of systems and processes with greater attention to customer needs, often called quality function deployment, better horizontal integration, and closer partnerships with suppliers, especially high schools.

Curriculum Development. Paralleling the project team phase was the development of curricula. The College developed training modules to educate staff in the fundamental principles and practices of TQ. Beginning in 1987, these modules were offered to other organizations and businesses through the College's contracted training department. The plan called for the inclusion of TQ principles and practices in appropriate courses in other curricula and culminated in the development of a Total Quality Management (TQM) certificate program.

Teaching and Learning. The final phase of the original plan was the use of TQ in the classroom to improve the teaching and learning processes. Many faculty members are applying TQ principles to classroom practice. Some are merging these principles with the Cross-Angelo "teacher as classroom researcher" model, while others are using the Project Learn model developed at Samford University. (Cross, Angelo, 1993; Baugher, 1992). Faculty and others are using the TQ model to assess the College's effectiveness in teaching both general education and specific program competencies. This outcomes assessment process using TQ principles was initiated in the College's self-study for regional re-accreditation.

To understand what it would take to implement TQ throughout the organization as the primary management system, DCCC staff reviewed and adapted the GOAL-QPC model (TQ wheel) to its own needs and strategies. In this model, strategic planning becomes the core activity by which TQ is implemented.

STRATEGIC PLANNING

To gain the synergy of people working together to transform an organization, the alignment of all levels and departments with the College's goals is essential. This "vertical alignment" was particularly important as the college attempted to empower people to exercise more responsibility in achieving the mission and vision of the organization. Without a vision and strategic goals with which to align, there is no common cause. Empowering people may simply increase the chaos. In addition to alignment, each department must optimize the sub-systems and processes that support the mainstream system of the college. Unit, or department, optimization is achieved through the Administrative Fundamentals process. As units are aligned and optimized, horizontal integration binds all systems and processes together to achieve more than any units can do alone. Horizontal integration emphasizes the cross-functional nature of systems and processes and the interdependence of all units. However, all of these elements only indicate how the vision is to be achieved, not what the vision is. The strategic plan builds the vision of the organization and

Figure 1

informs all of the other activities around the wheel. The strategic plan itself must be built upon the principles of TQ and contain a vision that empowers an organization.

All of the activities around the "wheel" create an environmental press that can change the culture of the organization to reflect the inherent values and principles of TQ. People are asked to change the fundamental way they do their jobs. Because this does not happen overnight, leaders of an organization must exhibit perseverance and patience. There must be a constancy of purpose, as Deming points out in the first of his 14 points, to instruct this perseverance and patience. Constancy of purpose requires a clear mission and vision that is well understood and shared by the staff and stakeholders of the organization. A strategic plan incorporates the mission and vision of an organization and sets out the strategic objectives by which the mission and vision will be achieved. TQ is a means to achieve important goals, not an end in itself. The strategic objectives are the goals, and TQ is the method by which they can be achieved with quality.

The Strategic Planning Process: Since quality is achieved by meeting or exceeding the needs and expectations

Figure 2

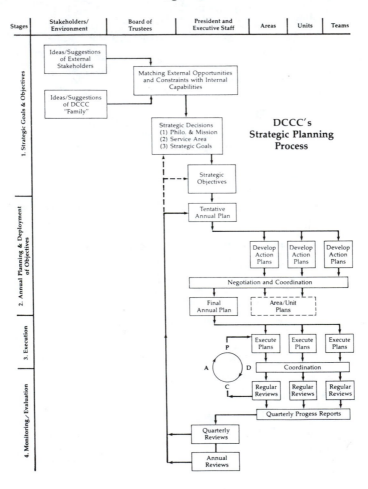

of customers, it is necessary to discover these needs and expectations in order to build an effective strategic plan. At DCCC a "search" process was developed to "find" these needs and expectations.

Various stakeholder groups (customers) were identified who could help in this process. Focus sessions were held with representatives of each of these stakeholder groups. Since DCCC is a public college, it is charged with a general mission embodied in legislation. Each group learned the mandated mission of the College, a brief history of past strategic goals and the extent to which they were achieved, and the broader climate of the external environment beyond the local community: state, national and international. Each group was asked to describe the vision they had for the College as it moved toward the 21st century, along with specific threats and opportunities they expected along the way, and to explain how they might recommend that these be met over the next 10 years. In short, it was important to find out what they thought should be done for them and their constituents during the next 10 years. These stakeholders (customers) became an integral and important part of the planning process.

Staff and faculty focus groups had a slightly different agenda. These focus sessions came at the end of the search process, and while they were asked the same questions, an additional task was required of them. They were asked to indicate their estimation of the capabilities of the College in relation to what the other groups had recommended. This material was distilled by a management and Board of Trustees team, and common themes from the stakeholder groups were identified. They discovered a convergence of needs and expectations among the stakeholder groups that fit the estimated capabilities, both actual and potential, of the College. At a two-day retreat, the trustees and executive staff digested this information, articulated a vision and selected a small set of strategic goals for the College that would achieve this vision by the end of the 20th century. Because of the inclusive nature of the search process, the resulting vision statement reflected a broad, widely-shared consensus. This vision and strategic goals were articulated in a publication titled *Vision 2000: A Work Plan for the Future* (1992).

In carrying out its mission, which commits the institution to responding to the area's changing educational and training needs, the College's enrollment is expected to grow substantially in size and diversity. The College's physical, human and financial resources will be expanded in scope and reach in order to accommodate the anticipated growth. The College will be regarded as a vital partner working cooperatively with other educational providers linking them to leverage our combined capabilities and resources. The College will also be widely recognized for its educational quality and for its organizational values which are manifest in its Total Quality culture and the quality of its graduates. DCCC graduates will be competent in their fields of study and proficient in the general education skills required to succeed in the new information age of the '90s and beyond.

The college established three goals and several strategies for each. What follows is a synopsis of these goals and objectives:

1.0 Provide access to affordable and comprehensive higher education to meet the needs of the community it serves.

    1.1 Continue to expand access to higher education for its constituents.

    1.2 Provide education and training required to build a world-class, competitive work force.

    1.3 Develop strategic partnerships with other organizations, both public and private.

2.0 Ensure the high quality of all educational services provided by the College.

2.1 Strengthen the general education core competencies, including the addition of the use of information technologies.

2.2 Achieve and gain recognition for excellence.

3.0 Acquire sufficient resources, and manage them efficiently and effectively.

3.1 Provide adequate facilities both on and off campus to maintain access.

3.2 Obtain funding from non-traditional sources, including fees for service, grants, gifts and contracts.

3.3 Manage the college to achieve both effective and efficient uses of resources.

This statement of the vision, goals, and strategic objectives forms the policy to be deployed by the staff. The principles of TQ are embedded in the vision and strategic goals of the college. The vision and goals are based on the needs and expectations of DCCC's customers. The plan focuses the college's attention on the excellence that can be achieved and recognized when stakeholders needs and expectations are met. The partnership strategy is based upon the principle that both customers and suppliers must be an integral part of an organization. An expectation that the college will use its resources efficiently and effectively is built into the plan.

Vertical Alignment. With the plan developed, it was necessary to select and plan the activities to achieve the vision and goals. Sessions were held with administrative staff to engage in dialog about the mission, vision and strategic objectives and develop College-wide and departmental plans aligned with the strategic plan. In a series of meetings, departments drafted plans, presented them to executive staff, and received feedback. The dialog about this operational plan re-occurs each year in May and June, just prior to the initial budget planning for the fiscal year beginning one year later. The give and take which occurs in this planning process emphasizes shared vision, constancy of purpose and the vertical alignment of all departments with the overall strategic plan. This planning process has become the backbone of the implementation of TQ across the College. The departments then work to implement the agreed-upon activities and periodically report to the executive staff about their progress. This entire process has enabled the College to improve the implementation of the strategic plan including TQ. It has helped staff identify the need for training, or retraining, as a department encounters barriers to the use of TQ to achieve their goals.

Recently, the president completed a series of visits with each department of the College. The purposes of these visits were to: 1) learn the mission and vision of each department as developed by its own members, 2) dialog with the staff in each department about the way in which their mission/vision carries out the mission/vision of the College, 3) learn how each department is implementing TQ in their daily tasks, and 4) learn the barriers they are encountering which prevents them from achieving their vision and goals. These sessions demonstrated that the mission and vision of the college were widely understood and shared across the College and that department activities were strongly aligned with the strategic plan.

Without a strong strategic plan, constancy of purpose would be more difficult to achieve. The strategic plan, if correctly conceived, gives all the employees of an organization the same information about the essential mission and vision of the organization. It empowers everyone to contribute to an ennobling enterprise, which is larger than anyone in the organization and more than any department can achieve by itself. If it is developed and redeveloped in a participative framework, it can become a widely-shared and self-administered plan. People support what they help create. In a public institution, the plan must be based upon the real needs and expectations of stakeholders.

No human activity is without its challenges, and creating alignment is no exception. Since alignment will not occur without effective communication, communication is the very first challenge. Others cannot be expected to pursue a plan that is ignored in the day-to-day activities of people in leadership positions; therefore, leaders must keep the plan foremost in their actions. No one can be expected to follow a plan if her or his own needs, expectations and frustrations are ignored. While customer needs come first, staff reactions and needs are important. It is essential to engage staff in frequent dialog about the plan, their reactions to it, their frustrations in implementing it, and even their disagreement with it or the activities expected to implement it. The resolution of these issues allows for a greater sharing of the vision and strategic goals of the plan so all staff members can "own" it. To do otherwise is to prevent the effective alignment which can develop the powerful synergy needed to achieve great things. The entire staff must know and share the importance of the goals. These are the responsibilities of the leaders of any organization.

ADMINISTRATIVE FUNDAMENTALS

After strategic planning, the next component essential to the success of an organization's transformation to TQ is to focus attention on how each and every unit can optimize their everyday capability to meet or exceed their customers' expectations and thereby contribute to the consistent achievement of the organization's strategic plans. An organizational unit, whether a department or division, has an inherent capability just as every process does. The task of those who manage and operate within a unit is, first, to understand that capability and then to strive to maximize it, one small improvement at a time.

When the college first introduced TQ, it did so through multiple waves of cross-unit project improvement teams. Project

---

teams continue to have an important place in our overall implementation strategy. They are a necessary ingredient in horizontal integration, the third component depicted in the continuous improvement wheel. However, as successful as they were, the project teams proved to be insufficient as a vehicle for infusing TQ more evenly throughout the College's operating units. For many staff, the project teams were seen as time-consuming interruptions to their normal routines when they went off to their team meetings to do their TQ "time." Quite a few staff seemed to appreciate the potential value of using the tools and techniques for improving their day-to-day work, but only a relative few actually put them to use. Many staff opted out, claiming they did not have the extra time.

After many initial project team successes, the college's TQ efforts stalled somewhat while we struggled to determine how to move TQ from being an extra-curricular activity to TQ being how the daily work gets done. In hindsight, we now realize that we had worked ourselves out on the same shaky limb many other U.S. organizations did when launching TQ programs. The headline of a *Wall Street Journal* article reporting on a recent study by Ernst and Young read, "Quality Programs Show Shoddy Results" (*Wall Street Journal*, 1992). According to the study, quality practices had reached lasting or meaningful levels in very few U.S. companies. One of the major contributors to this poor record was that most companies treated TQ as a separate program, isolated from day-to-day operations, and not as a way to meet business objectives. Unsuccessful companies were also long on awareness building and expectation raising, but short on skill building and support. Most importantly, they lacked implementation plans to help managers and their staffs develop their own plans for changing each unit's approach to managing those aspects of their daily work, which was critical to their success.

DCCC's executive staff sensed at the time what needed to

be done, but did not know quite how to do it. We could find no road maps to follow. After about a year of frustration, we had the good fortune to learn about Hewlett Packard's business fundamentals process. In an adaptation of this process, which we call our Administrative Fundamentals process, we found a framework for encouraging more staff to use TQ in managing and improving their daily work.

The Administrative Fundamentals process required all operating units to take two initial steps. The first of these was to define the unit's mission. In doing so, the staff briefly described how the work of their unit contributed to furthering the college's mission. This served two purposes. It reinforced the alignment process, described earlier, by allowing units to validate their understanding of how they fit in organization-ally. To most staff, this was an entirely new experience. Some learned for the first time what their unit's real mission was. In a few cases, units defined their roles too broadly and in others, too narrowly. For instance, one academic support unit had been "taken over" in terms of the volume of students being served from a single academic department. This skewing of services happened gradually and was never intended as a matter of conscious policy. The intention was still to keep the services open and available to support all departments. By having the unit define its mission, this discrepancy surfaced and its broader role reaffirmed. The second purpose of the unit mission statements was to provide guidance for the units as they identified their key processes. These were defined as the processes most integral to carrying our their unit's mission.

We have learned that the selection of a unit's key processes should not be underestimated. For some staff, choosing among their many processes, however routine or simple, was not easy. In their view, all their processes are important and related to their mission, or they would not be doing them. The result is often an indiscriminate list of virtually all the processes a unit performs. The purpose in choosing a short list is to encourage the staff to be focused in their application of TQ techniques. If applied conscientiously, these techniques, which involve more up-front planning and systematic data gathering, can take more time. The redeeming value, of course, is that this initial time investment will be recouped many times over through operating efficiencies. The risk is attempting to pay this kind of attention to too many processes at once; the staff may dissipate their energies and become frustrated and cynical about the value of TQ. Consequently, when selecting their key processes, it is vital that units choose only those few that are of strategic importance to the unit and the organization.

To help determine what might be of strategic importance to the organization, we used a staff planning retreat to reinforce the concept of the college as a system made up of interlinking processes. Although most staff had vague notions of the college as a collection of interdependent parts and that education was our main order of business, it was the first time that these concepts were explicitly discussed. The retreat provided an opportunity to discuss and reach consensus about how we, and

Figure 3

ADMINISTRATIVE FUNDAMENTALS

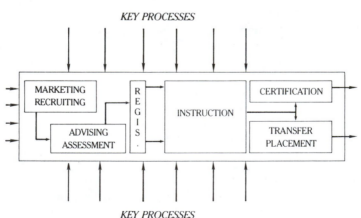

the processes we manage, interrelate in support of instruction, the college's mainstay process. The conceptual system that we drew up is depicted in Figure 3.

The staff retreat was followed with a "customer-window" survey of all administrative staff. Staff were asked to evaluate each unit's list of key processes on two scales: importance to the functioning of their unit; and how well they thought the process was performing. The survey results provided valuable feedback for narrowing their lists. In some cases, administrators had underestimated the importance of a process to its internal customers. In other cases, they overestimated the degree to which customers were satisfied.

In arriving at their "short" list of key processes upon which to focus their "quality" time, each process was weighed using several factors: its role in supporting the college's mission and goals, its relationship to the college's mainstay process and how well it was functioning as judged by its internal customers. Obviously, a process considered to be mission related, important to other units and in need of improvement, would head the priority list of processes targeted for TQ activity. Strategically, this would be time well spent – a case of trying to do the right things better.

This took us into the next steps of the Administrative Fundamentals process. Staff were charged with taking each of their key processes through the following sequence of steps:

1. Specify the outputs of the process
2. Define the process using a flow chart
3. Identify the internal and external customers of the process
4. Identify customers' expectations/requirements
5. Establish performance measures
6. Collect and review measurement data
7. Standardize or improve the process

Our first approach required all units to move ahead in unison. A deadline was set for having each key process documented through the third step, which involved identifying internal and external customers. Before the deadline, training workshops were held to familiarize or refresh staff in top-down flow charts and how to identify customers and outputs. The executive staff, which serves as the oversight committee for the college's TQ implementation, felt that the deadline had accomplished its purpose of getting all the units up to a minimum level of TQ activity. Process management responsibilities were established for the college's key processes, and the processes were defined and documented in an Administrative Fundamentals notebook. The notebook is a reference source that enables each staff member to understand the processes of his or her own unit as well as the processes of other units. It can also be used to identify the intersections between processes from different units.

Executive staff took this mandatory approach because it began to realize that the full synergistic power of TQ would not be achieved unless everyone was participating and unless all the College units were operating at their optimum levels. In making its strategic commitment to TQ, the College has come to recognize the scope of the necessary cultural transformation as well as the natural resistance and defensiveness of staff clinging to old habits. Some TQ proponents advocate the "champion" approach, where TQ "champions" are encouraged and supported in the organization, and valuable energy and resources not wasted trying to convert the resisters. DCCC took this approach in the beginning by including champions in project teams and encouraging them to become facilitators and trainers. This allowed some units to move ahead and provided successes to motivate others. However, for the institution, this resulted in the stalled condition that prompted the across-the-board Administrative Fundamentals approach.

Many concerns and objections were raised in attempting to engage everyone in the implementation process. As a result, executive staff created the TQ Steering Group, made up of a cross-section of middle-level administrative staff. The TQ Steering Group was given the following charge:

- ❖ To plan, support and steer implementation of TQ at the operational level
- ❖ To identify implementation barriers and solutions
- ❖ To develop and implement communication strategies
- ❖ To develop a training plan for all staff
- ❖ To pilot new initiatives

As their first activity, the TQ Steering Group surveyed their colleagues to find out the nature and extent of the concerns and the obstacles they encountered as they continued implementing the Administrative Fundamentals process. The list of concerns and obstacles fell into four categories: those related to time and competing demands, training, communication and interdepartmental issues. The training issues dealt mostly with the diversity of the staffs' experiences with Total Quality. They wanted customer-driven training that was "just-in-time" and geared to their skill level. They also wanted a case study approach that used real examples, especially DCCC ones, to help de-mystify all this "TQ stuff" and give them confidence to proceed on their own. The communication issues were similar in that they wanted more sharing of successful improvement activities. The interdepartmental issues were delegated back to the executive staff since one of their roles as custodians of the system is to manage the interfaces and intersections between processes.

A number of strategies were developed to deal with these issues. The most important issue to be resolved concerned individual time constraints and a generally negative reaction to the imposed deadline. To address most, if not all, of these

---

issues, the TQ Steering Group created a process which allowed each unit to develop their own process management and improvement plans. As part of these plans, each unit established a timetable for each of its key processes. This timetable allows them, with appropriate consultation with other affected units that might be customers or suppliers, to say when they can reasonably expect to work through the sequence of steps that were listed earlier. Their plans can then reflect the shifting time demands inherent in the unit's work cycle. For instance, units heavily impacted by the rush of activity at the beginning of a semester can pace their TQ activity according to their own deadlines.

An important value of the written improvement plans, which have been in effect for over a year, is that it has allowed everyone to assess their impact relative to other demands. Improvement planning has been integrated with regular institutional planning activities. As part of the periodic review process (we have recently gone from a quarterly to a trimester timetable), staff are expected to give progress reports on both their improvement plans and their annual work plans for achieving the College's strategic goals and objectives. This has proven to be successful by providing the opportunity for openly negotiating priorities and trade-offs so that all interested parties are aware of the implications and are consulted.

The emphasis during these trimester reviews focuses on the gaps between what was planned and what could actually be accomplished. The purpose, of course, is not to fix blame but to find ways to bridge the gaps. Sometimes this is done by providing more resources. Sometimes, when there are no more resources available, the expectations are lowered or deferred to a later trimester. Mainstreaming improvement planning in this way has lessened stress levels without sacrificing TQ. By design, staff are more in control of their work priorities and the change process.

Through the Administrative Fundamentals process, each and every staff member is empowered as a change agent. An essential part of their jobs is to constantly experiment with new and better ways of managing their work. At first, this means focusing on their key processes so that the organization can leverage its TQ efforts. However, as experience accumulates and staff get more comfortable with TQ methods, they realize that TQ is not synonymous with marathon project teams and complicated data-gathering techniques. They begin to appreciate that the big gains from applying TQ are in the small, incremental improvements. These small successes create the energy and motivation that carries TQ throughout the organization, transforming it unit-by-unit into a learning organization.

The Administrative Fundamentals process created a new momentum in DCCC's TQ transformation. Evidence of TQ activity abounds throughout the College. There are still a few "backwaters" where it is business as usual, but these have become the exception. Where are we on the road to becoming a learning organization in which TQ principles and techniques are the accepted way we do business, whether it's the business office, the business department, or Business 101? To answer this question, the TQ Steering Group, with widespread staff involvement, has drafted a TQ implementation vision. It is an attempt to be explicit about the kinds of behaviors that we will expect to see in each other and in each department and classroom as we move ever closer to the elusive goal of becoming a true TQ organization. We have just prepared a questionnaire to go to all staff that will attempt to assess where we are in our units and across the College in exhibiting these behaviors. The results will provide a new benchmark for ourselves and an opportunity to learn how we can progress even further.

CROSS-FUNCTIONAL MANAGEMENT

Without waiting for the survey results from staff, we already know that we have not paid sufficient attention to the issues related to horizontal integration. This is the third component of DCCC's continuous improvement TQM wheel. "Horizontal integration" is a term used to describe cross-functional management activities that focus on optimizing the capability of the entire organization. It addresses problems and issues that go beyond the purview of a single unit or department. At the conceptual level, it relies heavily on systems thinking and, at the technical level, on skills related to process design and redesign. At the practical, day-to-day level, it depends on good, old-fashioned "people" skills, or the "soft" skills as they are called today. In order to proceed in this area, we find ourselves dealing with such basics as teamwork, interpersonal communication (i.e., listening skills) and conflict resolution.

We have taken some strides in this area with our numerous cross-functional project teams and with our attempt to rethink the organization in terms of a system of interlinking units, all supporting instruction as our main function and purpose. We have even experimented with process redesign involving processes that cut across multiple departments. These are important first steps, but they have been largely ad hoc initiatives. As we move further in this direction, we realize that the organization of the College will have to change in significant ways. Some said, "Organizations are perfectly designed to get the results they get." We are proud of the results we now get but not satisfied, and we know that to do much better will require nothing less than a redesign of the College. We envision a horizontally-networked organization with staff at all levels reaching out to one another and joining as partners to work on problems and issues in teams and clusters of teams that cross functional and organizational boundaries. This vision is already beginning to show itself in the white spaces on the organization chart in the form of permanent cross-functional teams such as the Institutional Marketing Team and the TQ Steering Group.

PIECING IT ALL TOGETHER

When first introduced to TQ, many people are struck by the simplicity and common sense nature of the principles and techniques. They wonder what all the fuss is about. Those of us who have been at it for awhile and have discovered the profoundness that Deming speaks of, realize that it is far from simple when you try to put all the pieces together that are necessary to transform the culture of an organization and reap the full benefits of TQ.

Obviously, it makes no sense to have a strategic plan if staff are not committed to it and the organization is not capable of accomplishing the goals and objectives that are embodied in it. Nor does it make sense to have units within an organization that are optimized but going off in different directions. The full potential of an organization is only realized when all of its resources are fully in play and pulling in the same direction. For DCCC, this means paying proper attention to the three indispensable elements of Total Quality – vertical alignment, unit optimization and horizontal integration.

REFERENCES

"Quality Programs Show Shoddy Results," *Wall Street Journal*, May 14, 1992.

Angelo, T. A., Cross, K. P. *Classroom Assessment Techniques, A Handbook for College Teachers*, (2nd ed.) San Francisco: Jossey-Bass, 1993.

Baugher, K. "Student Quality Team Manual," Birmingham, Al.: Samford Unversity, 1992.

Richard D. DeCosmo has been president of the Delaware County Community College in Media, Penn., since 1980. DCCC enrolls about 25,000 students in its credit and community service programs each year.

Prior to DCCC, he was executive vice president of Moraine Valley Community College in Palos Hills, Ill., for five years. He was also dean of student and community services (1971-74) and dean of student personnel services (1968-71).

He started his career at Macomb County College in Warren, Mich., as an instructor in 1958, and subsequent to teaching was the director of admissions and then chief student personnel officer.

He holds a B.A. and M.A. in political science from the University of Detroit. His doctorate in education is from Loyola University of Chicago.

He is a frequent speaker on the topic of TQM at universities and colleges across the U.S.

Jerome S. Parker When Delaware County Community College began to experiment with the application of Total Quality Management principles to its own management operations, it was one of only a few colleges and universities to do so. Now, more than six years later, the College is widely recognized for the success of this pioneering initiative.

As dean of management systems and planning at Delaware County Community College and as a member of the College's Total Quality Implementation Team, Parker has had major responsibility for planning and supporting the transformation of the College's planning and management processes to reflect the principles of Total Quality. His specific responsibilities in this regard have included chairing the first successful improvement team and the TQ Planning Committee. He is a member of the president's executive staff, which has assumed ongoing responsibility for steering the implementation of TQ in both institutional and instructional management.

Parker has attended numerous Total Quality seminars and workshops, including Deming's four-day workshop and Masaaki Imai's week-long Kaizen seminar. He has conducted training sessions and consulted on such topics as the seven basic TQ tools, implementing TQ in a college setting, Hoshin planning, and TQ in daily management.

Parker received his undergraduate degree from Wesleyan University and his doctorate in higher education administration from the University of Wisconsin-Madison.

5

Is Quality a Manageable Commodity in Higher Education?

Dean L. Hubbard

What value do the concepts and techniques frequently referred to as "Total Quality Management" add to the process of change in higher education? Or do they simply muddy the waters by injecting alien terminology, assumptions and relationships into a very complex and intractable culture. The fact that educators prefer CQI (Continuous Quality Improvement) to TQM (Total Quality Management) suggests that the fit is not perfect. (The word "total" is difficult to interpret, while "management" diverts the focus from the leadership that is really called for.) Regardless of the terms one prefers, the question remains: Can substantial and lasting improvements be made in higher education by extrapolating from what seems to work in industry to what all agree is a very different culture?

Northwest Missouri State University began a quality improvement odyssey in 1984, a year before the moniker TQM was coined by the military and several years before an agreed-upon set of principles for managing quality began to emerge. Our initial efforts were sometimes poorly defined and certainly not deployed across all units in the University. Nonetheless, we began a process of systematically extrapolating from what was apparently working in industrial and service settings to our educational environment, particularly the academic side of the enterprise. During the 1986-87 school year, we finalized what came to be called our Culture of Quality plan for improving undergraduate education. The plan, now in its seventh year of implementation, contains 42 goals and 40 action steps. We are currently using the criteria for the Malcolm Baldrige National Quality Award as a template for renewing this plan.

After nine years, what do we have to show for our efforts? Well, for one thing, we have some notable successes (of which we are proud), some failures (which we would like to cover up), but most of all a pervasive conviction that quality is a receding horizon and therefore must be relentlessly pursued. The journey is not painless, nor are there any quick fixes. (I'd like to know what planet Phil Crosby was on when he entitled his recent book, *Quality Without Tears!*)

Incidentally, Northwest is a typical comprehensive, co-educational, publicly-supported, regional university. The University has a student enrollment of around 6,000, and a faculty of 235. The majority of students live in on-campus housing and come from within a 150-mile radius of the campus.

IMPLEMENTING TQM IN A UNIVERSITY SETTING

The Principles of Parsimony. If asked to rank CQI concepts in terms of relevance for higher education, first on my list would be the principle of parsimony. Dr. Nam Suh, professor of engineering at MIT, states it best: "The perfect design is associated with the assemblage of the fewest parts." We took that to mean fewer and more sharply-focused goals, clear definitions of quality appropriate to the task at hand, fewer administrative layers, fewer programs and fewer evaluative metrics. Planning efforts in higher education are usually too global, involve too many goals and fail to differentiate between the crucial and the trivial. One way to overcome this tendency is to apply the principle of parsimony.

We started by applying this principle to our mission. A sharply-focused statement was adopted which commits the University to "place special emphasis upon agriculture, business and teacher education, particularly as these professions contribute to the primary service region." Further, "All of the University's programs build upon comprehensive general education requirements."

Since adopting that mission, we have consolidated seven colleges into four, eliminated 34 programs which were undersubscribed or of poor quality, and phased out three-and-a-half full-time dean's positions and two vice presidencies. The result was a reallocation of over six percent of the Education and General budget away from administration and academic support areas to quality improvements in instruction. The portion of the University's Education and General (E&G) budget allocated to instruction grew from 48.5 percent (the national average) to over 59 percent. (According to John Minter, the 75th percentile is 51.5 percent for comprehensive universities.) Computed in constant FY92 dollars, $3,100,000 (10 percent of the Education and General budget) was shifted from physical plant, administrative and academic support services into instruction, even as services were improved. Figure 1, based upon audited financial statements, displays the reallocation of resources that has taken place.

Since the instructional portion of the E&G budget is where faculty salaries are funded, this change made it possible for us to increase faculty salaries at 147 percent of the rate of inflation during this same time period. The average salary of a

Figure 1
Constant Dollar Changes Since FY85
Northwest Missouri State University

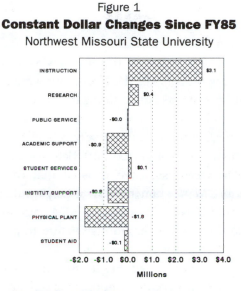

Computed in Constant FY92 Dollars

Figure 2
Salary Increase Comparisons
Northwest Missouri State University

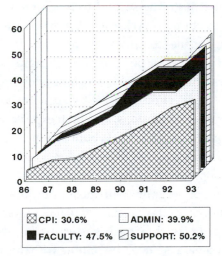

faculty member at Northwest climbed from $3,000 below national norms, as reported each spring in the *Chronicle of Higher Education*, to national equivalency.

Finally, the principle of parsimony was applied to the number of support services the University would attempt to manage. The result was out-sourcing the management of custodial, grounds, maintenance and the power plant to ServiceMaster Corporation (food service and the book store had previously been contracted out). Before signing the contract with ServiceMaster, we insisted that they agree to implement a TQM program in the areas they would manage on campus. Today, ServiceMaster and ARA, our food service vendor, are leaders in Continuous Quality Improvement at Northwest. A six- to eighteen-month backlog of maintenance projects has been eliminated. Eighty-five percent of students rank food service as good, very good, or excellent. The overall rating is 3.3 on a 5.0 scale, compared with a national norm of 2.9. Buildings sparkle and a general campus beautification program has been implemented. At the same time, campus maintenance costs have been reduced $1,700,000 per year.

Benchmarking. The second technique borrowed from industry was benchmarking. Robert Camp defines benchmarking as "the [continuous] search for...[the] best practices that lead to superior performance." (Camp, p. 12). Of all the techniques utilized in TQM, benchmarking appears to be the easiest fit to education. At least two benefits accrue. First, benchmarks raise expectations, and high expectations are the foundation upon which quality is built in any setting. Second, without benchmarks, goals have a tendency to be self-serving and status quo-preserving. Stated more bluntly, comparisons of one's students or programs with those from other institutions is the best antidote for the inertia that plagues most campuses.

In keeping with Camp's definition, Northwest benchmarked several sources, beginning with the institution's own faculty and students who were asked to submit "ideas for creating a culture of quality on campus." While different individuals and groups on campus spent a semester formulating ideas, a steering committee culled ideas from educational reform literature that had appeared over the previous decade. Various data regarding student characteristics and performance were gathered and compared to national norms. The 200 ideas gleaned from all these sources were synthesized and incorporated into a document entitled "Reviewing the Reviews: Suggestions for Reforming Higher Education." Of course, not all 200 ideas could be applied at Northwest, nor were all of equal value. In fact, some were mutually exclusive. Ultimately, 42 were selected as the goals which make up the Culture of Quality plan. Following is a sampling of accomplishments and/or activities initiated as a result of this process.

❖ The first comprehensive electronic campus in the nation was installed; it includes a computing station, two dedicated television channels, and a telephone which accesses a Touch Tone Talker in each residence hall room. The network includes more than 2,400 terminals, 400 microcomputers in 15 labs, 200 software applications and a computerized videodisc and interactive voice synthesizer tutorial system.

❖ Major writing assignments have increased 72 percent as a result of an across-the-curriculum writing program and the electronic campus.

❖ The semester was lengthened from 15 to 17 weeks. The net effect of this change was the addition of one month of instruction to the school year, or 16 weeks to the four-year college experience.

❖ An undergraduate research program is in place which has met with remarkable success. Since 1990, top students are required to participate.

❖ Over 50 events are sponsored each year designed to integrate the student's extra-curricular life with learning activities. Examples include distinguished lectures, art gallery exhibitors, music master classes, Black History Month speakers, guest lecturers, Greek Week presentations and residence halls guest lecturers.

❖ Seventeen "Institution-Wide Instructional Goals" were adopted by the faculty. These goals provide a context for all other action steps.

❖ A general education CORE was adopted, which encompasses the basic knowledge and skills necessary for successful completion of college and later functioning as a literate, educated citizen. The CORE must be completed by the end of the sophomore year.

❖ Freshmen experiencing difficulty in selected courses now have the opportunity to participate in supplemental instruction activities which not only help them in the targeted course, but also provide instruction in note taking, test taking, how to use a textbook as a learning tool and other similar topics. The result is that instead of spending three hours per week in, for example, chemistry, students may spend four or five hours.

❖ Advanced standing requirements are being developed whereby students will be formally evaluated at the end of their sophomore year.

❖ A faculty committee created a uniform course outline/syllabus format to ensure that the University's "Institution-Wide Instructional Goals" are integrated into the objectives of CORE courses.

❖ Over half of all departments have adopted or developed comprehensive senior exit exams.

❖ A new faculty evaluation system was developed by the faculty.

Currently, we are benchmarking selected major degree programs as well as some academic support systems. For example, our chemists have benchmarked labs at the University of Illinois and Marion-Merrell Dow, a major employer of chemists in our region.

Focus on the Customer. The third potent concept higher education can borrow from industry is to focus every service and process on the customer. Despite the intuitive appeal of this perspective, faculty generally have difficulty understanding how such an approach would play out in the classroom. In fact, at some universities TQM efforts have aborted over this issue. We concluded that in the classroom, the student, along with the instructor, are "suppliers" producing a "product" (knowledge) that a future "customer" (employer or graduate school) will evaluate. Even as the supervisor (instructor) and worker (student) in a TQM setting cooperate to understand and satisfy the customer, so students should be involved in instructional design and evaluation and empowered to assume more responsibility for their own learning. In other settings on campus the student is the customer in the typical sense of the word.

An even more sophisticated perspective was suggested by Merlin Ricklefs during a visit to campus. He suggested that what happens in a classroom has two components: curriculum and instruction. Clearly, the student is the customer of instruction. On the other hand, the next course in the sequence is the primary customer of the curriculum, followed by the first employer or graduate school, the accrediting agency and then the student, probably in that order. Discussing these perspectives helped us at Northwest resolve the issue of student as customer.

At Northwest, in the support services, a customer orientation was readily adopted. A permanent Continuous Quality Improvement Team was formed to identify and prioritize opportunities for improvement and to establish expectations. The team, chaired by a department director, includes faculty and students. One of their first accomplishments was to develop and post across campus the following pledge:

CULTURE OF QUALITY
COMMITMENT TO SERVICE

Northwest Missouri State University recognizes that quality service is an essential component of a quality university. Furthermore, we acknowledge that all of us – students, faculty, staff and administration – are at times providers and at other times recipients of services.

Accordingly, we pledge our best efforts to provide quality service to you by:

❖ Treating you with respect, fairness, and honesty
   Making you feel important and earning your trust

❖ Performing our tasks with competence and skill
   Giving you confidence in the quality of what we provide

❖ Communicating clearly and courteously the services provided
   Making it easy for you to know what you can expect

❖ Listening actively to your requests, comments and concerns
   Making it easy for you to tell us what you need

❖ Being flexible and open to new ideas
   Accepting you and valuing your knowledge

❖ Providing what we agree to deliver in a timely manner
   Enabling you to depend on us to help meet your goals

This same group has overseen the establishment of a Student Services Center, with the goal that students can transact 90 percent of their business with the University at a single location. In other words, instead of going to different buildings or offices to cash checks, pay bills, buy tickets, etcetera, students can do all of that at one centrally located counter.

Another task force redesigned the registration process, which used to take one or two days, so that it is now accomplished from the student's room or advisor's office via the electronic campus in less than 15 minutes.

Various assessment instruments have been adopted to understand and monitor customer needs, expectations and perceptions, including regular focus group sessions. The student senate sponsors an annual "gripe day" to garner reactions plus an "I Love Northwest Week" to celebrate successes. Maintenance and custodial personnel regularly survey administrators, faculty and students regarding the perceived quality of their services. Additionally, monthly building inspection tours are conducted to sites selected by a member of the president's cabinet.

Assessment for Prevention. One of the most challenging and potent lessons that educators can learn from the factories is that assessment efforts, if they are to be efficacious in improving quality, must focus on prevention and improvement, not ranking and sorting.

Historically, industry assured the quality of its products by placing inspectors at the end of the assembly line. Assessment under such conditions consisted of ranking and sorting what workers produced. Several problems attend such a system. First, it is very expensive. The cost of not making products right the first time includes wasted labor and raw materials, labor and materials needed for rework, warranty costs for marginal products that were shipped, to say nothing of lost customers, damaged reputation and the like. (Ponder the cost to education of remediation, attrition and under-developed talent.) Second, inspectors at the end of the assembly line suggest to workers that they are not trusted to do the job right the first time, thus lowering expectations and aspirations. As is often the case, expectations become self-fulfilling prophecies. Finally, the presence of inspectors highlights differences between management and labor. Under such circumstances workers tend to focus their attention on turf protectionism, cumbersome work rules and other adversarial strategies. All of these negative consequences can be observed in education.

Yet, it is incontrovertible that assessment and feedback are critical to the improvement of any process. Less obvious is the linkage between assessment systems and attempts on the part of those being assessed to "beat the system." Sometimes that means "cooking" or distorting the numbers. At other times it leads to focusing solely on that which is easily measurable while ignoring more important goals (for example, simple recall rather than critical thinking skills). Or, since assessment ipso facto clarifies minimum standards, minimums often become maximums. Once participants – be they students or employees – conclude that the primary reason for measuring how they are doing is so they can be sorted and ranked, they will shift their energies toward finding ways to circumvent, or at least compromise, the system.

This conundrum led Phil Crosby to advocate that inspectors be taken off the assembly line and that the focus be on prevention. Edwards Deming concurs with Crosby, but goes even further, admonishing administrators in his 14 points to "eliminate quotas or work standards, and management by objectives or numerical goals; substitute leadership." In higher education, most assessment is "inspection at the end of the assembly line" for purposes of ranking and sorting; relatively little diagnostic testing is done. Further, the primary beneficiary is the instructor who uses results to assign grades, not prevent failures. The key to at least attenuating these problems lies in shifting the primary focus of assessment away from ranking and sorting toward improvement.

At Northwest, two approaches to assessment were incorporated into the Culture of Quality plan in order to focus the results on raising expectations and preventing errors rather than simple ranking and sorting. First, an assessment program, deliberately designed to raise expectations, was put in place. Freshmen are asked to come to campus for a week-long orientation before school begins each fall. During that time, in addition to being introduced to the Culture of Quality, they are tested along several dimensions using a combination of locally developed and nationally normed tests. The information gleaned is used for placing students in appropriate classes and later as a benchmark against which progress can be measured.

At the end of the sophomore year, a nationally-normed test administered during Freshman Orientation is re-administered (to plot progress), and a writing sample is analyzed. Various departments also administer their own tests, examine portfolios and the like before the student is formally admitted to advanced standing. Three benefits accrue from such a program: (1) an opportunity is provided to ameliorate problems while there is still time; (2) a salutary kind of anxiety is induced on the part of freshmen as they look forward to this hurdle; and, (3) a more homogeneous upper-division environment is created which facilitates teaching to higher-order thinking skills such as analysis, synthesis and evaluation. This approach also avoids the practical problem with senior exams which are part of graduation requirements; namely, the reluctance to deny graduation after four years of promotion and presumed satisfactory performance.

At graduation, additional tests are given. The results are used to evaluate program effectiveness. Finally, five years after graduation alumni are surveyed in order to glean additional "customer" perspectives.

A second, less traditional, use of assessment focuses on improving both teaching and learning. In his book, *Higher*

Learning, Derek Bok suggests that testing drives student study habits (Bok, 1981). The first thing students do when beginning a course is find out how they will be tested. They ask the instructor, they query former students, they study the syllabi. Once they have a feel for the type of questions they will be asked, they adjust their study habits accordingly. Therefore, if instructors ask questions which force students to use higher-order cognitive skills such as analysis, synthesis or evaluation, students will prepare themselves for those tasks. On the other hand, if all the instructor demands is recall and understanding, students will study in those modes.

Since few college instructors have ever systematically learned how to construct questions which test to different cognitive levels, we focused faculty development on that task. Specialists were brought to campus to hold weekend workshops on the topic of teaching to, and testing for, higher-order cognition. Participation was extensive and enthusiastic. Thus, the stigma often associated with assessment was avoided, assessment was at least moved in the direction of prevention, quality of instruction was improved and the expectations of students were raised.

RESULTS OF CQI AT NORTHWEST

Northwest's experience suggests that doing things better does, in the end, pay off. Specifically, the dollar impact of Culture of Quality changes have been dramatic. For example, despite a severely declining population in its catchment area, enrollment grew 26 percent until it hit capacity. (The slight downturn experienced in 1992-93 appears to be the ripple effect of an unusually large freshman class brought in four years earlier which resulted in a larger-than-usual graduating class.)

Education and General fund balances went from a negative $962,000 to a surplus of over $1.2 million.

The University went from technical default on its auxil-

Figure 3
Enrollment Growth
Northwest Missouri State University

Student Enrollment (Thousands)

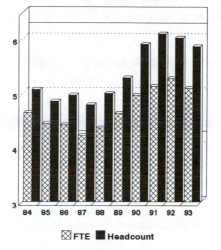

⊠ FTE ■ Headcount

Figure 4
Education and General Fund Balances
Northwest Missouri State University

Actual from audited financial statements.

---

iary bonds to a $1,700,000 surplus at the same time residence halls were being renovated, new furniture was installed and occupancy rates increased. The surplus has allowed the University to fund some large renovation/enhancement projects which would have been unthinkable in previous years.

Figure 5
Auxiliary Debt Reserves
Northwest Missouri State University

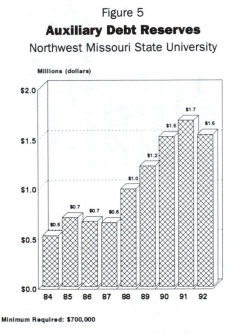

Millions (dollars)

Minimum Required: $700,000

During the energy crisis of the late 1970s, a decision was made to move the University away from fossil fuels. Since that time, this program has been wrapped into the Culture of Quality plan and expanded to include recycling. The use of fossil fuels has declined dramatically (see Figure 6), while energy costs as a portion of the total budget have declined. Equally important, the University has entered into a partnership with area communities to generate energy using pelletized waste paper products which previously had clogged landfills.

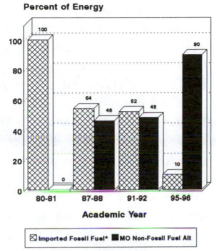

Figure 6

Thermo Energy Consumption

Northwest Missouri State University

Percent of Energy

* Missouri imports $9 billion of fossil fuel each year.

Figure 7

Growth in Assets

Northwest Foundation, Inc.

Millions

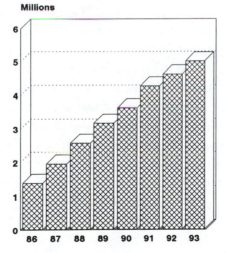

Finally, the Culture of Quality has generated enthusiasm among alumni, as evidenced by steadily-increased giving.

OBSERVATIONS AND LESSONS

Colleges and universities are exceedingly complex organizations. A typical campus encompasses a bookstore, dining establishment, hotel operation, police force, construction company, athletic club and entertainment center, all of which supposedly support and compliment a collection of fiercely competitive (internally) academic departments which deliver the institution's core product. Each of these segments share attitudes and technologies common to their industry, albeit tempered by their association with each other and with the traditions and expectations of academe. Beyond the Golden Rule, the assertion that any single concept can be applied in this multifarious environment seems exceedingly heroic. Indeed, any attempt to slavishly apply the Deming, Crosby, Juran or any other guru's model to every segment of an educational institution is probably doomed from the outset. Nonetheless, the system in all of its diverse dimensions – from the registration of students to the presentation of ideas – can be managed in ways that maximize quality outcomes. Furthermore, while there are identifiable differences between manufacturing a product and teaching a course or delivering a service, many of the principles and techniques used in managing manufacturing quality can be applied to managing educational quality. Likewise, some of the principles which undergird quality education have trenchant potential for manufacturing (for example, designing assessment to raise expectations).

Education can learn from the factories. Principles for ensuring quality which are grounded in a clear sense of mission, concern for people and high expectations can and should be emulated.

REFERENCES

Camp, Robert C. *Benchmarking: The Search for Industry Best Practices that Lead to Superior Performance* , Milwaukee: Quality Press, 1989, p. 12.

Point number 11 of Deming's 14 points.

Derek Bok, *Higher Learning*, Cambridge, Mass.: Harvard University Press, 1981.

Dean L. Hubbard has been president of Northwest Missouri State University since 1984. Prior to coming to Northwest, he served as president of Union College, in Lincoln, Neb.

Hubbard has earned degrees from Stanford University (Ph.D.); Yonsei University, Seoul, Korea (Korean Language); and Andrews University, Berrien Springs, Mich. (B.A. and M.A.).

Under Hubbard's leadership, Northwest has received national attention for its "Culture of Quality" plan to improve the quality of undergraduate education. Northwest was the first institution in the nation to develop a comprehensive electronic campus which includes a computing station, two dedicated television channels and a telephone, which accesses a Touch Tone Talker, in each residence hall room.

Hubbard is internationally recognized for his work in the field of Total Quality Management (TQM), particularly in the service sector. He is a member of the Board of Examiners for the Malcolm Baldrige National Quality Award and is a judge for the Missouri Quality Award. He chairs the Academic Quality Consortium and is a member of the American Society for Quality Control. He regularly lectures and conducts workshops on the topic of quality improvement.

Hubbard has been a commissioner and is currently a consultant/evaluator for the North Central Association of Colleges and Schools. He has evaluated 23 colleges and universities for accreditation on three continents.

In addition to editing this book, he has 20 published articles, five book chapters and numerous papers.

6

Forging Effective Business-Academia Partnerships

Robert M. Price

On June 5, 1989, President George Bush appeared before the Business Roundtable in Washington, D.C. and issued the following challenge: "Get involved – personally involved – with the schools in your community. Walk into that classroom – not as a CEO, but as a concerned parent, as a good citizen in your community."

As I listened to President Bush urge America's business leaders to "be a catalyst" for educational reform, I thought about my own experiences in Total Quality Management (TQM) and education. I had been involved in the quality journey of my company, Control Data Corporation, for more than six years. I also had been an active participant in the Education Committee of the Minnesota Business Partnerships and served as chairman of the Board of Visitors of the Fuqua School of Business at Duke University, but I had no idea how deeply I was to get involved, how intertwined those activities were to become.

The observations and lessons of the past four years have been instructive, deeply rewarding, sometimes painful, frequently frustrating and, above all, useful. The bottom line is that TQM is a conceptual framework for the most effective business-academia partnerships.

There is a myriad of initiatives to improve the quality of elementary and secondary schools in the United States. President Bush's challenge to the Business Roundtable, however, was striking.

Not only did it call for a 10-year commitment on the part of both the companies and their CEOs, but also by bringing it together as a Business Roundtable (BRT) effort, the initiative was more focused, more cohesive and, therefore, had a better chance of succeeding. Traditionally, business support of education has mostly consisted of "throwing money over the wall." Obviously, money is important, but I knew from Control Data's many complex and far-reaching collaborative efforts that a true partnership is where you bring intellect, know-how, emotion and commitment to a project.

Perhaps even more important was the structure of the initiative. It called for leadership from the top of the business community, the largest 200 companies in the U.S. and their CEOs. The activity, however, would take place at the state and local level where systemic change has to occur if, as a nation, we are to achieve our goal of excellence in education. Without its having been explicitly stated as such, this is exactly the framework of TQM, something already familiar to me in a business environment.

PART I: Business and K-12 Education . . .
The New Mexico Experience

As a result of President Bush's challenge, the Business

Roundtable established a 13-member CEO task force. As a member of that task force, I participated in the process of encouraging matchups between companies/CEOs and the governors and education leaders in each state. My own pairing was with New Mexico.

If there's a word that describes New Mexico, it's diversity. The state's population is culturally and linguistically diverse. Hispanics and Native Americans alone account for 55 percent of the population. With 88 school districts, ranging in size from a few hundred students in remote rural areas to many thousands in the city of Albuquerque, there's great demographic diversity. Like most states, the efforts at educational change in New Mexico are themselves diverse and highly fragmented.

At the same time, New Mexico has a very caring group of leaders. Business leaders, National Laboratory executives and governmental officials are sincerely concerned with the education process. There's an above-average desire to improve the quality of the schools.

My task was to help, to seek out and to support those most aggressively seeking change and improvement in education.

How to approach this task?

With large, complex systems, where problems are so endemic they frequently have ceased even to be recognized as problems, where every "solution" is at best a partial solution, it is necessary to take a pragmatic "bail and row" approach. Clearly it is essential to have a goal, an objective toward which one is "rowing." And this, in turn, calls for a clear understanding of how to get there, i.e., to have a well-articulated strategy. At the same time, if the boat is leaking severely, you have to bail hard just to stay afloat...you have to take the short-term action necessary to give your strategy time to work. Anyone who has had "bail and row" experience in a real boat knows just how hard this can be. Total concentration on either task will surely result in failure.

For example, any viable answer to the cost-effectiveness problems facing education involves widespread use of electronic educational technologies – communications and computers. However, these technologies cannot simply be "pushed" onto the system. It requires a strong "pull" by the practitioners – the teachers. That requires, in turn, an understanding which can only come from training in those technologies.

The challenge was to effectively engage the business community in this "bail and row" process and to help generate the "pull" as well as to help with the "push." Within six months, in the summer of 1990, through a partnership of the State Department of Education, the Governor's Office and business, the New Mexico Education Technology Institute (NMETI) was formed, and the first training sessions were held in five locations throughout the state. Through cooperative partnerships, the NMETI has continued each year since 1990 to conduct educational technology training. For 1993, the effort has been incorporated into an initiative by Sandia National Laboratory to train academic administrators. This effort, although modest in terms of total education need, demonstrated that collective action could produce results and help meet urgent needs.

In September of 1990, shortly after the NMETI effort was begun, the State Board of Education and the Commission on Higher Education jointly chartered the Education Technology Planning Committee (ETPC), bringing together key individuals from K-12 education, higher education, libraries, museums, the National Laboratories located in New Mexico, community representatives, state government agencies, parents and the business community. Thus, the task of "rowing" toward a long-term objective (or at least charting a course) began as well.

At the very first meeting of the ETPC, it became obvious that the fragmentation of reform and improvement efforts was the biggest challenge we faced. Each improvement or change initiative was a response to a particular problem or need. Some were simple augmentations of current teaching and programs. Some, such as Re:Learning,* were true systemic change initiatives. Whatever their scope, most required new educational technology investment. All of them competed for the already inadequate financial resources available to the educational system. Although this was not as obvious, they also competed for the available expertise in planning and management.

The committee, therefore, took the approach that the most significant thing it could do was to lay out a framework for collaboration and prioritization of needs, as well as a basic strategy for improving the utilization of educational technology.

It was felt that this approach was vastly preferable to a prescriptive one, i.e., specifying the number of computers or modems or video recorders (or whatever) per 100 students, which would simply result in one more program competing for scarce or nonexistent resources.

The ETPC produced a strategic framework, titled Challenge 2000, that has four basic elements: 1) Partnerships – the need for utilization of public-private partnerships; 2) Telecommunications – an approach to completing the state-wide educational telecommunications network; 3) Training – train and support teachers and faculty; 4) Technology in the schools – a structure and process for planning and providing the all important "pull" force for technology utilization in the learning process.

Underlying this strategy were several key principles:

The first of these principles is **increasing public aware-**

---

*Re:Learning is a joint secondary education reform effort based at Brown University and sponsored by the Coalition of Essential Schools. Theodore Sizer, a professor of education at Brown, is founder and director of the Coalition, which is a partnership of more than 500 schools nationwide committed to the re-design of their school programs.

ness. Public apathy about the need for education reform is a major contributor to the resistance being experienced by reform efforts. Most attempts to prod the public and government into action dwell on the negative and result in "bashing" the teachers and school administrators. In general, people cannot cope with so much negative rhetoric. So, they ignore it or reject it. It is essential that a public-awareness campaign show people the potential, the excitement, the reward and the fun, as well as the need for change in effective use of technology.

The second principle is **collaboration**. This is where business can help the most – providing management and technical expertise as well as money. By focusing and prioritizing these resources, they can be used to achieve the greatest state-wide benefit.

The third principle is **coordination** of systemic reform initiatives. To be effective, a strategy for technology infusion must be a part of systemic reform and restructure initiatives.

The fourth principle is the use of what can be called **"push-pull" methodologies**. This entails the development of a reservoir of available products, services and technical assistance – push. It provides training, financial and other incentives to practitioners and school systems to make use of that reservoir – pull.

The fifth principle is **a structure and process** for continuous improvement. A total solution cannot be prescribed in one grand plan. Rather, the process needs to be such as to allow the leaders and innovators in the educational system to rise to the surface. The process must recognize that technological change is dynamic and that appropriate utilization must be achieved step-by-step. That is, the infusion of technology will be on-going and needs specific oversight, management and assistance over a long period of time. Priorities, needs and understanding of those needs change.

Finally, it is essential that the process be built on the

precept of guidance, assistance and standards of excellence from "above," with initiative, planning and action from "below." Those closest to the work being done – the teachers – must plan for and **pull** technology into their work based on what is best suited to their needs. It cannot be dictated from above. They can be supported, motivated, encouraged and held to high standards.

In little more than a year, then, the BRT partnership had resulted in an important short-term action in technology training for educators as well as a collaboratively-developed comprehensive strategy for the future. The work had barely begun.

ORGANIZING BUSINESS SUPPORT

Many states have a state-wide business organization which provides public policy leadership. Some, like New Mexico, do not. So, in addition to the tasks of initiating some new immediately helpful and visible action and undertaking to develop a longer term strategic process, it was necessary to organize business support for education. This is never a simple matter, but it was made more difficult in New Mexico because of several considerations.

First of all, small business is predominant in New Mexico's economy. Small businesses have neither the time nor money to support major policy initiatives and, in any event, they identify much more closely with local problems and issues. Beyond that, of course, there was the sheer mechanics of dealing with their larger numbers and lower profile.

The problem was even further complicated by the larger businesses being mostly branch plants of companies headquartered elsewhere. These branch operations are mainly clustered around Albuquerque, so a state-wide business perspective or support effort is difficult to organize.

Also, in New Mexico, the National Laboratories are of unusual economic importance, so any envisioned business leadership or policy group would need to involve them.

Finally, any private-sector group must have the respect and be able to command the attention of the political leadership. At the same time, it is important that the group truly represent the private sector. It cannot become "politicized" in the sense of appearing to be just another instrument of the current administration; otherwise, it will have both a narrower public voice and likely not survive the vagaries of the political process.

In spite of these constraints and considerations, by October 1991, a group to be called the Governor's Business Executives for Education (GBEE) had come into being.

There was a lot of discussion about how the group could be most effective in helping to effect systemic educational change in the state. There were, once again, a plethora of educational initiatives, any one of which could consume the entire time and resources of the group and no one of which could truly be said to be the answer in and of itself.

The answer agreed upon was to promote, foster and support TQM as a framework which would best foster continuous improvement and local selection of initiatives which would best address local problems. Perhaps equally important, it would provide a common language for business people and educators – no small problem in forging effective business-academia partnerships.

This TQM approach was called Strengthening Quality in Schools (SQS). The Malcolm Baldrige Award assessment criteria will be used to obtain a base line and to measure future progress for each school district in the state.

BASIC PROBLEMS AND BARRIERS

From these experiences, implementing NMETI, producing the Challenge 2000 strategy, organizing the GBEE and its SQS initiative, it has been possible to better understand some of the problems of business-education cooperation and how to deal with them.

The problems in business-academia (K-12) cooperation fall into four basic categories:

1) Public awareness and understanding, not to mention mutual lack of understanding between academic professionals and business people, make effective communications to be mostly accidental, if it occurs at all.

2) As is well known, there are inadequate resources with which to address needs. However, the business person senses the opportunity for far greater productivity, to "do more for less" by re-engineering the system. However, the nature and structure of the system and its financing frustrate this opportunity. There is no ability to take "a one-time write-off" and then proceed on a new and better course. Front-end investment and on-going expense compete for the same dollar, and front-end investment normally loses.

3) The size, diversity and complexity of the educational system is simply beyond that experienced by most business people.

4) The need for persistence, in the face of political leadership change, dwarfs what most business people understand as change in leadership. This change is much more than the normal biennial legislative elections and quadrennial gubernatorial ones. For example, the average district superintendent tenure in New Mexico is less than two years.

DEALING WITH THE PROBLEMS

There are four strategies which effectively address these basic problems: collaboration, TQM, technology and measurement. They need to be employed jointly, for no one of them alone will suffice. The particular articulation of this approach will vary from one state and/or school district to another. The strategies are generically described here, with examples taken from the New Mexico experience.

COLLABORATION

The nature and magnitude of the financial problems mentioned above make collaboration with business a practical, common-sense course of action. Not only can business be a source of specialized and "matching" funding to help initiate systemic change, it can help bring perspective to the necessary prioritization process.

Collaboration necessitates improving mutual understanding and awareness. Business expertise in planning, process analysis and management can best be shared through substantive collaborative undertakings. Perhaps most important in the long run, business-academic partnership can help provide the long-term persistence needed to effect systemic change across multiple political discontinuities.

In New Mexico, the ETPC has been an effective example of collaboration in planning – not just business-academic, but involving all community partners in the learning process.

The SQS initiative of the GBEE brings the collaborative approach into specific action.

TOTAL QUALITY MANAGEMENT

The original mission of the GBEE in New Mexico was not, per se, to bring TQM to the school system. The mission was, in fact, simply to assist the state in improving education. As the GBEE thought about what the business community in New Mexico could do to improve education and to assist in the systemic reform of education, TQM emerged as the best answer. The Baldrige assessment will point where things are weak, what needs to be improved and, then, how these various tools can be used. It provides a framework for analyzing the flaws, and selecting programs and projects for improvement. Clearly, it provides the measurement process which is essential to the concept of continuous improvement over long time frames.

The education TQM effort in New Mexico will be further

assisted by the creation of a state quality council. This council is being created at the urging of New Mexico's U.S. senators and its governor. One of its principal priorities will be education. This education focus provides important reinforcement of the SQS initiative through both advocacy and recognition.

TECHNOLOGY

A concern for educational quality quickly focuses on the need to personalize the learning process. If each student's learning characteristics, approaches and needs can be dealt with on an individual basis, the learning of all students can be maximized.

The ability to manage the learning process at the individual level is not practical for larger, diverse groups of students without the aid of technology. The mere availability of communications, video technology, computer software and hardware is useless, however, without user training and integration of the technology into restructured learning systems.

Business-academic partnerships can be effective in overcoming these hurdles by marshalling the necessary resources for planning and training.

To this end, a voluntary partnership, called the Education Technology Coordinating Council (ETCC), was established by the State Board of Education and Commission on Higher Education. Like the ETPC, this permanent council has broad representation from the public and private sector. Most importantly, it also includes members from the major systemic change initiatives in the state.

Since all technological needs cannot possibly be met, it is vital to be able to prioritize and to present a more unified voice to the state legislature and business communities. Further, the ETCC helps to ensure that technological training occurs and that school systems have consulting and expertise available to them for their strategic technology planning.

MEASURING PROGRESS

There is an old adage, "You can't manage what you can't measure." It might be added as well, "You can't sustain continuous improvement without measuring progress." Anecdotal success stories, heroes and missionaries can generate enthusiasm and a lot of impetus for change, but any partnership – especially business-academic partnerships – need the revitalizing force of measurable progress. The excellence in education journey is a long and arduous one. Without meaningful measurement of progress, the partners will rapidly tire of the effort (and the effort is very large).

In New Mexico, the GBEE group chose the Baldrige assessment criteria as this basic measure. There are strong and weak aspects of almost any measurement criteria. The Baldrige is no exception, but it does provide a well-established and well-thought-out measurement system of quality performance.

Whether Baldrige criteria or some other vehicle, the key point for academic-business collaboration is to have measures and to understand that they, too, are a subject for continuous improvement.

VISION OF THE FUTURE

Perhaps the biggest accomplishment in New Mexico over the last three years is a more widespread understanding by leaders in government, education and business that you need a strategic framework for progress; a framework within which the various initiatives, the seemingly endless parade of "solutions" to educational problems, can be focused, measured and assessed. Such a framework also serves to clarify the goals and missions defining the roles of various players. It fosters collaboration and is essential to attracting the federal, business and private foundation financial resources that are required to supplement state and local funding.

In September 1992, the New Mexico State Board of Education released a document which articulated such a strategic framework. The report is titled "Consolidating Initiatives for Tomorrow's Education," with the subtitle "A Student-Centered Policy Framework for System-Wide Educational Change in New Mexico." A pictorial representation of this framework is shown in Figure 1. It is both broad and conceptual as well as specific and focused. It is the result of the leadership evident in the State Board of Education, the state superintendent of public instruction and the staff at the State Department of Education. It is also the result of collaboration with business people in New Mexico who, over the past three years, helped provide perspective and shared in a better vision of the future.

Figure 1
CITE Policy Framework

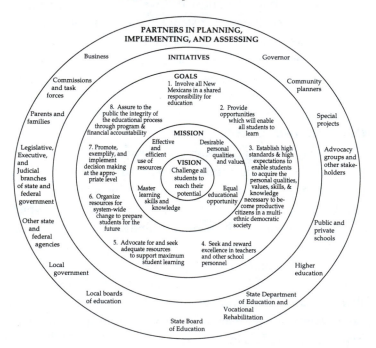

PART II: Business and Higher Education . . . The Fuqua School of Business Experience

Business' traditional relationship to higher education is three-fold: first, and most dominant, as the "customer" (the employer of students); second, as the philanthropic relationship (according to the most recent survey of corporate philanthropy by the Conference Board, contributions to higher education in 1991 totaled $337 million); third, as a major source of research funds for university researchers. The first two of these relationships are described best as arms-length. Even the third, research funding, has involved, in most instances, a low level of "partnering" interactions. [One exception to this worth noting is the university research funding provided by the Semiconductor Research Corporation, itself a collaboration of major semiconductor manufacturers.] Business' funding of academic research also continues to be limited unnecessarily by the confusion surrounding ownership of technology resulting from such research. Some universities insist on exclusive licensing rights, while others, under the banner of academic freedom, refuse to engage in proprietary research projects. Any substantial increase in meaningful business-academic research partnerships (as opposed to "grants") is dependent on resolving this matter.

THE CHANGING ECONOMICS OF HIGHER EDUCATION

The mechanisms for delivering quality higher education are enormously labor intensive. There has been little progress in terms of being able to deliver "more for less" to a greater number of students at less cost per student. The classic solution for post-secondary institutions is more revenue – either through higher tuition, more tax revenues (for state-supported schools) or larger gifts and grants.

All of these sources are becoming increasingly constrained and business, in particular, faces enormous competitive pres-

---

sure and thus resource constraints. Not only is money not as readily available for business philanthropy, but higher education is only one of many societal needs competing for available funds. These needs involve such pressing problems as families, youth-at-risk, support for early childhood development, and so on. Reflective of this, corporate donations to higher education are down considerably – from $410 million in 1990 to $337 million in 1991.

In short, those organizations, educational or otherwise, which can attract business support, are those with whom business has something more than a "money-over-the-wall" relationship, organizations in which business senses a genuine desire for and an active program of continuous improvement.

BUSINESS-HIGHER EDUCATION PARTNERSHIPS

So, the need for substantive business-education partnerships is very real. But partnerships do not just happen. They require a better understanding of one another's needs, problems and issues. That's easier said than done. What, for example, does the manager of a chemical plant have in common with the dean of a school of arts and sciences, or the president of a liberal arts college? What are they going to talk about? Most likely sports.

Now, however, TQM provides a way for business to meaningfully relate to the academic community. It is a way of sharing a common problem. The common problem is turning out a better-quality student – a student capable of participating more quickly and effectively in business processes and, for that matter, in the processes of society at large. Moreover, continuous improvement, with its focus on effective processes, offers at least the possibility of meeting the need for higher-quality education without relying on greater revenues from tuition increases or gifts.

TOTAL QUALITY AT FUQUA – SOME BACKGROUND

Business schools and other graduate professional schools enjoy an important advantage over much of academia. Advisory boards of professional people are, and have been for a long time, a standard mechanism for maintaining contact between the school and the professional community with which it is associated. Thus, the common dialogue aspect of effective partnering is already in place.

As chairman of the Board of Visitors at the Fuqua School of Business at Duke University, I have had a first-hand opportunity to observe and be a part of assisting the school in its TQM initiative (which is called "Continuous Improvement") and in establishing business partnerships to assist in that process.

A basic axiom of the effective practice of Total Quality is the necessity of top management commitment and leadership. Academic settings are no exception to that. Indeed, if anything the need is even greater than in a business environment. Academic leadership involves a much greater degree of persuasion, consensus building and example-setting, not to mention patience and persistence. Without the leadership of the dean, nothing will happen. Fuqua has been most fortunate in that regard.

As with many business organizations, a formal approach to Total Quality at Fuqua followed a period in which some practices such as "teams" have been experimented with, and a few individuals within the organization have become familiar with various TQM concepts, tools and practices. By 1991, with persistent pushing by the dean, such an effort was underway. A Quality Advisory Committee was established which included not only faculty and staff, but myself as a representative of the School's Board of Visitors.

In addition, an outside consultant was hired to conduct formal TQM training for staff and faculty who wished to participate. Although this was in many regards a very satisfactory experience thanks to the consultant's expertise and appreciation of the academic environment, a partnership with a business could also have been an effective arrangement. This will be discussed in a later section on problems and opportunities.

By 1990-91, Fuqua was also engaged in a major innovation in its academic calendar and curriculum which affected every aspect of its operation. Duke University operates on the semester system. The new approach at Fuqua divides the normal 15-week semester into two seven-week mini-terms plus a week-long "Integrated Learning Experience" (ILE) week at the beginning of each term. These ILEs are devoted to topics such as quality, diversity, leadership and strategic thinking. Classes also changed in duration, from one hour and fifteen minutes to two hours and fifteen minutes. The change has many potential benefits to both faculty and students. What is important to the discussion here, however, is that this change affects almost every aspect of the school, from course syllabus to class registration. So, continuous improvement was being initiated simultaneously with a major systemic innovation.

Areas For Collaboration

There are five areas in which business can contribute to an academic institution's total quality journey. None of this potential can be realized, however, without leadership and extensive dialogue as to the needs and objectives of both partners.

For the most part, academic institutions have undertaken TQM initially in non-academic functions – administration, support services, and so on. The principal reason for this seems to be the feeling that it is "too hard" to gain faculty support for TQM. While in no way arguing that it is not very difficult to do so, this is a mistaken approach.

The challenge to total quality is two-fold: one, to integrate its concepts and principles into the student's learning experience, and, two, to improve the learning experience itself through the application of those concepts and principles. Administration and support services are important and, without question, are fertile ground for demonstrating continuous improvement. However, they are not the core activity of an educational institution. It pays to start with the core.

Curriculum: Enhancing the curriculum is the most immediately fruitful area for business-academia partnerships. In fact, in the long term, this may well be the richest area of potential cooperation between business and the university. In every discipline, meaningful examples are an important part of pedagogy; with regard to TQM, the pragmatism and perspectives of business practitioners is essential.

Moreover, TQM concepts, principles and tools are part of a broad spectrum of disciplines from social sciences and psychology, to statistics and engineering, to finance and accounting. So, there is no small opportunity available with respect to curriculum. Business people will be forced to think more carefully and more explicitly about the knowledge and skills it expects from graduates. Academics will be forced to think about the content of courses from a new perspective.

Teaching Effectiveness: Faculty, as professional teachers, have an innate desire to be effective in leading the learning process. Having desire, however, is not the same as practicing continuous improvement. It does provide fertile ground in which a carefully-structured continuous improvement program in teaching effectiveness can take root. On the other hand, professionals of any ilk are not receptive to what they perceive to be either panacea peddling or fad-ism. This is no less true of academic professionals.

A broad-reaching partnership in which professionals in business and education share their experiences, concerns and use of new technologies to enhance the learning experience can be fruitful for both. Large business, in particular, devotes enormous resources to the training function. There is much to be shared.

Research: There are two different ways in which research can be involved in a TQM partnership between academia and business. One is the matter of doing research related to the practice of TQM. A business represents a "living laboratory" in which academic research can be carried out. Topics such as cultural change, organizational structures and corporate policies essential to TQM, or measures of organizational effectiveness, are but a few possibilities that are of vital importance to business. TQM research should also have the advantage of not being caught up in the technology ownership issue mentioned earlier.

The second way is that the concepts and tools of TQM can be applied to the academic research process itself. Research, like any creative process, is as Thomas Edison once said of his inventions, "One percent inspiration and ninety-nine percent perspiration." By sharing experiences in their respective creative processes, business and academia can learn much about ways to free creative people to be more productive.

Support Services: The myriad administrative and service areas of an educational institution are well-recognized opportunities, not just for continuous improvement but for substantial re-engineering. It is tempting, therefore, to make these "support services" the focus of any educational institution's TQM initiative, including that of a prospective business partnership. As noted earlier, this temptation should be resisted in favor of concentrating on those activities which are central to the academic function. That does not mean that these supporting functions should be ignored, however. Business clearly has a great deal to offer to its academic partner in this area.

Academic bureaucracies are, if anything, more cumbersome and more entrenched than those in business. This is partly due to the nature of the institution. The "line employees," the people with the responsibility to deliver the institution's services – knowledge and learning – tend to distance themselves from the "staff employees" and their functions. It's not delegation. It's closer to abdication. So, there is even less integration of functional objectives than in even strongly-partitioned business organizations.

Continuous improvement teams that are not only cross-functional but also involve faculty, staff and students offer an excellent opportunity to address this problem. Business-academic partnerships can help to provide perspective on the need for such activity as well as the opportunity to directly participate and share experiences in cross-functional teams.

Measurement: Measurement is the sine qua non of TQM. This is as true for higher education just as it is for any organization serious about the long-term journey of continuous improvement. It is possible to approach the whole subject of measuring progress by means of the Baldrige process. However, that in and of itself does not solve the measurement problem. Rather, it highlights the need for effective measurement and evaluation process for each major function involved in delivering the end service or product. At Fuqua, the approach has been to attack this directly. Measuring customer satisfaction in the business school setting means measuring the satisfaction of the key partners involved in the process: students and alumni, the business community, and the faculty and staff.

Measuring the elements which are involved in delivering the School's services means devising measures for things such as curriculum effectiveness, faculty development, MBA programs, doctoral programs, executive education, various administrative services, the external affairs function, and support services such as the library and computer services and facilities. Obviously, proven measures, or even reasonably good ones, are not readily available.

In exploring uncharted waters such as this, gaining insight and perspective from the experience of others is essential. Thus, devising effective measurements may be one of the most fruitful areas for collaboration. Nor is this a one-way street. Experience shows that business struggles with this measurement problem as much as educational institutions do. Much of the data gathering and analysis for a typical Baldrige assessment is brute force and expensive. In short, metrics for and "instrumentation" of the soft processes of business and industry is, at best, poorly understood and would greatly benefit from widespread collaboration.

PROBLEMS AND OPPORTUNITIES

The first basic principle of an effective partnership of any sort is that the parties involved have a clearly defined and understood intersection of strategic interest. This axiomatic principle is as true for collaboration between business and academia as it is between businesses or between business and government. It is all the more amazing that something so obvious is so frequently ignored, or at best, poorly articulated when collaboration is undertaken.

The second principle results from the first. Strategies change, and in today's world they change rapidly. Flexibility in strategy is essential if the goals of an organization are to be realized. Given the need for flexibility and change, it is necessary that collaboration be governed at the level where strategy is decided. This is the second fundamental of successful partnerships. Successful business-education partnerships will normally require the leadership and involvement of the CEO and the president of the institution. There is plenty of opportunity for organizations to rationalize their way into delegation of this responsibility. Such opportunities should be rejected.

The customer focus inherent in TQM represents a major opportunity to deal effectively with the first principle. Both business and academia have, or at least should have, an intense preoccupation with the quality of the graduates of the educational process.

The problem of, and need for, effective communication is no less in higher education than in K-12 partnerships. TQM helps to address this problem, but means guarantees an answer in and of itself. In fact, it can exacerbate the theoretical versus practical misunderstandings which muddle many interchanges between business people and academics. Moreover, fairly prevalent academic concern that TQM is but one more management fad that will, in time, give way to the next fad. No doubt the jargon of TQM will change, will be refined and improved as understanding grows. But the core of TQM is much richer than that. Its basic focus on customer need and satisfaction, on process analysis and improvement, on measurement and, above all, on human resource management provides both theorist and pragmatist as good a communication framework as could be desired. Given that framework, as is the case with meaningful communication of any sort, it is a matter of genuine interest in the needs of the other party.

Related to the communication problem and opportunity is, somewhat ironically, the problem of TQM training. On the one hand, any business organization successful in TQM is using an effective training program in team problem solving and basic TQM tools. The business people quite understandably feel that this is something meaningful they can offer a prospective partner – academic or otherwise.

On the other hand, the prospect of spending several days being lectured to on a subject viewed as mundane, rightly or wrongly, is not one which will thrill the average academic.

Yet, in this peculiar situation there is an opportunity for

the would-be partnership. The key is, once again, to focus on the student. Bringing TQM into the curriculum involves specific courses or learning experiences focused specifically on TQM as well as weaving TQM concepts and principals throughout the curriculum. At Fuqua, the one-week Integrated Learning Experience is important to the first part of that task. It also provides an opportunity for business people to work together with faculty, both in devising and improving the structure of the sessions as well as in actually delivering the "learning experiences."

This is a far more effective learning process for faculty (not to mention the business people) than simply sitting around listening and discussing or engaging in practice exercises.

Beyond the student, there is also the University staff. Instead of hiring professional consultants and trainers, the business partner and the institution can work together to develop a training program for the staff which will be delivered by the faculty of the institution itself. If the temptation is avoided to relegate all this to the statistics department, and participation is broadly structured, a most effective mechanism for exposure to and training in TQM for faculty will result.

One other problem is worthy of mention. It is the problem of time. Business people are generally downright obsessed with this problem. However that may be, effecting good partnerships takes time, and educational partnerships take considerably more time than average. So, business should think carefully before casually committing themselves to such an undertaking.

This is all further compounded by the widely-held business belief that academics have little, if any, pressure with regard to time constraints. This is a fatal flaw in the thinking of anyone wishing to have a partnership with an educational institution. The time demands on faculty are no less than those on business executives. To the muffled, or not so muffled, scoffing of the business reader I offer this first-hand advice: try it before you laugh.

Careful consideration of time involvement by both partners is as fundamental in these partnerships as any.

GROWTH IN BUSINESS-EDUCATION PARTNERSHIPS

In 1991, at a meeting of the Total Quality Forum, Robert W. Galvin, chairman of the executive committee of the board of directors of Motorola, proposed that business and higher education form total quality partnerships. The objective of these partnerships is to encourage colleges and universities to integrate Total Quality into their curricula and to research and practice Total Quality. This resulted in five corporations undertaking eight partnerships in 1992. In 1993, 12 corporations entered into 20 more partnerships. The 1992 and 1993 partnerships are shown in Figure 2.

SUMMARY AND CONCLUSIONS

In the preceding sections, the opportunity for more and more meaningful business-academic partnerships has been discussed in two very different environments. The fact that TQM can provide the motivation, the framework of communication and, beyond that, specific processes for partnerships in such diverse situations is not accidental. It is a result of the three pillars of the TQM concept: customer satisfaction, continuous improvement and people-doing-the-work.

By insisting on attention to outcomes, i.e., student learning, customer satisfaction redirects attention from the "me-you" focus of much business-academic discourse.

Continuous improvement, in turn, insists on meaningful measurement which can be related to specific process improvement. It inculcates a "there's gotta be a better way" attitude and thus provides a more substantive underpinning to a partnership. In particular, continuous improvement both

Figure 2
TOTAL QUALITY BUSINESS-EDUCATION PARTNERSHIPS

1992

IBM	Massachusetts Institute of Technology Rochester Institute of Technology
Milliken & Co.	Georgia Institute of Technology North Carolina State University
Motorola, Inc.	Purdue University
Procter & Gamble	Tuskegee University University of Wisconsin - Madison
Xerox	Carnegie Mellon University

1993

Aluminum Company of America (Alcoa)	Lehigh University
Corning, Inc.	Syracuse University
DuPont	Pennsylvania State University
Eastman Chemical Co.	University of Tennessee - Knoxville
General Motors	University of Michigan
Nalco Chemical	Illinois Institute of Technology
Northern Telecom	Duke University North Carolina Agricultural & Technological State University University of North Carolina - Chapel Hill
Procter & Gamble	Cornell University
The New England	Babson College
Texas Instruments	East Texas State University Iowa State University
3M	Florida Agricultural & Mechanical University Michigan Technological University Texas A&M University
Westinghouse	Duquesne University University of Maryland - College Park University of Pittsburgh Virginia Polytechnic Institute and State University

engenders an expectation for immediate results while at the same time nurturing the patience and long-term view, which is so necessary to achieving educational excellence.

The people-doing-the-work aspect of TQM is perhaps best expressed in the objective that each person in an organization must have a genuine belief that "what I think and do matters." It is the best hope we have that teachers – especially those in K-12 – may escape the suffocating embrace of educational bureaucracy. It also inhibits the debilitating finger-pointing by business people, e.g., at tenure as the root of all evil, which is so tempting when they encounter the frustrating obstacles to progress in educational reform.

It all comes down to the fact that most people in both education and business want to do well in their jobs, and they want the satisfaction that comes with superior outcomes. It is the job of management in both education and business to provide the policy framework, structure, processes and measures by which that can occur and be recognized.

TQM partnerships between business and education may, then, have their greatest value in helping management in both sectors achieve the insight and skill necessary to do just that.

Robert M. Price is retired chairman of the board and chief executive officer of Control Data Corporation.

Price became chairman and CEO in January 1986, succeeding Control Data's founder, William C. Norris. He had been president and chief operating officer since July 1980. He retired in May 1990 after 29 years with Control Data.

Price was named to his first vice presidential assignment in 1967, with responsibility for sales. He was appointed senior vice president and group executive for services in 1972, president of systems and services in 1973, and president of the Computer Company in 1977.

Under Price's leadership, Control Data established its quality program, called Total Quality Management Process (TQMP). Through TQMP, the company has made great strides in quality. In 1988, for example, the Small Disk Drive Division of Control Data's Imprimis Technology subsidiary was selected as a finalist for the first Malcolm Baldrige National Quality award.

Price also has been a champion of quality in Minnesota where Control Data has its corporate headquarters. He was an original member of the Minnesota Council for Quality.

Born in New Bern, N. C., in 1930, Price graduated magna cum laude from Duke University in 1952 with a bachelor's degree in mathematics. In 1958, he earned a master's degree in applied mathematics from the Georgia Institute of Technology.

Currently, Price is involved in quality, U.S. technology policy and education issues. In June 1990, he co-hosted with New Mexico Governor, Garrey Carruthers, The Business Roundtable's Governor-CEO Dialogue on restructuring of the U.S. education system.

7

Transformation: From Good to Better!

Richard N. Lennes

"Great ideas are the integrity of change...the backbone of improvement." If you agree with this statement and you represent top management, you may experience the same revelation I did.

Great ideas are essential. Ideas alone, however, are like throwing a stone in the water and getting no rippling rings that usually spread to all edges of the pond. The ripples of life are created by process and ultimately determine the success or failure of any change. That's what the school of hard knocks taught me. It started with a great idea – to provide staff recognition.

On a visit to Florida, I was introduced to the "Second Miler Award" as a means of recognizing employees. I created visions of the staff stumbling over each other to nominate their colleagues for that extra effort.

On the plane back to Minnesota, I organized the methodology. On the first nomination, a person was to receive a congratulatory letter from me, the president of the college. Along with the letter, each person was to receive a cap that said, "Second Miler Award." Each consecutive nomination was acknowledged. Upon reaching five nominations, their picture was to be placed somewhere prominent in the commons area of the college. In that way, everyone could view the achievement.

A dinner for two at a good restaurant was the recognition for receiving 10 nominations. Fifteen nominations qualified them for special recognition at the staff retreat at the end of the school year. Finally, the employee receiving the most nominations received a $1,000 value to be applied toward any professional national conference he or she wanted to attend the following year.

I was ready! Within two weeks, the plan was published, the procedure explained and the concept implemented. Nominations started rolling in. After a year, I felt the award process was a powerful tool for staff recognition. The second year, it struggled. The third year, it was discontinued.

Someone was honest enough to explain to me that it was viewed as the "president's thing." The staff was never given an opportunity to take ownership.

What a crushing blow! My intentions were good, and it was a great idea, but I violated the very basics of Total Quality Management (TQM) – empower the staff, and allow them right to ownership.

My management style had to be altered. Empowerment was frightening. We finally created a definition. At Hutchinson Technical College, empowerment means "provide the right, the responsibility and the accountability to serve the customer first within the vision of the college."

Suddenly it made sense. There must be a vision, it must

be communicated, and the customer concept had to be understood and accepted as part of our culture. Furthermore, empowerment would only be successful if adequate knowledge, skills and support were given to the decision makers.

The Hutchinson Technical College (HTC) went through a transformation. HTC had earned a reputation of being an innovative, state-of-the-art school. We stressed the attitude of evolving from good to better. Improvement didn't mean things were bad. Instead, any permanent improvement was an added value for the customer.

It was easy to imply that people were not working hard enough or good enough. It became necessary to reinforce that the focus of continuous improvement was on the process or procedure – not the person.

Decision-making closest to the level of implementation was our goal. I'd like to share five examples that represent empowerment, process improvement, and decision-making closest to the level of implementation. Each of these examples were implemented through the efforts of many people at the HTC over a five-year period.

IMPROVEMENT COUNCILS

Very early in my presidency, a desperate need for internal two-way communications surfaced; not just the traditional meeting or two, but an ongoing give-and-take atmosphere. Staff had to have opportunity for input and also expect timely feedback on action.

With the assistance of the staff, we established the Communication Improvement Council (CIC). Members were elected by peers and included four instructional staff, four support staff, one supervisory person and the president or a designee. The president could not chair the council, and all decisions were by majority vote.

It took a good share of the year for the group to gain trust

---

of the motives, but the members took it seriously and established scheduled staff (all staff) meeting times for the next school year, organized a "Better Idea" process, accepted the responsibility to plan the quarterly staff inservices and the end-of-the year staff retreat. One rule that was established and endorsed was that all staff meetings have a 50/50 format – 50 percent of the time for the CIC to discuss issues and gather input from staff, and 50 percent of the time for administration

The first year, staff and students submitted 92 Better Ideas to the CIC. Ninety-one of the ideas were implemented through a process of the CIC working with the appropriate staff. The Better Idea process was a phenomenal success because of two elements. First, the staff took complete ownership and viewed it as a nonthreatening process. Secondly, the CIC was quite clear that it would not discuss or deal with personnel issues.

The council improvement process was so successful that the CIC recommended an expansion of improvement councils to focus on other improvements and to get more people involved to champion improvement.

As a result, four councils were established the second year, including:

❖ Staff/Instruction Council
❖ Recognition and Celebration Council
❖ Image Enhancement Council
❖ Student Communication Council

The membership of each group was voluntary and had a staff liaison from the CIC. Empowerment included guidelines of responsibilities and authority, along with a budget that the council could use without administrative approval.

What a revelation! Staff involvement was great. Each council took their right and responsibility seriously – things happened, with staff feeling good about their achievements. Change was happening, and the "Good Ideas" had a better chance of survival because they were integrated as part of the process. Each council contributed to the improvement of the college and added value to customer services.

A few examples of council achievements seem appropriate to mention.

STAFF/INSTRUCTION COUNCIL (SIC):

1. Reformated procedure and software for curriculum development.
2. Designed and implemented a personal assessment instrument and a process to develop a personal improvement plan.
3. Designed and implemented written curriculum standards.
4. Designed system-wide electronic testing and grading network.

RECOGNITION AND CELEBRATION COUNCIL (RCC):

1. Developed and implemented a college-wide recognition process for student academic achievement.
2. Planned social opportunities for staff.
3. Designed informal and formal recognition for staff.

IMAGE ENHANCEMENT COUNCIL (IEC):

1. Determined long-range facility improvement recommendations for future budgets.
2. Used their own budget to:
   - ❖ Install vertical blinds in student commons area
   - ❖ Add a fully-furnished and landscaped patio area
   - ❖ Change "No Smoking" signs to "Thank You for Not Smoking"
   - ❖ Remove all displayed statements with the word "No" or "Do Not" from the institution
   - ❖ Eliminate signs and notices on walls and create bulletin-board space throughout the building

STUDENT COMMUNICATION COUNCIL (SCC):

The president met monthly for breakfast with students who represented every program. (Would you believe the students preferred pizza and coke to a nourishing traditional breakfast?)

As the students brought up concerns, my job was to involve staff

---

or students in resolving the issue. Many times, staff were invited to the next breakfast meeting to discuss or explain the issues. In most cases, the concern was resolved through effective communications.

Does this sound like a lot of structure? Not really. The perception at first may have been "more structure," but as involvement increased the perception changed to "opportunity." I'm convinced that if the "Second Miler Award" had been developed through the improvement council process, it would be an accepted part of the college's culture today.

STUDENT OPINION SURVEY

Wayne Fortun, president of Hutchinson Technology, Inc., says, "If you can't measure it, you can't improve it." How do you measure instructional effectiveness? Our research on quality taught us that to measure anything for improvement, it had to be systematized to insure regular and consistent use of the measurement method.

After considering many methods to measure instructional effectiveness, we decided it had to be:

1. Non-threatening
2. Reliable
3. Relevant to good instruction
4. A tool for improvement
5. Customer focused

Our effort ultimately became known as the Student Opinion Survey (SOS). Why survey? Why not evaluation or assessment? The word "survey" was used to help make it non-threatening.

Madeline Hunter's elements of instruction gave us a basis for identifying eight elements of good instruction for our instructional environment. After the eight elements were identified, we carefully designed 20 questions that provided an assessment of one or more of the elements. The necessary validation and reliability studies were conducted, software developed and inservicing conducted.

The SOS has been a part of the college now for seven years. Twice a year, students complete the survey based on their perception of the instructor. The vice president of instruction receives the computer profile on each instructor, and an aggregate by program and college. Improvement is illustrated by benchmarking the instructor's profiles in the form of an historical comparison.

Individual meetings are scheduled with every instructor to review the perception survey results. Instructors are asked to use the information as a tool for improvement. The SOS remains confidential and is not part of the permanent instructional file.

The quality process is truly at work providing reliable data for continuous improvement closest to the level of implementation.

WRITTEN CURRICULUM STANDARDS

Why is the curriculum format different in every program? Why does the curriculum list resources that aren't available? Why is the format so confusing? Why are there grammatical errors?

These and other questions were starting to surface from students, support staff and some faculty. You see, the Hutchinson Technical College curriculum is paper based. All curriculum was formated in packets called Instructional Units. Each unit indicated what activities the student must achieve, what resources to use, and at what level of competence the student must perform.

HTC instructional staff worked hard for many years to be one of the few institutions of higher learning to be completely competency based with personalized delivery.

We had reached a plateau where student's expectations were greater than in the past. Even though the staff was performing at a high level of output, the final product varied considerably.

So where do we start? We asked ourselves three important questions:

"Are we conforming to customer expectations?"
Answer: "We don't know."

"Why don't we know?"
Answer: "We lack standards that reflect customer expectations."

"Must we establish curriculum standards?"
Answer: "It is the only way to consistently comply with customer expectations."

Next, we designed expectation statements from focus groups and existing survey data.

Employer's Expectation: The employer expects that the curriculum will reflect the subject matter and standards that are requirements for success in that business or industry.

Student's Expectation: The student expects that written curriculum represents a professional published document that is current and organized for easy comprehension.

These statements were endorsed by a representative group of students and employers. The next question was, "What should we do about the expectations?" Do we engage in a curriculum-restructuring process and risk the unsettling emotions the staff will have to face with another change? Or do we look the other way and be satisfied with the status quo?

To answer that question, we asked ourselves, "What is the price of non-compliance?"

1. Student dissatisfaction

2. Deterioration of program and college reputation
3. Loss of existing and future students
4. Loss of employer partnerships
5. Loss of public confidence
6. Reduction of staff morale

When we applied this quality problem-solving process to determine the value of change, it became apparent that we must move to a new level of excellence.

Our goal was to design and implement a process of continuous improvement for HTC's written curriculum that will result in 100 percent compliance before the final product is released to the student.

Instructional staff had to be the designers. The design and implementation responsibility was empowered to the Staff/ Instruction Council (SIC). The following expectations were also given to the council:

1. Develop standards
2. Define the measurement process
3. Identify the support needed for successful implementation
4. Establish product recognition for 100% compliance

It took only a month for the SIC to develop and present the written curriculum standards. An additional three months of intensive work on the staff's part culminated in a detailed curriculum standards manual, procedures, product recognition and the support mechanisms to be successful. The staff were inserviced over the summer, and eight days of curriculum development helped each instructor to get started using the new standards.

The procedure designed by the SIC also empowered the program advisory committees to approve the curriculum content. The customer concept was consciously applied. Who is the customer as instructors identify the knowledge, skills and attitudes the students need to be successful for that occupation? The student? No. The student is the customer when the instructor delivers the content. Employers are the best advisors for content and are the ultimate customer when the students must demonstrate their knowledge, skills and attitudes in a work environment.

It wouldn't be fair to imply that everyone was waving a flag to celebrate the new process. As time elapsed, however, most instructors viewed the standards as a tool for excellence. We were very proud when the first curriculum guides were stocked in the bookstore, with the quality seal on the cover symbolizing the document had complied with all standards. Students applauded the effort.

But we're not done yet! What process do we use for future improvement of the curriculum guides? Every curriculum guide includes a student response form. The users (students) have an opportunity to submit their suggestions for improvement to the instructors. As you can see, this creates a loop for continuous improvement closest to the implementation level.

MERGER

The Minnesota legislature reduced the administrative units of technical colleges from 32 to 18, causing Hutchinson Technical College to merge with nearby Willmar Technical College. Marrying the two colleges would create one administrative unit, but unless the transitional process had legitimate credibility, we would create a monster.

A transition process was established seven months prior to implementation to ensure opportunity for staff ownership in the planning process.

Merger meant a new governing board. Interim appointments were made early to provide support for a smooth transition.

The first quality issue was conceptual. A pre-appointed

committee with representatives from each college made two conceptual recommendations to the board of directors. The board approved both, launching the formal planning process.

The first concept used an inverted organizational chart, with customers at the top symbolizing our reason for existence. The second level from the top were the direct service providers to the customers – the instructional staff. The board of directors were illustrated at the bottom, indicating they were most remote from the front-line delivery of student and employer services. The role of each level is that of a service provider to the level above, with the ultimate focus on the student and the employer.

The second concept was a transitional process which named a 22-member Quality Council responsible for the screening and approving process, and any procedures related to the merger.

Conceptually, the two decisions empowered a cross-functional quality team to design a customer-focused transition. The inverted organizational chart mandated that all decisions consider the customer first.

Almost immediately, the Quality Council created speciality teams. Their mission was to review existing process and procedures on both campuses, research other alternatives and champion their recommendations to the Quality Council. Each specialty team was inserviced on the "Eliminate, Simplify, Systematize, Automate" (ESSA) decision-making process.

ESSA is a step-by-step process to improve process or procedure:

❖ **Eliminate:** Carefully examine each procedure to eliminate unnecessary tasks.

❖ **Simplify:** Streamline each task so that the procedure is clearly understood and focuses directly on meeting customer expectations.

❖ **Systematize:** Create a workflow that insures consistency every time it is done. This step is absolutely a prerequisite to the fourth element: automate. If you can't chart it on paper, you can't automate a process or procedure.

❖ **Automate:** By this time, it is apparent whether or not the procedure is conducive to computerization. If automation has the potential of reducing cycle time and reducing human effort, do it!

Specialty teams championed their findings to the Quality Council. The Quality Council accepted, rejected or requested revision. All accepted recommendations were reported to the interim board of directors by the Quality Council instructional and support staff representatives.

Board and administration maintained a hands-off policy on the Quality Council's decisions and committed support for implementation. The merger planning process worked! Often it seemed slow, but the inverted organizational chart concept prevailed, empowering decision making closest to the level of implementation.

An added value is that the process is still producing quality results one year after the official merger took place.

ELECTRONIC INSTRUCTIONAL SERVICES

It all started one month after assuming the presidency. The computerization never stopped! It was not done for the sake of appearing high tech, but to reduce cycle time, provide data for making decisions and create a consistency.

It began with grading. Many staff got enthusiastically involved in developing software to create the grade reports necessary at the end of each quarter, and in producing the necessary documents for local and state reporting. That was barely complete when staff members designed software to record the grade data at the program level on a daily basis and electronically transfer the information to the central computer at the end of the quarter.

This meant networks, more computers, inservicing staff and someone to be responsible for spearheading the revelation. About the time the first wave of programs was getting on the grading network, the state of Minnesota provided software for curriculum development. After a process of acceptance and software refinement, we committed ourselves to "a computer for everyone." We accomplished that within a year and a half. Now every staff member had access to a computer.

Just when it seemed to be settling down, the state staff introduced another integrated software that would create a lesson. It would not work for Hutchinson Technical College because of our paper-based instructional units. The software, however, had some wonderful features that seemed appropriate for our instructional environment. We tried to negotiate an alternative format. Nothing seemed to be falling into place.

Meanwhile, the instructional staff had been storing up their anxiety over the frustrating situation. The Staff/Instruction Council was just getting organized. It seemed risky to turn such a sensitive issue over to a newly-formed council. On the other hand, maybe it was the best way to launch a new process.

The issue was turned over to the SIC with a set of guidelines. Wow, what involvement – 80 percent of the instructional staff got involved in some way. With strong staff leadership, the SIC involved themselves in a problem-solving process that took about two months. They provided feedback to the entire staff and met frequently to update administration. When they needed resources for decision making, they were provided.

Finally, the recommendation: develop a software specifically for the Hutchinson curriculum with human resources available at the college. This was not the decision the state wanted to hear, but the concept was endorsed by the Hutchinson administration. The responsibility to oversee the software development challenge was also placed with the SIC.

It should be no surprise to you by this time that the software did get developed and implemented, but before we could catch our breath, the state staff introduced a third software to create tests. The state immediately invited Hutchinson to get involved with the final development of the software. We accepted, and with the repeated conscientious work of the SIC, Hutchinson not only adopted the software for implementation, but went one step further. We wanted the software to not only create a test, but to allow the student to take the test electronically.

With a grant, we solicited an outside programmer to bridge that gap. The SIC again monitored this process and introduced the final product to the staff. It was truly an achievement!

How do all the loose ends get tied together? The systematized approach to grading and curriculum has the capability now to develop the complete curriculum, prepare curriculum-integrated tests, make the test available to the student on computer, electronically transmit the test grade to the appropriate program network, allow students to monitor their grades electronically and transmit the course grades to the central computer.

Most of this would not be possible without committed staff who are willing to take on a challenge and who are capable of viewing obstacles as opportunity. From a quality point of view, we reduced cycle time, provided data for decision making and created an automated process that insists on consistency.

Describing five examples of our transformation from good to better scratches only the surface of involvement and commitment that exists in the culture of Hutchinson Technical College. Empowerment was defined earlier as providing the right, the responsibility and the accountability to serve the customer first within the vision of the college. These are but a few examples of staff accepting responsibility and commiting themselves to customer-oriented decisions that drive us a little closer to our vision.

Richard N. Lennes As the immediate past president of Hutchinson Technical College, Hutchinson, Minn., Lennes remains active in the Total Quality process. He presently serves on the Minnesota Council for Vocational-Technical Education and is active in his own entrepreneurial activities.

Lennes' 36-year career in education includes high school and college teaching, school district financial management, school public relations, leadership in community education and post-secondary administration.

Active in community service organizations, Lennes has been president of the Hutchinson Chamber of Commerce, the Hutchinson Ambassadors and the Hutchinson Downtown Retail Association. Professionally, he has been president of the Minnesota Community Education Association. He has served on the Board of Directors for the Private Industry Council, The Central Minnesota Manufacturing Technology Services Board, Minnesota Chapter of the National School Public Relations Association and National Community Education Association.

His abilities have been recognized by receiving the Hutchinson Distinguished Service Award, Minnesota Honor Roll Teacher of the Year Distinction and Outstanding Leadership in Education Award.

Lennes holds bachelor's and master's degrees in business education from St. Cloud State University and continues to pursue education in quality management, computers, finance and marketing.

8

Continuous Improvement: Transition Through Service Systems

Susan G. Hillenmeyer

Continuous Quality Improvement at Belmont University is a four-year effort. We have learned much from our successes, and even more from our mistakes. It has been a remarkable learning time for many in the administration, staff and faculty of our institution. That said, the president's quality steering team found in an internal quality planning session that one part of the strategic quality plan was not as successful as we had hoped. Somehow, through all our learning about teamwork, continuous improvement, systems thinking and student quality teams, we assumed there would be a "halo" effect. We led ourselves to believe that with substantial focus on process improvement, miraculously, front-line service would also improve.

Process improvement is critical – measuring outputs, finding root causes and preventing errors. We also found that the human touch, personal helpfulness and a systems perspective in the way we do our business can make the difference between good companies and great ones, between good universities and premier ones. Through process-improvement teams, Belmont streamlined registration, posted grades faster, improved parking, delighted students with excellent cafeteria food, involved them in course feedback and a myriad of other such "satisfiers." Both staff and faculty served on most teams, and students played major roles in many of them.

Involvement and improvements were significant, yet there were many critical incidents in which people felt unable to serve students or their co-workers well. Students were often critical of the level of service they received, and there was great variability among work groups in their abilities to deliver quality service. Internal customer groups faced service barriers across the campus. We heard about it from everyone. *(Learning #1: Quality improvement brings with it a forum for more conversation, conflict and opinion. Welcome it, or be frustrated to distraction.)*

The steering team chose a strategy of providing education for continuous improvement of service. We surveyed customer service materials from over 20 vendors. Most of it was what we came to call "smile training." These materials focused on teaching employees to have better "attitudes." It was what Albrecht (1985) referred to as "charm school." We rejected these materials because:

❖ They were mechanical. ("When the customer says ...., you smile and respond ....")

❖ Language suggested was trite and stilted. (When faced with a policy you can't violate, you say, "I'm sorry you're feeling that way, but it's just the way we have to administer this. **But we really care about you!**")

❖ Business language and principles did not apply. ("The

---

customer is always right, no matter what." Our customers aren't always right, and we can't tell them they are. Our response may have to be, "Yes, you really **must** have an official transcript to be admitted, even if it is a great inconvenience to do so.")

The steering team started over. A team of front-line employees met and brainstormed all the issues of quality service they believed needed attention at Belmont University. *(Learning #2: If you ask people what their concerns and issues are, they'll tell you if you listen long enough.)* The list was extensive, but the following are among those with highest priority:

- ❖ Responding quickly to all customers
- ❖ Telephone systems, answering
- ❖ Changing "broken" systems
- ❖ Communicating bad news
- ❖ Dealing with difficult students
- ❖ How to deal with a real "mess up"
- ❖ Dealing with difficult internal customers
- ❖ Time and people shortage as it affects service
- ❖ Repetition of tasks
- ❖ How to avoid blaming
- ❖ Listening empathetically
- ❖ Being able to answer questions
- ❖ Collecting information on ways to improve service

Armed with this information, two members of the steering team began design of a curriculum for delivering quality service. In doing so, they related the course to Belmont University's vision: *To be a premier teaching university bringing together the best of liberal arts and professional education in a consistently caring Christian environment.*

Delivering Quality Service became a framework for improving the way we at Belmont University serve others. When organizations begin quality improvement activities, there can be a "tug of war" between the ideas of service and process improvement. Our goal was to leverage through quality improvement teamwork (reducing mistakes, improving turn-around time, etc.), while improving our service. We build loyalty to our organization through the exceptional way we care for people. Someone once said that the only thing another organization cannot duplicate is the competence, commitment and enthusiasm of its people.

During the course development, we found an innovative system that had excellent video support. We customized the material for applicability to the university setting and educated our training team in the Center for Quality and Professional Development on material use. The course is unique because it combines what we know about process improvement and systems thinking with the best of customer-service models. The following is an overview of the curriculum:

KEY CUSTOMER GROUPS AND SERVICE QUALITY

Participants identify key customer groups, both internal and outside their work area, then determine what they provide those groups or individuals. They identify in their work how they know what those customers think of service quality. In most instances, participants come to the conclusion they don't know, they surmise.

DIFFERENCES BETWEEN MANUFACTURING AND EDUCATION SERVICE

Participants discuss the ways manufacturing and education-service industries differ, including intangibility of output and language. Many people in education have a strong barrier to learning about quality because of the language. Many of us are "put off" by the industrial model language. **Customer, product** and **outputs** are terms so unfamiliar in academic settings that people avoid learning because they don't like the words. Old-style leadership would say, "Oh, come on now! You're smart people; just make the translation." We've learned the hard way that much dialogue around what words mean to us is vital. *(Learning #3: If you don't spend time talking about the language differences, you passively inhibit learning.)* The translation of these words is valuable, but the real value is in the conversation, really listening to each other for understanding. In the Delivering Quality Service course, when this kind of interchange takes place, there is remarkable similarity about what people believe is right and what they should accomplish, but the languages are very, very different.

❖ In manufacturing, you can measure output the same way the customer will – in concrete dimensions. (A stitching defect in the factory is still a defect when we put on a pair of socks.) In higher education, we don't know if service output is quality until it's received by the customer. (If someone thinks he is being helpful and the customer thinks he is being long-winded, by definition, there is a service gap.)

❖ Service output is perishable. We can't store it for delivery another time. It is difficult to separate the service output and the act of producing the service itself. (We can't put aside an irate student until we're ready to handle the situation when we're already face-to-face with the student.)

❖ By its nature, service is variable. There is natural variation in each person's response, and no two people react the same way. Despite this limitation, we strive to reduce variability, not for its own sake, but so that we can predict with certainty that Belmont can achieve its vision as a place where caring for each other is consistent practice.

VALUE OF CUSTOMERS TO THE UNIVERSITY

We calculate in dollar amounts the value of each major customer to our institution. Participants spend time actually multiplying known figures (tuition, housing, food revenue, average alumni contributions) by the number who enter. We calculate the dollar impact of a lost student, a lost business-community customer, a lost employee. These numbers bring into focus how important the service dimension is to our financial well-being. *(Learning #4: These are just the numbers we know. As Deming reminds us, "The real numbers are un-known and un-knowable." The cost of poor quality service in education is astounding.)* The "TARP Consumer Complaint Handling in America," an update study by the U.S. Office of Consumer Affairs, is a helpful resource.

MAKING A SERVICE COMMITMENT

Participants make service commitments for each major customer group, both inside and outside the institution, based on what those customers need and the level of service we will provide them.

WHAT'S DIFFERENT ABOUT OUR SERVICE?

Participants determine what will set their service apart from others' service. They "standardize" these. In the Center for Quality and Professional Development, for example, we print our materials on heavy-stock paper and put them into customized binders. For our breaks in classes, we serve warm, delicious chocolate chip cookies. These are the "little extras" every internal customer receives.

RECOVERING FROM FAILURES

During brainstorming, participants list incidents when they might not meet service commitments and then develop recovery strategies.

RESPONDING TO CUSTOMERS

Participants learn a system of responding to both positive and negative feedback from customers. It is a problem-solving model with a "twist." Instead of "smile training," the participant learns specifically what he or she is able to do for that customer as well as strategies for reducing anger, being proactive and maintaining personal dignity.

STRATEGY TO IMPROVE THE SYSTEM

Finally, participants learn the element that differentiates this quality service model from most others, a way for giving feedback to the **system**, Belmont University. Each time a Belmont person is unable to meet his or her commitment to a customer – internal or external – he or she documents that failure and reports it in a simple format to the steering team. The steering team collects the information and enters it into a spreadsheet format for display. This data collection gives comments on system problems and provides direction to the steering team in chartering improvement or planning teams around those service gaps.

This systems approach is critical to the institution. Dr. Paul Batalden, president of Hospital Corporation of America's Quality Resource Group, reminds us at Belmont that there can be many "activity-based" quality improvement efforts. We can have teams everywhere on campus, with large numbers of people involved, and still not improve the system. If teams don't see change in the system, they become "burned out" with the activity. To give an example of how this works in the Delivering Quality Service model, consider the following scenarios:

> At a mythical school, during the registration process, registration workers are in a hurry and sometimes rude. Students complain about the quality of service. The institution sends registration workers to customer-

service training and helps them be more "student centered." They learn to personalize service and make sure we value our students.

Next fall, registration workers are helpful, student-centered and caring. Lines are around the block because of all the "personal" service. The dean goes on a rampage about "poor service" because the lines are long and students are complaining about it.

This is a classic case of system failure. Deming's retort might be, "Everyone's doing his best! But the system is failing." A real example also illustrates the idea:

In a student quality team giving feedback about a laboratory assignment, the teacher discovered the laboratory assistants were not familiar with one of the software products students used. If they had trouble, they were out of luck unless another student could help. The professor **remedied the problem for the class** by asking for an assistant who knew the software product.

In both instances, there was **problem solving**, not system improvement. Not only should we help registration workers be more "student-centered," we should address the reasons they were having difficulty being so in the first place and improve the registration system. In the second example, not only should the professor address class needs, he or she should insist we examine the system of assigning laboratory assistants for all classes. *(Learning #4: If you only focus on problem solving, quality efforts will be short-lived.)*

One helpful learning is that we can use process mapping to find not only areas of waste and re-work in a process, but also to log service variability. In several instances, we posted a detailed flow diagram of a "broken process" for both customers and workers to study. They put different colored dots on the chart to depict 1) great variability, 2) significant resource allocation, 3) reported service gaps, and 4) most time spent.

The Delivering Quality Service initiative has completed its pilots in four important areas of service: Records, Admissions, Center for Quality and Professional Development, and Student Services. We have anecdotal information and course evaluations at this writing. The director of quality research gathers student census data every semester about student attitudes and our service in particular work areas. We will monitor results carefully so that in the true spirit of the PDCA cycle, we can improve Delivering Quality Service based on learning from our pilot efforts.

Finally, most quality authorities recognize the lessons learned from human resource leaders who say **hiring** a "service" attitude is easier than **changing** existing attitudes. While we are certainly working to improve the service systems internally, results from an internal customer survey instrument told us that the way we were bringing new people into the organization had much to do with their initial perceptions and attitudes. As a result, Belmont University teams developed an entire orientation system around our vision and values. The president's Internal Planning Group (deans and vice presidents) commissioned a video about what our vision means. Belmont shows the video, made entirely by Belmont students, faculty and staff, whenever we recruit and hire new people. We are printing new application forms listing the Belmont vision and the values to which we ascribe. To deliver consistent quality service, everyone must understand the vision of what we will become with their help. The recruiting and hiring process is the first step toward making the service model work.

REFERENCES

Albrecht, Karl and Ron Zemke. *Service America*. Homewood, Ill.: Dow Jones-Irwin, 1985.

Albrecht, Karl. *At America's Service*. Homewood, Ill.: Dow Jones-Irwin, 1988.

Batalden, Paul. Personal communication, Nashville, Tenn., March, 1993.

Deming, Edwards. *Out of the Crisis*. Cambridge, MA: MIT Press, 1986.

"Quality Service Everytime." Seattle: WMI, Corp., 1992

Rodgers, Buck. *Getting the Most Out of Yourself and Others*. New York: Harper and Row, 1987.

Senge, Peter. *The Fifth Discipline*. New York: Doubleday, 1990.

Zemke, Ron. *The Service Edge*. New York: New American Library, 1989

Susan G. Hillenmeyer is vice president for quality and professional development at Belmont University in Nashville, Tenn. She works directly with the president in leading Belmont's quality improvement effort and heads the Center for Quality and Professional Development, a campus unit delivering custom-designed training for area businesses. Hillenmeyer previously served as director of special projects for Belmont.

From Johnson City, Tenn., she is a graduate of East Tennessee State University and holds a Ph.D. from the University of Georgia. In 1981, Hillenmeyer returned to ETSU to complete a post-doctoral fellowship in higher education administration.

Much of her study and many of her publications deal with adult learning and quality improvement in higher education. She is an active consultant and public speaker. Her efforts center around quality systems, teambuilding and productivity as they relate to education and service industries. Currently, she is serving on the board of directors for the Tennessee Quality Award. In 1993, Hillenmeyer was named a Malcolm Baldrige National Quality Award Examiner.

9

Is There Hope for TQM in the Academy?

Trudy W. Banta

In his book *On Q, Causing Quality in Higher Education*, Dan Seymour (1991) cites four driving forces behind the current inclination of colleges and universities to be concerned about quality: competition, costs, accountability and service orientation. He describes each as follows:

❖ **Competition.** For all but the most elite institutions, it is a buyer's market in higher education. Both public and private institutions have to worry about preserving head-count enrollment: privates need tuition dollars, and publics need both tuition and state subsidies based on enrollment. In some markets, there is open and blatant competition for students among institutions.

❖ **Costs.** Throughout the 1980s, tuition rose faster than the consumer price index, and now students and the public want to know what more they are getting for their education dollar. In Indiana, public universities requested a 32 percent increase in state funds for the 1993-95 biennium and the legislature responded with the collective question, "What did you do with the last increase we gave you?"

❖ **Accountability.** Those who support higher education want to know how the dollars are being spent, and have therefore instituted regulations and reporting requirements to ensure accountability. My own career includes 10 years of dealing with Tennessee's performance funding program, which bases 5 1/2 percent of each public institution's budget on the results of a prescribed set of evaluation procedures, including testing students in general education and their major, as well as surveying alumni.

❖ **Service Orientation.** Professionals in higher education have set their own standards and have said, in effect, "Leave the money on the stump, and trust us." Those days are over. Now the public wants to be involved in structuring its public institutions to deliver better services by setting standards of quality and determining costs, and we are compelled to respond.

In 1989, I received a three-year grant from the Fund for the Improvement of Postsecondary Education (FIPSE) to work with seven institutions, both two- and four-year, to study the implications of Deming's quality improvement principles for higher education. We met for joint discussions twice a year for three years and established study groups on our individual campuses. In 1989, we felt there was a great need for a translation of Total Quality Management (TQM) principles from the language of business and industry to that of the academy, and thus, over the course of the project we produced a brief overview of quality improvement principles as they can be applied to higher education. Now – nearly five years since we wrote the

FIPSE proposal – there are hundreds of articles and several books on the topic.

The FIPSE project culminated in a meeting that took place in May 1992 in Knoxville. We invited the quality improvement coordinators of several universities that were acquiring some reputation for implementing TQM. The group of institutions included Samford University and the universities of Maryland, Michigan, Minnesota, Pennsylvania, Tennessee, Wisconsin and Virginia Tech. We considered at that meeting four topics:

1. The features of a quality-oriented institution
2. Barriers to achieving that vision
3. Ways to overcome the barriers
4. Target areas for future work

In this chapter, I would like to consider an extended list of the features of a quality-oriented institution that we identified on that occasion and identify some of the barriers we face in achieving these. I believe there is some hope for overcoming the barriers to continuous improvement within the academy, but nothing less than a culture change is required to do so.

FEATURES OF A QUALITY-ORIENTED INSTITUTION

To most academics, a list of characteristics of a college concerned about quality will sound simplistic, like a Dale Carnegie recipe for success. Yet the philosophy underlying TQM or Continuous Quality Improvement (CQI) is profound. Its implementation requires a fundamental change in the culture of higher-education institutions.

An institution with a serious commitment to quality:

1. Is committed to the need for **continuous improvement – forever.** Its people are always thinking about how to get better.

2. Identifies **whom it wishes to serve** and what these potential clients want and need. Client groups include stu-

dents, recipients of faculty research and service activities, and members of the community.

3. Addresses **the needs of its clients** in its mission statement.

4. Identifies the **values** that guide its actions.

5. Develops a **vision** of what it would like to be in the future.

6. Has **strong leadership** that **communicates** the mission, goals, values and the vision of the institution continuously to faculty, staff and students.

7. Identifies its **critical processes**: teaching, research and service.

8. **Aligns** the implementation of its activities with its mission and values.

9. Provides **continuing educational opportunities** for all employees, both in group process and in job-related skills.

10. Uses cross-functional **teams** to improve processes: works with its **suppliers**, builds quality into each process and ceases dependence on inspection to achieve quality.

11. Pushes decision-making to the lowest appropriate level, thus **creating** an **attitude of interdependence and trust** throughout the institution.

12. Bases **decisions** about the allocation of resources on **data**. Uses quantitative thinking, along with competence in group problem-solving skills and relevant statistical procedures. These should be in widespread use throughout the institution.

13. Views itself as a **learning organization**, one that:

❖ Produces student learning, research and service

❖ Studies, monitors and evaluates the processes that produce the products

❖ Makes active collaborators in the improvement process of all concerned, including faculty, staff and students, parents, suppliers, employers and community members

14. Recognizes and rewards those who conscientiously

---

work to improve quality.

(I think it is interesting that my list of features includes 14 points. It just turned out that way; I did not begin with the intention of addressing each of Deming's 14 points, and I have not done so. But like so many others working in this field, my thinking has been profoundly influenced by Deming's work.)

BARRIERS TO ACHIEVING THE VISION
OF A QUALITY-ORIENTED INSTITUTION

Daily we hear and read diatribes against TQM. In an article entitled "What's Wrong with TQM?," Boyett and Conn have described 10 mistakes that organizations investing heavily in training and TQM consultants often make. In effect, they say it's tough to change a culture based on individualism.

Within most colleges and universities, there are many faculty and administrators who hold views that provide an environment that is not conducive to establishing the concept of continuous improvement. Some of these views can be cited in connection with each of the 14 points just identified.

The first argument advanced by many is that American higher education is generally regarded as the best in the world. Faculty and administrators are often overheard saying things like, "We have excellent faculty, all doing their best. How can we improve on perfection?"

Many faculty assert, "**We** don't have customers. We know best what students need and how to do our research, so why should we ask anyone else? How dare anyone try to tell us how to do our work? We have academic freedom. Moreover, creative work cannot and should not be managed."

In considering the need for statements of values and vision, the campus argument goes: the strength of American higher education is its diversity. Breadth is important. The whole student experience is the sum of parts; that is, individual courses. There is no compelling need to agree on comprehensive program objectives for students because they can and should put their knowledge together themselves in their own way. What we hope to promote in students is critical thinking, which can neither be defined or measured. Faculty cannot, and therefore should not, try to agree on specific goals for student learning in college.

Communication is not very effective in most institutions. Faculty in many departments communicate with similar specialists in their discipline on distant campuses more often than with colleagues in their own department. Administrators think they do well by absorbing outside flack so that faculty can do their jobs. In fact, faculty may have been shielded so effectively that they don't know the wolf is at the door. Most don't recognize that the questions being asked by the public (about how and how much faculty work) are serious and are not likely to go away.

Within every institution, there are critical processes such as student recruitment and admission, orientation, teaching and evaluation. Cross-functional teams could be established to effect improvement in each of these areas. But how many universities actually approach their critical processes in this way?

An overall campus plan must guide college and departmental plans so that all work together. Few institutions have a set of plans that really guides day-to-day decision making.

Most universities train secretaries in word-processing and in the use of new software. Some training in human relations issues such as team-building is being offered through human resources departments, but often we do not provide the structure for immediate use of the concepts being taught. The opportunity to practice what is learned is as important as the instruction itself.

By virtue of their training and tradition, academics tend to work alone. Despite the fact that we carefully collect and analyze data in conducting our disciplinary research, we ignore data and use intuition in reaching conclusions about the impact of our work with students. We have few explicit goals for this work and therefore little direction for evaluating it. In general, we offer few rewards for studying or evaluating the processes of teaching and learning.

We say that we want good teachers, then we reward faculty for doing research as reflected in grants and publications. Jim Fairwether, at the Center for the Study of Higher Education at Penn State, has analyzed massive faculty databases supplied by the National Center for Education Statistics and has demonstrated clearly that the more faculty teach the less they are paid.

To outsiders, colleges and universities are viewed as big, bureaucratic places. Faculty are arrogant and unresponsive, not at all interested in evaluating their effectiveness. Both administrators and faculty pay far more attention to recruiting and ensuring the welfare of faculty than of students. We are seen as not interested in focusing our efforts, working together to set goals, or assessing our own progress. We teach the scientific method, but we don't practice it. When asked to explain what we are doing for students, we make it sound almost mystical. We say, in effect, "You put students and great minds together in periods of exposure of 50 minutes for four to six years, and out will come an educated student." "How do we know?" "Don't ask! We just know."

We are asked by parents and potential students:

❖ "Do your graduates get better jobs and make more money?" We reply, "Don't ask! We are not training people for jobs. Many of our students go on to the best graduate schools!"

❖ "How do you know which schools are best?" We reply, "Don't ask. We just know."

❖ "Are you one of the best schools?" Again we reply,

"Don't ask! Those rating systems they use are flawed. Our graduates live fuller, richer lives as a result of their education."

❖ "How do you know?" We respond, "Don't ask – it's immeasurable."

I want to emphasize that this is not a call to give up creativity and intuition and go to a recipe-like, step-by-step plan, just filling in the cells. Nor am I describing a quick fix. Managing for quality is not for short-term gain; it's a way of life. Simply stated, it will give more focus than we currently have to the doing and to the evaluation of our work in the academy.

THE NEED FOR A CHANGE IN
THE CULTURE OF HIGHER EDUCATION

Which of the 14 aspects of a quality-oriented institution are so important that we must do something about them? I believe that all 14 must be addressed, because they are conceptually interrelated. The need to provide evidence of accountability is not going to go away – it's well into its second decade and stronger than ever in Tennessee. Too many other public goods and services are competing with higher education for public dollars, and there are too many educational providers. Two- and four-year institutions, training firms, business and industry are all in competition for today's learner. Colleges and universities must use the resources they have to do **fewer** things **better**.

According to Roger Chaufournier, the quality leader at George Washington University, if TQM is to be accepted in higher education, faculty must recognize the need for change, acknowledge that new learning must take place, and be willing to take risks (FYI Column, 1992). Relinquishing control to an empowered workforce can be threatening. Finally, and perhaps most importantly for faculty, there must be a willingness for faculty to support the whole, even if this exacts a cost from the individual.

We **can** improve what we now do and we **must**. We do not necessarily need to adopt the philosophy of Kaizen – the Japanese concept of continuous improvement with a 200-year view of the future – but we could certainly learn from studies of Kaizen.

We must identify the individuals and groups that we serve, learn more about them, and be more responsive to their needs. We need to know the learning styles of our students and how to address those. Their goals should help to shape our approaches to courses and curricula. If we think of a customer as someone with whom we exchange something of value, it may be easier to recognize students as customers. We may know what students need to know, but they know how they learn best. They can help faculty become better teachers by providing continuous feedback about teaching strategies that work or don't work.

At Samford University in Birmingham and now at Belmont University in Nashville, Kathy Baugher has had enormous success teaching student teams to work with instructors to continuously improve teaching and learning. Students from quality teams help instructors make changes in their courses that will enable more students to comprehend the material being covered. Baugher has published a manual entitled "LEARN: Student Quality Team Manual" (Baugher, 1992) that guides student-team members to (1) Locate an opportunity for improvement, (2) Establish a team, (3) Assess the current process, (4) Research causes, and (5) Nominate a solution. In contrast to traditional course evaluations that furnish generic information for use in future classes and are given at the end of a class, student teams provide continuous evaluation throughout the class that can assist the instructor in improving learning opportunities for current students.

Bateman and Roberts (1992), professors in the Graduate

School of Business at the University of Chicago, ask students to complete a "fast feedback" at the end of every class. Questions include those from the "one-minute paper" strategy described by Angelo and Cross (1993): "What was the most important thing you learned today?" and "What was the muddiest point?" The questionnaire also asks about the helpfulness of the advance reading assignments for the class in preparing the students for the day's work. In response to open-ended questions, students suggest how the instructor could improve the assignments as well as what went on in class.

Bateman and Roberts report that their questionnaires have produced immediate responses by professors. When students in one class said they were having trouble hearing the instructor, a portable microphone was installed. Students wanted larger type on overhead transparencies and asked that the lights be left on while the overhead projector was in use. Students said they did not need to cover material read in advance in detail in class, so instructors were encouraged to move more rapidly to other material. Students also asked for more examples in class, and instructors have acted on that suggestion.

Faculty complain about the poor preparation of the students they must teach. We need to get closer to our suppliers – teachers in grades K-12 and other professors who teach the introductory and general education courses in our own institutions. We need to set our specifications carefully, communicate them, and hold to our standards. We can help our suppliers by providing training for them.

We must focus our statements of purpose (our mission) and our goals. We can emphasize our unique strengths in determining what the goals will be and thus be distinctive. Many faculty say it will weaken rather than strengthen higher education to specify goals for student learning. Yet we work hard to delimit problem statements to guide our own research.

We decry "fishing expeditions." We prize purposefulness. Why should we expect student learning to proceed without any sort of plan?

We must articulate the values that shape our behavior. Do these include religious beliefs, civic participation, honesty? How do we define and defend academic freedom? Does every faculty member simply teach his or her specialty in whatever way he or she likes? Is there any responsibility for what colleagues expect students to know after they complete one of these specialty courses? Do we ever discuss that with them?

We need a vision of the kind of institution we would like to create in the future. Here we could use Alexander Astin's (1991) concept of talent development: emphasizing the institution's responsibility to nurture and promote the personal growth of each student toward his or her maximum potential. In addition, Peter Senge's (1990) ideas about the learning organization can be instructive: the notion that there are five disciplines, or bodies of knowledge, that a successful organization must adopt. The five disciplines are systems thinking, personal mastery, mental models or images, shared vision and team learning.

We need strong leadership. Often the commitment of a college president comes from contact with government, business and industrial leaders outside academe. If we can't get help from outside the institution in persuading the CEO, respected internal people who are convinced of the need to change should try to influence the leadership. In the final analysis, we may need to recruit someone else for the job. Leaders need to communicate broadly in person and in writing. One must not shield faculty from problems. **All** need to be involved in finding solutions.

Collaboration on critical processes is important. Cross-functional teams of faculty and staff need to be trained to work together to improve every aspect of the services colleges provide.

Decisions about how we will spend our time – the activities we will undertake – should be made within the context of our mission, values and vision. We must be more concerned about education and training, both to do our own jobs and to help us become better collaborators. Then we need opportunities to **practice** the collaborative skills we learn in our training.

We must define our critical processes, work on them in cross-disciplinary teams, set our standards and work with suppliers to help them meet them. They need feedback about their performance just as we do. Faced with underprepared students, we should not lower our standards. We need to build quality into each process, not simply announce at the end of the process that we have failed with a particular student. Students need assessment, with feedback at many points along the way in their education.

We must involve everyone in problem solving by giving everyone in the academy the pride of responsibility for quality. If we believe higher education can improve society, then we ought to pledge to help more people complete their studies. This means working together to figure out how to do that.

We must cease to rely on intuition alone and begin to be systematic in using data to direct improvements. This is the contribution of outcomes assessment in higher education. The process of reviewing assessment colleagues' chapters for a book (Banta, 1993) has convinced me that despite the fact that few campus leaders who have guided assessment programs have background in educational research, the improvements undertaken in response to assessment findings are the very actions that decades of research show are most likely to improve student learning.

We must set goals in higher education and evaluate our progress in meeting them. We must also recognize and reward those who participate conscientiously in this process.

WHAT CHANCE HAS CQI IN THE ACADEMY?

In a letter written in December 1992 to the president of Indiana University, the Executive Committee of the Bloomington Chapter of the American Association of University Professors stated, "Any university, but most of all a major research institution, is a collection of specialists having expertise that extends beyond the knowledge of anyone else in the world. These specialists push forward the frontiers of knowledge by extending their own. Specialists do not thrive if managed closely by nonspecialists. At best they are slowed in their efforts to learn by having to drag along, by explanation, those who are not thinking at the same advanced level. At worst, specialists are stymied by the disapproval of their non-specialist evaluators."

In an article in the *Chronicle of Higher Education*, Michael McGerr (1993) argues that today America stands out among advanced industrial societies for its cultural resistance to organization. In the 1950s, Reisman's *Lonely Crowd* and Whyte's *The Organization Man* painted a picture of post-World War II Americans as victims of large-scale organizations that promoted a centralized, impersonal, homogeneous social system, with little room for individuals and individualism. But what has actually happened, according to McGerr, is that the fundamental value of individualism on which this country was founded has prevailed. Corporations have had little impact on our heterogeneous society, on the way we live our lives. "Managers, engineers and advertisers have not spoken the same language, and they have not drowned out other voices." Our society is "less organized, less modern, less susceptible to change than we have assumed." This suggests that TQM too shall pass because Americans cannot be comfortable collaborating to solve our problems.

But there are other voices. Bob Zemsky, director of the Institute for Research on Higher Education at the University of

Pennsylvania, has said, "More and more higher-education institutions are coming to see themselves as enterprises that need direction. A college or university is not a gathering place. It needs purpose and discipline." (See Lively, 1993.) In the future, external forces such as demands from students, public agencies and industry, are more likely to shape colleges than are internal deliberations. College is a service industry, and education experience is its product. Zemsky asks, "How do you re-engineer that experience so that it is more flexible and adaptable and meets the needs of its customers; so that it takes advantage of assets and doesn't become so costly that the market evaporates? We are in the business of re-engineering the education experience."

Estela Bensimon and Anna Neumann (1993) studied top administrative leaders in 15 colleges and universities by going to live on the campuses for a few weeks and interviewing presidents and their staffs. They found CEOs relying on close associates to help them make decisions because "the combined expertise of multiple minds" is needed to address the tensions of contemporary campus life. Bensimon and Neumann believe that the most important feature of a successful team is its ability to act like a social brain. Team members pool their intelligence in forging multiple perspectives; questioning, challenging and arguing; and monitoring and providing feedback. The team becomes a source of creativity and can serve to correct institutional dysfunction.

What does the future hold? Are we individualists valuing academic freedom who cannot or will not be brought together around a common set of goals? Or will we combine our brain power to collaborate in teaching and in accomplishing all our other responsibilities?

REFERENCES

Angelo, T. A. and Cross, K. P. *Classroom Assessment Techniques* (2nd ed.). San Francisco: Jossey-Bass, 1993.

Astin, A. W. *Assessment for Excellence.* New York: ACE MacMillian, 1991.

Banta, T. W. and Associates. *Making a Difference: Outcomes of a Decade of Assessment in Higher Educations.* San Francisco: Jossey-Bass, 1993.

Banta, T. W., Phillipi, R. H., Pike, G. R. and Stuhl, J. H. *Applying Deming's Quality Improvement Strategies to Assessment in Higher Education. Final Report.* Knoxville, TN: University of Tennessee, Knoxville, Center for Assessment Research & Development, 1992.

Bateman, G. and Roberts, H. "TQM for Professors and Students," unpublished manuscript, 1992.

Baugher, K. "LEARN Student Quality Team Manual." Birmingham, AL: Author, 1992.

Bensimon, E. and Neumann, A. *Redesigning Collegiate Leadership: Teams and Teamwork in Higher Education.* Baltimore, MD: The Johns Hopkins University Press, 1993.

Boyett, J. H. and Conn, H. P. "What's Wrong with Total Quality Management?" unpublished manuscript, nd.

FYI Column. *TQM in Higher Education,* 1992, 1(2), 6, 1992.

Lively, K. "State Colleges Grapple With Tough Decisions on How to Downsize," *The Chronicle of Higher Education,* Feb. 3, 1993, A23, A28.

McGerr, M. The Persistence of Individualism," *The Chronicle of Higher Education,* Feb. 10, 1993, A48.

Senge, P. M. *The Fifth Discipline: The Art & Practice of the Learning Organization.* New York: Doubleday, 1990.

Seymour, D. *On Q, Causing Quality in Higher Education.* New York: ACE MacMillian, 1991.

Trudy W. Banta is vice chancellor for planning and institutional improvement and professor of higher education at Indiana University-Purdue University Indianapolis. Prior to assuming her current position in August 1992, Banta was the director of the Center for Assessment Research and Development and a professor of education at the University of Tennessee, Knoxville. Since 1983, she has edited two published volumes on assessment, written over 60 articles and reports, and  contributed 12 chapters to other published works. A third edited work, *Making A Difference: Outcomes of A Decade of Assessment in Higher Education*, will be published by Jossey-Bass in 1993.

Banta has addressed state-wide conferences in 20 states and national conferences in China and Germany on the subject of assessing quality in higher education. She has also visited two- and four-year institutions in 28 states and Puerto Rico to consult with faculty and administrators on matters related to outcomes assessment. Her interest in CQI began in 1988 when she organized a consortium of seven institutions in Tennessee to study the potential link between outcomes assessment and CQI. The consortium received a three-year grant from the Fund for the Improvement of Post-Secondary Education, and participants concluded that a powerful synergistic relationship between outcomes assessment and CQI can exist when the leadership for both processes is carefully coordinated.

10

Maximizing Flexibility for Tenured Faculty Positions with CQI

Sandra Featherman
Valerie Broughton

INTRODUCTION

Quality improvement tools rarely have been formally applied to the allocation of tenure-track faculty positions, although decisions to increase or decrease the number of tenure lines in particular departments are among the most important judgments academic leaders make. Academic officers must adjust resources to account for program changes and planning goals. This is especially true during periods of budget constraints. Continuous Quality Improvement (CQI) processes can enable and improve the reallocation of tenure-track faculty lines.

In this chapter, we discuss the development and application of CQI procedures for faculty position allocation. The issues examined include institutional culture, budget constraints, applicability of CQI to faculty resource decisions, the selection of a cross-functional team, coupling planning objectives with resource allocations and developing implementable procedures.

Many academic departments regard their programs as fixed entities, with given numbers of essential courses and disciplinary responsibilities for which the present-size faculty cohort is the minimum required to meet needs. While departments frequently request additional positions, they rarely volunteer to give them up. Furthermore, faculty are extremely sensitive to efforts to reduce academic staffing within departments. The fragmentation and isolation of disciplines contributes to a belief that academic leaders who propose cuts do not understand the needs of the discipline and devalue the field of study which members of that department have made their life's work.

Quality improvement requires change. Areas of growth, emergent areas and programs of excellence need to be supported. In periods of resource growth, decisions can be made to increase staffing in one unit without cutting back others. During periods of retrenchment or budget stasis, however, it can become extremely difficult to alter a given configuration of faculty positions.

In the last several years, public institutions of higher education have faced serious budget cutbacks in many states. Academic leaders find themselves confronted with flat budgets, lack of flexible funds and hard choices. Changes that need to occur in faculty staffing needs frequently can only be met through internal reallocations. CQI techniques can be used to analyze need and to develop policies and procedures for wise internal reallocations of tenure-track faculty positions.

HISTORICAL OVERVIEW

Historically, at the University of Minnesota, Duluth, (UMD) the prevailing culture supported the notion that departments "owned" positions. When a faculty member from a department resigned or retired, it was generally assumed that the budget line belonged to the department. Departments would request the chief academic officer to approve the search for a replacement, arguing that monies to pay for the position were available from the funds which had supported the previous position. In addition, departments expected to retain the increment which resulted from the differential in salaries between the senior person retiring and the new entry-level position. The demand of the chief academic officer to approve replacement hires and recapture differential funds was seen as an infringement on departmental privilege.

This automatic return of open slots led to inefficient use of scarce resources. In any institution which is growing and changing, the need for tenure-track slots changes over time. Due to budget cuts, UMD has had to eliminate some departments and programs and merge others. At the same time, needs have arisen for expanded support for strong, high-demand programs, yet no new dollars are available. Furthermore, while many departments are quite responsible about exploring the potential use of new faculty positions, automatic replacement of lines has allowed some departments to retain positions without undergoing a rigorous needs analysis.

Departments wishing to retain or increase faculty lines should be required to examine the nature and direction of the department, changes occurring in the discipline and the needs which new faculty would address. Deans must demonstrate that position requests fulfill collegiate goals. The time frame necessary for such analysis is inconsistent with a policy of instant reallocation. Departments need sufficient time to fully explore serious questions regarding their future shape and direction.

The chief academic officer also needs adequate time for planning and response. Information about the opening of faculty slots does not become available at one given time. It becomes available in a piecemeal fashion as notifications are received of resignations, retirements or deaths.

A procedure needed to be developed that would allow appropriate planning time for the chief academic officer as well as for the departments and collegiate units. For the procedure to be acceptable to the units, it had to appear fair, be readily understandable and be easy to implement. The use of CQI processes enabled UMD to develop and implement a procedure that was seen as unbiased, clear and implementable.

CQI IN HIGHER EDUCATION

Total Quality Management (TQM) was developed as a quality control system at Bell Laboratories and used by war-materials industries during World War II. TQM was adapted by Deming and Juran to rebuild the Japanese economy after the war. Over the last two decades, a number of major corporations have used quality improvement principles to transform management and production operations in factories and offices across America, evidence that CQI practices can be successful within the United States. The practical attraction of CQI is the expectation that by using quality control processes, quality can be improved while costs are contained.

These dual characteristics appeal to higher education because institutions face internal and external pressure to increase quality, with bleak prospects for increases in resources. Assessment activities, undertaken to provide evidence of quality, have increased in the academy and now have a permanent institutional role. Similarly, over the past 20 years, retrenchment and reallocation planning has become a common feature in long-range planning in American higher education. Federal goals for education, media criticism, consumer poll results, requirements to report graduation rates and state policies on program coordination are all examples of external pressure on colleges to demonstrate quality. Student needs for enhanced academic and career advising, and institutional needs for modern instructional research equipment and facilities are examples of internal demands related to quality. The resistance to higher tuition levels, competition for student enrollments and decreased, or at best, stable governmental funding put stress on both public and private college and university budgets (De Cosmo, Parker and Heverly, 1991).

Deming's 14 points (Deming, 1986) for quality management provide the foundation for transforming organizations into enterprises with quality control. Other authors summarize or recast the main components of CQI (Heverly & Cornesky, 1992; Sherr & Lozier, 1991; Chaffee & Sherr, 1992). A focus on several major elements that relate to higher education institutions offers hope for quality improvement and controlled costs by emphasizing a few selected components: mission, needs of the customers or beneficiaries, systematic approach to operations or processes, and long-term thinking. While a number of colleges have adopted quality management initiatives, there are some barriers which impede meaningful adoption of quality management principles and tools (Winter, 1991).

Mission clarification and differentiation are familiar terms to college and university administrators. Mission statements have been staples in strategic plans for many years. CQI principles enhance mission statements by insisting that customer needs serve as the driving force behind a mission and that the mission express a commitment to quality. Although mission statements can be found on nearly all college campuses, faculty and staff may be unfamiliar with them or may not view them as meaningful. Quality management efforts require that mission statements guide decision making throughout the organization, and that employees have the knowledge and opportunity to contribute to the mission by studying and recommending changes in their work activities which will lead to quality improvements.

The identification of customers' needs requires identification of customer groups or beneficiaries, followed by data collection efforts to document actual needs. Of course, higher education has multiple customers, both internal and external. Students, parents, employers and granting agencies are examples of external customers. Internal customers are those inside the organization who depend on the work of others inside the organization. For example, faculty are the customers of academic administration, all staff are the customers of the payroll office, departments are customers of facilities management.

Patience and long-term view are characteristics associated with CQI. These are often problematic in higher education management. Emergency requests for budget reduction plans called for by many central offices, boards and legislatures for public universities rarely encourage long-term thinking and planning. The short tenure of many college administrators also may prohibit consistent implementation of procedures. CQI requires clearly-specified procedure and data to support any changes. Therefore, clearly-specified processes may compensate for turnover in campus leadership. Adopting a strategy on campus "X" because it worked on campus "Y" would violate the principles of patience and long-term view. The long-term view of an organization must be seen with the changing needs of the customers or beneficiaries in the foreground. The institution must position itself to respond flexibly to changing needs and demands.

Most faculty and academic administrators have experience investigating research problems in their disciplines. Just as the research process requires patience and systematic inquiry, so does CQI. Elements of research methods can be found in CQI principles as well: problem identification, experimental design, data collection and interpretation leading to conclusions. Systematic organizational improvement requires problem identification, process design, collection of quality indicators at each stage of a process, evaluation of the data collected, and – based on the evaluation – a redesign or improvement of the process. The cost of redesigning a process can be a significant error, costing time, effort and money to rework a decision. If an error occurs in a resource allocation process when that resource is faculty positions, it may take years to even have the opportunity to "rework;" that is, to reallocate a faculty position.

ACADEMIC STAFFING

Academic staffing is the key resource in college and university budgets. Seventy to 80 percent of academic operating budgets are attributed to salaries of instructional personnel. Mingle identified three crucial responsibilities of academic administration to maximize effective allocation of faculty resources: maintain flexibility, ensure faculty intellectual vitality, and respond to public demands for increased productivity. Mortimer identified another layer of complexity by identifying two factors exacerbating the challenge of managing faculty resources. Maintaining flexibility is crucial because program and curricular needs change faster than existing positions become vacant. And, most colleges and universities are operating with a decline in real dollars, which further limits administration's ability to reassign faculty resources.

Mortimer established four categories of staffing practices that provide opportunities to reduce instructional expenditures or reallocate academic personnel. A "position control" strategy is available at the time a position is created. The position could be established as a tenure-track position, a temporary full-time position, a part-time position, a position with fixed-length appointment, or perhaps other options available within the institution's personnel classification scheme. The position could be left in the department where the vacancy occurred or reallocated to a department where student demand requires additional staff. Another opportunity is to maximize institutional flexibility in managing the tenure process. Some institutions establish tenure quotas, tenure rates above which a department may not go. Other schools either extend the probation period or establish stricter tenure standards. Still others adopt up-or-out rules requiring progress through the ranks within given time periods. Finally, strategies such as post-tenure review, early retirement incentives, and retraining faculty in low-demand areas to qualify them to teach in high-demand areas are also worth consideration.

Each strategy has its advantages and disadvantages. Any one alone will likely be unsuccessful in maintaining flexibility, faculty vitality, and response to external demands for increased efficiency.

FACULTY RESOURCE ALLOCATION AT UMD

Three activities simultaneously occurring at UMD encouraged senior administrators to adapt quality improvement processes to planning and resource allocation. These were a series of cuts in the University budget, the chancellor's commitment to TQM training and the development of a campus-wide strategic plan.

UMD is a mid-sized comprehensive university within the University of Minnesota system. The UMD chief academic officer, the vice chancellor for academic administration (VCAA), is responsible for five collegiate units (College of Education and Human Service Professions; College of Liberal Arts, College of Science and Engineering, School of Business and Economics, and the School of Fine Arts), the library, information services, institutional research and research centers. The University has 69 undergraduate and 17 graduate programs. It receives $45 million in state funds annually and $20 million in externally-sponsored research projects.

Two external events made change necessary at UMD. The first was that state support did not keep pace with budget needs over the last five years. In order to fund inflationary increases, the University made substantial cuts in selected programs, personnel and support. Five separate budget-paring plans occurred within the five-year period. System-mandated budget cut exercises, where the campus was required to plan reductions in the operations and maintenance budget, have ranged from four to 10 percent, although the uncertainty of legislative funding required the University to plan for worst-case scenarios. The actual cuts at UMD were much less. Even so, unfortunately, the morale of faculty, students and staff suffered from the effects of the planning exercises. UMD has verified through experience Mortimer's claim that whether an institution grapples with resource limitations by increasing the number of students (generating more revenue) while holding the number of faculty constant, or holding the number of students constant while reducing the faculty (reducing expenditures), results can have adverse effects on faculty and student morale and on the quality of advising and instruction.

The other factor leading to change was the insistence of the University of Minnesota system on internal reallocation. This was exemplified first by a policy known as Commitment to Focus, which promoted the shift of resources to areas of excellence, and then by the present policy of internal reallocation from areas perceived as weak or declining to areas of growth or mission-relatedness. One program was closed as a result of the retrenchment, and five new faculty positions were created through the reallocation. Even before these reallocations were implemented, however, further budget cuts eroded some of the improvements intended in the reallocation process, causing a cutback of 9.5 positions in the 1991-92 academic year. During the past three years, it has been made clear that the only source of new faculty positions will be reallocations of the existing budget.

Because of the size of the student body and operating budget, UMD has limited capacity to reallocate resources. UMD's long-term resource commitments are great due to tenure obligations; 82 percent of the regular faculty are tenured. Only 10 percent are temporary and 12 percent are part-time. In order for UMD to employ position control or reallocation strategies, efforts had to be made to devise ways to move funds and positions from one area to another area without threatening the institution's basic vitality.

The one tradition that had to be changed, in order to control the allocation of faculty resources, was department ownership of the budget lines of their tenure-track faculty positions. This policy of ownership violated the three goals of faculty-resource management: to maintain flexibility, insure vitality and increase productivity. Fortunately, the senior campus administrators had been through TQM training over a two-year period. The chancellor had brought in a consultant to work with administrators in applying TQM methods to problem solving and daily management. Several process improvement teams were functioning with some success. This background of training in quality control provided a core of support and some know-how for attacking the problem of managing faculty line reallocations. The quality training management for senior administrators created an environment in which clear processes are valued. The task for academic administrators was to develop clear processes that everyone could feel comfortable with. The VCAA staff has set a goal to regularize routine processes and clearly present them to the campus.

Fortuitously, the University was involved in a strategic planning process, Vision 2000, during the same time that TQM training was occurring. The planning process required all units to examine their relationship to broadly-agreed-upon mission and vision statements, planning assumptions and goals. The campus had developed a certain amount of cynicism about the planning process. Previous plans had not been fully implemented or updated. Budget reductions had dashed hopes for growth or new initiatives. Many faculty members asked, "How can we plan when cuts are occurring?"

One of the planning assumptions was that funding would remain relatively stable over the next six years. Such an assumption was believed necessary to get the UMD community to focus on what it could do, as opposed to what was being done to it. People needed a sense of control over the planning process. The uncertainty about cuts had almost paralyzed the planning process.

The VCAA chaired the Campus Planning Committee. During the planning process, the VCAA made clear the intention to tie unit budget allocations to unit plans. All requests for fiscal resources would need to demonstrate how the requests related to the goals and objectives stated in the unit's Vision 2000 plan.

Thus, campus experience with budget adjustments, strategic planning and exposure to TQM principles provided the foundation for developing sound policies and implementation procedures.

POLICY DEVELOPMENT

The VCAA, in consultation with the deans, developed a policy specifying that when positions were vacated due to retirement or resignation (but not those due to negative tenure decision), departments would, in most cases, be granted permission to hire temporary replacements for one or two years, while departmental, collegiate and campus plans would be reviewed. Positions would be allocated on a permanent basis only after analysis of all vacated positions and departmental and campus needs. Funding to support the position at the new hire's salary level would be provided to the hiring department. Excess funds would remain in the vice chancellor's faculty position pool for the purposes of potentially creating additional positions and funding of faculty retention cases.

Generally, policies specifying the need for vice chancellor approval for new hires had been attempted at UMD prior to this effort. One difference between this and previous tries was that all campus administrators, and many faculty and staff had been through TQM training, and several examples of quality improvement projects had been presented at campus forums over the past three years. The administration knew that in order to improve faculty-resource allocation, the process should be specified and quality indicators identified to measure the success of the strategy over time, to relate it to the campus mission and to meet the needs of various campus constituencies.

Using CQI techniques, we developed a policy on faculty line replacements. All vacated tenure, tenure-track faculty lines will revert to the Office of the VCAA. In the case of lines vacated because of denial of tenure, positions will immediately revert to the department except under unusual circumstances. Vacancies created by resignations, retirement or death are replaced for one year with temporary faculty. During the temporary period, the departments are expected to engage in developing rationales for requesting the return of the positions. Departments must state how the new hire will help them fulfill departmental goals, and deans must consider how such requests will contribute to the overall collegiate goals and initiatives.

ROLE OF THE CQI TEAM

Senior academic administrators meet regularly with the vice chancellor and the associate vice chancellors as the Council of Deans and Academic Administrators (CODAA). Decision making is reasonably collegial and consential. There is an expectation that the criteria for such decisions will be explained and shared with the group.

A six-member, cross-functional team was recruited to develop a process flow chart for the faculty position allocation model. The team was charged with designing the policy implementation process. Team members first reviewed the purpose of the policy and then worked to develop guidelines for a fair and open application of the policy. The team met three times over a period of three months. The cross-functional team included people with responsibility for implementing policy to insure that those with practical experience determine that implementation is workable.

The team consisted of the budget officer from one collegiate unit, two deans, the budget officer from the VCAA Office and the two associate vice chancellors for academic administration. The collegiate budget officer provided insight into the impact of various implementation strategies on collegiate budget planning. The deans identified concerns about their roles representing departments and ensuring fairness among colleges. It was seen as advantageous for deans to be able to advocate for faculty positions by moving veto power to the VCAA. Also, the deans wanted to ensure that all collegiate units would be treated consistently and fairly. One associate vice chancellor was responsible for implementing the policy. The other associate vice chancellor represented faculty and department head views since he was a part-time faculty member and part-time administrator and had recently served four years as a department head.

Reaching agreement on policy goals was the first and most critical step the team had to take. Although four of the six members had been involved in the policy-formation stage, each had a different view of the policy's main purpose. The sharing of these viewpoints and a resolution of the differences needed to occur.

The clarification of the policy was critical. Without this stage, the faculty position allocation process might have gone the route of previous failed policy implementations. A policy on faculty positions reverting to the vice chancellor had actually been announced several years before but had never been implemented because there had been no agreement on how the implementation was to work. This step mirrored the CQI step of the team seeking approval from the sponsor.

Two additional meetings were devoted to drafting and reviewing a flow chart designed to specify the implementation procedures. The issue of exceptions to the policy demonstrates the type of details the team wrestled with. There was general agreement that deans should request exceptions to the policy rarely and that only very unusual circumstances would warrant such a request. When one team member suggested that the VCAA should always defer to a dean's judgment in these cases and approve all exception requests, another member responded that the policy was intended not only to help collegiate units reach goals, but also to accomplish campus goals. Since what a dean views as crucial to one college may be less critical than some competing request, the right of the VCAA to deny exceptions was supported by the team.

Once the team agreed on a process (Table 1, p. 174), the next step was to bring it for full discussion at CODAA. The flow chart and implementation guidelines were presented to the group. Questions were asked, some minor adjustments to the process were agreed to, and group support for the process was gained.

FACULTY POSITION REPLACEMENT POLICY

In November 1992, the Council of Deans and Academic Administrators approved the new policy on faculty line re-

---

placements. The policy established that all vacated tenure/tenure-track faculty lines revert to the VCAA. The process for requesting replacement of faculty lines vacated through resignation, retirement, or death entails a two-step procedure:

1. Requests for replacement are made by departments to the appropriate dean. Departments must include in their requests a rationale for rehiring in terms of how this will fulfill department goals. Deans will consider how such requests contribute to their collegiate goals and mission, and will then make formal requests to the VCAA. Those lines that are then returned to deans will normally be filled on a temporary basis (one year, renewable), as longer-term academic and budgetary considerations are evaluated. Decisions for temporary replacements are made as positions become vacant.

2. Further evaluation will take place during the temporary period. Following evaluation at the departmental level, requests for permanent replacements are made to the appropriate dean. Once again, departments must include a rationale for rehiring in terms of the long-term departmental goals. Deans will consider how such requests contribute to their collegiate goals and mission, and will then make formal requests to the VCAA. After this process, the VCAA, in consultation with the deans, will determine allocation of tenure-track lines. Decisions for permanent hires are made annually in conjunction with the budget cycle.

Considerable concern had been expressed about potential negative impacts of the policy on tenure review. Faculty expressed fear that weak tenure cases might receive favorable review in order to assure that a department would retain the faculty line. To reduce this incentive, it was agreed that in the case of lines vacated because of denial of tenure, positions will immediately revert to the department unless there are exceptional circumstances. However, if the faculty member leaves without taking the extra year, the position will usually be filled on a temporary basis, to be replaced with a tenure-track line the following year.

The policy was developed to provide opportunities for departmental, collegiate unit, and campus planning and flexibility. Implementation guidelines were provided to insure fairness and an open process. Procedures for requesting replacements were developed to be comprehensive, but not overly complex.

The following is the set of procedures given to the deans:

1. When a resignation, retirement or death occurs, a dean notifies the VCAA.

2. The dean then submits a plan for a temporary replacement to the VCAA for review and approval .

3. When the annual budget is prepared, the total funding for the faculty line is transferred from the department budget to the VCAA position pool. Funds to support temporary replacement positions are then allocated to departments and collegiate units as non-recurring, post-budget adjustments.

4. By May 31 of each year, deans submit prioritized requests for permanent positions they want to fill during the following year; requests must include department plans. During the summer, the size of the faculty position pool available will be determined and requests considered. VCAA decisions should be made by September 1 and searches may begin.

5. When phased retirements or terminal-leave agreements are approved, recurring funds to support those positions will move to the VCAA pool, and non-recurring funds will be allocated to the college to fund the terminal leave or phased retirement.

As the flow chart in Table I indicates, deans submit their prioritized collegiate requests for faculty positions along with needs for non-tenure track instructional personnel. Documen-

Table 1
Permanent Faculty Position Allocation Process

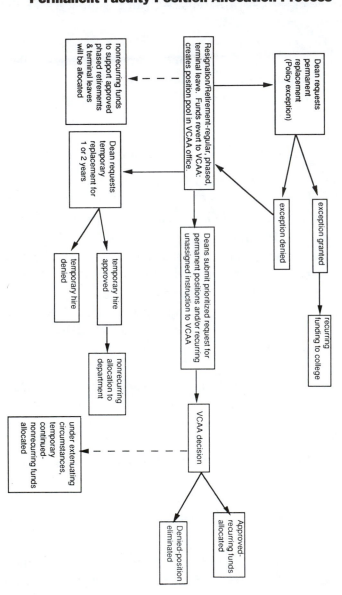

tation is to be included which addresses staffing needs, present workload, student credit-hour generation, program quality, disciplinary issues, and departmental and collegiate goals and priorities.

Deans may request new or replacement, temporary or permanent faculty lines. If a request is made for a permanent line, the VCAA may approve the request. Maintaining departmental program quality may sometimes necessitate an immediate return of a tenure-track line so that departmental responsibilities can be adequately met. Normally, however, when the request is made to fill a newly-vacated line, the expectation would be for approval of a one-year, temporary replacement. This would give the department, the college and the chief academic officer a one-year planning period. Approval for a temporary replacement would be withheld only under unusual circumstances, such as program reduction or clearly demonstrated over-staffing problems. After the one-year planning period, a decision will be made by the chief academic officer as to whether or not a tenure-line position should be allocated to the department. The annual decision on all tenure-track replacements will be discussed with the Council of Deans and Academic Administrators before a final decision is made and permanent funds are transferred.

BENEFITS

There are a number of benefits of the application of CQI techniques to faculty line allocation. First, departments and colleges are forced by the process to assess their present status. Mission, goals and objectives must be clarified and agreed upon. Clear processes are developed. This forces institutions to recognize stakeholders from the outset. Criteria and standards for judgment are required to be explicitly stated. This forces academics to face hard questions about what is valued and how it is to be measured. It also enables institutional culture to be changed by heightening recognition that a particular embedded process is not necessarily natural, benign or unalterable. Also, everyone knows what the rules are and can feel empowered by this knowledge.

The TQM training over the past several years for senior administrators has created an environment in which clear processes are valued. The Plan-Do-Check-Act cycle allows institutions to attempt innovative practices because the community knows that the process will be monitored and modified when evaluation warrants. Finally, evidence of the success or failure of the resource-allocation process will be checked, and any unsuccessful parts of the process can be changed.

Furthermore, because the chief academic officer has discretion to return positions to departments, the risk of policy failure is reduced. If the policy is found to be flawed or unworkable, reversion to the former policy could occur with little inconvenience. However, before any decision is made, the reasons for failure would be explored and the appropriate remediation pursued.

SUMMARY

CQI processes can be successfully utilized to establish procedures for ongoing, rational allocation of faculty resources. Even such difficult issues as the replacement of tenure-track faculty lines can benefit from the application of continuous improvement methods.

At UMD, an administrative process improvement team developed a policy for reallocation of faculty lines, and a cross-functional team charted the implementation process. The cross-functional team approach enabled us to gain early recognition of faculty fears about possible negative impacts on tenure review. Adjustments were made before a final policy was adopted.

The campus plan, Vision 2000, was completed at the same

time that the faculty position replacement policy was adopted. As a result, planning and allocation could be linked.

Five positions have reverted to the VCAA in 1993. One department has been reallocated a permanent position. The other four vacancies are being filled by temporary replacements. During the summer, requests for permanent positions will be considered, not just from departments with vacancies but also from departments wishing to expand their staffing.

There was great resistance to this process when it was first broached. There was doubt that it could work, or that the financial records and transfers could be easily tracked and managed. There were also fears that the policy might not last if the VCAA position were to change. What has happened, however, is that the process has been so well documented that it has been relatively easy to implement. People now understand it, it is operative, and even the historic rhetoric has changed. Vacant positions are now seen as belonging to the campus, through the VCAA, rather than to departments.

A culture has been changed for the better, a clear process has been charted, and allocations of faculty lines can follow from the articulation of goals in a rational and orderly fashion. The entire campus is learning that CQI mechanisms can be successfully applied to all areas of campus life, including academic programs.

REFERENCES

Chaffee, E. E. and Sherr, L. A. (ed.) *Quality Transforming Postsecondary Education*. ASHE-ERIC Higher Education Report no. 3, Washington, D.C.: George Washington University School of Education and Development, 1992.

Craven, E. "Managing Faculty Resources," in J.R. Mingle and Associates (eds.), *Challenges of Retrenchment*. San Francisco: Jossey-Bass, 1981.

DeCosmo, R., Parker, J. S. and Heverly, M. "TQM Goes to Community College," in L.A. Sherr and D.J. Teeter (eds.), *New Directions for Institutional Research*, San Francisco: Jossey Bass, 1991.

Deming, W. E. *Out of the Crisis.* Cambridge, MA: MIT, Center for Advanced

Engineering Study, 1986.

Heverly, M. and Cornesky, R.A. "Total Quality Management: Increasing Productivity and Decreasing Costs," In C. S. Hollins (ed.), *New Directions for Institutional Research,* San Francisco: Jossey Bass, 1992.

Mortimer, K. P. and others. *Flexibility in Academic Staffing: Effective Policies and Practices.* ASHE-ERIC Higher Education Report 1985, 1.

Sherr, L. A. and Lozier, G. G. "Total Quality Management in Higher Education," in L.A. Sherr and D. J. Teeter (eds.), *New Directions for Institutional Research,* 1991.

Winter, R. S. "Overcoming Barriers to TQM," in L.A. Sherr and D. J. Teeter (eds.), *New Directions for Institutional Research,* San Francisco: Jossey Bass, 1991.

Sandra Featherman is vice chancellor for academic administration and professor of political science at the University of Minnesota, Duluth. She previously served at Temple University as assistant to the president and director of the Center for Public Policy. Her Ph.D. is from the University of Pennsylvania.

Featherman is the author of numerous articles on educational policy and on the politics of ethnicity and gender. Her publications include "Barriers to Representation of Women and Blacks in Pennsylvania," "A Pluralistic Model of Public Sector Bargaining" and "Women in Higher Education Management in the United States and Canada."

A well-known speaker, writer and interpreter of political events, Featherman has appeared on numerous radio and TV shows, has hosted and produced a weekly radio program on educational issues, and writes a monthly newspaper column on government and politics.

Valerie Broughton is director of institutional research and associate vice chancellor for academic administration at the University of Minnesota, Duluth. Broughton manages academic personnel and budget for academic administration and directs the institutional research function at the University. She previously served at Wichita State University and in the Iowa Board of Regents Office. Her doctoral work was completed at Iowa State University, where she concentrated on  educational research and evaluation. She is a graduate of the 1989 Institute for Educational Management for College and University Administrators.

Her interest in studying the use of information to support decision making provided the basis for her interest in applying TQM principles in higher education.

She has been active in the Association of Institutional Research for nearly 10 years. Currently, she serves on the executive committee of that organization, and as the chair of the Data Advisory Committee. She recently contributed a chapter to a new issue of *New Directions for Institutional Research*, "Confluence Between Standard Operating Paradigms and TQM."

11

Faculty as Customers: Hard Lessons for Administrators

Robert L. Carothers
Jayne Richmond

In our times, what does not change in American higher education is only the daunting fact of change: more people, more differences, more education, more often. Knowledge itself grows exponentially, and it is fair to say that the creation, processing and distribution of knowledge is the business America is in today. More rapidly than we could have imagined, the ivory tower is now the vortex in the maelstrom of change.

At the same time that higher education has moved to center stage in America, however, the national economy has slumped into a recession that hangs on and on. Beginning in the late 1980s, nearly two-thirds of all colleges and universities were hit by budget cuts that have meant increased class sizes and fewer course sections, postponed hiring of staff and deferred maintenance of facilities, less research support and more pressure to help local and regional economic development. Doing more with less has clearly stressed both individuals and relationships. The signs are everywhere.

So, on one hand, the shift to an economy based on knowledge has vastly increased the importance of America's colleges and universities. On the other hand, it is clear that these institutions do not have the resources to meet vastly increased expectations, especially not if we array those resources in traditional ways. Moreover, public confidence in colleges and universities – and especially in their leaders – has declined sharply in the wake of scandals about student loan defaults, intercollegiate athletics, overhead charges for research and, most damaging, how we treat our undergraduates. The consequence has been an unprecedented scrutiny of the way colleges and universities do their work and an increasingly aggressive demand for reform.

ENTER TQM

It is in this context that TQM (or TQI or CQI, depending on local parlance) has appeared on America's college campuses. Developed in response to equally powerful challenges in other sectors of American enterprise, Total Quality Management has become a call for new leadership and new relationships, for organizations committed passionately to quality. At least on one level, TQM is a philosophy about work, people, relationships and shared vision. In a "quality" organization, we work to serve others (customers), and we do so most effectively when we invoke the power of teams who are focused on continuing improvement. If there is clarity in an organization about its vision and about the values which underlie that vision, each individual can be empowered to act creatively, largely without direction and supervision. The result is increased efficiency and effectiveness as well as more fulfilled workers. Or so goes the mantra.

TQM ON CAMPUS

Quality has been heralded by its advocates as a philosophy and strategy for higher education reform, a way to focus missions and improve processes, a way to help us both to "do the right things" and to "do things right." The critical paradigm shift in higher education, as in every other enterprise which has turned to TQM, has been to customer satisfaction, a concept truly alien in the university culture. While we talk a great deal about service in higher education, serving others **in the ways they define their needs** is very difficult for us. Many have found quality a fascinating intellectual subject, much easier to talk about than to live. Faculty, like physicians or priests or engineers, clearly believe that they are best able to decide what the customer, student or patient really needs, or what future employers or society needs. The special expertise of the faculty, like the special expertise of the physician or the engineer, gives them the insight and the responsibility (at least according to this argument) to dictate terms. After all, almost by definition, we know best.

The consequent hard facts are that where TQM has been made to work in higher education, at least to date, it has been at the margin, with those activities which parallel business enterprises off the campus. TQM is fine, say the faculty, for food service and residence life, for building and grounds, maybe even for the registrar or the bursar. And if the administration can use this new management system to make things work more smoothly at the purchasing office or over in personnel, that's okay too.

But TQM has seldom touched the heart of the university, its central academic mission. Where administrators have led the initiative for TQM, the effort has often been greeted with mistrust and skepticism by those faculty members crucial to the success of the enterprise. Many of our faculty, especially those in the liberal arts, have resisted the central metaphor of

TQM and have often taken offense at the language of quality, the origin of which is clearly in commerce. They begin their evaluation of the ideas of TQM – and the language which gives those ideas form – in the context of their own loyal membership and shaping experience in the academic community and its value system. They hear terms and phrases like "customers" and "conformance to standards" and "zero defects" and "statistical process control," language which confirms their worst fears: that the administration has turned their university over to the Philistine forces at the gate. The resistance to necessary change has often been strengthened, in fact, by the introduction of TQM jargon on campus, sometimes deepening the polarization of faculty and administrators.

Yet, if TQM is to be the catalyst by which systemic change in colleges and universities is to be facilitated, we cannot allow the faculty to sit it out on the sidelines. We will not achieve the reform demanded by those who must invest in us by improving only the way in which we distribute financial aid or clean the classrooms (although these must change as well). Change must come to the most fundamental aspects of our institutions, including the role of the faculty and the priority given to teaching and learning. To do so, leaders of colleges and universities must affirm their basic belief that these organizations exist to serve others, and they must do so by way of acts and deeds, not simply by intensifying their rhetoric. For most administrators attempting to lead the quality revolution on campus, the time to "talk the talk" has drawn to a close. It is time for those who would lead to "walk the walk" of service.

A NEW PARADIGM FOR LEADERSHIP

The leadership attitudes and skills which will advance the agenda we have adopted are distinctly different from the hierarchical, authoritarian models most of us have experienced and learned. But we will not change the organizations we seek to lead unless we ourselves are different and behave differently. We will not enable or empower others to adopt an ethic of service – a displacement of self for others – unless we ourselves become servants. The key concept may lie at the root of the word administration, that is, to "minister to" the enterprise, another and useful way of thinking about how we are to serve.

The concept of the servant and servant as leader is a difficult one in Western culture, even counter-intuitive. First developed by Robert Greenleaf, the phrase itself has a Zen-like feel to it which runs against the grain of our usual ideals of purposeful, decisive leadership. But, increasingly, we understand the fundamental truth in this paradox, that those who have a personal commitment to serve the higher needs of others have the greatest opportunities for transforming the organizations in which they work.

Meeting these higher needs of others requires above all an understanding of the other, achieved first through a process of disciplined listening. This is the critical step in the process by which the leader accepts and affirms those she or he would serve. From this careful listening comes an authenticity, a relationship built on a genuine caring about the other's growth and well-being. The servant leader takes seriously each person she or he would serve and takes that person's work seriously as well. The goal of such a leader is not control, but of making the other whole, capable and confident. The goal, purpose and object of his or her processes is empowerment.

Administration, under this model, is an exchange, an intense conversation, aggressively participatory, minimizing hierarchical distinctions, authority and power. To that conversation, the leader brings his or her own vision of the organization and its future, but he or she also recognizes that everyone else in the organization has a vision as well. From this continuing conversation comes a new and shared vision, and an exchange of energy between leaders and members in which both experience enhanced confidence and the permission – the freedom – to act.

In moving others toward fulfillment of this shared vision, the servant leader relies upon persuasion and remains engaged with the group's members, as well as with the issues and feelings important to them. Such persuasion is in sharp contrast to the coercion or manipulation common to most traditional organizations, to forcing or guiding people into beliefs or actions they do not fully understand or accept. Reliance upon persuasion means that the president, the provost and the dean cannot be distant or aloof, cannot rely upon charisma or the trappings of office to influence others. In this model, both the leader and the member must respect the integrity and autonomy of the other, and each must encourage the other to find his or her own intuitive confirmation of the rightness of the action chosen.

In matters of style, then, the new leader is both self-effacing and confident. Because the leader has confidence born of mutual support, she or he can tolerate ambiguity. Even in the chaos which seems to characterize higher education today, the leader remains centered and focused on empowerment. As a steward, the leader's chief duty is to those served. In that sense, the servant leader is distinguished from other leadership types because she or he enriches the members rather than diminishing them. The result is that the members become wiser, freer and more autonomous, rather than confused, frightened and more dependent.

This empowered other, in turn, acts to affirm and reinforce the leader, empowering him or her to continue to provide authentic leadership. The symbiotic nature of this relationship is immensely important, particularly in universities, where constituent interests are so diverse and are often in major and minor conflict. This kind of joint visioning process can be the key to a mutual interdependence born of self-confidence and trust (rare commodities in our institutions today!)

In a wonderful report to the Kellogg Foundation, Sulayman Clark of Hampton University writes about the experience of interviewing Nelson Mandela, Walter Sisulu and Julius Neyerere. Each of these leaders has sought to transcend, writes Clark, the racial, political and tribal differences which prevent South African society from reforming itself, through a vision of a new, democratic and non-racial nation, sustained in that vision through years of persecution and imprisonment by the support of those they lead. He cites John Gardner, who speaks of leaders like Mandela as people who can "articulate goals that lift people out of their petty preoccupations, carry them above the conflicts that tear a society [and a university!] apart, and unite them in the pursuit of objectives worthy of their best efforts." Such servant leaders are effective because they have the ability to see through appearances and through differences of opinion with regard to the particular, and to hear the common good which is revealed by listening closely to those one would lead.

Nowhere is this paradigm of leadership better suited than in colleges and universities, where traditional models of collegial governance seem increasingly unable to respond to the accelerating rate of changes demanded of our institutions. In organizations made up of teachers and learners, the leaders must practice the teaching arts at a very high level, enabling all members of the community to learn.

THE FACULTY AS CUSTOMERS

As difficult as the concept may seem to some, we believe that college administrators who would be leaders must begin by serving their faculty as customers. If, as Peter Drucker says, a customer is anyone who can say "no," faculty members surely meet the criteria! Remember: customers are the beneficiaries of our services or products, and every institution has both external and internal customers. Our external customers are current, prospective and past students; their parents; our donors; state legislators; high schools and community colleges; employers and vendors, to name only a few. Our internal customers include every person who works in every office on campus and in every academic department. In reality, the university is a complex web of customer relationships, each one affecting the success of the institution as a whole.

Perhaps more than any other group, however, the faculty are the customers of the administration. Everyone, of course, must work toward continuous improvement, because the survival of the institution depends on it. But faculty have a unique role in the equation, because for the given student customer at a given point in time, the faculty are the university. This is particularly true because faculty are largely unsupervised professionals acting on their own initiative. We must depend on faculty to make quality happen for students – our most important external customers.

But in the difficult times in which we now live, faculty morale – that ubiquitous term used so often on campus to describe the willingness of the faculty to initiate action on nearly anything – is suffering. In faculty offices and labs around the nation, there is a low-grade frustration among our colleagues, resulting in a generalized loss of community feeling or citizenship. Much of the dissatisfaction comes from a muddled sense of mission and a conflict of values, particularly surrounding our commitment to the teaching and learning process.

The opportunities for improvement in faculty morale, however, are everywhere. There is no more powerful and sustaining way to improve morale than advancing the sense of congruence between institutional and personal goals. To do so, we must restructure the university to diminish the perceived boundaries between faculty and administrators, such that both groups work together on a commonly-defined mission. This will not happen until administrators are committed to serving faculty as fully-informed customers who articulate their needs and aspirations as mirror images of institutional goals.

As in any serving relationship, fear is the great inhibitor of success, and today the academy is deeply fearful. In the face of rapidly-accelerating change in the university, many faculty feel a loss of control in their lives and fear that the worst lies ahead. The best way to deal with this anxiety is to increase the time administrators spend listening carefully to the needs of faculty members and talking with them about the way the institution is serving those needs. Shaped by our belief in continuous improvement, this conversation must be set in the context of these faculty customers better serving the needs of our student customers. If administrators are to effect real change, they will do so only by guiding the faculty through the power of careful listening and subsequently through a conversation that informs and persuades.

For most administrators, this is tough stuff and hard to sustain as a pattern of personal behavior in the face of growing criticism from those to whom they are responsible. Many outside the academy – the business community, board members and legislators – argue that the problem with our current model is that it is excessively faculty centered, that too few faculty members care about their undergraduate students and that the tenure system prevents accountability in that regard. These critics demand that administrators **direct** faculty to focus more attention on their students and on the learning process.

But the record is clear that these attempts at coercion or intimidation simply don't work and are, in fact, counter-productive in our efforts to cause positive change. Rather, what is now needed is authentic leadership from presidents, provosts and deans, leadership that is expressed in the deep commitment to serve students through serving faculty. This begins, again, with systematic listening. Like many who believe they know best, we make the common mistake of moving forward on the basis of assumptions about the needs and expectations of customers without data to support those assumptions. In addition to the development of personal listening skills, it is extremely important to have a systematic process for assessing the needs of the faculty and the performance of the administration in meeting those needs. Carefully-designed surveys and focus groups can be very helpful in off-setting anecdotal information which is likely to be highly selective in nature. Like every other organization which aspires to quality, we need to hear not what we want to hear but the needs and expectations of our customers **as they define them**.

Once we have achieved this congruence of institutional and personal goals, nearly anything is possible, including bringing the quality philosophy directly into the learning process. There are already many faculty members who have used TQM successfully in their individual classrooms for the continuous improvement of teaching and a better integration of assessment and productive feedback on student performance. We need to remember that it will be **faculty** who will infuse TQM into our academic programs and **faculty** who will produce the research which will lead to the transformational learning process we seek. It will be **faculty** who will use TQM in a more global way to rethink the design and delivery of the curriculum. And it must be **faculty and administrators** proceeding **together** from a common sense of mission and a common agenda who will take TQM from the institutional margins to the heart of our reason for being.

PARTNERSHIPS FOR BETTER TEACHING AND LEARNING

Armed with real knowledge about their mutual needs, administrators, faculty and students can build new partnerships to work together in a purposeful way to affirm the agenda for positive change. Purposeful communities are characterized by a compelling vision, by leadership and by incentives that motivate specific actions which advance the agenda. Our vision involves making teaching and learning central to the mission of our institutions, and we have a model for servant leadership which will work. But we must now plan carefully to assure that our incentive systems link faculty work to institutional goals.

The culture of higher education has traditionally focused on the individual. Our recognition and reward system has reinforced individual achievement, both for students and faculty, creating a competitive environment even within academic departments and disciplines. Yet we know that quality happens best at the team level, where the combined insights and skills of the group exceed the performance of any one individual. But those seeking to advance TQM must ask themselves why, given our reward system, anyone would want to participate in process improvement teams, a critical component of continuous improvement.

The appropriate corrective, however, lies again within the ken of the faculty. Administrative leaders must begin by asking the right questions about incentives and listening for the answers. The challenge is to devise reward structures which stimulate group thinking and team efforts, and which reinforce the successful efforts of departments or centers toward the end of advancing the vision. Funding team travel, for example, or granting released time for collaborative research projects produces better results for the university than simply distributing across-the-board salary increases. The truth of the matter is that in universities we are seldom organized for teamwork, rarely trained for it and generally not very good at it. However, the interaction of motivated individuals committed to a common goal can build the kind of high-morale, high-performance community that reinforces and sustains improvement efforts.

That successful interaction is what must be recognized and rewarded on a consistent basis.

While all quality improvement – large and small – in colleges and universities is important, we believe that the really pivotal improvement will happen in the teaching and learning systems of the institution and in the development of a new team dynamic there. The benefits of this new paradigm for students will include:

❖ Ownership of their own educational processes

❖ Increased efficiency and effectiveness of learning through active and collaborative involvement in the learning process

❖ Building important personal and professional relationships with faculty

❖ More personalized and customized curricula

❖ Decreased costs, as the administrative processes of the university improve and overhead is reduced

For faculty, these improved systems will mean:

❖ Increased student involvement and performance, with the collateral benefit of increased student retention

❖ Improved quality of those services which assist faculty in achieving their personal and professional goals

❖ Improved quality of relationships with colleagues and students

❖ New pride of membership in an institution recognized for quality

❖ New freedom to innovate and create

TRAINING AND DEVELOPMENT: NEW SKILLS TO BE LEARNED

One of Deming's most difficult concepts to internalize is the admonition that "every person working harder will not do it." Quality is not an add-on, not something we can do in addition to what we have always done. While trying to work harder is a common first response to a threat to the traditional paradigm, TQM is rather a different way of doing things, an illustration of Edward DeBono's "lateral thinking." DeBono likens us to the soldier hunkered down in a foxhole with artillery rounds falling on him. The soldier works feverishly to improve the foxhole, adding sandbags and camouflage to his structure. As his pride in the work grows, his reluctance to leave it increases as well. But the artillery has zeroed in on him, and his survival depends upon leaving that wonderful foxhole and moving on, either to a new defensive position or, better yet, to an offensive action which will silence his opposition and put him on the road to victory. This kind of lateral thinking – letting go of strategies whose time has passed and taking the risks associated with new and creative initiatives – is what quality improvement is all about.

So an important part of our challenge is developing in administrators, faculty and students the skills necessary to transform once-comfortable beliefs, behaviors and organizational structures. While this effort may seem a diversion from the pressing problems immediately before leaders, in the long run it may be the critical success factor. Nearly all of us require new understanding and skill in group and interpersonal dynamics, in priority setting and decision making, in the use of TQM tools of process, and in the use of statistical tools of performance assessment. Benchmarking, the use of "best in class" processes from whatever source accessible, can take us outside the perimeters of our own experience to see the issue from a fresh perspective. A large metropolitan hospital may have devised a successful patient "advising" system that can be adapted creatively to serve students. A regional library system may have the best record of recruiting minority professionals. Or a local manufacturer may have set the pace in moving to a new facility. We need to look internally to the university as well, seeing how other departments and other disciplines evaluate research, for example, or how they communicate classroom strategies to new professors. In each case, a careful study of highly efficient and effective processes can allow us to broaden our sense of the possible and set appropriate performance standards.

In establishing such a professional development program, however, it is important once again to listen first to what faculty themselves need and expect by way of skills training. Since it is entirely possible that the role of faculty in the quality effort will not be well understood at first, the conversation between administrators and faculty must be set in the context of continuous improvement of service to faculty themselves, and ultimately of students and other significant customers. The university's incentive and reward system should be structured in such a way as to recognize and reinforce faculty participation in professional development programs that advance the performance of the relevant group in the change process, not just those which improve individual performance within traditional areas of expertise. We should also attempt to reinforce the development of student-centered learning experiences through the integration of students into the faculty's research activities, and by encouragement of students to participate in collaborative research projects and on effective research teams.

INCENTIVES FOR FACULTY INVOLVEMENT

TQM places heavy emphasis upon recognizing and rewarding those groups and individuals who advance the institutional vision. The recognition process may actually be more important than the reward system, but both are necessary to the process of enhancing performance. Within colleges and universities, the current incentive system might best be described as dysfunctional, sending mixed signals to faculty members about what behavior is important within the institutional culture. The most obvious illustration lies in the dichotomy between teaching and research. Educational leaders often talk about the centrality of the teaching mission and the importance of collaboration with the community served by the university, but they tenure and promote faculty almost exclusively on the basis of published research. Less obvious, but equally significant, is the current customer orientation advanced by administrators, yet matched by very little recognition of those faculty who do, in fact, treat their students as valued customers, spending precious time in and out of class building the students' confidence and competence, the hallmarks of empowered people.

In fact, it is probably fair to say that the handling of the faculty incentive system by college administrators borders on mismanagement of the institution's most valuable asset. Faculty in general feel unappreciated and unsupported by administrators, and whether or not this feeling is based on fact, it is nonetheless a real feeling. And such feelings are very costly. Because faculty do not sense that they are held in high regard by administrators, they are unlikely to embrace an agenda for change championed by those they fear or distrust. An effective incentive system to promote positive change by faculty members must begin with strong positive regard by administrators for faculty as individuals and as groups, and for their work. When faculty members ask the inevitable question – "What's in it for me?" – we should not undervalue removing the barriers to pride in work well done.

From this positive perspective, we can move to incorporate leadership with and among faculty into the paradigm of continuous improvement in a way that captures their hearts and minds. To do so, we must create an "organizational momentum," a social dynamic that enlists departments or other groups of faculty members in taking new responsibility for leading change. We should focus on supporting and extending this dynamic, consciously choosing to reinforce those who provide the help we need. As administrators, we should be careful to use the information we gain from aggressive listening to shape the incentive program. We should be equally careful not to proceed from our own assumptions about what would provide the appropriate incentive to a given group of faculty members. In this endeavor, preconceived notions vanish quickly, and surprises are more common than the anticipated!

Indeed, if we can get the incentive systems right, faculty satisfaction may well come to serve as an important index of quality, as we shift the institution's priorities to understanding and meeting the needs and expectations of the faculty as the driving force in improving educational quality. Each administrator must find the courage to take charge of the rewards, making changes large and small which she or he has learned by listening will impact behavior. Clear, measurable goals need to be established, rewards defined and the connection between goals and rewards articulated. This admonition may seem too obvious to mention, but it is rarely undertaken in our enterprise. If we want faculty to change, then we must be prepared to reward innovation, reinforce pride in work well done, enhance the pleasure in serving and join in the fun of celebrating success with those who make us a quality institution.

HARD LESSONS LEARNED

In the quality movement, many administrators have seen faculty members as mountains too large to move, focusing their efforts for continuous improvements on the college's business and support services, where direction is more easily given and taken. On those campuses whose leaders have been brave enough to try, the defense by the faculty of the traditional ways of doing business has been spirited, leaving administrators fuming over the intransigence bred by tenure. And it is true that nearly any one of us will resist change that threatens our perceived privileges, whether those prerogatives belong to the

---

faculty or to administration. But it is also a hard truth that there will be no successful reform in higher education that does not engage faculty as the primary agents of change.

Each of us, says Maslow, is a bundle of needs. Effective leadership is based on understanding the needs of others and working to meet them in such a way as to meet the needs of the organization as well. Administrators, faculty and students want the same thing: to be part of a strong learning community, to be a member in a high-morale, high-performance team. And that need cannot be met, that vision cannot be realized, unless we all work together to improve the quality in the teaching and learning system of the institution.

Administrators and faculty must accept ownership and accountability for the performance of the institution, both its academic performance and its fiscal integrity. Accountability requires measurement of customer satisfaction first and then of the stewardship of resources toward that end. While higher education has, in general, been reluctant to keep score with any consistency, it is clear that if we want to win, we will have to mark the scorecard much more carefully. Once we have that critical assessment of what we do that best satisfies our customers' need and expectations, then we can work to get better, setting aspirations high and celebrating progress toward realizing them. Based on what we know now, we can begin to divert resources to faculty development toward the ends of better teamwork, more interdisciplinary collaboration, the creation of student-centered learning environments and more.

When faculty embrace these strategies and implement change, we must be ready to recognize and reward those efforts both for work well done and as models for their less enthusiastic colleagues, even as we affirm our regard for those faculty members whose commitment has yet to mature. If we ourselves are committed to persevering in this endeavor, we too can succeed, doing the right things, doing things right, rebuilding the structure of higher education through the total quality movement.

Jayne Richmond is an associate professor of human development, counseling and family studies at the University of Rhode Island, where she prepares graduate students for careers in higher education administration. Currently, she is completing a year of study as a Fellow with the American Council on Education, chiefly at the University of Central Florida. During the previous year, she served as a special assistant to the president of the University of Rhode Island, working particularly on initiatives for change. Since 1991, Richmond has been investigating the application of quality management techniques in higher education. She is a frequent speaker and panelist at conferences and workshops on TQM and continuous improvement. Richmond holds the B.A., M.Ed., and Ph.D. from the University of Florida, Gainesville. She is also a graduate of the HERS program at Bryn Mawr College.

Robert L. Carothers is the president of the University of Rhode Island, where he has served since 1991. Prior to his appointment at Rhode Island, he was the chancellor of the Minnesota State University System, and, before that, president of Southwest State University. He also served as professor of English, dean of arts and humanities, and vice president for administration and student services at Edinboro University of Pennsylvania.

Carothers was the author of the Q-7 quality initiative in Minnesota, an effort which harnessed the public and private leadership of that state to define the standards of performance required of both secondary school and college graduates for the new century. During his tenure as chancellor, the Minnesota system built and opened a new branch campus in Akita, Japan. Carothers credits this experience and his work with IBM in their Rochester, Minn., facility for his "conversion" to quality. Since coming to Rhode Island, Carothers has been the state's champion for TQM, focusing particularly on the leadership styles and skills needed for the new paradigm.

A graduate of Edinboro University in English, Carothers received his M.A. and Ph.D. from Kent State University and his Juris Doctor from the University of Akron. He has been active in leadership development for two decades now and more recently has worked with and written about quality management in higher education.

12

Partners in Progress: An Integrative Approach to Educational Quality

Linda L. Baer
Bea Walker Knodel
Jon Quistgaard
Ivan Lee Weir

INTRODUCTION

Although the movement toward Continuous Quality Improvement (CQI) as a means of transforming American industry gained genuine acceptance in the 1980s, it was not until the 1990s that most institutions of higher education began to seriously consider that the CQI concept also holds promise for them, particularly in light of the global changes taking place as the 21st century approaches. Academic institutions, perhaps predictably, have begun to appreciate the new promise that the quality movement brings at precisely the time they found themselves in a world of economic uncertainty and facing a new kind of consumer demand. This consumer demand has been stimulated by an unprecedented and accelerated rate of global change, a domestic job market that is tightening while it faces global competition, a virtual disappearance of the expectation of long-term tenure in one job, and the emergence of students and employers alike who demand genuine career relevance from higher education.

Clearly, then, while colleges and universities have often had difficulty in responding to externally imposed quality initiatives, current pressures require a rethinking of both the traditional roles and the processes of higher education. Attention to quality improvement has been dictated by a whole array of changes taking place not only in academe, but across society and around the world. These changes include an ongoing information explosion; an increasingly global outlook; unprecedented technological advances; and rapid, worldwide political and economic change. At the same time, there are new pressures very directly tied to higher education itself. Seymour, in *Causing Quality in Higher Education* (1992), identifies four contributing motivations which account for much of the urgency in the current discussions regarding the place of the quality movement in higher education. The motivations he noted are 1) survival in an increasingly competitive environment, 2) the escalating costs of doing business, 3) the trend toward making organizations more accountable for their actions and outcomes, and 4) the concomitant blurring of the distinctions between "products" and "services."

If institutions of higher education are to function effectively in the 21st century, they must take these concerns seriously. At the same time, universities must recognize that not only their world, but the world of work for which they are preparing their students, continues to undergo dramatic changes. Information and technological change in the marketplace has resulted in revolutionizing the work place. Workers at all levels are becoming aware of the need to train and retrain. Positions are viewed increasingly as temporary because they, too, are continually evolving to satisfy changing economic needs (Drucker, Reich, and Thurow). And education – the traditional avenue into careers that formerly assured lifelong employment – must be viewed not as something to be completed in four or five years, but as a process of lifelong learning that is a necessity to avoid obsolescence. Rather than increasing in value with time, education is becoming a rapidly-depreciating commodity, even while the cost of obtaining a higher education continues to escalate. Clearly, the need for quality, and for CQI in higher education, has never been greater.

A clear definition of educational quality is, however, only beginning to emerge. The "ivory tower" university of the past half century will give way to a far more society-sensitive university in the future. The 21st-century university must prepare students for the real world, that is, for the ever-changing career and economic realities they will face. Taxpayers and students, noting the ever-rising costs of a university education, expect to see rising and demonstrable returns for their investment. Universities must leave the production model of higher education in which success is based on head counts, credit generation, grades, and degrees and move toward a learning environment which emphasizes an involvement that will empower students with a high-quality "tool kit" to meet new challenges. (Astin, Boyer). It is, however, as Seymour (1992) points out, easier to describe and define quality than it is to develop, reinforce and sustain it.

THE MINNESOTA QUALITY INITIATIVE

In 1990, the Minnesota State University System recognized the critical importance of enhancing the quality of the education delivered by the seven universities in the system. A Blue Ribbon Commission, made up of representative citizens and employers from across the state, indicated very clearly that they believed, above all else, that the central dynamic of the future will be continuing and accelerating change, and that a high-quality, post-high-school education is the strategic resource necessary for the future and for the people of Minnesota. The commission identified seven specific indicators of quality as critical to an education designed to meet the needs of students, employers and the economy of the state of Minnesota. The indicators they identified were 1) preparation for college, 2) higher-order thinking, 3) multicultural sensitivity, 4) global awareness, 5) scientific and quantitative literacy, 6) readiness for work, and 7) citizenship in a global society. Bemidji State University added as an eighth indicator, a sense of community, to this list.

To begin the movement toward increased quality in higher education called for by the commission, the Minnesota State University Board articulated five fundamental steps to be followed. First, commitment and involvement were demanded from the Board itself, the chancellor, the seven state universities, and the system's constituents throughout the state. Second, the Board expressed a belief in the importance of assuring that all system employees would participate in the quality initiative. Third, input from all participants, including students, parents, and employers as well as faculty, staff and administrators, was solicited. The fourth step was to recognize the need for review and evaluation as a part of the CQI process. The final step was to engage in a process of continuous employee improvement through an upgrading of employees' knowledge, skills and abilities, together with advances in goal setting, problem solving, decision making, and team building.

Promoting institutional change requires a shared vision throughout an organization. Faced with declining resources and the demographic potential of 50 percent attrition in the faculty ranks, the Bemidji State University administration recognized the need to refocus the University. They chose to view the Board's quality initiative, which had been given the name "Q-7," as an opportunity to infuse a vision for enhanced quality education over the next decade into the University's long-range planning activities. This choice, however, was not without risk. Across the system, commitment to Q-7 was viewed by faculty with attitudes ranging from polite skepticism to outright cynicism and due to the origination of the Q-7 initiative from the state university board office, many faculty members believed they had not been adequately included in the development of the process. A dynamic strategy was needed to recognize obstacles and work on opportunities for institutional change in the University from the bottom up.

CREATING A CLIMATE OF INSTITUTIONAL CHANGE

One barrier to institutional change in Minnesota is an incentive system (i.e. method of calculating budget allocation) that is based on enrollment numbers. In this reward system, student failure is defined as the responsibility of individuals rather than the responsibility of the institution that creates an environment that permits failure.

To begin to change the institutional climate from one that permitted failure to one that promotes success, a grass-roots movement to gain a Q-7 foothold was devised to include students, staff and faculty in the Q-7 process on a University-wide basis. With financial support from a legislative appropriation dedicated to Q-7 and additional monies from the office of the University vice president for academic and student affairs, a series of idea-intensive, pragmatic steps was initiated. First, every program, department, discipline and division was asked to provide two-, five- and ten-year plans. On the basis of this information, the University developed a campus-wide Q-7 plan. Next, a number of mini-proposals from programs, departments and disciplines across the campus were funded, each designed to advance one or more of the Q-7 quality indicators. Subsequently, departments or units which had carried out successful projects were encouraged to apply for continuation funds, and proposals for new projects were solicited. In this way, some excellent projects were sustained, and the best of the proposed new projects also received funding. At the same time, activities designed to bring about major changes in the institutional environment were undertaken.

AN INTEGRATIVE APPROACH: THE BEMIDJI MODEL

While grass-root projects aimed at enhancing one or more quality initiatives were occurring, an assessment and evaluation process was designed to determine the extent to which students, faculty and alumni were receiving or providing the education that was really needed. The assessment plan (included in Figure 1) has its basis in recommendations from the Blue Ribbon Commission, who had included readiness for work or career among their indicators of high-quality university education, and from research by Astin (1987), Stark (1989) and others who found that an increasing number of students indicate that getting a better job is an essential expectation in the decision to attend college.

After several versions were explored, the final "Bemidji Model" that was settled upon is shown in Figure 1. The Bemidji Model includes a significant feedback component informed by the assessment of student, faculty and alumni perceptions of their involvement with the quality indicators. The Q-7 indicators that were identified by Bemidji State University faculty and staff as the foundation on which an excellent university education should be based are 1) higher-order thinking, 2) scientific and quantitative literacy, 3) global understanding and 4) multicultural perspective. Three aspects of the assessment of these variables are discussed below, including the frame of reference of the assessment, and the operationalization of the variables and measurement characteristics.

The Bemidji Model is intended to portray a general, unified perspective designed to serve the administrative and curricular needs of the university. It is based on educational,

Figure 1
The Bemidji Model

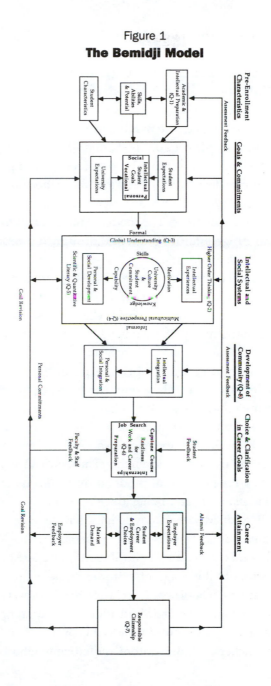

economic and measurement theory. Readers of Tinto (1987), Astin (1987, 1991), Boyer (1987), Chickering (1969), Gordon and Arvey (1975), Holland (1985), Pace (1984), Stark, et. al. (1989), Pascarella and Terenzini (1991), Tiedeman and O'Hara (1963), and Willingham (1985) will recognize some similarities between their models and The Bemidji Model.

The primary purpose of The Bemidji Model is to convey that an educated person must be prepared to compete in a global economy structured to reward those persons whose knowledge, skills, capabilities and commitments are competitive on a worldwide basis. The model was designed to reflect the natural progression of students through the process of obtaining a higher education.

The model is based on a value-added approach to educational attainment that begins with the students' preparation and background (See pre-enrollment characteristics in Figure l) and culminates in a globally-educated citizen who is ready for employment and a career (career attainment), and is also ready to contribute to the well-being of his or her community (responsible citizenship). The model identifies actors, activities and outcomes that are primary elements in each aspect of education, and through continuous feedback loops, adjusts to changing educational competencies, societal expectations, and work-force and market requirements. The feedback loops and evaluation components of the model provide mechanisms for institutional planning and policy development.

The Bemidji Model acknowledges that the precursors to a baccalaureate degree are adequate preparation at the elementary and secondary levels (pre-enrollment characteristics). The relevant actors at this stage of a student's development are children, parents, school boards, schools, teachers and general societal actors (such as religious leaders, grandparents, etc.). The university is also a contributor to this process insofar as it trains the teachers, administrators and citizens who have an effect on children. Underlying The Bemidji Model and the Minnesota Q-7 initiative are enhanced preparation in science, mathematics, writing, multicultural awareness and understanding, geography and expression (goals and commitments). These subject areas are closely related to higher-order thinking, global understanding, multicultural perspective, and scientific and quantitative literacy – which are the indicators identified by the Blue Ribbon Commission on Quality (intellectual and social systems).

Although the quality indicators are among the traditional elements found in a liberal education, The Bemidji Model envisions them in a broader context by incorporating the idea of the education of a symbolic analyst or knowledge worker (Reich). This focus includes the critical importance of education that can be utilized in professions and careers and enhances one's ability to accommodate change. Among the actors who contribute the quantity and quality of a higher education are students, faculty, staff and administration, all of whom must create an integrative culture (development of community) of learning that includes CQI.

Students' occupational and career goals are linked to their expectations of a higher education and its relationship to the work place. A noticeable difference between students of the 1990s and those from earlier decades is an increased emphasis on personal well being and a desire for career attainment perhaps brought about by the added cost of a higher education (Boyer). In recent years, universities have begun to focus on providing capstone courses, internships and the identification of other opportunities for students to become directly involved with the work place while attending college (choice and clarification of career goals).

Readiness for work involves actors from the university – students, faculty, administration, staff and alumni – as well as actors from business, education, industry, government, professional groups, not-for-profit and for-profit agencies, and voluntary associations. Readiness for work connotes that students thoroughly understand the array of career options, occupations and professions that will be available to them in the future, and that they will, in all probability, change careers and jobs five to seven times during their working lives. Thus, students must obtain a general education extending far beyond a single discipline or specialty. Rather, their education must afford them transferable skills and capabilities to enhance rather than hinder their ability to adapt to change.

The outcomes portion of The Bemidji Model (career attainment) focuses on expectations, choices and demands of employers, students and the marketplace. By obtaining feedback from alumni and employment sectors of the economy, The Bemidji Model anticipates a process of continuous improvement that takes into account global, economic and marketplace conditions.

ASSESSMENT AND EVALUATION

The questions used to assess higher-order thinking, scientific and quantitative literacy, global understanding and multicultural awareness have the common characteristic of asking the respondent populations – students, alumni and faculty – whether the teaching and learning process has prepared students to perform symbolic analytic activities. Symbolic analytic activities are defined as those activities that prepare students to engage in abstract and creative thinking. Students, for example, are asked, "Considering your college education so far, to what extent are you being prepared for each of the following?" Then, a list of items for each variable is presented. An important consideration in each question is that respondents are asked not what they know because of their college educations, but what they have learned to do because of their college educations. From the perspective of a student, the variables are designed to represent an array of survival skills needed to succeed in the global economy of the 21st century. As such, these skills are not discipline specific, but are behavior or capability specific. That is, it is not only what one knows that is important, but also what one knows how to do with that knowledge and how one can gain more knowledge for adaptation purposes as jobs, the economy, or the state of knowledge changes.

OPERATIONALIZATION OF VARIABLES

Higher-order Thinking. Higher-order thinking, also described as critical thinking or the ability to reason abstractly, was identified by Robert Reich in his discussion of the intellectual tools needed in symbolic analytic professions. Reich argued that in order to become a symbolic analytic thinker, one had to engage in the behaviors and develop the skills used by persons in upper-level professions. Although many skills are involved in symbolic analytic thought, Reich labels four basic types: "abstraction, system thinking, experimentation and collaboration" (Reich, p. 229). Relying upon Reich's narrative, an 11-item index of these skills was developed, including viewing knowledge as a system of causes, consequences and relationships; using equations, formulae and analogies in problem solving; communicating concepts through reports, designs, scripts, and projections; using analytic and persuasive abilities to bring about change; and utilizing teams to identify, plan and communicate solutions to problems.

Scientific and Quantitative Literacy. A similar method was used to develop measures for each of the remaining variables. Figure 2 shows the 11 items used to assess scientific and quantitative literacy. Underlying these 11 items, again, is a set of behaviors in which a learner must engage to develop an understanding of scientific and quantitative thought processes. Instead of following the lowest-common-denominator approach often adopted in many educational settings to reach a maximum number of students, the symbolic analytic approach challenges students to reach for the highest level of intellectual skill. Thus, reading articles from scientific journals, performing experiments, processing numerical data, questioning underlying assumptions and becoming conversant with computer technology are all part of scientific and quantitative literacy.

Global Understanding. Two dimensions of global understanding were operationalized. The first dimension included the more traditional factual approach to learning related to global understanding. Some items in the measure of academic global understanding were discussion of differences in meanings of words from one language to another; examination of relationships of climate changes to world food production; discussion of the significance of racial, ethnic and cultural differences, and of differences in political structures; and comparisons of world markets. The second dimension of global understanding that was operationalized was experiential. The experiential items involved learning to speak another language, studying or living abroad, visiting with international students, listening to and reading international news, and joining groups that intervene in international problems. Each of these items required the learner to have participated in an activity with an international scope.

Multicultural Awareness. The dimension underlying the items used to assess multicultural awareness was the ability to recognize and act in a responsible manner on a range of cultural issues. Items were concerned with value comparisons and judgments, employment and other socioeconomic issues faced by minority persons, familiarity with communications of minority groups, and involvement in the lives of persons of different ethnic, cultural and gender groups.

Figure 2

Items Used to Assess
Scientific and Quantitative Literacy

How often did you **do** the following in your undergraduate college years?

Please circle one answer for each item.

a. Read articles from scientific and/or research journals? — Often / A Few Times / Once / Never

b. Used a mainframe or microcomputer for data analysis? — Often / A Few Times / Once / Never

c. Planned and performed experiments largely on your own or with a team-mate? — Often / A Few Times / Once / Never

d. Collected and analyzed numerical data? — Often / A Few Times / Once / Never

e. Wrote about information contained in a table? — Often / A Few Times / Once / Never

f. Discussed the meaning of science and/or mathematics from a philosophical perspective? — Often / A Few Times / Once / Never

g. Critically examined differences in qualitative and quantitative research methods? — Often / A Few Times / Once / Never

h. Reviewed literature by examining what several writers said about the same scientific or mathematical issue? — Often / A Few Times / Once / Never

i. Learned to question the underlying assumptions involved in scientific and/or mathematical thought? — Often / A Few Times / Once / Never

j. Worked on a paper that was to be published or presented at a professional meeting? — Often / A Few Times / Once / Never

k. Studied the ethical and political values involved in doing scientific research? — Often / A Few Times / Once / Never

MEASUREMENT CHARACTERISTICS AND PILOT TESTING

During the instrument construction phase of the project, faculty members representing various disciplines most directly related to the key variables were asked to supply items and comment on the items selected for the measures. Pilot tests were used to ascertain readability and understanding of the questions and items.

Ordinal measures using a Likert-type scale of the amount of exposure to topics contained in each item were used for each variable. For example, for higher-order thinking, respondents were asked if they had experienced the item to a HIGH degree, a MEDIUM degree, a SLIGHT degree or NOT at all. The responses for scientific and quantitative literacy, academic global understanding and multicultural awareness were OFTEN, A FEW TIMES, ONCE or NEVER; for experiential global understanding the responses were VERY MUCH, SOME, A LITTLE and NONE. For computational purposes, each item was scored from 1 to 4, item scores were averaged, and average scores were interpreted as to whether they indicated bottom, lower, higher, or top fourths of the range of possible symbolic analytic training. Based on pilot tests involving representative samples of students, alumni and faculty, alpha coefficients ranging from .78 to .85 were found for each of the variables which, according to Angelo and Cross (1993) who conducted similar studies, is within an acceptable range.

AN EMPIRICAL EXAMPLE

The information presented in Table 1, characterized as intensity of preparation, is commonly referred to in industry and business as "time on task." The percentages are the result of three surveys conducted with random samples of students and alumni, and a survey of all permanent instructional faculty during 1992. Although any conclusions that may be drawn from Table 1 should be viewed as exploratory since the instru-

---

mentation has not been widely tested, some interesting results have been identified.

One result is a remarkable consistency in the percentages of students and alumni (former students) concerning their perceived level of instruction in the items represented in the variable scientific and quantitative literacy. When viewed in the light of faculty perceptions, both students and alumni felt they had received much less exposure to the items included in the variable than did the instructional faculty.

A second result apparent from the data in Table 1 is that more can be done insofar as time on task or intensity of the educational experience is concerned. Over half of the students, alumni and faculty believe they are receiving or providing less than 50 percent of what is theoretically possible in instruction for scientific and quantitative literacy.

Table 1

Intensity of Perceived Preparation for Scientific and Quantitative Literacy According to Students, Alumni and Faculty Expressed in Percentages

| | Type of Survey Respondents | | |
	Students N=622	Alumni N=750	Faculty N=151
Intensity of Preparation			
Top Fourth	5	5	17
Upper Middle	28	30	30
Lower Middle	42	43	30
Bottom Fourth	25	23	23

CAREER ATTAINMENT MEASURES

An outcome or final objective of a university education is assumed in The Bemidji Model to be a satisfactory occupation or career. Often-used strategies (e.g. U.S. Census categories) for classifying occupations were not used because they do not take into account the dynamic changes that are occurring both in the work force and in the economic sectors of society (Reich).

A perspective encompassing the work place of the 21st century was adopted as the framework for developing baseline occupational data. This perspective was derived from Reich, who identified all occupations as belonging to one of four conceptual categories in his recent book, *The Work of Nations* (1991). He labeled these categories routine production services, in-person services, symbolic analytic services and all other services. "All other" is a category which includes teachers and government workers, among others. This typology of occupations and workers has the advantage of simplicity; it takes into account the education, skills and capabilities expected of employees; it anticipates economic changes that can be expected; and provides for an ordinal level of measurement.

Reich's typology was operationalized for this study by using the first three categories (See Figure 3).

Figure 3
Three Categories of Occupations

Assume that, upon graduation from college, you had been offered three jobs, each being equal in pay and other benefits. You were required to **choose the job** for which you had received the best education and training. Based on the **education and training you received as an undergraduate at your university**, which job would you have chosen? (Please circle number of one answer.)

1. **A job that required you to produce the same kind of product, or perform the same kind of activity many times over to the best of your ability.** In this job, your work is rewarded by the **QUANTITY** of effort, production or services you render.

2. **A job that required you to use your skills to provide a service directly to people when they determined they needed it.** In

this job, your work is rewarded by your ability to provide acceptable **SPECIALIZED SERVICES** to the consumer.

3. **A job that required you to work with others to identify problems, solutions and markets for your ideas or product.** In this job, your work is rewarded by your ability to adjust to highly unique situations, and do tasks and **CREATE PRODUCTS OR IDEAS** of high value, although few in number.

[Figure 3 shows the form of the occupational question used with alumni.]

In appropriate formats, the occupational question was used with samples of students, faculty and alumni. Alumni were asked to provide information concerning the job they would have chosen and also information concerning the job they presently held. Table 2 shows the percentages of each group according to their occupational choices.

Table 2

Three Types of Occupations for the 21st Century Expressed in Percentages of Student, Alumni and Faculty Respondents

	Type of Survey Respondents		
	Students N=622	**Alumni** N=750	**Faculty** N=151
Job Classification			
Routine Production Services	8	6 (10)	3
In-person Services	46	51 (54)	40
Symbolic Analytic Services	42	42 (32)	57

[Numbers in parentheses represent jobs currently being held; all other percentages are for jobs that the respondent would choose, or in the case of faculty, jobs for which they are preparing their students.]

The data in Table 2 show a high degree of similarity for students, alumni and faculty concerning occupational categories that students are being prepared for and in which alumni have been prepared. It is interesting that faculty believe they are preparing students for higher-level jobs (symbolic analytic) than indicated by either students or alumni. Alumni believe they were prepared for higher-level jobs than they are currently holding. Thus, faculty expectations about the education they are providing for students are greater than the expectations students and alumni have for themselves. Attainments, on the other hand, are less than expectations.

CONCLUSIONS

The movement toward enhanced quality in American universities and colleges began in the 1930s. American universities have always striven for quality, and for this reason they are attended by students from throughout the world. What is new about the recent focus on quality is its association with approaches taken by business and industry (Corneskly et. al.).

There is much to be learned from the pursuit of continuous quality improvement. Quality in the academy, when defined at all, has been traditionally calculated in terms of numbers of students who enroll, faculty loads and student credit hours. Students were allowed to succeed or fail on their own merits, and the system became self perpetuating. The roles of administrators are often reduced to managing crises rather than leading by conveying an understanding of the process and goals of higher education.

Faculty are trained in discrete disciplines. Loyalty and specialization often are focused on disciplines rather than the broader values of the university. As a result, there has been a greater emphasis placed by faculty on promoting disciplinary subcultures rather than on promoting the larger campus culture. Thus, for many faculty, CQI represents a threat to their individuality and expertise rather than a conscientious team approach to the needs of higher education for the 21st century.

While the Blue Ribbon Commission presented a voice

from employers, labor and citizens of Minnesota, Reich's vision of the world of work was needed to develop a clear, conceptual model that directed our attention toward the skills needed to accommodate the changes in the 21st century. In *The Work of Nations*, Reich provided a portrait of what to expect in terms of workforce and employment changes and indicated the types of skills workers at all levels will need to meaningfully contribute in global economy. Although the highest level and best jobs will still require a considerable amount of disciplinary knowledge characteristic of a traditional higher education, the symbolic analytic professions will also require the refined ability to adjust to change.

The university of the 21st century will have a dual responsibility. First, there will be a need to develop a plan in which change will be fostered in relation to infusing quality into the curriculum for both faculty and students. Second, managing quality strategically requires a proactive approach to problem solving that can be learned and applied to the process of continuous improvement.

Support for this research was provided by the Q-7 Implementation Team, Bemidji State University. The data were collected by the Center for Social Research at Bemidji State University.

REFERENCES

Angelo, T. A. and Cross, K. P. *Classroom Assessment Techniques,* San Francisco: Jossey-Bass, 1993.

Astin, A. W. Green, K.C. and Korn, W. S. *The American Freshman: Twenty Year Trends.* Los Angeles: Cooperative Institutional Research Program of the American Council on Education and University of California, Jan. 1987.

Boyer, E. L. *College: The Undergraduate Experience in America.* New York: Harper and Row, 1987.

Chickering, A.W. *Education and Identity.* San Francisco: Jossey-Bass, 1969.

Corneskly, Robert A.; et. al. *Improving Quality in Colleges and Universities.* Madison, WI: Magna Publications, 1990.

Drucker, P. F. *Managing the Future.* New York: Dutton, 1992.

Holland, J. L. *Making Vocational Choices: A Theory of Vocational Personalities and Work Enviornments.* Engelwood Cliffs, N.J.: Prentice Hall, 1985.

Pace, C. *Measuring the Quality of College Student Experiences.* Los Angeles: University of Southern California, Higher Education Research Institute, 1984.

Pascarella, E. T. and Terenzini, P. T. *How College Affects Students.* San Francisco: Jossey-Bass, 1991.

Reich, R. B. *The Work of Nations.* New York: Alfred A. Knopf, 1991.

Stark, J. S., Shaw, K. M. and Lowther, M. A. *Student Goals for College Courses: A Missing Link in Assessing and Improving Academic Achievement.* ASHE-ERIC Higher Education Report no. 6 Washington, D.C.: School of Education and Human Development, The George Washington University, 1989.

Thurow, L. *Head to Head.* New York: William Morrow and Company, Inc., 1992.

Tiedeman, D. V. and O'Hara, R. P. *Career Development: Choice and Adjustment.* New York: College Entrance Examination Board, 1963.

Tinto, V. *Leaving College: Rethinking the Causes and Cures of Student Attrition.* Chicago: University of Chicago Press, 1987.

Willingham, W. W. *Success in College: The Role of Personal Qualities and Academic Ability.* New York: College Entrance Examination Board, 1985.

Linda L. Baer received her B.A. in sociology from Washington State University in 1970, her M.A. in 1975 from Colorado State University and her Ph.D. from South Dakota State University in 1983.

Prior to her appointment as vice president for academic affairs at Bemidji State University in 1990, Baer taught in the Rural Sociology Department at South Dakota State University. She chaired that university's Assessment Review Committee. Since 1990, she has been working on long-range planning and the quality initiative at Bemidji State University. This has included the development of a conceptual model of quality, exploring the operationalization and measurement of quality indicators, and implementing programs to enhance quality at the departmental and university levels.

Baer is currently the senior vice president of academic and student affairs at Bemidji State University.

Bea Walker Knodel joined the Bemidji State University Department of English in 1964 after several years teaching English, speech and journalism in the public schools. She has served as director of freshman English, director of women's studies, and chair of the Department of English. Her Ed.D. in English education is from the University of Northern Colorado.

Knodel has been closely involved with the Minnesota State Universities' Q-7 quality initiative. She was a member of the resource team that worked with the Blue Ribbon Commission which made the initial recommendations on quality and access to the state universities and was also a member of the Preparation Standards Task Force. Currently, she serves on the System-wide Facilitation Team as well as on the Bemidji State University Q-7 Implementation Team.

Jon Quistgaard received a B.A. in government from the University of Arizona in 1970. He earned both a master of arts in government in 1972 and the Ph.D. in political science in 1977 from the University of Arizona. More recently, Quistgaard's research interests have focused on organizational behavior, conflict resolution, comparative education and the international political economy.

Quistgaard has published in the area of international organizations, drawing upon sociological role theory in the *Journal of Conflict Resolution* and *International Organization*. He is a frequent presenter and consultant in the area of international education.

Quistgaard has held numerous administrative positions at Bemidji State University. Presently, Quistgaard is the dean of graduate studies, library and special university programs.

Ivan Lee Weir received his Ph. D. in sociology from Washington State University in 1978. After several years with the Department of Rural Sociology at WSU, he accepted a position in the Urban Studies Center at the University of Louisville. Weir currently teaches sociology at Bemidji State University, and serves as the founding director of the Center for Social Research.

The Q-7 Blue Ribbon Commission made its recommendations for seven indicators of quality to the State University System in Minnesota two years ago, about the time Robert Reich published his book, *Work of Nations*. As part of the implementation team, Weir and his colleagues began the conceptualization of a model that would meld the search for quality with the changes Reich indicated will be demanded of the workforce of the 21st century.

13

Quality Assurance Within Higher Education in the United Kingdom

Richard G. Fisher

Higher education in the United Kingdom (U.K.) is a national system of independent institutions where rarely does an institution choose to operate outside of direct government funding. Therefore, as a collective of higher education institutions (HEIs), all are equally subject to the Acts of Parliament, and to the policy and allocations of government. Compared to higher education in the United States, it is similar to a state where planning, legislation, funding and accountability resides.

Comparing the U.S. HEIs to their U.K. counterparts, in any brief way, is sensitive to misinterpretation. However, it may be contextually helpful for the uninformed reader to have a minimal reference.

❖ Research universities to universities (now including

the former polytechnics, though some may choose to be primarily access, teaching and applied-research oriented, therefore comparable to U.S. comprehensive universities)

❖ Comprehensive universities to non-research rated universities and broad based colleges of higher education

❖ Colleges to colleges of higher education (some U.K. colleges tend to specialise, e.g., nursing, teacher education)

❖ Community colleges to further education colleges which have a broad mission

❖ Technical colleges and institutes to some further education colleges

Due to the unique nature of the two systems and individual institutional missions, readers are urged to seek specific information before making precise comparisons.

This chapter reviews the history and present state of policy and management of higher educational institutions in the U.K., concentrating on the universities with regard to social change, accountability, quality assurance and continuous improvement.

SOCIAL CHANGE

Historians and futurists have addressed the social transition of the late 19th century from an agrarian to an industrial society. In the late 20th century, the transition has been from the industrial to an information society. Alvin Toffler (1990), in the third of his three-book work on these transitions, states that global society is in the midst of a "powershift" among three types of power: violence (force), wealth and knowledge. In the agrarian era, the predominant power was violence, while in the industrial era it has been wealth. During the "third wave," the predominant source of power is knowledge and communication.

Higher education is accepted as being the sector of society most capable to advance a nation's knowledge power base.

Therefore, it is imperative that government and HEIs concur on the nature and scope of knowledge as power and understand the implications for the state of education as a primary provider. A common social goal must be an interdependent approach to both stimulate the power source and flourish from the results.

GOVERNMENT PERCEPTIONS OF HIGHER EDUCATION

Elected representatives of the public hold it reasonable to expect an organisation founded on the principles of the search for truth, and creation and dissemination of knowledge, to apply these same principles for improvement and accountability of its performance. However, public officials are perplexed by appearances that HEIs are slow in adapting to the changing social issues and needs, and organisation best-practices. This is a major charge by officials. Their claim is that the very institutions that consider it legitimate to investigate and to criticize others in society appear most reluctant to apply research to their own operations (Ewell, 1992).

Middlehurst (1991) suggests a similar paradox within U.K. universities. As some of the oldest institutions in our culture, Universities present a paradox in relation to change. Change is intrinsic to their core intellectual activities, but has not impinged seriously on the characteristics of academic organisations which are still recognisable from their medieval origins.

This paradox is a significant perceptual barrier to a consistent, collaborative relationship between the government and HEIs.

Government has, during the 1980s to the present, been increasingly concerned about the outcomes and management of higher and further education, as it has been for all public services. Since the deep budget reductions of 1981, "evaluative" interests and actions have greatly accelerated. Neave (1986) suggests that this is the result of three developments: the need to limit social expenditure; the need to direct student enrollment to high-potential employment fields; and the need to develop courses that meet the needs of the marketplace. Worldwide, these factors, among others, have generated state working sessions, reports and legislation on access to, quality of, funding for, and management of post-secondary and higher education. The government has sought a greater accountability over outcomes of education as a public service.

HIGHER EDUCATION INSTITUTIONS' PERCEPTION OF GOVERNMENT

Over this and the previous decade, HEIs perceive that they have been on a policy and funding roller coaster without sufficient stability to expand teaching and research potential. Since 1981, the U.K. government policy has increasingly directed how higher education will be managed, including no further tenured staff and required staff appraisal (Middlehurst, 1991). HEIs have cause to believe that government is determining curriculum content and teaching methodologies by looking at funding by subject field-research ratings, numbers of funded students by subject field, and assessment for funding by subject field delivery, among other policy, funding and assurance activities. This "intrusion" upon traditional institutional autonomy has been met with various means. The HEIs, through the leadership in their sector organisations, have proposed diverse actions to keep pace with mandated changes, and in many instances to take the lead. However, the caution of Stephen Bailey may have crossed the mind of more than one higher-education leader.

"...the precise border between the state and the academy is, and must be kept, fuzzy. For if a precise delineation is sought...the state has more than the academy of what it takes to draw the line" (Berdahl, 1990).

His implication is that the power of wealth will predominate. The "golden rule" of funding has recently sparked debate about the future funding independence of at least one prestigious U.K. university. However, there is only one "private" HEI (native institutions) in the U.K., a small college.

HISTORICAL CONTEXT

This official relationship began over 100 years ago when, in 1889, the universities requested £50,000 (approx. $76,000) from the government. Treasury formed an ad hoc committee to administer a £15,000 (approx. $22,800) award. Twenty-eight years later, the University Grants Committee (UGC) was established to receive university requests, advise the Parliament and administer block grants to the universities.

In 1963 the "Robbins Report" recommended the expansion of access to and support for HEIs. However, the report presented the universities with a caution that would become pronounced in subsequent years.

> ...progress – and particularly the maintenance of a competitive position – depends to a much greater extent than ever before on skills demanding special training. A good education, valuable though it may be, is frequently less than we need to solve many of our most pressing problems (Robbins, 1963).

A new government brought to the 1980s a philosophy of privatisation, focus on economic development and less national funding with more entrepreneurial initiative. In 1981, the financial restructuring period began with the UGC making drastic cuts in grants to universities and colleges (Middlehurst, 1991). In 1985, amidst growing discontent and anticipating government interest to seek greater restrictions on institutional autonomy, the Committee of Vice Chancellors and Principals (CVCP) established a commission to look into management of the universities. The "Jarrett Report" called for overhaul of management, a strategic plan for each university performance indicators (internal, external and operational), internal information and external comparison of universities (Jarrett, 1985). HEIs became "Jarrettised" with sufficient savings that preserved all of the universities.

In this same year the government stated:

> There is continuing concern that higher education does not respond sufficiently to changing needs. This may be due in part to disincentives to change within higher education – including over-dependence on public funding, and to failures in communication between employers and institutions (Department of Education and Science, 1985).

The government believed that higher education could improve its effectiveness and efficiency by: being more responsive to the needs of the economy; depending less on public funds; being more selective in the allocation of resource funding to centres of excellence; and being more cost conscious.

These same policies were restated, in broad terms, in the White Paper on "Higher Education: Meeting the Challenge." This policy document stated that HEI's performance would be judged by reference mainly to students' achievements (DES, 1987). It also called for a new funding relationship between the government and the institutions of higher education.

The government's endeavour to gain accountability abruptly changed when, in 1989, it replaced the UGC and its counterpart, the Polytechnics and Colleges Funding Council (PCFC), with the University Funding Council (UFC). The change was substantial, from a system of block grants primarily expended at the discretion of the university, to funding through contractual agreements for the provision of specific services in return for sums of money. Universities were now to bid for students through course/subject field enrollment targets. Research funds would be primarily influenced by the research selectivity exercise presented by the UGC in 1985-86 and first implemented in 1988 (Jones, 1989), but now referred to as Research Assessment as completed for 1992.

In the U.K., the government seeks evidence of assurance that the funded provision is being efficiently and effectively purchased, that there is fitness for purpose. This assurance is mandated by the "Further and Higher Education Act 1992" (Donaldson, 1993).

During these events, the higher education leadership was active through the CVCP and Committee of Directors of Polytechnics (CDP), developing approaches to guidance and codes of practice, program review, performance indicators, staff appraisal, staff development, academic and corporate plans, and quality audit. Notably, the CVCP published a "Green Paper on Total Quality Management" (Crawford, 1991).

The government has unequivocally spoken and acted upon its value for higher education as an essential economic component of the public interest. Higher education leaders have responded by proposing and implementing new management procedures and by strengthening self-examination and quality enhancement functions.

PRESENT SITUATION

With the passage of the "Further and Higher Education Act 1992," the binary line between the universities and polytechnics was removed, with all such institutions gaining university status. Also, funding for the universities was devolved into separate Higher Education Funding Councils for England, Scotland and Wales. Hereafter, specific reference will be made to the status of quality assurance in Scotland.

> The Funding Council is obliged by the "Further and Higher Education Act (Scotland) 1992" and the Letter of Guidance from the Secretary of State to undertake

assessments and to have regard to the outcome of such assessments when determining funding for institutions (Donaldson 1993).

Assessment of provision was begun by the Scottish Higher Education Funding Council (SHEFC) after a pilot project and extensive university consultation was completed in the fall of 1992. The council agreed at its eighth meeting on January 15, 1993, to implement an initial programme of quality assessment (SHEFC, 1993). Similar directions have been formulated by the other funding councils (Harvey, 1993).

The CVCP, which now includes the "new" universities (old polytechnics), reorganised quality self-examination activities under the Higher Education Quality Council (HEQC) which is owned by the universities (Quality Support Centre, 1992). This independent body has three divisions: quality audit, quality enhancement, and credit and access. The universities are continuing the tradition of self-examination to sustain internal assessment for the provision of education.

QUALITY ASSURANCE

The promulgation of academic, behavioral and operational standards is a central responsibility of educational institutions.

Universities have always been concerned with academic excellence, guaranteed by formal systems of peer review and external assessment. However, Quality Assurance is part of the language of a different approach to quality. This report identifies a number of major themes that universities need to address which are implicit in this approach: fitness for purpose; need for a strategic approach; meeting customers' expectations; a cycle of continuous improvement; and a cohesive system of interconnected processes (de Wit, 1992).

de Wit has accurately highlighted that there is a different approach to quality than the language and method from 10, even five, years ago. Societal change has brought about a democratisation of thinking and action with regard to expectations about quality and how it is to be achieved.

All participants in higher education, i.e., universities, government, funding councils and customers, are stakeholders in the assurance of quality.

Quality Assurance encompasses all the policies, systems and processes directed to ensuring maintenance and enhancement of the quality of educational provision in higher education (Donaldson, 1993).

The following are quality assurance activities of the Funding Councils and/or HEIs in Great Britain. The focus of current activity is, for the most part, on the formal teaching and learning provision.

Quality (Student Achievement). A high evaluation accorded to an educative process, the students' educational development has been enhanced; not only have they achieved the particular objectives set for the course but, in doing so, they have also fulfilled the general educational aims of autonomy, of the ability to participate in reasoned discourse, of critical self-evaluation, and of coming to a proper awareness of the ultimate contingency of all thought and action (Barnett, 1993).

This definition of quality is presented as the Department of Education and Science (1987), and Jim Donaldson, director of the SHEFC Quality Assessment Directorate (1993), places importance for outcomes on student achievement, both during course of study and in post-graduation employment.

Planning. Universities have been completing formal academic and corporate plans (Trainer, 1991; Jackson, 1993). The process flows through the academic and administrative units to university committees and councils/senates to the court. SHEFC requires a five year university strategic plan (Sizer, 1992) and a 10-year building and estates strategic plan (Sizer,

1993), which will require 10-year academic and corporate plans.

Fitness for Purpose. Each independent HEI determines aims, purposes and objectives. In 1993, the SHEFC, through its Quality Assessment Directorate, stated:

"'Quality' does not lend itself to easy or precise definition. There is general agreement, however, that in this context the quality of any activity may only be assessed in relation to the purpose of that activity" (Donaldson, 1993).

Quality Control. Quality control is an institutional responsibility. Quality control relates to the arrangements (procedures, standards, organisation) within HEIs which verify that teaching and assessment are carried out in a satisfactory manner (Donaldson, 1993).

Quality Audit. Quality audit is the process of ensuring that the quality control arrangements in an institution are satisfactory and effective (Donaldson, 1993).

The HEQC's Quality Audit Division conducts institution quality audits on an on-going rotational basis through a system of self-evaluation and peer review.

Quality Assessment. Quality assessment is the process of external evaluation to the actual provision of education. It is a statutory responsibility of the funding councils (Donaldson, 1993).

SHEFC administers this responsibility through a Quality Assessment Directorate. Self-examination and external examiners are central to this process, as will be performance indicators (a funding council's joint working party is charged to develop qualitative and quantitative indicators). A Quality Framework, listing the aspects of the "definition of quality of provision against which quality process should be conducted," (Donaldson, 1993) is provided for use in the self-assessment process. Emphasis is on outcomes, particularly the student experience, assessed against institutional purposes.

Quality Enhancement. This HEQC Division serves as a catalyst for, and facilitator of, the generating and sharing of information and knowledge for the advancement of quality in higher education (Quality Support Centre, 1992). The objective is to enrich university standards and self-examination to address improvement and external communication.

Program Review. Numerous institutions employ academic course review to support development as well as assessment expectations. This will continue as a pre-audit/assessment preparation to identify areas for improvement. Institutions are now considering or have implemented program review for non-academic programs and services (e.g., Exeter, Northumbria).

Peer Review. British higher education is based on the tradition of peer examiners for validating student achievement, course provision and degrees. With the initiation of program review, audit and assessment, the system is strained to find sufficiently capable and available professionals to stay abreast of the demand, while at the same time not detracting from primary teaching and research remits (Brookman, 1993).

Staff Appraisal. Universities are required to conduct appraisal for academic and academic-related staff and have programmes for all staff (University of Sheffield) (DES, 1987). The outcome is to be used in staff development. Numerous universities use appraisal outcomes in the consideration of permanent status and promotion, while others do not (University of Glasgow).

Staff Development. The scope of staff development remits is varied, as are most programmes in over 100 diverse institutions (Opinion and Perspective, 1993). Efforts for teaching, allied and administrative staff are underway at the universities (e.g., University of Nottingham, University of Sheffield, University of Stirling).

Quality Circles. Quality circles are found at several institutions, including Aston and Nottingham. These are the "Western" circles or teams, not the original Japanese Quality Circles. There are other improvement teams active in institutions (e.g., Wolverhampton, South Bank).

British Standard 5750. BS 5750 is a method for demonstrating that a management system works in the way it claims to do. It measures the consistency of the administrative system that supports teaching and learning (de Wit,1992). International Standard 9000 was based on BS 5750.

Performance Indicators. Performance indicators (PIs) are quantitative representations of the objective and subjective outcomes of education and operations functions for achieving provision of education (Burrows, et al, 1992). PIs will be a part of the quality assessment process (Donaldson, 1993).

Instruments. Standardised instruments for assessment are little known or used in the U.K. due to the extensive system of peer examiners. Surveys are used, though not widely, in instances when opinion or satisfaction and importance is assessed, e.g., student satisfaction or use (University of Central England).

Total Quality Management. Whatever the current perception of TQM is in academe, universities over the next few years will be under increasing pressure to state their missions, objectives and goals more clearly, and will progressively be supported only to the extent of perceived national needs in the market niches that they have chosen and according to the quality that they are believed to deliver (Crawford, 1991).

SHEFC has included the concept of TQM in the assessment approach. The introduction of a system of quality assessment based on evidence arising from institutional self-assessment exercises at subject level is consistent with that found in industry and reflects Total Quality Management practice (Donaldson, 1993).

TOTAL QUALITY MANAGEMENT CASE EXAMPLES

Institutions in the United Kingdom which have implemented TQM have done so, in whole or in part, for reasons of survival, student achievement, customer/supplier satisfaction, operational enhancement, financial and provision accountability, reputation and/or cultural transformation. The four case examples which follow indicate the diverse nature of institutional activity. The author has had a telephone conversation with the responsible officer, a review of documents, plus a site visit at Aston, East Birmingham and Wolverhampton.

University of Aston: The theme of quality has been embedded in Aston University's strategic plans for long-term success during a decade of change brought about by the national policy to restructure the British Higher Education system. The philosophy and techniques of quality management have been applied as a means of ensuring continuous improvement and progress towards Aston's mission to be a leading technological university. The strategic plan has led to major projects, including academic restructuring to ensure that departments cover disciplines consistent with the mission, and the provision of an appropriate high-quality support infrastructure. The plan for growth is rooted in the concepts of understanding who the "customers" are, in understanding their needs and serving them well. The formation of a Quality Council has marked a further stage in the realisation of an integrated Quality Management programme. The purpose of the council is to review the University's processes and critical success factors in order to identify key areas for improvement.

An extensive education and training program has been launched, and there has been experimentation with the vital quality management technique of "Quality Function Deployment" (Clayton, 1993).

Quality circles are a component of the University programme. The In-House Laundry Service Quality Circle was nominated by the University for the "1991 Michelin Award of the National Society of Quality Circles." (Contact: Marlene Clayton, Director, Staff Development, Aston University).

University of Wolverhampton. The Corporate Code of Practice explains how our key service: THE DESIGN AND PROVISION OF LEARNING EXPERIENCES is delivered to various clients – students, employers, firms and society – and sets out our commitment to achieving high quality. As an institution, our criteria for quality services are that they shall:

- ❖ Be fitted for the purpose
- ❖ Provide client satisfaction
- ❖ Be of a grade at least equivalent to that of other suppliers

The University of Wolverhampton supports the principles of Total Quality Management as expressed in the director's statement:

> The staff at the University of Wolverhampton is committed to providing high-quality services – regionally, nationally and internationally – to its wide range of student and other clients regardless of their gender, creed or nationality. This provision is aimed at developing the relevant knowledge, skills and competencies to meet the future needs of industry, commerce and society. We will foster a cost-effective, do-it-right-the-first-time culture by understanding and conforming to the requirements of our tasks at all times.

Thus, every member of staff of whatever status, in whatever section, will try, through the agreed procedure, to contribute to the identification of quality problems, ineffective work habits and non-conformances in our Quality System, thus helping to ensure corrective and preventive action within the University (Doherty, 1992).

The University is progressing toward a BS 5750 certification visit. The "Corporate Code of Practice" and "BS 5750 Quality Manual" are in place, with supporting documentation. Quality Improvement Teams are functioning and a system of internal quality audits is in place. (Contact: Susan Storey, Head, Quality Assurance Unit, University of Wolverhampton, Walsall Campus).

South Bank University. In December 1991, the Total Quality Initiative was begun, with a full announcement to staff in March 1992.

"Total" means simply that everyone is involved at all levels and across all functions of the University. TQ involves nothing less than a wholesale change in corporate culture and ethos, involving commitment to quality and to serving the needs of customers at all times and in every way (Geddes, 1993).

Steps in the journey for South Bank include:

❖ Define quality
❖ Define Total Quality
❖ Define management structure and role
❖ Define concepts and principles of TQM
❖ Define quality characteristics

Departments and schools:

❖ Identify inputs and outputs
❖ Identify transformation processes
❖ Create aims statement

❖ Draft quality standards and benchmarks

Thirty-four customer/supplier work groups were formed to negotiate Quality Service Agreements by the following steps:

❖ Agree to quality standards
❖ Prioritise quality standards
❖ Establish quality benchmarks
❖ Establish customer care procedures
❖ Monitoring and review arrangements
❖ Finalise the agreement.

BS 5750 is being considered by departments and the University. (Contact: Chris Clare, professor and director of planning and information, South Bank University).

East Birmingham College. "East Birmingham College is a medium-sized, further-education college on the outskirts of Birmingham...." (Thorpe and Green, 1991).

In a TQM cultural transformation context, this opening line in a summary of college TQM is low-key. However, after a site visit and reading East Birmingham College material, there is little that is low-key about this culture! This is an organisation that made a commitment to cultural change through investing in people. It is not "there," wherever "there" will be, but after six years staff members profess a positive change in staff morale, customer feedback, programme and organisation function, physical appearance and testimony. All of the formal elements are present in principle and practice.

BS 5750 is a part of the TQM programme with certification gained two years ago as well as several re-certifications.

The principal, Tony Henry, lost his office space because of his resource philosophy that "if you don't use it, you lose it." The staff informed him he was not using "it" (leading by moving around). The office is now a conference room, with a desk and computer in the corner for the principal's work area!

Another piece of convincing evidence, of which there are many, was the electronics area. The area consisted of an entry core with the laboratory to the left, classroom to the right, and the project-team area to the forward-right. Open arches provide unhindered sensory and physical access to all areas. During the site visit, a teaching staff member worked at a computer in the core area while nearby a staff member talked with a student. In the projects area, a group of students worked at one of the round tables. In the classroom, students were conversing. The philosophy was in practice. (Contact: Marion Thorpe, quality manager, East Birmingham College).

SUMMARY

The relationship between the British government and the higher-education sector is wholly intertwined by policy, funding and quality assurance. Institutions are independent to determine aims and purpose, and the content and method for achievement of the teaching and research provision.

Management of the higher-education sector has been under continuous change (Watt, 1992). That path has been one of accountability for the provision of education on the basis of value for money and contribution to the well-being of the economy, which intensified in the 1980s.

Educational outcomes must address goals stated in government and funding-council policy, enrollment targets, and subject field and research assessment.

Quality assurance is based on fitness-for-purpose assessed against aims and purposes stated by the institution.

The evidence of quality assurance must be documented by the university, including performance indicators collaboratively determined by HEIs and funding councils and verified by external examiners.

There is assessment of teaching and research provision by

subject field with the results considered in course-specific funding agreements. This contractual relationship is completed by consultation between the respective funding council and each university.

There is an increasing recognition that quality assurance must mean more than accountability. It must mean continuous improvement of academic and management operations (Harvey, et al, 1993, and Donaldson, 1993).

The implementation of TQM has been selective, as each institution determined the need (Burrows, et al, 1992). Most universities are too preoccupied with the mandated assurance processes and daily operations to consider a further commitment of effort such as TQM, which is generally viewed as a business-industrial model with uncertain outcomes for education.

There are numerous institutional, or units within an institution, programs of TQM and continuous improvement (e.g., Aston, Bradford, East Birmingham, Edinburgh, Leeds Metropolitan, Northumbria, South Bank, Wolverhampton). These should harvest success that will be reviewed by the HEIs for benchmarking.

BS 5750 has been primarily implemented in the further education colleges (e.g., East Birmingham and Sandwell), though the University of Wolverhampton plans a certification review in November 1993.

Quality circles (teams) have been successful at several institutions (University of Nottingham – halls of residence; University of Aston – Central Laundry Service; and East Birmingham College – staff teams).

THE FUTURE

Two necessary partners, education and government, prioritise primary social values, human and economic development based on their individual circumstances, including experience, philosophy, context and outcome needs. Tension over inputs, e.g., resources, and outcomes, e.g., education, training and research, escalates during a period of social change, particularly when coupled with economic recession. Quality, as a philosophical, thus relative, term, must be defined by the two partners under point-in-time circumstances. This can best be accomplished when the participants commit to a planning process to set forth specific outcome criteria and input factors unique to individual and collective needs. Thereafter, institutions should be free to determine the educational content and method, and specific data elements and measures to communicate achievement of the criteria.

Government and higher education institutions should commit to a long-term management style for policy, funding and assessment that is transparent, defines future-market factors, sets goals and criteria, maintains and develops diversity, is sensitive to stability and viability, promotes special initiatives, supports flexibility and innovation, rewards good management, and acknowledges effectiveness and efficiency in meeting the provision of education (Sizer, 1993, Annex). A national plan (e.g., three to five years) to define market factors, and to set goals and criteria should be completed in a similar manner as institutions complete a corporate plan. Once agreement is reached, HEIs would be free to use best-practices to implement, evaluate and communicate results.

It is recommended that continuous improvement of the provision of education and management support systems be the common value that bonds education and government. This concept is inherent in the developmental interests, human and economic, of both parties. Adopting continuous improvement principles and best-practices will create a common language and style that may transform an occasionally uncertain and contentious relationship into one that is more steady and viable over time.

Continuous improvement principles of leadership commitment, fitness for purpose, strategic approach, fact-based common language, enabling involvement, systems innovation, and meeting/exceeding expectations all contribute to a cultural transformation that can benefit participants, specific and general. Such an approach takes the emphasis from differing views and places effort on a shared value that can encompass the individual values of all parties in the education relationship.

The philosophy of continuous improvement and use of best-practices to direct a systems approach to learning organisations can be a distinct benefit to HEIs, and to their customers and clients (Senge, 1991). In an era of knowledge and communication, power HEIs, as a primary source of this power, should set the standard by serving as the premier learning organisation.

This project was completed during a Fulbright Fellowship United Kingdom Academic Administrators Award, 1 February to 1 June, 1993. The host institution was the University of Stirling, Scotland. To both organisations, and to all those who extended full professional courtesy, deep appreciation is given. **Editor's Note:** *The author chose to retain British spellings for authenticity in this chapter.*

References

Barnett, R. *Improving Higher Education: Total Quality Care.* Buckingham: The Society for Research in Higher Education and The Open University Press, 1992.

Bailey, S. In R. Berdahl "Public Universities and State Governments: Is the Tension Benigh?" *Change,* 1990, 71(1), 38.

Brookman, J. "Breakpoint Reached by Examiners." London: *The Times Higher Education Supplement,* 1993, *1060,* 5.

Burrows, A., Harvey, L. and Green, D. *Quality Assurance Systems: A Review of the Applications of Industrial Models to Education and Training.* Birmingham: Quality Higher Education Project, 1992a.

Clayton, M. *Towards Total Quality Managment in Higher Education - Aston University: A Case Study.* Birmingham: Aston University.

Crawford, F. "Total Quality Management." London: Committee of Vice Chancellors and Principals, Occastional Paper, 1991.

Department of Education and Science. *The Development of Higher Education into the 1990s*. London: Her Majesty's Stationary Office, Cmnd 9524, 1985.

Department of Education and Science. *Higher Education: Meeting the Challenge*. London: Her Majesty's Stationary Office, 1987, Cmnd, 114.

de Wit, P. *Quality Assurance in University Continuing Vocational Education Universities*. London: Department of Employment, Council for Adult and Continuing Education, 1992.

Doherty, G. D. *Code of Corporate Practice*. Walsall: University of Wolverhampton, Nov. 17, 1992.

Donaldson, J. "Quality Assessment Arrangement for 1993-94." Edinburgh: Scottish Higher Education Funding Council, *Circular Letter*, Mar. 2, 1993, 9(93).

Donaldson, J. *Conversation with the Author*. Edinburgh: Scottish Higher Education Council, Mar. 4, 1993b.

Ewell, P.T. "Defining the Quality Driven Institution." *Assessment Update*, 1992, 4(5), 1-2, 4-5.

Geddes, T. *Presentation: Total Quality Initiative*. London: South Bank University, Mar. 23, 1993.

Harvey, L., Burrows, A. and Green, D. *The Quality Assessors*. Birmingham: Quality Higher Education Project, 1993.

Jackson, M. *Academic Plan 2002/3*. Stirling: University of Stirling, 1993.

Jarrett, A. (chr.). *Report of the Steering Comittee for Efficiency Studies in Universities*. London: Committee of Vice Chancellors and Principals, 1985.

Jones, P. K. *Report on the 1989 Research Assessment Exercise*. London: Universities Funding Council, 1989.

Middlehurst, R. *The Changing Roles of Leaders and Managers*. Sheffield: Committee of Vice Chancellors and Principals/Universities Staff Development Unit, 1991.

Neave, F. "The All-Seeing Eye of the Prince in Western Europe," in Moodie, G.C. (ed.) *Standards and Criteria in Higher Education*. Guildford: Society for Research in Higher Education and NFER Nelson, 1986, 157-170.

Opinion and Perspective. "Training Beyond the Primitive." London: *The Times Higher Education Supplement*, 1993, 1063, 14, 17-22.

Quality Support Centre. "A Guide to the Changes in HigherEducation," *Higher Education Digest*. Milton Keynes: The Open University, 1992, 14, supplement.

Quality Support Centre. "A Guide to the Changes in Higher Education, Part II," *Higher Education Digest*. Milton Keynes: The Open University, 1993, 15, supplement.

Robbins, Lord (chr.). *Robbins Report: Higher Education*. London: Her Majesty's

Stationary Office. Cmnd. 1963, 2154.

Senge, P. *The Fifth Discipline: The Art & Practice of the Learning Organization.* London: Doubleday, 1991.

SHEFC. *Eighth Meeting: Information for Institutions.* Edinburgh: Scottish Higher Education Funding Council, Jan. 15, 1993.

Sizer, J. "Strategic Planning in Scottish Higher Education Institutions." Edinburgh: Scottish Higher Education Funding Council. *Circular Letter,* 1992, 11.

Sizer, J. "Strategic Planning in Scottish Higher Education Institutions: 1993 Strategic Plans and Annual Planning Statements." Edinburgh: Scottish Higher Education Funding Council. *Circular Letter,* 1993, 8a.

Sizer, J. "Recurrent Grants for Teaching and Research for 1993-94." Edinburgh: Scottish Higher Education Funding Council. *Circular Letter,* Mar. 17, 1993, 14b.

Thorpe, M. and Green, M. *Total Quality Management.* Birmingham: East Birmingham College, 1991.

Toffler, A. *Powershift: Knowledge, Wealth and Violence at the Edge of the 21st Century.* London: Bantam, 1990.

Trainer, J. *Corporate Plan 1994/95.* Stirling: University of Stirling, Oct. 24, 1991.

Watt, H.D. "Managing Change While Maintaining Quality: The Challenge to the Universty of Glasgow." Glasgow: Course Paper, 1992

Richard G. Fisher is a member of the faculty of the Counseling and Student Personnel Department at Mankato State University. From 1979 to 1993, he served Mankato State as vice president for student affairs. Previously, he served as dean of students and then vice president/dean of student affairs at Marshall University.

Fisher recently completed a Fulbright Fellowship under the United Kingdom Academic Administrators Award Program on the topic of CQI in British higher education. The fellowship was served at the University of Stirling, Stirling, Scotland. Fisher led the initiation of a Quality Transformation using team-based management in the Division of Student Affairs at Mankato State. He has made numerous presentations on the topic of CQI. His degrees were awarded by the University of Dubuque and the University of Iowa.

14

Juran's "Quality Planning Road Map" as a Framework for Mission Development

Neil Story
Bruce H. Allen

Total Quality Management (TQM) is a system designed to engage an entire organization in planning and implementing a continuous improvement process, a process intended to result in the client's delight. It requires an organization to look to its core processes and to find ways of systematically improving them.

While TQM was first applied to business organizations, attention has more recently turned to its use in higher education, and particularly to academic programs in higher education. That attention has increased as criticism of higher education has strengthened, and nowhere has that criticism been sharper than of collegiate schools of business. Business schools have been charged with producing graduates without the skills required by employers needing to compete aggressively in modern global markets (Blum, 1991; Fuchsberg, 1990; *Business*

Week, 1992). Numerous critics have argued that business schools suffer from "practical irrelevance" because of misdirected, esoteric research, because of faculty with little actual managerial experience, and because of a failure to emphasize important factors such as ethics, multiculturalism and adaptation to technology (Blum, 1991; Fuchsberg,1990; *Business Week,* 1991).

The criticism of business schools, as of higher education programs in general, goes to the question of their quality. And so it is not at all surprising that business schools have begun to look at their core process – learning – in light of TQM principles, and have begun to systematically plan to improve learning. This chapter is the tale of how one business school, Central Michigan University's College of Business Administration (CMU/CBA), came to identify and articulate learning as its core process, and how it took its first steps toward putting in place a system for improving that process by defining its mission and goals. It is the tale of a college initially not oriented toward TQM – one which is now beginning to recognize its own need for that learning, but one which seems somehow to have found itself on the right road to quality, a road mapped out in *Juran on Planning for Quality* (Juran, 1988). It is the tale of how that College collectively developed and articulated a mission, a mission no one would have conceived of before the mission development process began, and one that succeeded in delighting its faculty and, we believe, its students and their employers.

MAPPING THE ROAD:
JURAN AND THE CATALYSTS FOR CHANGE

The professional accrediting agency for business schools, The American Assembly of Collegiate Schools of Business (AACSB), meeting the criticism of business schools and reflecting TQM principles, significantly altered its accrediting standards in 1991 to require each member school to be evaluated on continuous improvement toward fulfilling a self-defined mission. The CMU/CBA, facing re-accreditation review in 1993-94, adopted a process for developing a College mission in the summer of 1991, a process and subsequent development work which, as it turned out, closely followed Juran's "quality planning road map." AACSB's alteration in accreditation and CMU/CBA's adoption of a mission development process were the catalysts for change in the College, while Juran's was the map which that change began to follow.

Juran's Quality Planning Road Map

At the heart of TQM lies the duty of an organization to fulfill a customer's needs, to delight the customer. That fulfillment, that delight, is the ultimate measure of quality. The first move in providing quality is to plan for it. Juran has taken that first move and identified 10 specific steps, an "invariable sequence of steps," a "quality planning road map."

Figure 1
The Quality Planning Road Map

The planning road map requires that the customers be identified, their needs (in their own language) be determined, those needs be translated (into our language), that units of measure and "sensors" to evaluate quality be established, that a product be developed and optimized to meet those needs, that a process to produce the product be developed, optimized and test piloted, and that the process then be put into operation. The first three steps in Juran's road map, identifying customers and their needs and translating those needs into our language, mark out what is commonly called the mission-development process. And it is those steps which CMU/CBA's mission-development process followed.

Catalysts for Change

Two events were the initial catalyst for change. First, in 1991 the AACSB announced that henceforth a significant portion of its decision to award accreditation would depend on a school's ability to show substantial continuous progress toward achieving an appropriate, self-defined, periodically-reviewed mission. No longer were accreditation candidates to be straitjacketed in a business-school mold shaped by AACSB. Rather, within reasonable limits, each school was free to fashion its own unique mission. The catch, of course, was that that very mission set the standards for judging a school's candidacy. This shift by the accrediting body has been the most powerful contemporary impetus for the renewal of business schools. One other critical requirement was appended to AACSB's mandate: significant faculty participation in mission development, implementation and review. The essential ingredients were thus assembled for business schools to look at core processes and devise systems for continuously improving them. To be accredited, a school must demonstrate (and the emphasis is on demonstrate) that it can "effectively create, deliver, evaluate and improve instructional programs; and make innovations in the instructional process" (Evangelauf, 1991).

The change in standards had a major impact upon the CMU/CBA. Whereas the AACSB had applied a predictable and defined set of standards in the past, the new standards would be based upon a new mission statement which had not yet been developed. The CMU/CBA was to be held accountable to demonstrate outcomes which indicated at least continuous improvement toward achieving its mission. This change posed a serious challenge! The consequences of inaccurately defining the mission, or not providing compelling evidence of its attainment, would be the loss of accreditation which CMU/CBA had worked so hard to obtain.

The second catalyzing event occurred within the College in the summer of 1991. AACSB's standards had been announced and the College had to somehow respond with a strategy for re-accreditation. Initial discussions leaned in the direction of cosmetically patching up the old mission statement and getting on with the day-to-day work of running a business school. But a group of four department chairpersons vigorously argued to undertake a fundamental, grass-roots review of the College and its work, a TQM-oriented agenda and essentially an application of Juran's road map model, even though doing so would consume a great deal of time and faculty resources. The four were persuasive, and the dean endorsed a Statement of Recommended Process for Developing the College of Business Mission, a statement drafted by the four and embodying their vision.

What was striking about the drafting of that statement was that the four chairpersons were widely respected by the college's faculty as being open and fair minded. Furthermore, they were, as are all chairs at this University, viewed more as members of the faculty, leading members to be sure, rather than members of the administration. Thus, faculty ownership was much more likely to be achieved than if some renewal process had been imposed from the top. And, just as importantly, the dean's approval and support was quickly achieved. In fact, as a tangible product began to appear, administrative support became even more encouraging and enthusiastic. So seeds for the initial behavioral requirements for significant change, participation and support throughout all levels of the organization, were sown at the very start.

The Statement of Recommended Process is worth examining for a moment as a model of what, in hindsight, appears to be a wise mission-development process, a type of process endorsed by a number of well-respected authors (Drucker, 1973; Hubbard, 1992; Juran, 1988). The Statement first marked out a philosophy and a set of values, then described the main tasks and subtasks of a mission-development process and, finally, recommended a process for developing and ultimately monitoring the mission.

The Statement's philosophy and values, simply stated, proved to be workable, providential and inspirational. The language used is instructional:

> In recent years, organizations have achieved success in development of missions, goals and strategies via a broad-based, participative process. Thus, the planning process is designed to obtain a diversity of viewpoints from external and internal "customers" of the organization. The results from such a process include: identification of a wide spectrum of ideas, a partnership and joint ownership of the process and outcomes, and facilitation of a team approach in execution of strategies. It is essential that each participant in the planning process approach the task with:
>
> ❖ An open mind to accept and consider new information
> ❖ A broad-based, holistic perspective, looking beyond provincial self-interest
> ❖ A tolerance and respect for new ideas

❖ A realization that the organization's destiny is to be determined by our collective decisions and actions

❖ A view that we will be able to achieve more in a mode of teamwork than we will as independent entities

The broad-based, participative philosophy described above, when made operational in the College's mission-development process, requires the following:

❖ Extensive faculty involvement

❖ Identification of relevant College of Business stakeholders and solicitation of their input

❖ Evaluation of stakeholder input

❖ Dissemination of information about the process and outcomes

❖ A procedure for formally accepting the resulting mission statement

❖ Allocation of sufficient time and resources to the process

The tasks to be performed in developing a mission were outlined in some detail by the Statement, and clustered around three activities: planning, executing and reviewing. As for planning, a steering-committee structure was recommended and charged with the following "fundamental process elements:"

❖ Conduct an initial survey of faculty, asking for their views about future directions for the College of Business

❖ Utilize small, faculty focus groups to explore survey results

❖ Identify appropriate stakeholders and solicit their input

❖ Share stakeholder input with faculty and provide a means for faculty to discuss the implications of information provided by stakeholders

❖ Provide an opportunity for faculty to make recommendations to one or more drafts of mission and goal statements

❖ Provide formal acceptance procedure (possibly secret ballot) of a proposed statement of mission, goals, objectives and strategies

As for execution, the Statement set the challenge to manage the mission-development process to a successful conclusion. A successful conclusion is one that achieves a comprehensive, college-wide mission statement; measurable and realistic goals and objectives; strategic directions for the College; and, implementation plans and programs.

As for review, the Statement recommended that a process be established for continuously assessing the College's performance and, in light of those assessments, to periodically review the mission, goals, objectives and strategies.

In sum, both the catalyzing events and documents for change in the CMU/CBA were TQM oriented: The AACSB's new standards for accreditation and the College's adoption of the Statement of Recommended Process. The latter statement in particular echoed Juran's quality planning road map.

ON THE ROAD:
DEVELOPING A MISSION

As a result of the Statement, a Mission Development committee was elected by the faculty, and authority was granted to the committee to add additional members as it saw fit. Representation was from each of the College's departments, as well as a representative of graduate programs. Over time, the committee asked two of the four chairs who had drafted the Statement to sit with it, and their participation was invaluable.

The committee's work thus far, for it is still continuing, has fallen into three categories: identifying stakeholders, surveying stakeholders, mapping competitors and articulating a mission and goals. These conform to the first three steps of Juran's model.

Identifying Stakeholders

The committee's first task was to identify stakeholder groups. That task was swiftly accomplished. Five stakeholder groups were identified within the College: undergraduate and graduate students, alumni, business faculty and business chairpersons. Four stakeholders outside of the College (but within the University) were identified: academic department chairpersons (whose departments were in some instances suppliers to or customers of the College, and in any event were jointly responsible with the College for University graduates); deans of other colleges and the provost; the president and Board of Trustees; and the directors of the University's external degree programs. Finally, the committee identified seven stakeholder groups external to the University: current employers, potential employers, Michigan community colleges, accredited business schools in Michigan, parents of business students, potential (future) students, and the state legislature (and in particular its Higher Education Appropriations Committee).

Surveying and Mapping

The second task of the Mission Development Committee was to survey the stakeholders. All surveys followed the same general format; demographic and parallel information sections were followed by a section soliciting information specific to the particular stakeholder.

A good deal of time went into the design and administration of the surveys, at least six months in all. That time, as matters later turned out, was time well spent. For one, it gave the committee members time to get to know and work with one another at a task which was not immediately threatening to any member or department. Consensus forged here laid the groundwork for future consensus when decisions became more difficult.

For a second, it permitted the committee to evolve a drafting technique, the use of a principle drafter, which was to serve it well throughout its work. Each committee member was given primary responsibility for drafting the survey for one or more stakeholders. No survey would be administered unless it had received the approval of all of the committee members, and there was, in fact, a good deal of suggestion-making and reworking of all of the surveys. But, the principle drafter was given a good deal of discretion in deciding how to meet suggestions and concerns, and considerable weight was given to the drafter's judgment. While most surveys went through four or five drafts before they were even pilot tested, the use of principle drafters saved time in the long run and produced a better result. The committee was able to do what a committee does best – react to specific text placed before it – and was able to avoid what committees do worst – writing as a committee.

A third productive use of time was to bring students into the surveying process. Four advanced marketing-research students doing independent study were assigned to assist in drafting and piloting the student surveys and in structuring focus-group interviews with small (five- to eight-person) groups of graduate and undergraduate students. The marketing-research students gained valuable practical experience in their chosen profession, including a formal presentation of their work to the Mission Development Committee, and the committee gained valuable assistance in its work. We believe the use of students set an important example, one which should be followed in the future.

The surveys, largely constructed on a Likert scale with some open-ended questions at the close, were designed to elicit information of two types: what precisely the responding stakeholder expected from the College, and the degree to which those expectations were met or unfulfilled.

The surveys and other available data provided a wealth

of information to the committee. Some results were consistent across groups surveyed, while others varied among stakeholders. In general, the committee found that the College's graduates had a reputation among employers for good, but not outstanding quality, and a reputation for a strong work ethic; that faculty had good academic credentials, were productive teachers and researchers, were well prepared in the classroom, and prepared graduate students well for the transition to the professional business world, but undergraduates less well; that further strengthening in the areas of computer facilities and instruction, international experience, and undergraduate analytical and communication skills was necessary; that relations with the business community needed to be strengthened, particularly in the areas of internships and fund raising; and that significant work to improve faculty collegiality across department boundaries was necessary. That summary does not do justice to the enormous detail generated by the surveys, nor the difficulty that the committee had in coming to consensus on the conclusions to be drawn from that detail.

It is worth noting that the committee viewed the stakeholder surveys as an opportunity, in some cases a first opportunity, to open a dialog with the various stakeholder groups, and so approaches were made in such a way as to make possible and invite continuing discussion with the groups. Particular attention was paid to the faculty, and on numerous occasions reports and results were provided to the faculty. Every effort was made to make faculty aware that their perspectives were encouraged and welcomed, and that mission development was a grass-roots, organization-wide affair.

While the survey process was proceeding, the committee also did some strategic mapping. It identified universities that were competitors for the students thinking of coming to our University, and business schools whose graduates competed directly in the job market with our graduates, and mapped those institutions and ours on dimensions of cost, size and quality factors. That mapping helped the committee better visualize our College's competitive position and played a role in the mission statement that was ultimately developed.

Articulating a Mission

As the committee had been designing, administering and evaluating the results of surveys and mapping, it continued to wrestle with the notion of what kind of mission statement could be developed. The answers did not present themselves magically. In an important sense, the answers had to be invented; a shared commitment had to be shaped and forged. The transition from collecting data to crafting a vision was very difficult. Not only had six months of thinking and talking and surveying and mapping not produced any ready answers, a crucial threshold still had to be crossed. Would the committee opt to cobble together a mission that would hopefully satisfy AACSB accreditation requirements, a mission that replicated the traditional three-legged stool (teaching, research and service)? Or would it be able to transcend the familiar and articulate a mission that truly drew on the talents and resources that the College had available to it? To be sure, the four chairs in their earlier draft of the Statement of Recommended Process opted to go beyond the old and familiar mission. But this was a different committee, and the decision had to be made anew. The decision was made, and the committee opted to leave tradition behind. But that crossing was not easy. And the committee was in some confusion as it did so.

Over a six-week period, ideas started to cluster around two key components of what eventually became the mission statement. First, survey comments made by students, faculty and employers led the committee to believe that any earlier emphasis on teaching as a central mission was misplaced, and that clearer direction could be gained by focusing on learning.

Thus emerged the **learning-centered focus**. In the words of the mission statement as finally drafted:

> At the heart of our mission is the need to foster and further our students' learning. Student learning – not teaching, not research, not programs and courses, not even students per se, but student learning – is central to our mission. Teaching, research, programs and courses, students themselves, are all parts of the process of learning, but they are not the product. Student learning is the product. Student learning is a joint product of the amount of effort and preparation that the student brings to the task (strong work habits, a sense of purpose, basic competencies and liberal studies) on the one hand, and, on the other, the quality and quantity of interactions the student has with others (faculty, other students and, in the College's case, business professionals). We are dedicated to building an environment which expects, supports and demands active student involvement in learning, and to developing a system of assessment which monitors student learning and its components and is used for continuous improvement of learning.

The second key component emerged from lengthy discussions of student, alumni and employer survey results. All three wanted students to be better prepared to make the transition from college to work. One way of doing that is to increase the number of contacts between students and business, hardly a novel proposition, but one around which a very clear consensus developed. Thus emerged the **business-connected focus**. In the words of the mission statement as finally drafted:

> But no process of transition is ever complete until students have had an opportunity to see their studies being put to work in the professional world. The College is committed to increasing and strengthening its ties with business professionals in order to enhance

student learning, to provide role models, to improve opportunities for student placement, to better enable the faculty to make linkages between the academic world and the world of practicing professionals, to develop additional funding sources for the College, and to provide services to the business community compatible with our mission.

To sum up, again in the words of the mission statement as finally drafted:

These two dimensions, learning centeredness and business connectedness, are synergistic: progress in one enhances progress in the other. Both dimensions are critical to the success of the College.

We should make clear that by the time these two components first emerged, after eight months of work, they did so only in terms of their labels and some oral language about what they might mean. The committee and the faculty became committed to them as central, driving concepts, but we were not yet able to articulate them in writing, or to see their depth and power. The language quoted above evolved only after a further three months of work. The committee went to the faculty at the end of the 1991-92 academic year, with a report that it was preparing, to propose a shift in the College's focus from teaching and research to learning centeredness and business connectedness, and it listed under each a few tentative goals. The faculty responded with considerable support and enthusiasm, but further articulation had to await the beginning of the 1992-93 school year.

When classes reconvened in the fall of 1992, the Mission Development Committee, taking into account faculty feedback from the previous spring, asked the faculty to prioritize and comment on the sets of goals arranged under the learning-centered and business-connected labels. The faculty responses could be characterized in a variety of ways, but it was plain that they felt a lack of coherent sense of each mission dimension, and that business connectedness found far less favor with the faculty than learning centeredness did.

By October 1992, and after the faculty response, the committee began to solidify its understanding of the two concepts, determined that such a thrust, if truly carried out, would make the College significantly different from its competitors, and concluded that pursuing a strategy of differentiation based on those two characteristics would make the College successful. Moreover, two additional components emerged to join the learning-centered, business-connected components. One was the notion of **superior value**, ultimately defined as "a small college focus on learning, with a professional school experience, at a public university tuition." The other component that surfaced was to develop a culture in the College that would allow us to make the transition from where we were to where we wanted to go. Thus emerged the fourth component, dubbed **faculty professionalism**.

The committee then reverted to its earlier strategy of using a principle drafter. One member of the committee was entrusted with distilling the views of the committee into a written draft. Then draft after successive draft was written, the committee debating each section, each paragraph, each sentence, sometimes each word. At each step, the committee furthered its understanding of the key concepts and began to envision in concrete detail what it might be like to live in such an environment. Finally, in late November of 1992, the committee took the completed draft to the faculty for discussion. After spirited discussion, and after revisions were made as a result of faculty suggestions, the mission statement was put to a vote. A document the likes of which no one could have conceived when the development process had begun 15 months earlier (including a four-month summer hiatus), a document much different from the direction the College had been drifting, passed overwhelmingly (51-1).

Buoyed by the success of the page-and-a-half mission statement, the committee began working on a more detailed set of goals. Four guidelines were set for the project: the goals statement had to be faithful to and congruent with the mission statement; it had to be more detailed and explicit than the mission, laying out clear criteria for action; the goals had to be stated in a measurable form; and the goals had to set the College on a course of continuous improvement. Development of the goals document took four months. A draft document was presented to the faculty, at a faculty meeting and with individual faculty members who had suggestions for revision. That goals statement too passed by a very large margin (48 - 7).

THE ROAD AHEAD:
MEASURES, STRATEGIES AND IMPLEMENTATION

The development and adoption of the mission statement completed the first three steps of Juran's 10-step quality planning road map. The development and adoption of the goals statement partially completed the fourth through seventh steps. The third document, (yet to be developed), an objectives and implementing-strategies statement, will complete Juran's 10-step road map. At that point, planning will be finished and the College's new directions will become fully operational.

Two notes are worth special mention here. First, no operating organization has the luxury of suspending operations for a significant period of time and planning its future; operations must continue as planning takes place. And if planning indicates that certain changes in operations are immediately desirable, in anticipation of the new plan's completion, then implementation of those changes should take place prior to the completion of planning. That is particularly true for CMU/CBA, which undergoes accreditation review in 1993-94, and which must show significant improvement in achieving its newly-defined mission. So some strategies, including a critical faculty development program on learning-centeredness (active learning, continuous improvement and learning outcomes assessment) have already begun to be partially implemented, and a few others, currently under discussion, may begin pilot operations in the near future.

A second item worthy of note is that Juran's quality planning road map is only that; it is only a **planning** road map. Once planning is completed and implementation is in full swing, two other phases come on stream: quality control and quality improvement. In the control phase, procedures to monitor the effectiveness of the new mission, goals, objectives and strategies are put in place. In CMU/CBA's case, those control procedures will be largely, though not exclusively, related to learning outcomes. In the improvement phase, results from the control procedures will be fed back into the mission, goals, objectives and strategies to improve the processes leading to the College's ultimate product – student learning. Thus, the first cycle is complete, and the stage is set for continuous improvement.

CONCLUSION

We have described the process undertaken by the CMU/CBA in developing a new mission statement, a statement ultimately approved overwhelmingly by the faculty. The process described closely follows Total Quality Management planning concepts expressed in the writings of Juran. Juran's quality planning road map serves as a framework to view the mission-development process used by the CMU/CBA. The College has fully completed the first three steps of the road map by identifying multiple internal and external customers, by doing in-depth marketing research to define customer requirements and expectations, and by translating those requirements and expectations into a mission statement. The CMU/CBA well exemplifies the TQM philosophy, and is consistent with reported activities where the business schools at Penn and Texas have applied TQM in revamping their graduate business programs (*Business Week*, 1991, 1992). But the CMU/CBA process has been used more extensively to encompass its overall mission and entire programmatic structure.

Much has been learned by implementing this mission-development process. First and foremost has been the continuous grass-roots involvement of the CMU/CBA faculty as the driving force. As research data was collected, mission statement drafts were crafted, and revisions were completed, frequent faculty contacts and meetings were made to obtain oral and written feedback. When the final draft was introduced for a vote, the Mission Development Committee presented it as the faculty's statement. The faculty agreed and endorsed it by a 51-to-1 vote. The faculty took ownership of the mission statement and its philosophies because they were based upon customer input, and upon an interactive process of translation into a format which was relevant to the CMU/CBA's faculty and environment.

A second thing learned was that language does matter in articulating a mission. Language was continuously revised and sharpened to express precisely the vision of the College and to achieve consensus on that vision. Interestingly, the language of TQM did not play a significant role. Even in a business school, talk of students as customers strikes the wrong chord. The committee itself spoke in terms of stakeholders, and the mission statement's only TQM-like references were to continuous improvement and to the product of the College being student learning. Perhaps in deference to higher education, the term TQM when used in academe should be altered to TQL or CLI: "Total Quality Learning" or "Continuous Learning Improvement."

The third lesson involved time and timing. Time is always limited, and that has the beneficial effect of spurring accomplishment. But the pressure to hurry up and get on with other things must also be resisted. Adequate time must be provided to enable the faculty to come to consensus and develop a shared commitment. Timing, as it turned out, was crucial for the success of the College's mission-development process. AACSB's change in standards came long enough before the College's re-accreditation review to give it time to think deeply about its mission. Moreover, the process came at a time in the College's history when it had a mature and stable faculty, one to whom the learning-centered focus appealed a great deal.

TQM has clearly served as a road map for a renewal of the CMU/CBA. The experience has been (and will continue to be) time consuming and, at times, frustrating, but there are no short cuts. Private industry experience has already sufficiently proved that TQM is not a quick fix. But our experience is that results are well worth the time spent. The adaptation of TQM, married to a strong outcomes assessment component, will be the essential operational framework that will enable Central Michigan University's College of Business Administration to be successful well into the next century.

REFERENCES

Blum, D. "Business Schools Rush to Revise Curricula in Response to Critics and Competition, " *The Chronicle of Higher Education*, Dec. 4, 1991.

"Calling in the Consultants to the Classroom," *Business Week*, Nov. 16, 1992, 92-95.

Drucker, P. F. *Management*. New York: Harper and Row, 1973.

Evangelauf, J. "Business School Accrediting Group Revises Standards in Effort to Improve Teaching and Foster Innovation." *The Chronicle of Higher Education*, May 1, 1991, 11+.

Fuchsberg, G. "Business Schools Get Bad Grades," *Wall Street Journal*, June 6, 1990, B1.

Fuchsberg, G. "Under Pressure, Business Schools Devise Changes," *Wall Streeet Journal*, April 21, 1991, B1.

Hubbard, D. L. "Crafting a Statement of Mission: Some Observations Regarding Meaning Form and Content," Collection of Papers on Self-study and Institutional Improvement, North Central Association, 1992, 108-115.

Juran, J. M. *Juran on Planning for Quality*. New York: The Free Press, 1988.

"Wharton Rewrites the Book on B-Schools," *Business Week*, May 13, 1991, 43.

"Where the Schools Aren't Doing Their Homework," *Business Week*, Nov. 28, 1988, 84.

Neil Story is a Michigan business attorney, and he is an associate professor of business law & regulation and coordinator of general education at Central Michigan University. His memberships include the State Bar of Michigan, the American Bar Association, the Society for Professionals in Dispute Resolution and Phi Beta Kappa. His books include *Perspectives on American Law* and *American Business Law*. He is a member of CMU-CBA's Mission Committee.

Bruce H. Allen is currently professor and chair, Department of Marketing; and associate director, Center for Instructional Technology in Marketing, at Central Michigan University.

Allen received his B.B.A. at Michigan State University, M.B.A. at the University of Akron, Ph.D. at the University of Cincinnati and Post-Doctoral study at the University of California at Berkeley.

Allen has been an active consultant for 20 years and has held executive/managerial positions in health care and the private sector. During the mid-1980s, he served as vice president for marketing and planning at a multi-hospital system located in California, where he was a pioneer in developing systems which improved quality of service. As a manager in higher education, Allen has been translating his health care expertise to higher education applications. He has authored over 40 articles, and has published in many professional journals.

15

Human Resources Improvement at the University of Pittsburgh

Shirley Tucker

As a pilot study, we are applying the principles of Continuous Improvement in the Office of Human Resources at the University of Pittsburgh. I serve as a charter member of the guidance team, a team composed of staff members whose task is to provide both the infrastructure and ongoing support for the Office of Human Resources Continuous Improvement Program. This chapter traces the guidance team's history and major accomplishments. The disappointments and frustrations we weathered suggest caveats to those interested in applying a Continuous Improvement Program to the administrative organizations in institutions of higher education.

DESCRIPTION OF WHAT WE DID
Background

Founded in 1787, the University of Pittsburgh is an urban

University enrolling more than 34,000 students locally from western Pennsylvania and world-wide from over 100 foreign countries. The Office of Human Resources (OHR) provides for the needs of about 9,700 faculty and staff of the Pittsburgh campus.

The decision to implement a Continuous Improvement Program (CIP) in the Office of Human Resources was made by the director after an attempt to introduce a CIP University-wide was deemed to be premature. The OHR would serve as a pilot test to identify and overcome obstacles to acceptance by University employees. Our revised plan is to work with one autonomous work unit (called a Responsibility Center) at a time.

Structure

It was our original intention that all 40 members of the OHR would participate in the Continuous Improvement Process by serving on a team and, initially, 35 people did.

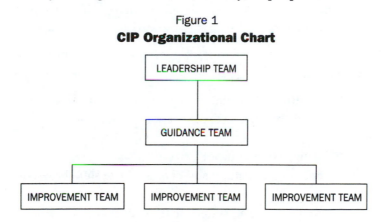

Figure 1
CIP Organizational Chart

The leadership team includes the director, the five section managers, the coordinator of special projects and the systems analyst. The guidance team initially included eight staff members serving in professional and support positions. The three cross-functional improvement teams began with 18 staff members.

The manager of employee development was charged with bringing a CIP into the organization, establishing its structure, and providing training and support services until the leadership and guidance teams were ready to oversee the process. Figure 2 depicts the flowchart for our CIP, with the functions of the guidance team marked with an asterisk (*).

Mission and Values

The first undertaking was developing a mission statement and values that everyone in the OHR could agree to. To accomplish consensus, we alternated between meeting as a total group and meeting in our sections. Virtually every word in the mission statement was discussed; values were clarified, reworded, elaborated, eliminated and/or combined. Once consensus was reached on the OHR mission and values, we signed the document with a quill pen. Each of us has a framed copy of the mission and values in our office.

Ideally, the Continuous Improvement Program in the OHR would:

❖ Educate staff in quality improvement principles

❖ Recognize that everyone is both a customer and a supplier

❖ Solicit customer input

❖ Enable staff to study and change the system based on data

❖ Provide an atmosphere that encourages continuous improvement, risk-taking and support

Figure 2
CIP Process Flowchart

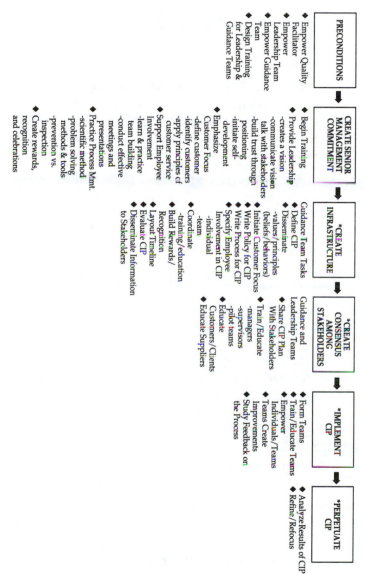

PRECONDITIONS
- Empower Quality Facilitator
- Empower Leadership Team
- Empower Guidance Team
- Design Training for Leadership & Guidance Teams

CREATE SENIOR MANAGEMENT COMMITMENT
- Begin Training
- Provide Leadership
  - creates a vision
  - communicate vision
  - build trust through talk with stakeholders
  - initiate self-positioning development
- Emphasize Customer Focus
  - define customer
  - identify customers
  - apply principles of customer service
- Support Employee Involvement
  - learn & practice team building
  - conduct effective meetings and presentations
- Practice Process Mnt.
  - scientific method
  - problem solving methods & tools
  - prevention vs. inspection
- Create rewards, recognition and celebrations

*CREATE INFRASTRUCTURE
- Guidance Team Tasks
- Define CIP
- Disseminate
  - values/principles (beliefs/behaviors)
- Initiate Customer Focus
- Write Policy for CIP
- Write Process for CIP
- Specify Employee Involvement in CIP
  - individual
  - team
- Coordinate
  - training/education
- Build Rewards/Recognition
- Layout Timeline
- Evaluate CIP
- Disseminate Information to Stakeholders

*CREATE CONSENSUS AMONG STAKEHOLDERS
- Guidance and Leadership Teams Share CIP Plan With Stakeholders
- Train/Educate
  - managers
  - supervisors
  - pilot teams
- Educate Customers/Clients
- Educate Suppliers

*IMPLEMENT CIP
- Form Teams
- Train/Educate Teams
- Empower Individuals/Teams
- Teams Create Improvements
- Study Feedback on the Process

*PERPETUATE CIP
- Analyze Results of CIP
- Refine/Refocus

Table 1
University of Pittsburgh Office of Human Resources

MISSION

Our purpose is to be an innovative leader in providing quality service to the University Community.

CONTINUOUS IMPROVEMENT PROCESS POLICY

The Office of Human Resources will meet the valid needs of the extended University community by continuously improving its services so that they are timely, correct, consistent, courteous and cost-effective.

VALUES

We promise commitment to these values and involvement in fulfilling them.

❖ Mutual respect and honesty are the foundation of all our relationships.

❖ We best serve the University when we pool our resources and work as a team.

❖ Being assertive, expressing ourselves while respecting others, promotes an effective work environment.

❖ We create a positive environment by being supportive, fair and just.

❖ Explicit and realistic expectations and the freedom to go beyond them are essential ingredients of empowerment.

Initial Training

Before the teams were formed, we all participated in a two-day training session about basic CIP concepts as well as tools and techniques for team problem-solving. See Table 2 for a list of topics.

Selection of the Guidance Team

Prior to the inception of our CIP, the guidance team members served on the OHR orientation committee. We de-

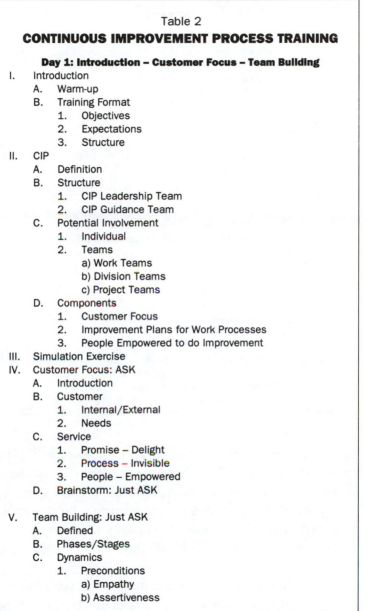

Table 2

CONTINUOUS IMPROVEMENT PROCESS TRAINING

Day 1: Introduction – Customer Focus – Team Building

I. Introduction
- A. Warm-up
- B. Training Format
  - 1. Objectives
  - 2. Expectations
  - 3. Structure

II. CIP
- A. Definition
- B. Structure
  - 1. CIP Leadership Team
  - 2. CIP Guidance Team
- C. Potential Involvement
  - 1. Individual
  - 2. Teams
    - a) Work Teams
    - b) Division Teams
    - c) Project Teams
- D. Components
  - 1. Customer Focus
  - 2. Improvement Plans for Work Processes
  - 3. People Empowered to do Improvement

III. Simulation Exercise

IV. Customer Focus: ASK
- A. Introduction
- B. Customer
  - 1. Internal/External
  - 2. Needs
- C. Service
  - 1. Promise – Delight
  - 2. Process – Invisible
  - 3. People – Empowered
- D. Brainstorm: Just ASK

V. Team Building: Just ASK
- A. Defined
- B. Phases/Stages
- C. Dynamics
  - 1. Preconditions
    - a) Empathy
    - b) Assertiveness

continued on next page

continued from previous page

      2.   Communications
         a) Non-verbal
         b) Verbal: Listen, Respond/Express, "I" Statements,
            Feedback, Consensus
      3.   Beliefs/Behavior
      4.   Conflict Resolution
      5.   Purpose
   D.   Meetings
      1.   Agenda
      2.   Minutes
      3.   Process Skills
   E.   Ten Team Troubles
   F.   Brainstorm: Just ASK

Day 2: Improvement Plans
Creating Improvement Plans: Just ASK

I.   Introduction
   A.   Overview of Process
   B.   How Improvements are Identified
   C.   How Teams are Formed
II.   Developing Improvement Plans
   A.   Clarify Team Goals
   B.   Initiate Problem Solving
III. Steps of Problem Solving
   ONE: Determine if Problem Exists
   TWO: Analyze Data and Develop Alternatives
   THREE: Implement Best Solution Experimentally

signed and implemented a program for welcoming new OHR hires and familiarizing them with our office. The CIP coordinator asked us to become the guidance team, and we all agreed to be responsible for providing the infrastructure for the office. Along with the leadership team, we would provide support for the improvement teams, specifically, and for the CIP process, generally.

The leader of the orientation committee assumed the role of leader of the guidance team by acclamation because of the enthusiasm and energy she devoted to the process. Although at each meeting we rotate the roles of meeting leader and recorder, she is our spokesperson to others in the OHR.

Guidance Team and the Infrastructure

We had read Peter Scholtes' *The Team Handbook* as part of the initial training, and we consulted it frequently. For example, we adapted his suggestions when we developed our formats for the minutes and agenda.

With the advent of the CIP, the guidance team saw a need for regular meetings of the entire staff. Over time, we encouraged the director to schedule staff meetings once a month. The guidance team leader agreed to work with the director on planning the agenda for each meeting. After about 10 months, we identified a time that is most convenient for all 40 of us and have scheduled the monthly staff meetings for the rest of the year.

During the initial implementation of the CIP in the OHR, the guidance team had concrete assignments which produced visible results. In contrast, the role of the leadership team was unclear to many of its members. We guidance team members felt the managers could support the CIP as part of their supervisory role by encouraging discussion of the CIP at section staff meetings and by teaching staff that the CIP responsibilities are integral to the job rather than nonessential additions to it.

Quality facilitators from non-academic organizations echo the need for people to perceive quality efforts as intrinsic to their jobs, rather than as supplementary and nonessential. One manufacturing company representative spoke of the company's first three years implementing quality throughout the organization. After all this time, several managers still see quality as added-on rather than as integrated into their responsibilities. This was true at another company after five years.

Improvement teams comprised of staff from several sections of the OHR were contrasted with teams operating within a section. People volunteered to be on the improvement teams, although some were encouraged informally by individual guidance team members. Only a few people chose not to participate.

We developed three improvement teams, which all began at the same time, and provided a liaison/resource person from the guidance team for each improvement team. The liaison could be called upon to assist in procedural (i.e., nonsubstantive) matters and would attend meetings when invited.

The Three Improvement Teams

(1) The orientation improvement team evolved from an orientation committee that was revising the orientation of new hires to the University (not to be confused with the OHR orientation committee).

(2) The front desk improvement team was chosen to standardize procedures for receptionists on three floors of the OHR based on recommendations from all the OHR staff.

(3) The manager of employee development suggested that we have a data improvement team. This team was charged with identifying what data we were now collecting, determining if some could be eliminated, and providing a mechanism to share it among ourselves.

The initial procedure was that at the beginning of each weekly guidance team meeting, each improvement team would send a representative to provide progress reports and discuss any issues or questions with us. However, this procedure was not implemented because of resistance from the improvement teams over issues of power and control. Moreover, some questioned the need for coming to guidance team meetings because minutes from guidance team and improvement team meetings are posted on bulletin boards in the office to provide updated information for everyone.

The First 10 Months

The guidance team is continuing to deal with problems that arise from lack of direction from the leadership team. Since putting the infrastructure in place, we have not begun a large-scale project, although designing a mechanism for rewards and recognition has been on our futures list for three months.

The three improvement teams have all lost members primarily because of perceived time pressures and dissatisfaction with the pace of problem solving. Again, these issues are common in non-academic organizations. The orientation improvement team has suffered from conflicting opinions about appropriate behavior. The front desk improvement team stopped meeting for several weeks and has recently begun again. They have narrowed their scope from three reception areas to one. The data improvement team lost three of five members. The other two people are progressing according to their timeline for reaching their objectives. None of the three improvement teams is ready to offer recommendations for improvements after 10 months.

EVALUATION PART 1: WHAT WORKED

We learned a great deal about what not to do in establishing a CIP in a small organization. Since our efforts are intended to be a pilot study, we have accomplished our original purpose. Otherwise, the list of successes is much shorter than the list of caveats.

We were pleased that the mission and values for the OHR were developed by consensus. Because the entire office worked together successfully, the process itself, as well as the outcome, was important.

The guidance team was successful with its internal team building and with providing formats for the agenda and minutes.

Overall, commitment to CIP was strong among some individuals, but not throughout the organization. Similarly, some individuals, rather than all improvement team members, worked to reach their goals.

EVALUATION PART 2: WHAT WE'D DO DIFFERENTLY
Schedule Values Identification Sessions Differently

After a brief explanation to the total group, each work unit (section) should develop its own mission and values statements. People would begin by talking about the part of the OHR that they are most familiar with and might develop greater team commitment. We would then return to the total group and combine our statements for all of the OHR. This process should be completed within a month because the time spent is perceived as a measure of importance.

Schedule Training Differently

As a prerequisite to CIP training, we would work with everyone until they developed basic skills in assertive communication. CIP requires that we work in teams and cooperate throughout the office. Therefore, we all need skills in taking responsibility for our own needs, opinions and preferences.

Once assertive skills met our standards, we would begin initial training. We would provide the entire office with an overview of the CIP process, an introduction to the Scholtes handbook and a discussion of the benefits to individuals.

We would then work with a team only as it became operational. We would focus on group-centered leadership and the overall Plan, Do, Study, Act (PDSA) process followed by just-in-time training on job-specific skills practice.

We would also train a group of facilitators to assist the improvement teams in the process involved in a CIP. It should be made explicit to team members and facilitators alike that the facilitator's responsibility is to monitor and evaluate the pro-

---

cess and not the substance of the meetings. Facilitators may offer suggestions about how to proceed, including a recommendation for additional training. This facilitator should not be a team member so that evaluating substantive ideas would not be a part of his or her role.

Training for team leaders, as well as these facilitators, should be comprehensive, including the rationale, tools and techniques for implementing CIPs. Afterwards, as with all the teams, just-in-time training would be ongoing.

The Relationship Between the Leadership and Guidance Teams

The leadership team did not provide the leadership to the OHR that the guidance team expected. Unfortunately, we did not analyze the reasons for their not walking the talk. Following the watchword of quality, we should have treated the leadership team as our customers. We should have followed the CIP process to gain their commitment or else we should have changed the CIP structure to limit their responsibilities to what they were willing and able to do.

The guidance team expected the leadership team to support the CIP as follows:

At section staff meetings –

❖ Solicit progress reports from members of improvement teams and those working on individual or section projects

❖ Discuss information from the leadership team related to CIP

❖ Ask staff to read bulletin boards

❖ Discuss items in the minutes that can be applied to the unit

❖ Solicit ideas to improve work processes

❖ Initiate projects, especially for individuals who are not on teams

When someone (staff or manager) speaks negatively about any aspect of the CIP, as appropriate –

- ❖ Clarify misperceptions
- ❖ Present a positive point of view
- ❖ Work to improve the situation for the person
- ❖ Locate the source of the problem

Serve as a role model –

- ❖ Make changes in their own management procedures
- ❖ Identify areas of weakness and areas where fear prevents appropriate interactions; plan how to overcome them
- ❖ Consider the members of the OHR staff as resources to help them do their job better – what the manager's staff do well reflects well on them and vice versa
- ❖ Think about how each section can better contribute to the "big picture" (the OHR, in general)
- ❖ Follow the OHR's values, especially respect (themselves, their staff, other managers and those who receive the OHR services)

Because the OHR is a small organization (about 40 people), there is less built-in bureaucracy. Perhaps one team fulfilling the functions of both the leadership team and the guidance team would be more effective. This team (call it the support team) would consist of the director, selected managers and staff, and an outside facilitator.

The support team would allow time at the beginning of its meetings to hear progress reports from the improvement teams, section-specific teams and anyone in the office with a CIP issue to address. No matter whether the structure includes a leadership team and a guidance team or one support team, every effort must be made for the director to champion the CIP in the office and throughout the University. Others outside of the OHR should positively anticipate the CIP coming to their areas.

Intervention For a Team
Having Difficulty with the Process

Here we refer to three needs: (1) the need for just-in-time training, (2) the need for facilitators for each team who are not members of that team, and (3) the need for an overall coordinating function.

Considering the third issue, the guidance team was reluctant to require improvement teams to report to them as planned because of the ambiguity of the leadership role in the office. The guidance team was concerned that others would react negatively to the guidance team's assuming the leadership role. We needed someone who could look at the CIP, taking the entire office into account. This person would be the CIP coordinator for all of the OHR. A University staff or faculty member serving as the CIP coordinator could bring a very useful perspective from outside the OHR.

Liaison Between the Guidance Team
and the Improvement Teams

For reasons stated above, we strongly recommend that a non-team member serve as facilitator at each improvement team meeting. Both guidance team members and others may receive training to serve as facilitators and as such would be responsible for helping the team follow CIP procedures and for identifying the need for just-in-time training.

Selection of Members of Teams

At first, we thought that everyone should be on a team and, more specifically, on a cross-functional team. The three improvement teams were cross-functional, with members volunteering or being encouraged to join a team. In retrospect, it is advisable to carefully select who is on what team based on their expertise as well as their interest. No one should join a team half-heartedly.

Also, we would recommend that sections develop internal improvement teams. Involving people in unit-specific improvements makes CIP more immediate and real, and it facilitates commitment to working toward meaningful goals.

OVERALL RECOMMENDATIONS

The philosopher Voltaire suggested that in the overall scheme of things, we must each cultivate our own garden. For quality initiatives in higher education, we recommend that you grow your own gardens, starting quite small. Instead of encouraging everyone in the organization to participate, select the first participants very carefully. Start with only one improvement team, nourish it and water it. When it flowers, begin another improvement team. We must garden to build commitment to the quality process. We assume the interest is there and that it is easier to sell the idea by starting small. Thus, we recommend that you begin with an improvement that is on a small scale and that can be solved in a timely manner. Make sure that progress is proclaimed with enthusiasm as each step in the quality process is reached.

Although speedy solutions are perceived as desirable, speed should be secondary to following the CIP process. Therefore, spending time on selling the concept of continuous improvement is vital no matter how much time it takes. It is essential to successful implementation.

Training on basic assertive communication skills should precede CIP training if people (at all levels) are not comfortable with these skills. Initial CIP training should focus on the benefits to individuals, work units and the University. This awareness training would be scheduled for one half-day. After the awareness training, comprehensive training would take place for the support team and one improvement team that was selected to begin first. Others would be trained when they begin to work on an improvement team. In addition to learning about data collection and analysis, team members would learn of their specific roles and responsibilities. Since training immediately precedes beginning to work on a team, people will have the opportunity to apply what they learn without delay.

Beginning small will make monitoring the process easier, as will having an outside coordinator to oversee the process office-wide.

It is important to celebrate the successes as the CIP process moves forward, not just at the time solutions are approved. Part of the infrastructure that the guidance team is responsible for is a rewards and recognition program which we will be working on as you are reading this book.

Continuous improvement requires that we learn from our mistakes. Based on our discussions with local groups who are involved in quality efforts from both manufacturing and service organizations, we are missing opportunities to learn from each other. Because we act independently, we are repeating each other's mistakes. The more we can learn from others, the more successful we'll be in our transition to quality, customer-driven organizations. Therefore, we highly recommend not only keeping up with the literature, but also meeting with people from regional educational and non-educational organizations to openly share what you have learned from experience – both successes and caveats.

Finally, it is recommended that the PDSA cycle is a useful tool for planning to introduce quality management to an institution of higher education. Comprehensive planning can help you avoid the difficulties we faced. Of course, learning from difficult situations is essential to continuous improvement. Plan so you avoid mistakes, learn from the mistakes you hadn't anticipated, and share that wisdom with other CIP practitioners.

Shirley Tucker has been the program consultant for employment development in the Office of Human Resources at the University of Pittsburgh since 1985.

In this capacity, Tucker serves on the guidance team of the Continuous Improvement Process, conducts workshops to introduce the concept of TQM to University staff, creates and conducts training programs, develops training for individual departments within the University, consults with departments regarding organizational development, develops special projects related to employee development and assists in the implementation of the University-wide performance appraisal program.

Tucker is active in the Women's Association of the University of Pittsburgh, a social and philanthropic organization, and the American Society for Training and Development, a professional organization.

Tucker earned a B.A. in English (Phi Beta Kappa) from the University of Michigan, an MAT in teaching English from Harvard, and a Ph.D. in educational psychology from the University of Pittsburgh.

16

Voice of the Customer: Using QFD as a Strategic Planning Tool

Burt Peachy
Daniel Seymour

The meeting was in its third hour. For the first two hours, the president and vice presidents of this small college made a detailed "state of affairs" to the Board of Governors. Things did not look promising. Enrollments had been on a steady decline. A survey of students who had been accepted, but had chosen to enroll elsewhere, suggested that the college's academic programs were seen to be weak. "I am not sure that I could get a job after I graduated," was how one person put it. Another said, "I didn't see any real-world applications." There was also a general discontent over the lack of computers.

Several major recruiters had chosen to stop coming to campus last year. According to the placement director, the recruiters said that the college's graduates had not performed well in management training programs for a number of years. The President's Advisory Board had confirmed the problem. Some of the board members said that other colleges and universities in the area were perceived to have higher quality programs, that their graduates could really "hit the ground running."

Things were going from bad to worse. The financial picture was becoming a real problem, and the local press had run a story on the enrollment decline. The question that had dominated the discussion in the last hour was the obvious one, "What do we do now?"

The dilemma is a universal one. Organizations are in the value-adding business. They take raw materials, convert or transform that input and present it to a would-be customer as output – a product or service that, hopefully, is needed or wanted. But what happens when the product or service is perceived to be second rate? What happens when the customer goes elsewhere? What happens when the microchip manufacturer or airline or college discovers that "quality" is a term used by customers to describe other manufacturers, other airlines, other colleges, and not themselves. What happens then?

Quality Function Deployment (QFD) is a strategic tool that enables an organization to capture customer's expectations and to translate those expectations into organizational language and action. QFD facilitates the analysis of product or service quality characteristics and allows these characteristics to drive internal improvements to processes that create the product or service. It also allows an organization to prioritize its process improvements and to systematically develop a plan for improvement; that is, what we do now.

Devised in 1978 by Japan's Yoji Akao, a professor at Tamagawa University, QFD has been winning adherents since being transplanted to the United States in the 1980s as part of the quality movement. Its primary benefit is that it provides a structured and systematic process to identify and imbed the "voice of the customer" into the operations of an organization. As such, it enables the organization to reallocate resources into areas and activities that have the greatest impact on customer satisfaction. It can also decrease costs. Instead of designing products or services according to internal likes, wishes and whims and then having to redesign after the customer complains, QFD helps the organization to do it right the first time. While rework is reduced, communication is increased. An extensive enumeration and clear articulation of customer requirements allows everyone within the organization to use a common language. Everyone is using the same baseline from which to guide their own thinking and actions.

Finally, QFD can increase the efficiency of organizational operations. It focuses and coordinates skills within an organization around a single item – in this case, customer requirements. The result is a better alignment of activities. A common vision is manifested in the goals and priorities of individuals who work together, synergistically, to add value that has worth to the users of the product or service.

Quality Function Deployment begins with surveying a customer base to define needs and priorities. Once such needs and priorities are quantified, the QFD process correlates customer requirements with internal functions or processes. By matching needs and priorities with internal processes, employees then have a "map" of their system and can identify what processes and process characteristics need to be improved to meet customer requirements. A matrix is used to visually describe this process which can then pinpoint where improvements need to be addressed and in which order.

Can QFD make the transition to education? Can a tool that has helped Polaroid, Ford, General Electric and Texas Instruments improve performance have the same effect in higher education? We believe that it can.

THE VOICE OF THE CUSTOMER: EDUCATIONAL IMPLICATIONS

The concept and practices of CQI are driving a new perspective about customer relations and services. Heretofore, service attributes reflected our own experiences, idiosyncrasies and individual tastes. We seem to think that, because we work within the system, we know what is best for our customers. These efforts blind us to the real information that we need in order to make better decisions. Information that can only be provided by customers. As reported in a recent edition of *Business Week*, we must go way beyond, "May I help you?" We must listen to customer's needs and expectations, by processing that information, and nurturing and developing a customer base (Armstrong/Symonds, 1992). As one of the coauthors has suggested, "A customer orientation relies upon a user-based definition of quality. From this perspective, quality is defined by the user in terms of 'the capacity to satisfy wants.' Quality is a perception, and that perception becomes the user's reality" (Seymour, 1992).

In the past, translating customers' needs and expectations into organizational improvements was a haphazard process at best, since a user's "reality" might not exist in institutional language. For example, an organization may perceive its processes to be customer-oriented, when it is in fact really oriented to making the work of its staff easier. By gathering customer information and using a tool or method to systematically match their needs to our organizational functions and processes, we can inform and direct our work toward meeting and perhaps exceeding customers' expectations; to add, in the eyes of the customer, real value to the services we provide.

In education, for example, shifting to a customer orientation in the curriculum development process should improve our capacity to meet real needs. Whether it is a redefinition of competencies to meet our external customers' requirements (business, receiving academic institutions, society) or to re-engineer the actual curriculum development process toward a more flexible and robust system capable of responding quickly to external needs, a customer focus can be a catalyst for positive change. Another application could be within a localized unit such as counseling, where student satisfaction may be paramount. Failure to identify and address student needs might drive them away from this important college service. In other words, embracing customer needs and expectations in every facet of our educational operations, in localized workplaces and broad institutional functions, is essential to a true quality effort.

Finally, listening to the voice of our customers may have its most pervasive impact when applied to our institutions' strategic planning process by generating visions and goals around a comprehensive understanding of our customers' needs and expectations. This will afford us the opportunity to "design in" quality up-front, to reduce rework, and to move dramatically from a reactive mode to a pro active approach to planning. By using this information to focus and coordinate the skills, processes and functions within our schools, we can design and then deploy services that our customers want and will continue to desire.

PLANNING STRATEGICALLY

The formulation and implementation of strategy, according to Peter Drucker, is the task of thinking through the mission of the organization; that is, asking the question, "What is our business and what should it be?" This leads to the setting of objectives, the development of strategies and plans, and the making of today's decisions for tomorrow's results (Drucker, 1974). More specifically, formal strategic planning introduces into an organization a new set of decision-making forces and tools. The most important ones are as follows:

Simulates the Future: A great advantage of strategic planning is that it simulates the future – on paper. Simulation should make managers better planners by forcing them to see, evaluate, and accept or discard a wide range of courses of action.

Applies the Systems Approach: In large, complex systems, the best solutions in each of the divisions or parts do not fit together to form the optimal comprehensive solution. Strategic planning helps us to look at the whole.

Forces the Setting of Objectives: The objective-setting requirement in strategic planning is a powerful mechanism for focusing attention and inspiring action.

Framework For Decision-Making Throughout the Organization: One of the most important attributes of effective planning is that it gives guidance to people throughout the organization in making decisions that are in line with the mission and vision.

Basis For Other Management Functions: Planning interacts and supports other management functions such as budgeting, staffing, and new product or service development.

Performance Measurements: A comprehensive strategic planning effort ensures that performance-related measures are taken to establish how well the organization is doing compared to its objectives.

Reveals and Clarifies Future Opportunities and Threats: The systematic collection and evaluation of data provides the organization with a broad view of a changing environment (Steiner, 1979).

Figure 1 illustrates a general strategic planning model in which an analysis of strengths, weaknesses, opportunities and threats drives a series of performance goals. The gap analysis is a "check" stage in which results are compared to goals, and strategies are adjusted accordingly.

What is the role of planning in higher education? According to George Keller in his 1983 book, *Academic Strategy: The Management Revolution in American Higher Education*, "Ameri-

Figure 1
Strategic Planning Model

can higher education has entered a new era that requires better planning, strategic decision-making, and more directed change. To accomplish this, colleges and universities need new procedures, structures, and attitudes." Keller goes on to argue that strategic planning in academe is critical for several reasons. First, it means that colleges and universities will become more active, instead of being passive, in the face of the forces that affect them. It will also help institutions look outward and recognize competitive market conditions.

It follows, then, that strategic planning in education asks and answers key questions with a sense of priority and urgency in an orderly manner. Questions such as the following come to mind: What are we trying to achieve? What are our underlying philosophies and purposes? What services do we want to offer? What are our markets? Who are our key competitors and what advantages do they have? What major changes are taking place in our environment that will affect us?

How does QFD relate to the strategic planning process? As Figure 2 shows, Quality Function Deployment can be used as the "engine" that drives all planning and process improvement efforts.

Figure 2
QFD-Driven Strategic Planning Model

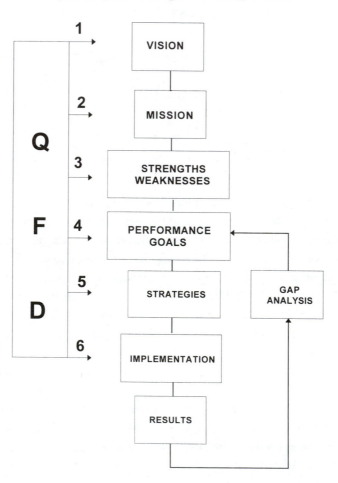

The information gathered and systematically analyzed in this way can assist the institution's leadership in planning their vision, goals, objectives and annual strategies around the needs of customers, rather than second guessing what should be improved. The following questions show how QFD customer data informs the strategic planning process:

1. Where are we going? What is our expectation-exceeding vision?
2. Why do we exist? Who are our customers?
3. Are our priorities correct? Do our strengths align with customer expectations?
4. Do performance goals reflect who our customers are and our desire to exceed their expectations?
5. Do our strategies enable us to exceed those expectations?
6. Does everyone in the organization understand questions 1-5? Are they given the resources, authority and incentives to act accordingly?

Through this process, a major paradigm shift can be affected within the campus leadership to turn from an inward planning process to one that focuses on gathering information from sources outside the institution and to rate that information against our processes and functions. This summary information can assist the leadership in prioritizing its planning efforts and focusing improvements on the most important functions that address customer needs.

QFD AND EL CAMINO COMMUNITY COLLEGE'S PLANNING PROCESS: A CASE STUDY

Step One: Gathering Customer Information

In February 1993, the president of El Camino College convened three separate focus groups representing our major customers: students; faculty and staff; community, business, and academic leaders from four-year institutions who receive our students. These three separate groups were asked the same question: "From your perspective, what needs do you have that El Camino College must fulfill in its function as an educational institution?" Through brainstorming, affinity diagramming and weighted voting, the needs for each group emerged. Each of the weighted categories were accompanied by a narrative section that focused on specific suggestions and/or problems as perceived by members of each customer focus group. This information was developed into a summary document for use by college personnel and the results returned to each focus group for their information. For the purposes of this example, we have focused on the external customer grouping that reflects the interests of community, business and four-year schools.

Community Focus Group Summary
(Weighted Averages: 10 = high; 1 = low)

Teaching Improvement (Weighted Average = 10)
- ❖ Focus on teaching students how to learn, collect, analyze and use data rather than on the **what** or content of knowledge
- ❖ Improve communication skills by involving students in dialogue and class discussions
- ❖ Concentrate on computational skills
- ❖ Create awareness of topics beyond one's own discipline (e.g. arts and literature)
- ❖ Improve teaching by team-teaching and cross-discipline techniques
- ❖ Improve training programs for staff and faculty to include total quality skills
- ❖ Develop a student teaching program

Institutional Stability (Weighted Average = 10)
- ❖ Accountability
- ❖ Financial Responsibility
- ❖ Maintain access and quality as an institution which serves "the people"
- ❖ Academic success for all students.

Secure, Stable Funding Sources (Weighted Average = 9)
- ❖ Secure stable sources for funding
- ❖ Secure non-state resources
- ❖ Build legislative ties

Lifelong Learning Opportunities (Weighted Average = 9)
- ❖ Provide reasonably-priced opportunities for:
  - ❖ Life enrichment
  - ❖ Career changes
  - ❖ Skill enhancement
  - ❖ Job promotion
  - ❖ Self-confidence
  - ❖ Teamwork skills
  - ❖ Better trained workforce
- ❖ Enforce positive benefits of work ethic
- ❖ Provide growth and enrichment programs, especially for retired adults
- ❖ Build confidence within students
- ❖ Provide a reasonably-priced education for all to use
- ❖ Provide better-trained people

Transfer Education (Weighted Average = 9)
- ❖ Provide higher education awareness and academic enrichment opportunities for students to increase their eligibility for higher education enrollment
- ❖ Continue to provide affordable and quality academic preparation for lower-division transfer students designed to facilitate their successful transition to four-year higher-education institutions
- ❖ Increase and enhance the dialogue between El Camino College and its feeder transfer institutions on behalf of the transfer function

Vocational Education (Weighted Average = 9)
- ❖ Upgrade training for entry-level positions in the workforce. Training should focus on new technologies. Expansion of vocational courses. Graduate students with complete skills for employment. Provide remedial education for underprepared students. Expand 2+2 programs with local high schools.

Cultural Diversity (Weighted Average = 8)
- ❖ Develop a diverse teaching staff using a culturally-sensitive

curriculum to provide validation of important ethnic values that reflect our multicultural society.

Business/Education Partnerships (Weighted Average = 8)
Benefits to business:
- ❖ Improved business practice
- ❖ Teach ethics
- ❖ Improved communication with local business
- ❖ Provide college-sponsored business forums
- ❖ Develop specific training & retraining
- ❖ Provide a site for government-funded projects to aid local business

Ongoing Institutional Planning (Weighted Average = 7)
- ❖ Develop an ongoing strategic planning process
- ❖ Provide 5-year/10-year master plan
- ❖ Marketing for future development
- ❖ Identify and prioritize processes for improvement
- ❖ Concentrate on quality faculty even at the expense of administration
- ❖ Provide an economic base for community development

Computer Training For All Students (Weighted Average = 6)
- ❖ Provide a computer-oriented curriculum
- ❖ Provide computer training for the general public without regard to its application to a specific course
- ❖ Aggressively seek new educational applications of technology
- ❖ Develop computer-taught and computer-assisted curriculum to reduce teacher time and effort and increase teaching and learning effectiveness

Interpersonal Skills For All Students (Weighted Average = 6)
- ❖ Teach psychological coping skills
- ❖ Develop group communication skills
- ❖ Promote psychological well being
- ❖ Personal & community spiritual development
- ❖ Create an awareness of the social impact of non-social decisions
- ❖ Teach common-sense skills

Community Resource and Education (Weighted Average = 6)
- ❖ As a responsible entity in the community, provide a forum for

educational, political, environmental, economic and other
societal issues
- ❖ Provide opportunities for developmental courses that mirror
society's needs, such as gerontological science and wellness
programs
- ❖ Provide a center of excellence for community arts development

Focus on Global and International Issues
(Weighted Average = 5)
- ❖ Include global and international issues in the general curriculum, in faculty and staff development programs and in student
support services

Nurture Alumni Involvement (Weighted Average = 5)
- ❖ Develop an ongoing program to involve alumni in college
activities and support functions

Maintain and Expand Facilities (Weighted Average = 4)
- ❖ Investigate developing a sports complex
- ❖ Continue to develop cultural venues
- ❖ Maintain the safety and beauty of the campus

STEP TWO: MAPPING THE COLLEGE'S SYSTEMS

At the same time the focus groups were meeting, a
representative group of management, faculty, staff and students was formed as a "Systems Team" whose task was to
develop a matrix of all functions and units, or "systems,"
within the College. From the initial meeting, it was clear that
the membership had differing levels of understanding about
what functions El Camino College performed. As a result of
this lack of common perception, it was decided that each
member of the team would research College functions by
talking with others and, when re-convened as a group, would
collate this information into an El Camino College Systems and
Functions "Map. " The result of this process is the following
grid:

El Camino College
Institutional Systems and Functions
(3/24/93)

Teaching & Learning
Course Development
Developing Student Outcomes
Honors Program
Instruction
Instructional Support Staff
Planning Instructional Capacity
Program Development
Scheduling of Courses
Specialized Instructional
    Facilities – Planetarium,
    Museum, etc.
State & Federal Compliances

Student Growth
Outside the Classroom
Counseling – Adult Re-entry,
    Career, Transfer
Early Outreach
Honors
Matriculation – Advising,
    Assessment, Counseling,
    Follow-up, Orientation,
    Placement
Student Affairs – Clubs,
    Leadership, Student
    Government
Student Equity – EOP&S,
    Project Success, Puente,
    Yes I Can
Student Mentoring
Student Retention – CARE,
    Early Alert, EOP&S, Project
    Success, Puente, Tutoring,
    Yes I Can

Learning Support
(Adult Re-entry)
(Foreign Student Program)
Articulation
Career & Transfer Counseling
Computer Labs
Counseling
Instructional Services
ITV
Learning Center
Library
Matriculation
Media Services
Special Resource Center
Technical Services
Testing
Tutoring

Leadership
Accreditation
Annual Planning – Short Term
Governance
Institutional Effectiveness:
    Planning – Assessment &
    Evaluation
Interaction with Board of
    Trustees
Leadership Development
Legal Aspects
Program Review
Strategic Planning – Long
    Term

El Camino College
Institutional Systems and Functions
(3/24/93)

Student Enrollment
Admissions
Articulation Council of High
 Schools
Enrollment Management
Evaluations re: Graduation
 Requirements & Certification
Outreach & Recruitment –
 F-I Visa
Records
Registration
Residency Checks
School & College Relations
Special Services
 a. F-I Students
 b. Veterans' Services
Student Recruitment
Testing & Assessment

Auxiliary Services
Athletics
Auxiliary Services Board
Bookstore – Other Books &
 Supplies, Text Sales
Campus Police
Child Development Center
Food Services – Cafeteria,
 Catering, Snack Bar
Marsee Auditorium
Parking Facilities –
 Investment
Parking Operations
Student Health Services
 Substance Abuse Programs

Financial Services
COLLEGE:
Accounting for:
 "Auxiliary Services"
 Student Programs
Budget Planning & Development
Cashiering
Developing Financial Resources
Money Management – Accounts
 Payable, Managing Invest-
 ments, Payroll
Purchasing – Contracts, Risk
 Management
STUDENT FINANCIAL SERVICES:
Financial – FOP&S, Yes I Can
Job Placement – College Work
 Study, Community Service
 Learning Program, Human
 Resource Systems (Student),
 Student Placement, Voca-
 tional Education
Student Financial Aid & Scholar-
 ship Services

Human Resource Development
Affirmative Action
Collective Bargaining
 a. AFT b. CSEA c. Police
Evaluating Performance
Health Benefits/Insurance
Labor Relations
Professional Development
 a. Faculty b. Management
 c. Staff
Recruitment & Hiring
Workman's Compensation

El Camino College
Institutional Systems and Functions
(3/24/93)

Facilities Management
Campus Security
Environmental Safety & Health
Facilities Planning –
   Short Term
   Mid Term
   Long Term
Facilities Maintenance
Inventory Management
Mailroom
New Construction
Off-Campus Facilities
Operations
Warehouse

Communications
Information Systems –
   Electronic Mail/Telephone
   Information Training
   MIS to State
   Provider of Data
   Schedule Planning
Printing –
   Instruction, Newsletters,
   Public Presentations,
   Student Information:
      - Catalogue
      - Class Schedule
      - Mandate Data,
   Public & Media Relations,
   Community Newsletter,
   (ECC Report), Newspapers,
   TV & Radio
Student Publications –
   Myriad (Humanities),
   Warrior Life (Student
   Magazine), Warwhoop
   (Student Newspaper)

Research
Institutional Research
   a. 5-Year Plan
   b. Matriculation
   c. Program Review
Market Research

External Relations
Alumni Relations
Business Partnerships
   a. Support from Business
   b. Training Needs for Industry
Center for the Arts
Chancellor's Office/BOG
Community Services
   a. Civic Center
   b. Program
Contract Education
ECC Foundation
Economic Development
   a. California Manufacturing
      Technology Center
   b. ECC Quality Institute
   c. Small Business Center
Governmental Relations
   a. Federal Government
   b. State Government
K-12 Partnerships
   a. 2 + 2
   b. Tech Prep

Step Three: Matching Customer Needs to College Functions

Utilizing the outputs from the customer focus group summaries, the "Systems Team" began matching customer needs to college functions. Using correlations (5=high; 3=medium; 1=low; and 0=no correlation) the team looked at each

El Camino College
Quality Function Deployment Matrix
(Correlations: 5=high; 3=medium; 1=low; 0=none)

GROUP: COMMUNITY/BUSINESS/EDUCATION

Weight Factor	Customer Requirements	TEACHING	LEARNING SUPPORT	HUMAN RESOURCE DEVL	LEADERSHIP	STUDENT GROWTH	EXTERNAL RELATIONS	RESEARCH	STUDENT ENROLLMENT	FINANCIAL MGMT	AUXILIARY SERVICES	COMMUNICATIONS	FACILITIES MGMT
10	Teaching Improvement	5	5	1	5	1	5	1	1	0	1	3	3
10	Institutional Stability	5	3	3	5	5	1	5	1	1	3	5	5
9	Funding: Secure Stable Sources	5	0	1	5	5	0	5	1	1	3	5	5
9	Lifelong Learning Opportunities	5	5	5	1	1	1	1	0	3	5	0	3
9	Transfer Education	5	5	5	3	5	3	3	1	1	1	1	3
9	Vocational Education	5	5	5	3	5	3	3	1	1	1	1	5
8	Cultural Diversity	5	5	5	5	5	5	3	0	1	3	3	5
8	Business/Education Partnerships	5	1	1	5	1	1	1	1	1	1	1	5
7	Ongoing Institutional Planning	5	1	1	5	1	1	5	3	1	3	5	3
6	Computer Training For All Students	5	5	0	1	0	0	0	3	0	0	0	3

El Camino College
Quality Function Deployment Matrix
(Correlations: 5=high; 3=medium; 1=low; 0=none)

GROUP: COMMUNITY/BUSINESS/EDUCATION

Weight Factor	Customer Requirements	TEACHING	LEARNING SUPPORT	HUMAN RESOURCE DEVL	LEADERSHIP	STUDENT GROWTH	EXTERNAL RELATIONS	RESEARCH	STUDENT ENROLLMENT	FINANCIAL MGMT	AUXILIARY SERVICES	COMMUNICATIONS	FACILITIES MGMT
6	Interpersonal Skills For All Students	5	3	5	1	1	1	1	0	3	3	0	1
6	Community Resource and Education	5	1	3	3	3	1	3	1	3	3	1	5
5	Focus on Global and International Issues	5	3	1	3	1	1	1	1	1	1	0	5
5	Nurture Involvement of Alumni	1	1	0	5	1	0	1	0	5	5	1	3
4	Maintain and Expand Facilities	3	0	0	3	3	0	3	5	1	0	1	5
	TOTAL	69	38	38	48	37	18	35	18	25	32	22	54
	WEIGHTED TOTAL (Correlation Factor X Weight Factor)	527	294	297	355	295	145	271	115	177	239	175	383
	Index Number	4.58	2.56	2.58	3.09	2.57	1.26	2.36	1.00	1.54	2.08	1.52	3.33

college function and correlated each customer need to that particular function. Matrices were developed for each customer group (students; faculty/staff; community/business/four-year schools) and a final summary matrix was produced that combined the needs of all three groups into a synthesized matrix, shown on the previous page and below.

El Camino College: Quality Function Deployment
Summary of Community Focus Group & System Team

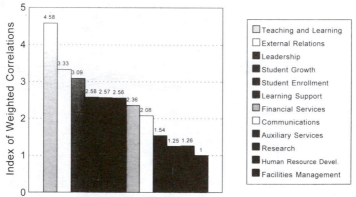

Summary of Results

By matching the weight of each customer requirement to the correlation of the college's functions, it is possible to develop a composite weighted average for each college function. From these results, it is possible to develop an index number that ranks each college function to the total needs of the community customer group. From the results of this QFD process, it is possible to deduce that the areas of teaching and learning, external relations, college leadership and student growth outside of the classroom are functions and processes that have the highest priority in meeting customer needs. Therefore, it is now possible to develop planning activities that will address our customers' needs with this "blueprint" which shows us which functions to work on.

Stages of QFD and Improvement Activity

The following is a summary of the stages of activity to demonstrate where the Quality Function Deployment activity is properly placed within a planning process towards continuous improvement:

- ❖ A survey is administered to customer/customers to ascertain their needs
- ❖ Employees "map" the processes and functions in their system
- ❖ The employees analyze customer priorities and quality requirements
- ❖ Quality Function Deployment Matrix developed
- ❖ The team prepares a process improvement plan by addressing priority functions
- ❖ When completed, the team returns to the QFD Matrix to identify the next process to improve, OR
- ❖ The team "benchmarks" the best practices of a competitor, OR
- ❖ Re-survey the customer to see if their quality requirements have changed.

CONCLUSION

QFD is a way to make "opportunities" come alive in an organization. It is a way to inform the strategic planning process by enabling organizations to prioritize customer demands, develop innovative responses to those needs, and orchestrate a successful implementation involving all units. It does this by correlating customer expectations with critical processes that produce customer services.

There are two compelling reasons why academic administrators need to consider a QFD-driven approach to strategic planning. First, the principles underlying QFD apply to any effort to establish clear relations between organizational processes and customer satisfaction that are not easy to visualize. Most colleges and universities have little understanding of precisely who their customers are and even less information about how their customers view them. Moreover, we do not know how well our products perform in the marketplace. Graduates are given a diploma, a warm and hearty farewell, and sent off to compete in corporate America. We engage in scholarly research and publish books and articles but do not know what, if any, impact such efforts have on any of our customers. QFD forces us to ask our customers about their expectations and requirements. It makes the "opportunities" part of strategic planning real.

The second reason why QFD-driven strategic planning is needed in higher education is that it urges us to think through processes and the characteristics of the processes that we use to produce our services. Our colleges and universities operate as a large collection of independent units – adjoining caves, if you will – with little knowledge of what goes on before or after them. We slice and dice our work. Each person does his or her job, then tosses the work over the wall. Instead, we need to think and act as if the entire institution is a series of customer supplier/customer linkages so that the extended process produces a needs-satisfying service. Again, QFD forces us to think less about the boxes on the organizational chart and more about the cross-functional processes that reflect how work flows through the organization.

It is the linkage between the "voice of the customer" and "how we work" that makes a QFD-driven strategic planning process a valuable way to pursue the mission and vision of an educational institution.

REFERENCES

Akao, Yoji. *QFD. Integrating Customer Requirements Into Design*, New York: Productivity Press, 1990.

Armstrong, L., and Symonds, W. C. "Beyond 'May I Help You?'," *Business Week*, January 15, 1992, 100.

Drucker, P.F. *Management: Tasks, Responsibilities. Practices*, New York: Harper & Row, 1974, 611.

Hauser, J. R. and Clausing, D. "The House of Quality," *Harvard Business Review*, May-June, 1988, 63.

Marsh, S., Moran, J.W., Nakui, S., Hoffherr, G. *Facilitating and Training in Quality Function Deployment*, Methuen, MA: GOAL/QPC, 1991.

Seymour, D.T. *On-Q: Causing Quality in Higher Education*, Phoenix, Ariz: Oryx Press, 1992, 45.

Adapted from Steiner, G. A. *Strategic Planning: What Every Manager Must Know*, New York: The Free Press, 1979, 37 - 41.

Daniel Seymour is the president of Q-Systems, a quality management consulting firm, and he is a visiting scholar at the Claremont Graduate School. Since receiving his B.A. from Gettysburg College, and M.B.A. and Ph.D. degrees from the University of Oregon, Seymour has worked in industry, and as a professor and administrator at the College of William and Mary, the University of Rhode Island and UCLA. He is a Fulbright scholar and the author of 10 books in business and higher education, including his recent best-selling book for the American Council on Education and Oryx Press entitled *On Q: Causing Quality in Higher Education* (1992). The book is in its third printing.

Burt Peachy is associate dean of institutional planning and staff development at El Camino College in Torrance, Cal. As quality coordinator at El Camino, Peachy is involved in the training and implementation of Continuous Process Improvement practices at the College. In addition, he is actively engaged as a consultant to higher education and presents training workshops throughout the country.

Of recent note, Peachy is spearheading an academic/business quality training partnership program for Sony Corporation of America in their California Logistics and Distribution Center.

Peachy holds a B.A. degree in humanities from the University of California - Riverside and an M.A. degree in theatre from California State University - Long Beach. He has done additional graduate work in communications at the University of Southern California.

17

Systems Thinking

Leslee M. Brockett
Clyde E. LeTarte

INTRODUCTION

Educational organizations, like all other organizations in this country, face the need for fundamental change in how they are managed. The organizational change that has occurred over the last 100 years has been primarily incremental rather than fundamental in nature. Incremental change occurs when core structures and thinking are modified, updated and adjusted, while the fundamental structure remains in place. Fundamental change necessitates going back to the beginning and rethinking the base structure. The new term for this is paradigm shift.

Jackson Community College has conducted a comprehensive review of our organizational structure and management. Fundamental change in the way we think about our organization is the result of our paradigm shift to systems thinking.

SYSTEMS THINKING – WHAT IS IT?

The whole notion of systems thinking was new and novel at Jackson Community College (JCC) in early 1990. One of our earliest experiences with this concept was a picture of a system/process flow chart (Addendum A), whereby resources enter the system, the organization conducts value-adding processes to produce a product, results/outcomes are achieved and customers' needs are met. We could understand the simplicity of this concept as it applied to producers of a discrete product, for example, in a manufacturing environment. However, applying this concept to the "product" of education first required a transformation in our way of thinking and the way we viewed our organization. Second, we needed to understand what the elements of a system were. Third, we needed to understand the relationship among the various elements of a system.

What is systems thinking? Peter Senge, author of the *Fifth Discipline*, describes it this way: a shift of mind from seeing parts to seeing wholes; a framework for seeing patterns and interrelationships rather than things; a discipline for seeing the structures that underlie complex situations.

Our first step toward understanding our organization as a system began with discovering the answer to this question: "How does work get done in our organization?" In other words, how do we produce our products and services? A traditional answer to this question once led us to proudly display the latest version of our organization chart (Addendum B). It told us who reports to whom; it reflected a hierarchical or vertical picture of the organization; it reflected how authority is distributed. However, it did not answer the question, "How does work get done in the organization?" In order to answer that question, we developed an understanding of the horizontal, rather than the vertical or hierarchical, view of our organization (Addendum B). We were challenged to view the entire College as a system, with various sub-systems operating within.

WHAT ARE THE ELEMENTS OF OUR SYSTEM?

Much of our training was conducted by Deming supporters. We learned early on about Deming's 14 points. Members of our Continuous Quality Improvement steering team had the privilege of attending a Deming seminar. In our quest for CQI, we were charged with advocating Deming's fifth principle: "Improve constantly and forever the system of production and service." However, we were unaware of what our "system" of production and service was. We could not improve it until we understood it. So, we needed to answer these questions:

1. Who are our customers and what are their needs?
2. What are our products and services?
3. How do we know if our products and services are any good?
4. What are the outcomes and results we expect to produce?
5. What are the systems that produce our products and services?
6. What are the resources required to operate the systems?

By answering these questions, we developed our "system map," and, over time, developed an understanding of system interrelationships, of the structures and processes underlying the complexity of our organization, and began seeing the whole, instead of just the parts. The evolution of our understanding of this system is still in process. Our conceptual view of the JCC system has changed several times and will change further as our learning continues to evolve. Our system map, in its current form, details our current thinking regarding system interrelationships.

CREATING OUR SYSTEM MAP

JCC's system map reflects the major systems and the multitude of sub-systems that constitute our total organization. We first identified the major systems in the organization, which assisted us in visualizing the organization as a whole, in terms of both structure and process (Addendum C). Those major systems include: supplier systems, management/planning systems, administrative/support systems, and producer systems. We also identified the primary sub-systems underlying those major systems. Each sub-system has been identified with a "mail-box address." Each of those sub-systems is managed by a "system owner, " usually an administrator in charge of that function. Faculty and students assume the greatest responsibility for the teaching and learning.

As all sub-systems are flow charted and documented, we will see more clearly the linkages and connections among the sub-systems. As improvements are made on a sub-system, we will have knowledge of the impact that changes have on other connected sub-systems.

Supplier/customer relationships will be easily recognized. Workers will be able to answer the questions, "Who do I depend on, and who depends on me in the system?"

A significant impact of our system map on the organization is that workers see where they "fit" in the organization; they see how their sub-system contributes to the success of the whole, and they clearly understand the purpose and goals of the organization, as identified in our producer systems.

We used the analogy of an orchestra during our initial overview training session for all staff to describe the concept of JCC as a system, with many varied sub-systems operating within it. We imagined what being a great orchestra would require:

❖ Every member is a master at playing his or her own instrument and has a method for continuously improving his or her own performance

❖ Every member knows how his or her part contributes to the performance of his or her own section and practices with them regularly to improve

❖ Every member and every section knows how they contribute to the performance of the entire orchestra

❖ Every support function knows its role in helping the orchestra make beautiful music and works to continuously improve its service to other functions and to the orchestra

❖ There is regular feedback from every member and from audiences, patrons and professionals about their needs, and the organization anticipates future needs

❖ Each member of the organization shares a vision of perfection, contributes joyfully to its pursuit and is valued for his or her contribution

Coincidentally, our understanding of system interrelationships has proven helpful in achieving another of Deming's 14 points – "break down barriers between departments" – as faculty and staff from across the organization cooperate and collaborate on system improvements.

ACHIEVING OUR PURPOSE

The producing systems that constitute the work of Jackson Community College are: 1) teaching and learning, and 2) community development. Those two primary activities are what we're all about! This is what we produce to achieve the purpose and aim of our organization and to meet the needs of our customers.

Our direct customers, those who "receive" our products and services are: other educational institutions, employers, and community and society. These customers receive individuals (our students) who possess knowledge, skills and abilities to perform on the job, transfer to other institutions, and perform in community and society. In this way, community development also occurs.

A striking revelation that occurred within the past year is the realization that students are not our direct customers, but are instead internal customers. This view has been debated extensively by members of the faculty and staff as well as by members of our Board of Trustees. Our belief is that students are active participants in our producer system; in essence, students are "co-producers." The learning that occurs is a cooperative effort between students and the faculty who instruct them. This belief came as the result of a shift in our way of thinking about the interrelationships between students and faculty.

Dr. Michael Walraven, dean of instruction, describes this relationship: "If our core process is learning, our core product must be what is learned. Accordingly, our products, those things which we market to our customers, are knowledge, skills and abilities. These products are produced by the interaction of faculty members and students, working together for common goals. While the instructor assumes responsibility for the initial design of the process, the student shares the responsibility for putting the process to work and ultimately embodies the products of learning."

SYSTEM IMPROVEMENT

As our understanding of our organization as a system was still evolving, we began training employees in the skills, tools and techniques of improving systems. Our first five breakthrough team projects were focused on improving subsystems. They were: career services system, financial aid system, telephone answering system, course schedule production system and purchasing system. These systems were selected as initial practice projects for training purposes, since, at the time, we were novices at system improvement.

To make meaningful system changes and improvements,

team members first needed to understand how the current system worked. Our employee training, conducted by two nationally-renowned trainers, Carole and David Schwinn, covered six principles for total quality transformation. These six principles are: customer needs, systems, variability, knowledge, planned change and people. The "systems principle" states that customer needs are satisfied through purposeful activities, or systems; systems are created to satisfy customer needs. All systems have a purpose, output, resources and processes. Addendum D provides further details regarding the systems principle.

In addition to the breakthrough team projects mentioned above, various staff members began using their newly developed skills of CQI in day-to-day work situations. One particular project that had good results had to do with the course scheduling system. Employees who worked directly in this system made changes to the system by placing a certain number of sections of high-demand courses on "closed reserve" in an attempt to reduce course offerings by 20 percent. The concept here was that as scheduled classes began to fill up, a closed reserve section could be opened as needed. This reduced the prospect of having many sections with lower enrollments and increased the likelihood of offering fewer sections, with a greater number of students per section. In essence, courses were scheduled "on demand."

The changes worked. We were able to reduce the number of sections that semester, while increasing average class size. This resulted in a considerable savings to the institution, since fewer adjunct faculty were needed to teach extra sections. System improvement was achieved! However, we overlooked the interrelationship between course scheduling (opening reserve classes as needed) and textbook ordering. As closed reserve sections were being added, the bookstore was not included in the information loop; therefore, textbooks for these various new sections were not ordered in advance. Imagine the irritation of students who were unable to purchase necessary books until several weeks into the semester. We learned what we had been preaching – that action on one system impacted another. One aspect of systems thinking, our ability to see the interrelationships and connections between different systems, will help us avoid this kind of situation in the future.

MANAGING SYSTEMS

As our knowledge and understanding of systems has evolved, so has our understanding of the role of managers. No longer just supervisors of people and tasks, managers are now responsible for managing systems. Of the many problems faced by any organization, expert opinion suggests that at least 85 percent are system problems and are the responsibility of management; the remaining 15 percent or less are problems with people. Traditional management practice rewarded those who could create a quick fix to problems, with little thought given to longer-term repercussions. While fire-fighting is still a necessary evil, recognition for superior management will go to those who understand systems thinking, who manage complex systems effectively and who implement systemic improvements, not just quick solutions. In order to make systemic improvements, managers must know how to: identify systems, standardize system processes, implement improvement, study the results and plan continuous improvement.

The challenge that lies ahead is in our ability to create new systems, not just improve current systems. We will undertake in the near future a variety of "design projects," whereby new systems will be created to meet current and emerging customer needs. We will again need to answer the six questions mentioned previously, as well as determine where the new systems will fit in the existing system map. The exciting aspect of design projects is that we will create new systems from a blank slate.

CONCLUSION

We are now at a point in time where management has made the shift in thinking as described previously. This restructuring of our thought process has given us a collective vision of where we need to go and what we need to do. We have begun the process of involving all employees. With that involvement comes deeper strength and commitment, in addition to new ideas. This is an evolutionary process. What we describe today may not – probably will not – be the same as that described a few years into the future. We are a learning organization that will continually test old ideas and adopt new ones. The exciting part of what we are now embarking upon is in releasing the power of the organization to improve, with freedom for each individual to feel important and to be involved in the effort.

According to Deming, "If you want to be world competitive in quality and productivity, it's management's responsibility to create the system for continuous improvement." Jackson Community College has created a system for improvement; we call it QI3 – Quality Improvement, Involvement, Initiative. Our ultimate goal is alignment within the organization in how we think – our paradigm; how we are structured – our systems; and how we behave – our actions. One element of the QI3 process is our focus on system thinking. Improving constantly and forever our systems of production and service will ultimately make Jackson Community College a world-class educational institution.

REFERENCES

Senge, P. *The Fifth Discipline: The Art & Practice of the Learning Organization.* New York: Doubleday, 1990.

Deming, W. E. *Out of the Crisis.* Cambridge, Ma.: Massachusetts Institute of Technology Center for Advanced Engineering Study, 1986.

QIP, Inc./PQ Systems, Inc.: *Foundations for Leaders and Foundations for Teams,* 1991.

Non-System View:

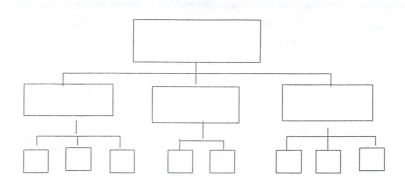

System-based View:

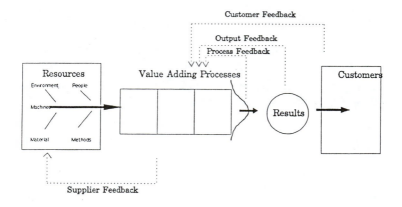

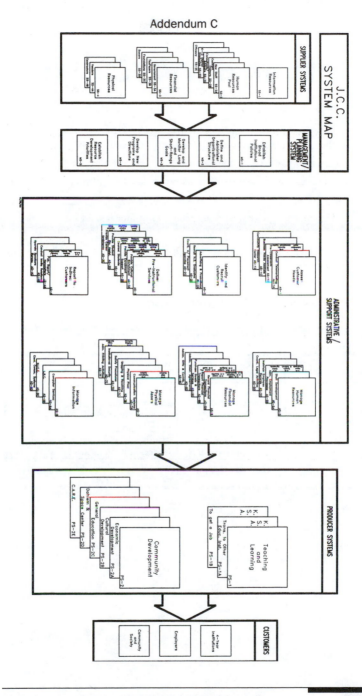

THE SYSTEMS PRINCIPLE

Customer needs are satisfied through purposeful activities, or SYSTEMS.

1. A system is a set of related entities that receives inputs, adds value to them, and produces output to achieve a defined system purpose.

2. Organizations/enterprises are systems created to satisfy customer needs.

3. Organizations/enterprises are made up of interrelated sub-systems.

4. All systems are subject to the same risks: interaction and suboptimization.

5. All systems have common characteristics.

Characteristic	Definition	Answers the Question
Purpose	Aim, mission, primary concern	Why does the system exist? What need does it fill?
Output	Products, services, information (Includes quality measures)	What does the system produce to achieve purpose? (How do you know the output is any good?)
Resources	Physical, financial, and human requirements	What is required to produce products, services, and information?
Processes	Sequence of events	What steps are required to transform materials to output?

Leslee M. Brockett is the dean of community and business services at Jackson Community College. In that capacity, she provides leadership and supervision for job re-training programs, contract training, continuing education, community outreach and off-campus extension center programs and services. She has worked at Jackson Community College since 1986.

She is currently involved in two projects to study and improve the competitive position of Michigan's community colleges in the areas of workforce development, economic development and training.

Brockett is a member of the JCC Continuous Quality Improvement lead team, and participated in the original planning and training conducted by Florida Power and Light Co.

Brockett holds a B.S. degree in education from the University of Akron and an M.Ed. degree from Kent State University in higher education administration.

Clyde E. LeTarte assumed the JCC presidency 10 years ago during a period of economic fallout that was changing the fabric of the Jackson community.

Recognizing that the college would have to develop new programs and services to help local businesses remain viable and to re-train the growing numbers of unemployed workers, he immediately directed resources toward that end. Jackson Community College faced the economic downturn of 1991 with sound academic and job training programs in place and skilled teachers ready to help. The institution now boasts an enrollment of more than 7,000 students, a rise of nearly 15 percent during his tenure.

Before coming to JCC, LeTarte served Triton College in Illinois for four years as vice president for academic affairs. He holds a doctorate in education from Michigan State University.

18

Implementing TQM in a Research University

Patricia Kovel-Jarboe

The University of Minnesota - Twin Cities Campus began the process of adopting Continuous Quality Improvement in 1991. Through a series of both conscious and out-of awareness decisions and application of the Plan-Do-Check-Adopt (PDCA) cycle, Minnesota has developed (and continues to evolve) a strategy for implementation of Total Quality Management (TQM) in a research university.

Research universities differ from other post-secondary institutions, not just in the purpose, scope and range of their activities, but also in the values and expectations of their students, staff and faculty. Thus, it stands to reason that the adoption of Continuous Quality Improvement and its exact nature in the research university may also vary from models found elsewhere in higher education.

WHAT IS CQI AND TQM?

Quality is hardly a new concept in higher education, but over the last few years it has come to be used in a new way. In the past, when we spoke of quality, we tended to mean richness of resources. Thus, more majors, a larger library collection, the number of National Merit Scholars or other quantitative measures would be taken as indicators of quality. The evolving view of quality takes it to mean the degree to which student and other stakeholder needs and expectations are consistently satisfied (Seymour, 1992).

Total Quality Management (TQM) or Continuous Quality Improvement (CQI) is a comprehensive philosophy of living and working in organizations; it emphasizes continuous improvement; its fundamental purposes are to improve quality, increase productivity and reduce costs (Chaffee and Sherr, 1992).

Based on what major proponents have to say, five elements characterize quality improvement as practiced in higher education (Chaffee and Sherr, 1992; Miller, 1991; Harris and Baggett, 1992).

1. It is focused on an identified **process** or **system** that can be described (flow charted) and linked explicitly to other processes and to institutional goals. Typically, quality improvement works on processes (or systems) in an organization, one by one, redesigning them to make them simpler and thus reducing the opportunities to make mistakes.

2. It is designed to identify, understand and meet **customer needs**. The staff member waiting to be paid and the financial controller are both users of the travel reimbursement process; both sets of opinions should count. For introductory calculus, students, instructors of subsequent courses, employers and graduate schools should all be involved in defining quality.

3. It relies on **data** to define needs, describe problems and arrive at solutions. Quality improvement uses scientific methods to analyze data, construct and test hypotheses and evaluate results in order to solve problems.

4. It involves those who make decisions about improvements and is sponsored by an appropriate manager or decision maker. Quality improvement requires more than participation; it necessitates the **empowerment** of those who work in and on a process day to day to identify problems, generate solutions and satisfy customers.

5. It **respects individuals** and their contributions whether they are customers, team members, administrators or colleagues. Quality improvement does not permit administrators to abrogate their management responsibilities, but it does rely on the capacity and responsibility of all players to make things better.

Despite the complementarity between these characteristics and many of the values which characterize higher-education institutions, Continuous Quality Improvement has been a hard sell in the academy and especially in research universities. (When Minnesota began its implementation of TQM, we were able to identify only a handful of peer institutions that had adopted or were planning to adopt CQI.)

THE UNIVERSITY OF MINNESOTA - TWIN CITIES

The University of Minnesota - Twin Cities is a comprehensive, research university (Carnegie Research I) located in an urban area of approximately 2.5 million people. It is the state's land-grant university as well, and its only research and Ph.D.-granting institution. These combined roles make Minnesota unique among peer institutions.

(The UM system also includes campuses at Crookston, Duluth and Morris and a graduate center in Rochester. The character and missions of these campuses differ significantly, and they are not discussed here.)

Like other major research universities Minnesota prizes its autonomy; it receives only about 25 percent of its funding from the state of Minnesota, with the second largest source of income being grants, contracts and gifts. During the 1980s, the University of Minnesota went through several retrenchments; in 1991, when the Quality Improvement Initiative was begun, the University had just undertaken a $58 million internal reallocation and restructuring to be spread over five years.

The University of Minnesota - Twin Cities has approximately 38,000 students studying in 24 colleges and another 22,000 registered in extension classes. Of these students, 10,000+ are in graduate and professional schools. About 10,000 degrees are awarded each year. The University employs about 6,000 academic employees (faculty and administrative positions). The University has a Board of Regents, appointed by the governor, charged with establishing policy and oversight for the full range of University activities.

In the mid-1980s, a strategic plan entitled "Commitment to Focus" was developed and adopted. The central goal of that plan was to increase quality (and thereby achieve excellence) by focusing institutional resources in areas of strength or great potential strength and curtailing other programs. As a result, the University of Minnesota had increased its admission standards, decreased undergraduate enrollments and sharpened its research profile by the early 1990s.

Throughout these efforts, the University had maintained a strong tradition of faculty voice in institutional governance. Tremendous value was placed on operating the University in ways that emphasized its academic nature and its ideal as a community of scholars and learners. But there was tension between those who espoused the need for professional management and those who viewed management as a concept without application in the academic environment and these tensions had increased in recent years.

THE DECISION TO ADOPT CQI

The formal decision to adopt Continuous Quality Improvement came midway in the current president's second year in office, but it was a decision that had been some time in coming. In assuming the presidency, the University's senior administrator had expressed his belief that "something more" than a good plan and clear vision would be required to move the institution into the future. The quality movement was something that he'd heard about and thought warranted further investigation.

Meanwhile, the vice president for finance had been approached by a University-industry group urging him to lead the University in adopting TQM. As a newcomer to the world of higher education, his most recent position being in health care administration, the VP was familiar with the quality movement and acceded to the group's urging. He became an early campus advocate for quality and also offered a set of support units where improvement practices could be tried.

Some introductory training was provided to administrators and managers in finance and operations units, and to a handful of other University administrators. This training did not emphasize real or potential applications of Continuous Quality Improvement in education or service organizations but tried to cover the conceptual framework for quality, the use of statistical process control and the process improvement tools. A few pilot projects were initiated subsequent to the training. With no further training and the untimely death of the sponsoring VP, some of these fledgling efforts continued, but in rather desultory fashion.

One of the associate academic vice presidents who participated in the finance and operations training saw the potential to apply continuous improvement to not just administrative processes but also academic and student support systems. He was able to gain the backing of the academic VP and president, who readily understood that real improvements in key institutional processes would have to involve both academic and administrative units. At this point, the responsibility for what was later named the Quality Improvement Initiative was placed in the Office of Academic Affairs. The associate vice president was charged with the task of further examining the advisability of implementing Continuous Quality Improvement on a large scale and, if advisable, organizing the effort.

Although not well articulated at the time, this decision – to locate responsibility for continuous improvement on the academic side of the University – has proved to be key in gaining the attention (and ultimately, we hope, the support) of faculty.

In May 1991, after two days of consultant-led training for the president and his cabinet, the formal decision was made to move ahead with quality improvement and to hire a coordinator.

THE STRATEGY

On the occasion of his inauguration, and reiterated at subsequent University events, the president had spoken of the need "to change our ways to preserve our values." This became one rationale for the adoption of Continuous Quality Improvement.

We knew the importance of administrative commitment to the support of any quality improvement effort, but we also knew that a purely top-down decision to move in this direction would encounter major resistance in the environment of a research University such as ours. Our challenge was to design an implementation that would be true to the values and practices of continuous improvement, while at the same time remaining true to the values and traditions of the academy.

Our initial strategy had several components:

Involve academic, administrative and support units. Other educational institutions that we observed had been successful in adopting CQI, first in administrative areas and then later in academic and student support offices. But, we feared that doing so at Minnesota would send a message suggesting that CQI was really something most suited for business processes. We decided that it would be best to try to involve all areas of the University from the beginning.

Start slowly and develop in-house capacity to support the effort. As noted above, we did not think that a top-down, comprehensive implementation would work in our culture. Nor, did we believe that extensive reliance on consultants would encourage the effort. By starting slowly and building our own infrastructure and expertise, we thought we would have the best chance of arriving at a model that would last.

Balance risks and visibility in early projects. By balancing risks with visibility in our early efforts, we hoped to have the advantage of attracting attention and creating awareness without making too many public mistakes. The advantage of using the PDCA cycle as a model and metaphor for what we were doing was that it allowed us to try things on a small scale and examine the results before moving forward.

Take advantage of units with high interest and low resistance. Units with high levels of interest would, we thought, be more likely to stick with the improvement process until results could be achieved, as well as being more likely to sign on in the first place. We wanted to find out the nature and extent of any resistance we would encounter, but we felt that we could do so without getting resisters involved in projects or other activities.

Eschew reliance on a single quality guru or rigid model. In an institution the size of the University we decided the likelihood of an ideal or model fitting every situation and unit was extremely small. Rather than start out with a single approach and try to rigorously enforce it, we decided to focus on essential characteristics and a general model or framework and let people make adjustments to meet the needs of specific situations or units.

Given the strong role of the faculty in institutional governance and the tradition of faculty resistance to adoption of business practices, we were concerned about creating either of two equally damaging perceptions. We did not want to appear to ignore academic concerns, nor did we want to force academic units to participate before they felt ready. Our decision was to implement three pilot projects, two of them in academic support services, and to try to get a better sense of what resistance we might encounter.

BARRIERS TO ADOPTING CQI

Through informal conversation and focused group discussions with faculty, we found several common themes associated with resistance to TQM in our University. Many of the same themes were also heard among other University groups, although in general we found greater interest and receptivity among administrative, clerical and technical employees.

Clearly, the **language** of quality was a problem for faculty. The terminology was seen as too oriented to the business world, too glib and lacking in rigor. After several discussions, some key ideas had emerged – that "total" couldn't possibly be, and that moderation should be our watchword; that "quality" is like pornography, undefinable and subject to community standards; and that "management" is barely tolerable, and not something to be sought out. In a similar vein, faculty were also concerned about the top-down nature of quality programs and what they perceived to be a faddish "all or nothing" approach that did not allow for reasoned debate and disagreement.

It was also clear that the concepts and practices of quality were viewed as **atheoretical**. This contributed to the belief that TQM was just a fad and like other fads, it would pass. Because much of the literature of quality did focus on practical, hands-on issues, it was understandable that even relatively informed faculty would hold this view.

Finally, there was a group of faculty who were informed enough about Continuous Quality Improvement to use its tenets against it. They pointed to the **lack of data** about application of quality practices in education. Until a convincing case, using real data from peer institutions, could be presented, Minnesota should hold off on adopting TQM. Likewise, some faculty set themselves up as customers of the University administration; since the faculty weren't asking for TQM, why should they be expected to accept it?

Since our goal was to implement Continuous Quality Improvement in our academic as well as administrative units, we knew that we needed to be able to address these concerns in order to be successful. But, as a participant in one of our initial training session noted, "When I look around the University at its hundreds of processes and systems, I can see it doesn't matter who the customer is – everything is set up to meet the needs of the senior faculty." Even if this is an extreme view, it suggests that there is a good reason for faculty to be cautious in giving their support to quality improvement. Optimism came from the knowledge that most faculty do care very deeply about their students and about the many other groups who stand to benefit from University activities.

THE FIRST YEAR

In terms of the Plan-Do-Check-Adopt (PDCA) cycle, our first year was a period of planning and small-scale experimentation to collect data which would allow us to design an appropriate system. Three pilot projects were initiated and completed; several training sessions for leaders, facilitators and teams were held; a steering committee was established and it developed a workplan; and much discussion took place, especially among administrative groups.

As soon as some of the barriers to adoption were identified, we developed a background paper which was circulated widely within the University. The paper described our quality improvement initiative and tried to establish it within the framework of the scientific method. It introduced a minimum of TQM jargon and attempted to defuse, implicitly and explicitly, some of the arguments against Continuous Quality Improvement. (Quality improvement is not the only campus initiative. We used the terminology deliberately to draw attention to the effort while at the same time putting it in a familiar context. We do not generally use the term Total Quality Management internally to describe what we're doing, although some University staff do.)

The three pilot projects were focused on major, cross-functional institutional processes. A registration project identified reasons why students were unable to complete the registration process with a single attempt; the project ultimately produced solutions for improving the process by eliminating several different kinds of barriers. A second project resulted in improvements to the processes by which prospective students are informed, admitted and advised of housing and financial aid decisions.

The third of the original pilot projects examined the causes of increasing volume of intra-campus mail and looked at customer needs and expectations; the project team put forward a set of recommendations which are still being implemented.

All project teams used the same model for process improvements, but each adapted or modified some steps; we have encouraged people to do so, reasoning that the model – like the problem-solving and management/planning tools – should structure rather than drive Continuous Quality Improvement. We believe that this is one way we can allay the fears of those who see TQM as too rigid and prescriptive for the academic/research environment.

The next paragraphs provide a few words of description about our teams and improvement process.

Most of our teams, pilot and subsequent, have had five to nine members. We use sponsors to support and give legitimacy to improvement efforts, typically the sponsor for a project is the administrator to whom the team leader reports. The sponsor is responsible for the initial charge to the improvement team and for implementation of the solutions generated; he or she is not usually a member of the team.

The team leader is the person who has day-to-day responsibility for the process being improved or is someone who shares in that role. If the team is not an ongoing work team, together the sponsor and team leader identify others to serve on the team and invite their participation. Each team is assisted by a facilitator from outside the immediate scope of the project; usually this is someone recruited through the coordinator's office. Each project which receives outside facilitation is asked to identify someone from the project or another involved unit(s) who will be trained and later assigned as facilitator on another project.

Over time, we expect the need for "outside" facilitators to drop. We want our staff to internalize the practices that lead to Continuous Quality Improvement, but until we have reached that goal, we have found it useful to have someone on each team whose primary responsibility is ensuring that the improvement process and quality tools are used and used appropriately. The facilitator is also the person who is most able to assist the team leader in managing the group's dynamics.

The basic improvement model we use consists of eight steps:

1. Target a problem or process for improvement
2. Identify customers and assess their needs
3. Select a specific issue
4. Describe (flow chart) the current process
5. Establish performance measures or benchmarks
6. Collect and analyze data
7. Develop solution(s) and test their effectiveness
8. Implement the new process/solutions

As noted earlier, while teams are encouraged to follow the process, they may add steps or take the steps in a different sequence, depending on the process they're improving and the opportunities/challenges they encounter. Some projects need to first ensure that the process they plan to improve is in control.

From the pilot projects, we received feedback about the training and team support that had been provided. We have, as a result, moved to a just-in-time approach to training. This means that we provide each team leader, facilitator and sometimes team members with an overview of the improvement process, basic information on group dynamics and an introduction to quality tools. With this training, teams get started. We then work with the team leader and facilitator to anticipate what skills and tools will be needed at each step of the process. Leaders and facilitators work in partnership to teach the rest of the team what it needs to get the job done.

Based on feedback, we are improving the support system for leaders and facilitators by providing additional kinds of training, peer-support networks and all-project discussions on a quarterly basis. We have plans to establish a computer-based discussion on quality that will allow sponsors, leaders and facilitators to raise and respond to questions from their peers. (We will also cross-post information from various electronic lists dealing with quality.)

In 1992, the president established a Quality Improvement Steering Committee. The committee has members from a variety of units involved with or interested in continuous improvement. Clerical, technical, administrative and academic staff are all represented. Several members of the faculty serve, including one who has been active in campus governance. The committee is chaired by the senior vice president for finance and operations.

Charged with developing and implementing a quality work plan, the Steering Committee is a working group that meets monthly (or more often) and carries out assignments between meetings. In addition to identifying activities and strategies for supporting continuous improvement, the committee developed performance measures for the various components of the work plan. It also drafted a vision for quality which provided a starting point for senior administrators to develop an institutional vision statement. This activity is being undertaken as part of the institution's strategic-planning process. To date, the vision has not been developed nor released, although this is set for the near future.

STEPPING UP THE PROCESS

Beginning in 1993, we tackled a number of challenges in moving Continuous Quality Improvement from the stage of planning, experimentation and data collection to an established and integrated part of the University's operations. We have about three dozen projects underway and several hundred staff and faculty who have received training in the basics of quality improvement. As noted earlier, we are using the data we've collected on the improvement system to strengthen and fine tune it.

One way of thinking about what's been done to this point is to compare it to the elimination of variance in the University system. On a small scale, we have attempted to create an awareness of the principles and practices of continuous improvement and have brought them to bear on a handful of critical processes. We have begun to achieve some of the small gains that can result from getting our processes into control. We must now face the task of real improvement – deciding which of the institution's critical processes should be targeted for change, fitting the philosophy of Continuous Quality Improvement into the planning process of the University, and changing the budget and reward systems to reflect our commitment to quality.

INSTITUTIONAL RESPONSE TO CQI

The various segments of the University population have responded to the quality improvement initiative in diverse ways. The Board of Regents has been interested, but not particularly aggressive, in pushing for adoption of Continuous Quality Improvement. They are, as might be expected, particularly interested in the issue of accountability and have seemed more inclined to a view of quality which focuses on inspection (for example, audits) than on quality as a result of attention to customer needs, process control and system redesign.

Senior administration has been largely supportive of the project efforts which have occurred but has failed to really integrate the philosophy of continuous improvement in their individual functions or the institutional processes for which they have responsibility. Some remain skeptical about the benefits that might come from continuous improvement and would argue that more time is needed to determine if the pilot improvement projects have yielded significant benefits or mere changes.

Middle managers are indeed in the middle. They do not perceive that the institutional commitment to quality is real or will last. They view their own roles as perhaps the most vulnerable to change or elimination if CQI becomes the University's way of life and, thus, they have serious reservations about supporting the effort. They point, and rightly so, to the lack of alignment between the rhetoric in support of quality and the traditional organizational reward systems. Despite these reservations, middle managers do see some opportunities for their units in adopting at least some of the practices of quality.

Faculty members, at least in small numbers, have been involved in some of the projects, are engaged in the teaching of quality concepts and have exhibited a surprising lack of resistance to the quality movement on campus. They continue to have difficulty with the language of quality – customer is still a "red flag" term in many departments – but otherwise appear to be unconcerned. We do not know if this results from the way in which we introduced Continuous Quality Improvement, because we had overestimated the degree to which faculty would be resistant, or simply because many are still unaware of our attempts to implement CQI. Given the intensity of faculty resistance to Continuous Quality Improvement observed by the author at the 1993 meeting of the American Educational Research Association, the second possibility seems remote.

Clerical and technical staff are sometimes in the middle like their managers; other times they are extremely eager to implement TQM and frustrated that some of their peers and managers are so uninterested. Layoffs have been necessary in recent months, and staff express concern that efficiencies resulting from quality improvement efforts might lead to additional layoffs. Though no layoffs have yet been attributed to our quality initiative, this fear is real and will probably continue unless we are able to gain wide agreement on other means of handling any staff reductions.

Students have not been a significant part of our quality initiative except in their role as critical customers. Those students who are aware of the University's new emphasis on Continuous Quality Improvement applaud it. Enrollment in quality-related courses has increased in the past two years, and the new MBA curriculum integrates continuous improvement across all courses.

RESULTS

While the University is not fully satisfied with the results of its quality improvement initiative, we see a number of successes as well as problems. Most of the projects have continued to completion; this means that teams have persevered through any difficulties to the point of producing solutions. But, few projects have completed the implementation of those solutions, although most are still being pursued. And, it is still too early to measure with certainty the results of implementing those solutions.

In looking at projects and team members, we have observed some benefits that we had not anticipated, although perhaps we should have. (The findings reported here are based on interviews and surveys with individuals who have participated in training and/or an improvement project. Results have not yet been fully analyzed or reported.) Almost all team members report feeling a greater sense of connectedness to the University as a result of having been on an improvement project. Most also report a better understanding of their roles and assignments. Involvement in continuous improvement, either through teamwork or participation in training, appears to increase individual's optimism about the University's future.

We have observed an increase in the use of terms and

concepts from the quality movement; while we know that use of the rhetoric does not necessarily mean accompanying use of the philosophy and practices, we regard adoption of the language as an important step in attitude formation. As noted in the section on response to the quality initiative, support for continuous improvement has developed in almost every internal constituency; however, there are still significant problems to be overcome.

As more University staff become interested in quality, the tensions of changing such a large organization become more apparent. Research universities have tended to encourage the individual entrepreneur or faculty star. Even our reward systems for administrative, technical and clerical staff have mirrored those applied to the faculty. While teamwork may not have been officially discouraged, institutional reward systems have certainly not been designed to support it. The requirement for teamwork to carry out continuous improvement is perhaps fortunate in coming at the same time that the research community is acknowledging that good research is becoming more interdisciplinary. The combined pressures of these two forces may be enough to speed changes in values and reward systems to include greater support and encouragement for team efforts.

NEXT STEPS

Earlier comments alluded to the need to integrate the philosophy of continuous improvement with the University's vision and critical processes; this is probably the most important issue facing us. Without this integration and the resulting alignment (horizontal and vertical) within the institution, we cannot continue to say that the University of Minnesota is committed to Continuous Quality Improvement. One example of the kind of integration needed is to move support for quality improvement training from its current home in the coordinator's

---

office to the human resources function. This will ensure that new employees are exposed early to the organization's emphasis on continuous improvement and will reinforce the idea that Continuous Quality Improvement is the way University of Minnesota staff carry out their assignments.

As this takes place, we also need to deal with other issues facing us. For example, we need to continue to seek the involvement of faculty and middle managers in specific improvement projects. We need to determine the means by which the Board of Regents can support and encourage the improvement initiative. We need to work at integrating continuous-improvement concepts and skills into the curriculum, and we need to find ways to involve our students in applying, as well as learning, the principles and practices of quality.

CONCLUSIONS

So far, the strategies we adopted for our implementation of Continuous Quality Improvement seem to be serving us well. We would be prepared to recommend them to others in similar situations. But, our experimentation has shown some areas in which we would recommend changes to our colleagues in other research universities.

We would try to involve all segments of the campus community as early in the implementation process as possible, while at the same time avoiding forced projects in units without readiness. Since none of us should expect the quality transformation to occur overnight or even in a few years, we think a slow start that leads to a solid foundation is preferable to a quicker but mandated adoption. It may be obvious, but we believe it's harder to change a culture you don't understand. A slower start allows time to learn about the current culture and, as a result, allows for the development of appropriate change strategies. We think it's improbable that an off-the-shelf model of continuous improvement will fit most research institutions;

---

it's important to take the time to develop your own customized version.

Among the changes we would recommend is earlier attention to establishing measures to indicate when the organization will be ready to move from testing and experimentation to full-scale implementation. Such measures might include: number of projects completed, nature of their results, percent of faculty and staff expressing interest, degree of integration with key university processes, etc.

Likewise, we would place more emphasis on the measures of administrative commitment and set firm timelines for achieving them.

We would choose our pilot projects carefully and would probably make them more narrowly focused. We think cross-functional projects make good sense as pilots, but they can be more difficult to organize and make it more difficult to track results. In most organizations, they have the advantage of high visibility and clearly signal that Continuous Quality Improvement is different from what it is replacing.

We would try to balance the practical side of continuous improvement – process-improvement projects and problem-solving tools – with a greater emphasis on the philosophical and conceptual aspects of continuous improvement. We have found it much easier to establish improvement teams and incorporate the improvement model than to instill the new way of thinking that is essential to Continuous Quality Improvement.

If we weren't already involved in Continuous Quality Improvement, would we start? The answer is "yes." We wouldn't do it exactly as we have done, but we would use many of the same strategies.

REFERENCES

Chaffee, E. and Sherr, L. *Quality: Transforming Postsecondary Education.* ASHE-ERIC Report no. 3. Washington, D.C.: George Washington University, School of Education and Human Development, 1992.

Harris, J. and Baggett, M. (eds.) *Quality Quest in the Academic Process.* Birmingham, Alabama: Samford University, 1992.

Miller, R. (ed.) *Applying the Deming Method to Higher Education for More Effective Human Resource Management.* Washington, D.C.: College and University Personnel Association, 1991.

Seymour, D. *On Q: Causing Quality in Higher Education.* New York: American Council on Education/Macmillan Publishing Co., 1992.

Patricia Kovel-Jarboe has been the University of Minnesota's quality coordinator since May 1991. Since joining the University of Minnesota in 1980, she has held various administrative and professional positions, primarily in the areas of instructional technology and distance education. She is an adjunct faculty member in the Department of Speech-Communication, and she also teaches an administrative development course on teamwork.

Kovel-Jarboe has a Ph.D. in communication with an emphasis on organizational communication and master's degrees in communication and library science from the University of Minnesota. She has been active in the development of the Academic Quality Consortium, a new organization which advances the concepts of CQI to provide a foundation for the transformation of higher education.

19

Schoolhouse of Quality

Robert E. Bush
Betty J. Bush

INTRODUCTION

In the 1950s, the Toyota Ship Building Division experienced construction delays, conflict in system design, production misalignment, assembly slowdowns and failure to deliver ships as scheduled. In order to meet production goals and delivery dates, internal stress between departments and employees was at an unacceptable level. The Toyota experience was not unlike the phenomenon associated with many assembly plants. Indeed, the American auto industry functioned with the same conflict model as was experienced by Toyota. As a result, it often required six years for a car to move from the conceptual design phase to the showroom floor. The buying public all too commonly experienced similar frustrations as they purchased products or services in the marketplace.

The experiences of Toyota and of American auto industries sound all too familiar to American educators. Educators today are similarly faced with inordinately high stress levels, resulting from issues such as uncontrollable student drop-out rates and high school students who fail to perform at minimum level. Pressures from governing agencies, irrelevant and out-dated curricula, inordinately high professional burn-out rates and a vast array of other issues also contribute to tremendous stress on teachers at all levels, parents, administrators and, especially, students. Many issues faced by education today are the result of poorly-designed, outdated or irrelevant curricula, which fail to meet the needs of students and communities. Often the preschool-through-college curricula fail to encourage the necessary skills and knowledge bases which are relevant to the employers in the world of work and the world of dynamic change.

THESIS

The thesis for this chapter is based on the assumption that many of the processes used by educators are similar to or identical to those employed in industry. If the reader accepts this assumption, then it is logical to pursue how Toyota and selected American auto industries escalated their 1950s products and services to "world class" level in the 1980s and 1990s. Education should search this body of knowledge to identify successful strategies and principles which can be implemented in resolving a variety of educational issues.

RATIONALE

World-class industries employ numerous Total Quality Management (TQM) and statistical process control techniques and measures to bring about their corporate, cultural trans-formations. Industries use a model commonly called the **House of Quality** as a basic design process to execute an approach titled Quality Functional Deployment (QFD). The strategy for using QFD is to employ a series of **"Houses"** to resolve design, product development, production, manufacturing and marketing issues. In all cases, cross-functional (interdisciplinary) teams manage the **"Houses"** to eliminate isolation or individuals for work units. The combined effort leads to a better product or service, delivered in a shorter time period and at less cost. This is accomplished in the name of customer satisfaction.

We will address one technique, **The House of Quality** (Hauser and Clausing, 1988), and how it relates to one educational issue – curriculum redesign. For the purpose of adapting the model to education, the name has been changed to **The Schoolhouse of Quality**. We believe that the same industrial model techniques can be used to design school curricula and address other educational issues.

It is appropriate at this point to examine a number of perceptions of QFD as reflected in the literature written about quality. Smith and Reinertsen (1991) define QFD as "... a rather elastic label used for a variety of decision-making techniques that rely heavily on matrices to present and analyze information systematically." Shores (1990) defined QFD as a way "...to deploy the voice of the customer horizontally from product development through manufacturing quality control." Schonberger (1990) postulated that all versions of QFD seemed to have certain things in common:

"... they oblige the product development team to reach out to the customer to define and rate needs, and they require that competitive analysis be done." Schonberger additionally comments that "... the added benefits of the matrices and other procedures are gravy." Caplan (1990), like Schonberger, states that "QFD places more emphasis on the customer's considerations and provides a mechanical method for organizing the decision processes...."

CONCEPTS AND TERMINOLOGY OF QUALITY

In the above reflections, several words or phrases hold special significance and warrant further explanation. Customers are the key drivers behind the quality movement. For any Total Quality Management/Continuous Quality Improvement concept or quality implementation programming to be successful, a customer or set of customers must be identified. The QFD process requires customer needs as a basis for the design process and assessment. It is paramount, therefore, that a committee (preferably a trained functioning team) charged with curriculum redesign first define the customer base. No external source can make this judgment, but a judgment must be made. Few curricula are designed with customer needs in mind, starting at pre-school and continuing through elementary, middle school-junior high, high school, technical school, college, and finally graduate and professional schools.

Process, as associated with QFD, is a key strategy that implies that all activities associated with designing, planning and teaching from the curriculum can be measured or assessed for effectiveness and reliability. When customers' expectations are met or exceeded, the process calls for a celebration. When the effort falls short, the planning assumptions should be reevaluated. The first step in the process is to **plan** a new strategy or improvement, then **do** an experiment on a small scale to test the new hypothesis. Results must then be **studied**. If the results are positive, the team is ready to **act** on the change by incorporating the successful strategy into the process or curriculum. Feedback results in more Continuous Quality Improvement activities. If the experimental strategy proves unsuccessful, it is necessary for the team to re-initiate the process by developing a new strategy.

This simple **"Plan, Do, Study, Act"** cycle was first described by John Dewey over 100 years ago. Its simple design will never fail if an honest attempt is made to implement the

---

cycle.

The cycle requires the work of a **team**. A cross-functional team is a trained group of individuals who represent a broad base of disciplines and customer representatives. In the case of a curriculum team, multi-grade-level teachers would be involved as well as representatives from elementary, middle school, junior high and high school; parents; university; technical school; labor; government and industry. Such a cross-functional team is necessary if a truly collaborative effort is to be successful in meeting reasonable customer expectations.

Schonberger (1990) refers to "competitive analysis" as another requirement. For QFD to be truly successful, one must compare or **benchmark** the process results with "best in class" or "world class" to determine the degree of comparative success. Without such comparison data, a team might be misled as to their true level of success or degree of accomplishment. Another way to describe benchmarking is a recognized standard of performance for a given product or service. The following definitions further explain benchmarking as used in industry.

Balm's definition (1992):

> The on-going activity of comparing one's own process, product or service [curriculum] against the best-known similar activity, so that the challenging but attainable goals can be set and a realistic course of action implemented to efficiently become and remain best of the class in a reasonable time.

Xerox Corporation's formal definition (Camp, 1989):

> Benchmarking is the continuous process of measuring our products, services and practices against the toughest competitors or those companies recognized as industrial leaders.

Finally, **time to market** refers to the time required to design, produce, test, manufacture and market a new product

---

or service. Fifteen years ago, it took the United States auto manufacturers nearly six years to build a newly-designed car. Today, by employing QFD techniques, it is around three years; the goal is two years.

Traditionally, it takes years to design, produce, test, distribute and teach a new curriculum. We must reduce the time required to redesign curricula, as the redesign must be a dynamic, continuous process in order to stay current in a rapidly-changing world. Each working day, 6,000 scholarly papers are written, for a total of 1,500,000 manuscripts annually added to the knowledge base. If educators are to take advantage of this information explosion, a process must be in place which allows changes to occur in a timely, organized and systematic manner.

With these key words and phrases, a profile emerges which establishes the criteria for the development of a cross-functional team. This team employs a process for curriculum design which will analyze information and data in a systematic fashion against benchmark standards to meet customer needs in less time. Before considering how the Schoolhouse of Quality is constructed, one must examine specifically how QFD applies to curriculum design.

Quality function is defined in terms of customers' needs or expectations of the curriculum. **Deployment,** as used in this context, refers to the strategy selected to deliver the curriculum to the customer in an appropriate time frame.

In the 1970s, the Toyota Kobe shipyard in Japan was the first to develop a series of matrices (**House of Quality** Model) to pictorially integrate design, production, and manufacturing processes. Customer needs (specifications) were also integrated into the spread sheet or map to illustrate how the entire process came together to produce a product in a timely manner. Matrices are used by management to show relationships between a variety of variables.

Webster's Ninth New Collegiate Dictionary defines matrix as "... something within which something else originates or develops...." Basically, it is a simple graph with information or data depicted on the abscissa (horizontal) axis and information flowing along the ordinate (vertical) axis. The intersection of any two data points originating from the two axes reports "new relationships" or performance levels. For example, if the team wanted to know the relationship between learning achievement and time on task, a simple graph or matrix would pictorially illustrate the resulting relationship.

In the **Schoolhouse of Quality** model, a series of matrices is brought together to resolve conflicts, set priorities, rank customer needs and benchmark against "best in class" or "world class" standards.

The rationale for using the matrix as a tool for curriculum planning is based on the need for a clear picture or map to illustrate the process the curriculum team is undertaking. The process clearly quantifies the rationale used to establish priorities and statements of value added. Juran (1992) offers the following rationale for serious consideration in matrix planning. For clarity, we have inserted words or phrases to base the selected statements in the curriculum development process.

❖ The numerous combinations of customers and needs require a structured approach to product [curriculum] development

❖ The spreadsheet [also matrix, quality table, etc.] is the major tool used during a structured approach to quality planning

❖ Criticality should be viewed from the standpoint of both customer and the supplier

❖ In case of internal [elementary, middle or high schools within the district] monopolies, it is often possible to secure competitive information from outside suppliers [other districts]

❖ Past behavior of customers is a useful leading indicator, a predictor of future behavior

❖ Product [curriculum] developers should use customers' perceptions as inputs to decision making, since customers act on their perceptions

❖ A major benefit of modern methodology is that it forces the [curriculum] designers to quantify certain elements that in the past were often glossed over

❖ Concurrent planning is likely to become the dominant form [for curriculum design] during the next century

❖ Choice of inputs should not be a monopoly

❖ The spirit of teamwork generated during completion of a project [curriculum writing] does not stop with the completion of the project; it carries over into the day-to-day operation as well

❖ [Curriculum] Goals should be written out

❖ [Curriculum] Goals should be approved by the appropriate authority

We also suggest that the curriculum team should produce, in writing, a document of shared values as a ground rule guide for working together as a team and that all team members sign the document, with copies distributed to each member.

CONSTRUCTION OF THE MODEL

The following discussion will be simplistic by design. As the curriculum team becomes more comfortable with the Schoolhouse model, its complexity can be expanded to meet the individual needs of the team. The construction of the Schoolhouse matrix will be accomplished section by section. This process will illustrate the importance of the individual matrices and the emerging interrelationships.

The model is driven by reasonable customer requirements for the curriculum, based on data gathered from questionnaires, focus groups and other techniques. The team begins the process of collecting what the customer perceives as essential for the curriculum. This process may identify hundreds of items or expectations. The team will use a variety of quality tools and statistical process control techniques (GOAL/QPC, 1988) or the team's expertise, to cluster similar items and eliminate duplication. This clustering technique of customer attributes is referred to as "bundling" (Hauser and Clausing, 1988). Customer attributes are described in broad terms by customers to reflect their needs or expectations. The team must decide on the descriptions that best define the customers' "bundled" attributes (see Example 1).

Example 1

Bundles	Customer Attributes	%
World Of Work	Critical Thinking	15
	Communication Skills	15
	Content Area Knowledge	15
	Decision Making	10
	Responsibility	15
Social Skills	Team Work	10
	Values Education	10
	Human Dynamics	10

The team's cross-functional professional expertise and customer knowledge is then used to determine the "relative importance" of each attribute. It is extremely important to weigh what customers say versus what they do (Hauser and Clausing, 1988).

This requirement may cause dissention and polarization of the team if not carefully executed. The team membership must use consensus as a technique to reach a decision. The importance of the team's "shared values" can play a major role in supporting team consensus. The scale used by the team to determine "relative importance" is a team decision; however, a scale which totals 100 percent is typical (see Example 1).

In public education, curriculum developers do not traditionally think in terms of other schools as competitors. However, in many communities, a significant portion of the public perceives private schools and home-based instructional models as viable alternatives to public education. Additionally, with the option of free choice, all schools will be competing for students in the future. Having identified customer attributes in Example 1, these attributes now serve as a basis for the comparison of the team's existing curriculum and the curricula employed by team-selected competitors. The same customer populations which generated the customer attributes now rank the attributes on a one-to-five scale for the existing curriculum. The same process is followed for the A and B competitor curricula. This process has brought the team to the point where they have received customer perceptions of what the customer wants in the form of a new curriculum as expressed in their statements of customer attributes. The same customer group has provided the team with feedback as to how they perceive the existing curriculum in comparison with two or more competitors (see Example 2).

The customers have indicated what to do in the curriculum, and educators determine how to do it. The team must now

Example 2

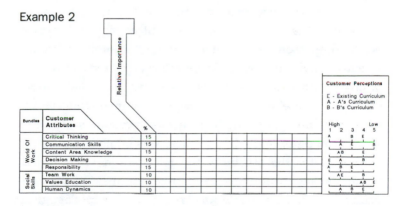

express the curriculum in pedagogical characteristics for the instructional program. This information is entered along the top of the matrix. Specifically, this process identifies those pedagogical characteristics that are likely to affect one or more of the customer attributes. It is critical that all pedagogical characteristics are measurable, i.e. test scores, third-party benchmarking, performance ratings, portfolios, demonstrated skills, etc. (see Example 3).

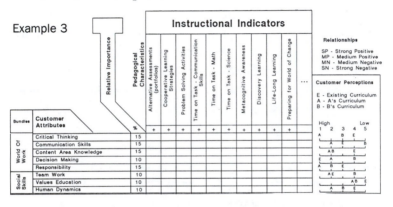

A series of positive and negative signs are used to signify opportunities which can enhance or reduce the curriculum impact on a specific customer attribute. A negative sign indicates a reduced impact of the pedagogical characteristic on the customer attribute. Conversely, a positive sign indicates a positive impact on the customer attribute. A customer attribute which is unaffected by pedagogical characteristics (neither positive nor negative) provides a new and uncharted opportunity to increase the impact of the curriculum on the instructional program. For example, if in 1980 a customer attribute stated "computer literacy" and there was no pedagogical requirement for the attribute, the team could have added "computer instruction" to the curriculum, making the curriculum much more viable for the future. If no pedagogical characteristic can be matched to a customer attribute, the team needs to search for "overlooked" customer attributes which may have been compromised in the "bundling" process. The pedagogical characteristic may also be judged ineffective or unnecessary and be eliminated (see Example 3).

The matrix is now in place for the team to make vital decisions by making notations within the structure of the House using "relationship" symbols as listed in Example 4. The resulting "relationship matrix" reflects how each pedagogical characteristic affects each customer attribute. The team leaves blank those relationships which have no effect. As identified earlier, consensus by team members is the guiding principle to complete the matrix. The team identifies a set of "relationship" symbols and/or color codes that best meets their needs to complete the matrix (see Example 4).

Example 4

Instructional Indicators

Relationships
SP - Strong Positive
MP - Medium Positive
MN - Medium Negative
SN - Strong Negative

Customer Perceptions
E - Existing Curriculum
A - A's Curriculum
B - B's Curriculum

Bundles	Customer Attributes	Relative Importance %	Alternative Assessments (portfolios)	Cooperative Learning Strategies	Problem Solving Activities	Time on Task - Communication Skills	Time on Task - Math	Time on Task - Science	Metacognitive Awareness	Discovery Learning	Life-Long Learning	Preparing for World of Change	Customer Perceptions
			+	+	+	+	+	+	+	+	+	+	High 1 2 3 4 5 Low
World Of Work	Critical Thinking	15	SP		SP		SP	SP				SP	A B E
	Communication Skills	15		SP	MP	SP	MN	MN				SP	A E B
	Content Area Knowledge	15				MP	SP	SP				SP	A B E
	Decision Making	10		SP	SP							SP	E A B
Social Skills	Responsibility	15		SP							SP	SP	A B E
	Team Work	10		SP						MP		SP	A E B
	Values Education	10							SP		MP	MP	A B E
	Human Dynamics	10		SP								SP	A B E

Having married the voice of the customer with pedagogical characteristics, the team now employs benchmarking to evaluate the competitors' curriculum outcomes against the team's existing curriculum. The "objective measure" requires the use of measurable data for comparative purposes. Note that the same competitors are used for measuring "objective measures" as were used for "customer perceptions." The authors suggest that the team consider measurement judgments in terms of quantity and quality. This requires the use of a third-party benchmark team to assess the pedagogical characteristics and give feedback to the cross-functional team. This eliminates bias in evaluation (see Example 5).

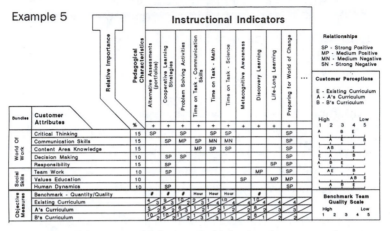

Example 5

Instructional Indicators

Relationships
SP - Strong Positive
MP - Medium Positive
MN - Medium Negative
SN - Strong Negative

Customer Perceptions
E - Existing Curriculum
A - A's Curriculum
B - B's Curriculum

Bundles	Customer Attributes	%	Pedagogical Characteristics	Alternative Assessment (portfolios)	Cooperative Learning Strategies	Problem Solving Activities	Time on Task - Communication Skills	Time on Task - Math	Time on Task - Science	Metacognitive Awareness	Discovery Learning	Life-Long Learning	Preparing for World of Change	High 1 2 3 4 5 Low
World Of Work	Critical Thinking	15		SP		SP		SP	SP				SP	A B E
	Communication Skills	15			SP	MP	SP	MN	MN				SP	A E B
	Content Area Knowledge	15					MP	SP	SP				SP	AB E
	Decision Making	10		SP	SP								SP	E A B
	Responsibility	15		SP									SP	A B E
Social Skills	Team Work	10		SP						MP			SP	A E B
	Values Education	10								SP	MP	MP		A B E
	Human Dynamics	10		SP									SP	A B E
Objective Measures	Benchmark - Quantity/Quality			#	#	#	Hour	Hour	Hour		#			Benchmark Team Quality Scale High 1 2 3 4 5 Low
	Existing Curriculum			4 3	9 3	10 2	2 3	1 4	1/2 4		10 4	4	4	
	A's Curriculum			5 8	8 2	6 3	1 2	2 1	1 2		8 2	3	3	
	B's Curriculum			10 2	10 2	11 2	1 3	3 3	3 3		8 1	2	2	

One dimension of the **House** which relates to pedagogical characteristics may reflect conflict or enhance customer attributes. The **Schoolhouse of Quality** roof matrix provides for the recording of the interactions for enhancements or conflicts. Once again, the same "relationship" symbols are used to record the degree of positive or negative correlations. Blanks will appear in the roof matrix where no apparent conflict or enhancement exists (see Example 6).

The **House** is nearly completed, but there remains one additional critical structure to be constructed. In order for a house to be structurally sound, it must rest on a solid foundation. The foundation section is composed of a number of qualifiers; "technical difficulty" (scale determined by team members), "degree of importance" (totals 100 percent), "estimated cost" (totals 100 percent of proposed budget) and measurable "curriculum targets" as established by the team for implementation. It is important to note that this section is based on team judgment (see Example 7).

Example 6

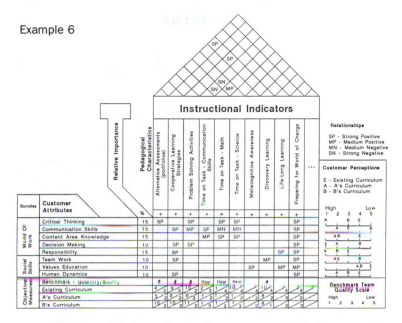

		Relative Importance	Pedagogical Characteristics	Alternative Assessments (portfolios)	Cooperative Learning Strategies	Problem Solving Activities	Time on Task - Communication Skills	Time on Task - Math	Time on Task - Science	Metacognitive Awareness	Discovery Learning	Life-Long Learning	Preparing for World of Change	Customer Perceptions High 1 2 3 4 5 Low
Bundles	Customer Attributes	%		+	+	+	+	+	+	+	+	+	+	
World Of Work	Critical Thinking	15		SP		SP		SP	SP				SP	A B E
	Communication Skills	15			SP	MP	SP	MN	MN				SP	A E B
	Content Area Knowledge	15					MP	SP	SP				SP	A B E
	Decision Making	10			SP	SP							SP	E A B
	Responsibility	15			SP							SP	SP	A B E
Social Skills	Team Work	10			SP						MP		SP	A E B
	Values Education	10								SP		MP	MP	A B E
	Human Dynamics	10			SP								SP	A B E
Objective Measures	Benchmark - Quantity/Quality						Hour	Hour	Hour					Benchmark Team Quality Scale High 1 2 3 4 5 Low
	Existing Curriculum			4 3	9 3	10 2	2 3	2 1	1/3	4	1/4 4	4	4	
	A's Curriculum			5 2	8 2	6 3	1 2	2 1	2 1	2 8	2	9	9	
	B's Curriculum			10 2	10 2	11 2	1 3	1 3	1 3	2 8	1	2	2	

Relationships
SP - Strong Positive
MP - Medium Positive
MN - Medium Negative
SN - Strong Negative

Customer Perceptions
E - Existing Curriculum
A - A's Curriculum
B - B's Curriculum

The **House** is now physically constructed. The integrated matrix accommodates facts, units of perceptions, units of measurement and professional judgments in one formal document. A series of matrices can now be constructed to reflect subsets of the curriculum issues. The matrix graphically represents customers' expectations of a curriculum in the form of attributes; customers' comparison of the existing curriculum with competitor's curriculum; pedagogical relationships; objective measures to quantify curricula through benchmarking; and relationships between pedagogical characteristics which conflict with or enhance each other. The matrix serves as a vehicle for the team to make decisions regarding specific targets for improvement of the curriculum. Decisions can be made with team consensus as to technical difficulty, importance and estimated cost of each target for improvement.

One might use other models or shortcuts to derive a strategic plan to implement subsets of the curriculum. However, failure to include any of the critical elements discussed

Example 7

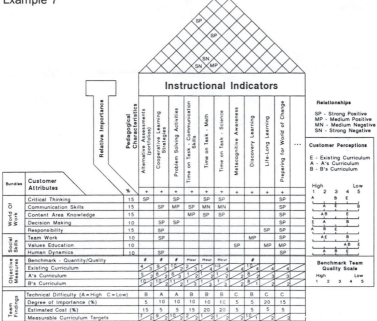

Instructional Indicators

Relationships
SP - Strong Positive
MP - Medium Positive
MN - Medium Negative
SN - Strong Negative

Customer Perceptions
E - Existing Curriculum
A - A's Curriculum
B - B's Curriculum

Bundles	Customer Attributes	%	Alternative Assessments (portfolios)	Cooperative Learning Strategies	Problem Solving Activities	Time on Task - Communication Skills	Time on Task - Math	Time on Task - Science	Metacognitive Awareness	Discovery Learning	Life-Long Learning	Preparing for World of Change	Customer Perceptions
			+	+	+	+	+	+	+	+	+	+	High 1 2 3 4 5 Low
World Of Work	Critical Thinking	15	SP		SP		SP	SP				SP	A · · B E
	Communication Skills	15		SP	MP	SP	MN	MN				SP	A E B
	Content Area Knowledge	15				MP	SP	SP				SP	A B E
	Decision Making	10	SP	SP								SP	E A B
	Responsibility	15	SP								SP	SP	A B E
Social Skills	Team Work	10	SP							MP		SP	A E B
	Values Education	10							SP		MP	MP	A B E
	Human Dynamics	10		SP								SP	A B E
Objective Measures	Benchmark - Quantity/Quality		#	#	#	Hour	Hour	Hour		#			Benchmark Team Quality Scale High 1 2 3 4 5 Low
	Existing Curriculum		4,3	9,3	10,2	2,1	1,1	1/3		10,4	4	4	
	A's Curriculum		5,2	8,2	6,3	1,2	2,1	2,1		8,2	3	3	
	B's Curriculum		10,1	10,1	1,1	2,3	3,1	3,1		8,1	2	2	
Team Findings	Technical Difficulty (A=High C=Low)		B	A	A	B	B	B	C	B	C	C	
	Degree of Importance (%)		5	10	10	10	10	10	5	5	20	15	
	Estimated Cost (%)		15	5	5	15	20	20	5	5	5		
	Measurable Curriculum Targets		7,2	9,2	10,2	2,1	2,1	2,1		2,10,1	2	2	

above could result in the team's failure to meet customer expectations.

The most important value of the model is its requirement for all players to gather at the table to better serve the customer. For too long, government, business, education and society in general have functioned independently of one another. The customer has paid the price for this isolation.

APPLICATION

Presently, the **Schoolhouse of Quality** model is being used to determine the level of acceptance of the National Malcolm Baldrige Criteria as an assessment device for public schools in Missouri. The Missouri Quality Award proposes the use of the Baldrige criteria for assessing schools wishing to be involved in the Missouri Quality Award process.

We suggest that the **Schoolhouse of Quality** model can

be used in many ways to assist educators in the planning process. Possible applications include:

❖ Construction of a new instructional facility

❖ Organization of a school district's transportation system

❖ Measurement of students' performances as they transition through grade levels

❖ Customizing instructional programming to meet specific marketplace employee qualifications

❖ Development of a nutrition program to meet specific student population needs

❖ Development of a strategic plan for a site-based management model

❖ Development of an interactive network between public schools and teacher-training programs

We have used the **Schoolhouse of Quality** to demonstrate how process, voice of the customer, perception, professional expertise and benchmarking are balanced against numerous resource variables (time, dollars, talent, expertise, technology or cultural acceptance) to yield and enhance a product or service. The model demonstrates the integration of numerous variables to produce what is perceived by the customer as "quality."

REFERENCES

Balm, G. *Benchmarking: A Practitioner's Guide for Becoming and Staying Best of the Best*. Schaumburg, Ill.: QPMA Press, 1992.

Camp, R. *Benchmarking: The Search for Industry Best Practices That Lead to Superior Performance*. Milwaukee, Wisc.: Quality Press, 1989.

Caplan, F. *The Quality System*. Radnor, Penn.: Chilton Book Co., 1990, 78.

GOAL/QPC. *The Memory Joggers: A Pocket Guide of Tools for Continuous Improvement*. Methuen, Mass.: GOAL/QPC Press, 1988.

Hauser, J. and Clausing D. "The House of Quality," *Harvard Business Review*, May/June 1988, 63-73.

Juran, J. *Juran on Quality by Design*. New York: The Free Press, 1992.

Shores, A. R. *A TQM Approach to Achieving Manufacturing Excellence*. Milwaukee, Wisc.: ASQC Quality Press, 1990.

Smith, P. and Reinertsen D. *Developing Products in Half the Time*. New York: Van Nostrand Reinhold, 1991.

SUGGESTED READINGS

Berry, T. *Managing the Total Quality Transformation*. New York: McGraw-Hill, Inc., 1991.

Imai, M. *Kaizen*. New York: McGraw-Hill, Inc., 1986.

Robert E. Bush has been vice president and director of the Center for Applied Research at Northwest Missouri State University in Maryville, Mo., since 1985.

Bush, who holds a doctoral degree in educational administration with emphasis in higher education from the University of Missouri-Columbia, is directing a thrust involving the transfer of technology through applied research for regional economic growth and development to improve the quality of life within the northwest region of Missouri.

In 1990, the University of Missouri System and Northwest Missouri State University jointly initiated the Quality Productivity Institute. Bush's role is to bring the University's faculty of approximately 250 persons in some 60 disciplines into partnership with business/industry, agriculture, health services, government and public education for regional economic development.

Bush has also been a faculty member at Northwest since1968.

Betty J. Bush is an associate professor at Northwest Missouri State University in Maryville, Mo. She holds a B.S. in education and a M.S. in reading from Northwest. Her Ph.D. is in reading education from the University of Missouri-Kansas City.

She has taught at the elementary level in Missouri and Oklahoma, and has been on the faculty at Stephens College in Columbia, Mo.

Bush has received numerous awards, including the Helen Kemper Fellowship, Teacher of the Year nomination, Distinguished Lecturer and the International Freshman Year Advocate Award. She has also been awarded the Governor's Award for Excellence in Teaching.

Bush has presented at numerous international conferences throughout the world, including the International Freshman Year Experience at St. Andrews, Scotland, the Citizens Ambassador Delegation to Moscow and St. Petersburg, Russia and the U.S./China Joint Conference on Education in Beijing, China.

20

Total Quality Management in Education

E. W. Gore, Jr.

INTRODUCTION

Total Quality Management (TQM), as it had evolved in industry over the last several years, is appropriate to educational institutions. The experience in industry, properly interpreted, will allow very effective application of TQM in education. TQM is a management approach that can provide an integrating focus for all members of an organization. As a central concept, it combines continuous improvement coupled with a focus on the requirements and expectations of the organization's customers.

There are a variety of approaches, tools and techniques that have been applied successfully. These include a reliance on the leadership of the organization to state and communicate a clear vision and mission for the organization, and the creation of a culture that expects a dedication to quality, individual responsibility and community service. Most definitions of TQM also include a management system that depends on facts, a strategic-planning system that includes quality as a long-term goal, a human resource system that treats all employees with respect and recognizes the importance of employee participation and empowerment. The tools and techniques that have been used to implement TQM include the use of teams, statistical process control, process analysis and improvement, and a variety of problem-solving techniques.

The central concept of TQM, continuous improvement, is fundamental to education. Where else could the idea of a culture oriented to continuous improvement be more appropriate than in institutions whose purpose is to support improvement and individual growth? TQM can enhance the quality of the educational experience by addressing the entire organization.

It is apparent that conditions exist in education similar to those that caused business leaders to apply TQM in industry. Competitive pressures are increasing, new areas of emphasis are developing, enrollments are under pressure, the demand for improved effectiveness is getting stronger and higher costs are forcing an examination of alternatives by both schools and prospective students. Changes in educational technology are accelerating as is the pace of technological change in our global economy, all resulting in the need for continuous and rapid change in programs offered by educational institutions.

Clearly, there are barriers to implementing TQM in education. Many of those barriers are similar to what we encountered in industry, and some are more severe. It took a crisis in many organizations before the leadership realized that there might be a need for change and improvement. It took exceptional leaders to embrace the idea that they might be the root cause of unsatisfactory results, and that changes in their behavior and the vision and culture of the organization were required. It frequently took careful internal selling to get a management team ready to accept the idea of TQM in their organization.

As an example, I once had the experience of meeting a new client who started our discussion by telling me that he had managed the company's operation in Japan; therefore, he knew all about quality circles and statistical process control and did not need to learn anything more about the subject of quality. He went on to tell me he knew the CEO wanted a quality program; therefore, I had his support and to let him know if I needed anything from him as I worked with "his people." There are educators who have a similar impression that they know it all and that they are neither the cause of any problem nor part of any likely solution. There are those who think that quality is something for the factory; others who think it is just for those institutions that have huge endowments and command the highest tuitions; and perhaps most disturbing, those who think it is just a fad, without supporting scholarly research, and therefore not appropriate for their institutions. Properly applied, we can expect TQM to impact the quality of teaching by encouraging a culture more open to change, teamwork, cross-functional cooperation and new technology. The focus on the customer and the environment will lead to a better understanding of the specific customers of the institution and their needs, a tendency to change more rapidly, and an atmosphere that will make continuous change desirable rather than an uncomfortable experience as it is in many cases.

There have been, and will continue to be, successes in industry in the application of TQM. Increasingly, we are seeing glowing financial results from major corporations that embraced quality in the face of a crisis. Many of these have been working steadily for years and are now in positions of leadership in their industries. There have also been some rough spots on the road toward implementation and many organizations have had false starts. These frequently were the result of following a particular approach that had worked in another organization. Any institution which pursues TQM will need to carefully design an approach consistent with its particular needs and situation. As we have learned, there is no one best approach (Best Practices Report, 1993). It is a very complex process that involves every element of an organization and requires commitment, patience and endurance. An organization must carefully assess its status, thoughtfully build on its existing strengths and work on its areas for improvement. However, there is a considerable body of experience with TQM, and it is time for education to capitalize on that experience. The concept of continuous improvement as a way of life throughout an organization is appropriate, the opportunity for improvement exists, the need to get entrenched functions to work together is apparent, and the tools and techniques that have evolved in industry can be adapted and applied.

There are some elements of TQM, as it is practiced, that seem particularly relevant. These include: the role of the leadership, the articulation and deployment of a vision and the development of culture; management by fact; a focus on teambuilding and processes that cross functional boundaries; management and enhancement of human resources; benchmarking; cycle time reduction; and customer focus, satisfaction and measurement.

LEADERSHIP, VISION AND CULTURE

The senior management of educational institutions will need to provide the same dimensions of leadership that have been required in industry. This may be as difficult for many educators as it has been for many business executives. The individual who rose to the top in education may be no better prepared to be a transformational leader for the entire organization than an individual who grew up in the ranks of finance, marketing, engineering or manufacturing. Yet the needs are the same. If there is to be a significant and permanent change in quality, there must be a change in the institution's culture. We now understand much better how to accomplish such change. It starts with a vision of the institution as it can and should be. It requires leaders who are respected, trusted and committed to that vision, and who can communicate it convincingly and consistently throughout the organization. Some of the special characteristics of educational organizations make this aspect of TQM particularly important. These include the complexity of the stakeholder group, the unique role and significance of faculty, the organizational structure, the existence of tenure and teachers' organizations. Just as the need for creating a common purpose, trust and a feeling of importance and participation were necessary in industry to effect permanent change, they are mandatory in education.

TEAMBUILDING, PROCESS
AND FUNCTIONAL BOUNDARIES

As education makes the transition to TQM, it will deal with functional barriers similar to what most businesses encountered. Many early efforts at quality improvement stalled. Often this came at the stage when people were excited, participation was working, but department-level teams with recommendations for defect root-cause elimination were thwarted and discouraged because they could not get their ideas implemented. In these early efforts, when the cause of the problem was in another function and no basis for a common effort had been established, it was often impossible to get the necessary changes made. We learned to overcome this difficulty by focusing on processes and the internal customer-supplier relationship as a way to get cross-functional cooperation. In effect, we learned to work on the business processes in the non-manufacturing areas and service organizations in the same way we worked on improving operational processes. This type of process focus will pay off in educational institutions as well. It will be valuable to identify key processes that result in important support to all types of customers, define and document them, assign owners, establish measurements and a spirit of satisfying internal as well as external customers, and work across functional boundaries. Industry is learning to apply this approach by encouraging teamwork and working cooperatively across functional barriers to involve all functions early in the product-development process. Educational institutions will need to get faculty and administrators to work together on such processes as registration, advisement and student services, and may well benefit from applying problem-solving tools, teambuilding and group leadership techniques that have worked in industry.

Employees of educational institutions are familiar with working in committees and, as a result, it may be easier to foster cross-functional teams than it has been in industry. It may not be so easy to develop recognition that there are internal customer-supplier relationships that cross these functional barriers. For example, it is not always understood that faculty are primary users and customers of many institutional services, but clearly this aspect of a quality process can apply.

MANAGEMENT BY FACT

The concept of management by fact is based on the belief that sound decision making requires complete, timely, relevant information to replace intuition, instinct and hearsay. With a focus on quality and meeting the needs of the customer, this includes the need for new measurements such as quality and customer satisfaction. Similar to industry, many educational institutions do not have good systems for supporting management in this area. Creation of empowered employees depends on providing them with the information necessary to make good decisions and to see the results of their actions. This

---

places significant new demands on the information systems function.

The focus on business processes in industry has had a significant impact on requirements for applications and support from information systems (IS) as well as on the organization and management of information system. There was an immediate demand for support of new measurements and different structure for many databases and applications in order to support newly-defined processes. This was frequently followed by a change in priority from support of organizational functions to the need to provide application support for process changes that the new focus was causing, and to support the flow of work through these newly-refined processes. Rather than supporting large, mainframe-oriented applications, IS often found itself pressured to provide support to smaller units within changing processes. At the same time, new emphasis on distributed systems, networks, and the availability of new application development tools have further impacted the way IS operates and is integrated with the rest of the organization. Generally, there has been a change to smaller, decentralized organization units or teams, oriented to providing support to user groups; thus accelerating the trend already underway to expand IS away from control applications and the financial organization. It is also apparent that a focus on business processes, as they are improved to better meet the requirements of the real customer, can result in more stable IS requirements.

Similar impacts will occur in education. In the same way that businesses learned to look differently at the needs of the entire organization, we can expect that as educational institutions start to focus on their processes, a very different set of demands will be placed on their IS functions. There will be a need to re-examine databases and data structures as well as applications systems. In many institutions, as teams of faculty, administrators and students attack some of the key processes together, it can be expected that there will be a significant demand for increased support from IS. As an example, it is conceivable that an integrated advisement and registration support system with a common student database accessible by teachers, advisors and administrators could become a very useful tool to instructional as well as administrative processes. There may be an entire set of applications that can contribute to making the institution more effective and efficient in providing education. These can be expected to surface and become practical, once the proper focus and environment is in place.

BENCHMARKING

There is a history of openness and willingness to share knowledge and experience that will allow educational institutions to take advantage of benchmarking more readily than businesses. It is a much more familiar concept to both educators and administrators. However, there is a need for a more structured focus on benchmarking specific processes as more institutions participate in formalized quality management efforts. Communication among institutions highlighting successes with the identification, definition, ownership and improvement of key processes should become a valuable and widespread activity.

CYCLE TIME REDUCTION

It is conceivable that TQM, with its focus on improved cycle time, is itself an example of the need for TQM in education.

TQM has evolved without significant leadership and support from business schools. Many schools are just now becoming actively involved by making quality a more significant part of their curriculum. Generally, this has been driven by people in industry and not by institutions seeking to understand what their customers need or want. Other institutions are beginning to support and encourage research into what works, why and the relationship to other disciplines. Still others are beginning a TQM focus in their operations. But all of this activity comes well after large numbers of industrial organizations throughout the developed world have been implementing formal quality efforts for years. Why does education seem to be behind? Is it possible that cycle time improvement, one of the central issues in TQM, plays a role?

There are several observations that seem applicable. First, the lack of scholarly research on the subject of TQM may be holding back implementation. If it were possible to more clearly relate the practices of TQM , with management theory as it has developed over the years, the implementation in both industry and educational institutions might well be expedited. Specifically, there are several subject areas where theory and practice seem to be very close, but there is, at a minimum, a different vocabulary. These areas include leadership style, planning and organizing, influencing and motivation, measurement and control. As an example, the leadership characteristics which appear to be most consistent with success in TQM are well described in the literature as transformational leadership. There is a great deal in common between marketing concepts and the customer focus of TQM. It would be useful to clearly describe the relationships among such topics.

There is a need and obligation for education – in this case business education – to be in the forefront with new ideas, and to originate and lead the introduction of new concepts such as TQM. However, with TQM, education has been more of a follower. As the pace of change in our society continues to accelerate, education will have to learn how to adopt new ideas and introduce new "products" at an ever-increasing rate. TQM is helping businesses compete through a focus on improving the cycle time of processes for new product development and adopting new concepts, and it helps education in the same way.

A better understanding of who the customer is, what his or her expectations are, teamwork, benchmarking and process improvement are some of the quality techniques that might apply, along with cultural change oriented toward being more innovative. It is also apparent that the standards of ISO 9000* certification could be productively employed in educational institutions.

HUMAN RESOURCE MANAGEMENT AND ENHANCEMENT

Total Quality Management depends on the participation and support of the people in the organization. Over the last several years, it has become increasingly well understood that effective quality improvement requires the enthusiastic support of everyone, at all levels. A variety of techniques have been used to achieve high levels of employee support including communications, measurements, quality circles, teams, team building, employee empowerment, training, education and incentives. Some of the unique aspects of many educational institutions make this an area where the approaches developed and applied in industry need to be most carefully adapted.

The key resource in any organization is its people. This is most true in a service organization where the people are the product and the only means a customer or prospective customer, has to judge an organization. In an educational institution where the primary customer is present in the facility – sometimes 24 hours a day – it is evident that the people have an overwhelming impact on the perceptions of the customers. The faculty, often represented by an entrenched organization and including tenured members, is the basis of the primary product and has the most impact on perceived quality of the product: education. There is also, in many cases, distinct sepa-

---

*ISO 9000 is a set of quality standards used by those in industry. Various levels of certification are achievable.

ration between the faculty and administrative personnel which needs to be carefully considered. It is important that the roles and skills of all personnel be addressed so that there are no less important or second-class groups. If an organization is to achieve total quality, the person on the phone answering an inquiry needs to be just as professional and well equipped in that role as the senior professors are in theirs. As a result, the way that human resources are involved in Total Quality Management is particularly significant.

The existence of teacher organizations and tenured faculty is both a potential barrier to effective implementation and a significant strength. Although there may be a perception that tenure gives a faculty member too much security and that teaching and research loads, coupled with tenure, may make it easy for faculty members to be "too busy" to participate, their commitment to the institution is a powerful offsetting factor. It is highly possible that given a clear vision and proper environment for participation, these critical human resources will become a leading force for change.

Also, educational institutions frequently have long histories, extended communities, and deeply-ingrained cultures which can make change difficult. On the other hand, by properly involving, for example, a strong alumni group or a dedicated faculty, a deeply-ingrained culture can become a powerful force for working to preserve and enhance the organization's viability. An active leadership – able to clearly articulate a need and a vision – is required to gain the support and trust in these areas.

It is important to carefully assess the attitudes, perceptions and needs of all the institution's human resources early in the process and to have a plan for their involvement. The primary need is for the institution's senior management to articulate a vision that will enable these valuable resources to participate in moving ahead without fear and distrust.

It is equally important that careful thought be given to the development of this vision so that it is accepted and endorsed throughout the institution and its extended community, and so that it becomes a real factor in the daily life of everyone involved. The need to drive out suspicion and create a common purpose that supports TQM are especially required in education.

CUSTOMER FOCUS AND SATISFACTION

Any TQM process needs an overall measurement to assess progress. Customer satisfaction can provide such a measure. Thus, a measurement should be established that can provide an ongoing indication of how well customers are receiving what they want and expect from the organization. It will also be useful as an indicator of dissatisfaction, and therefore of defects. A clear identification of the customers and their expectations is required, along with a definition of the organization's products. It is particularly useful to define this measurement so as to provide a comparison with the customer satisfaction that competitors are achieving.

An educational institution is very much a service organization, with customers and products or service offerings. Ultimately, to improve and succeed, any organization must satisfy the needs and expectations of its customers. For educational institutions, defining the ultimate customer and his or her needs and expectations is complex, and satisfying them can become a matter of balancing apparently conflicting demands. Generally, there is no lack of direct contact by every member of the organization with at least one element of the customer set: students. Although it cannot be assumed that access and sensitivity always coincide. On the other hand, many other elements of the customer set are not so readily visible, such as business managers who may or may not hire graduates, parents or employers who are actually paying the tuition, accrediting organizations, or alumni who might contribute funds or other support. Within these major segments there can be significant sub-segments with differing priorities. Potentially, these include undergraduate and graduate students, minorities, commuters and residential students, athletes, and all the other special-interest groups within a student body. Educational institutions, perhaps more than industry, have a prominent role in their communities and unique responsibilities. All of these elements must be identified and understood, and their needs reflected in the strategy for the TQM process.

It is not always obvious what the total product for each element of the customer set is, or what the processes are, for delivering all aspects of the product. As with industry, those total products must be defined consistent with the expectations of the customers and the vision and purpose of the institution. The processes for their planning and delivery must be identified, and responsibility for the management and improvement of these processes must be assigned. Then, the responsibility for interacting with the various customers can be clarified and understood, and the measurements of satisfaction defined and established.

A ·focus on defections as a measure and as a focus in planning for quality may be particularly useful for education (Reichheld, Frederich and Sasser, 1990). Clearly, the longer a student maintains his relationship with an institution, the more profitable to the institution the relationship becomes, including the important transition from student to grateful alumnus. It may well be true that a focus on defections and analyzing their causes will identify the sources of dissatisfaction of much of this customer set. It seems logical that any educational institution can benefit from such a focus and should consider it in the formulation of its quality process and measurements.

However, a defection measurement cannot be the only measurement of customer satisfaction, nor will it provide the only source of customer dissatisfaction. For example, many programs are structured so that once started, it is difficult to transfer or defect to another institution. In such a program, when a student becomes disenchanted or unhappy, there is frequently no way to find out or understand the cause of his or her dissatisfaction. In fact, at many institutions, the environment surrounding grades and graduation is such as to ensure that any student dissatisfaction is obscured. It may be that the first symptom will be when that graduate does not participate as an alumnus, and by then it is too late. It is possible that by then the same issue has become a major problem or that the graduate has discouraged several prospective students and they are already enrolled at other institutions. Designing and installing satisfaction measures is as important in education as it is in industrial and service organizations. It is difficult work, demanding careful analysis of the institutions goals, and the needs and expectations of its customers and stakeholders.

SUMMARY

Educational institutions occupy a unique position in our society and perform a particularly critical role. Many have a long history of sustained growth and excellence. Many more are subject to increasing pressures. Many of these can benefit from the experience gained by industry in applying what has evolved over the last several years to become Total Quality Management. Many of the techniques and approaches can be used, and the experience gained in industry can help educational institutions manage their own effective, continuous improvement. Most important, creating a culture and environment dedicated to continuous improvement in industry has led to improved product quality, improved profitability, and increased market share. We can expect similar results in education.

REFERENCES

Ernest & Young. American Quality Foundation. *Best Practices Study, American Society for Quality Control,* Milwaukee, 1993.

Reichheld, F. W. , Sasser, W. E. Jr., "Zero Defections: Quality Comes to Service." *Harvard Business Review,* Sept./Oct. 1990.

E. W. Gore, Jr. is assistant professor of management at Sacred Heart University in Fairfield, CT. He teaches courses in management, international business, marketing and Total Quality Management to both undergraduate and MBA students. He is currently a candidate for a doctorate in management and information systems and is writing his dissertation in the area of information systems and Total Quality Management. He has a master's degree from Columbia University and a bachelor's degree from M.I.T.

Gore is also an examiner for the Malcolm Baldrige National Quality Award. He has worked as a consultant and as general manager of a consulting firm in information systems and quality management. Employed by the IBM Corporation in a variety of marketing, information systems and management positions in both the U.S. and international operations, he was, for several years, the executive responsible for the initial implementation of Total Quality Management in the U.S. marketing and service organization. This involved defining an approach to applying quality management practices to a service environment; defining and installing measurements including customer satisfaction; ensuring awareness; encouraging participation and empowerment; identifying key business processes and providing for their ownership, definition, documentation, measurement and improvement; and providing training and education.

21

Quality Quest: A Community's Catalyst for Progress

Gary W. Evans
Darrell W. Krueger

EDUCATION STIMULATES ACTIVITY, ADVANCEMENT

Emerging now as a recognized leader in the area of quality-enhanced education, Winona State University in 1989 was an institution not unlike many other former teacher colleges founded before the dawn of the 20th century.

A natural metamorphosis had moved it from its roots as the first teacher training institution created west of the Mississippi River through a 130-year maturation process that by 1989 had broadened its mission to that of a comprehensive university serving primarily the residents of southeastern Minnesota and western Wisconsin.

Targeted by some state policymakers for elimination as the result of the recession of the early 1980s, unparalleled growth in student numbers across the ensuing decade had successfully ended that threat and resulted in the University being recognized by Minnesotans as a solid institution. Yet there was little to distinguish it from its sisters in the Minnesota State University System or many other institutions across the country.

A series of elements, however, were present that to an astute observer gave evidence of the potential to create something uncommonly good.

The growth that swelled enrollment from 4,202 in 1979 to 5,767 in 1988 enhanced the viability of each of the institution's five colleges and increased full-time equivalent faculty size from 190 in 1979 to 241 in 1988. Recruitment of teaching faculty had resulted in excellent additions, complementing an already strong core of instructors. These improvements had gone almost unnoticed, however, as the institution sought to put to rest the fears that accompanied threats to its existence.

As Winona State was nurtured back to viability and into favor with the state's policymakers, planning was underway for the nation's first composite materials engineering program. Promoted first by Minnesota Governor Rudy Perpich in response to a burgeoning city and area strategic industrial thrust in advanced materials, an arduous engineering approval process was ultimately successfully negotiated, due in large measure to support from the local community in general and its industrialists in specific.

A PROGRESSIVE EDUCATION PIONEER

That support was neither unexpected nor precedent-setting because Winona, a Mississippi River community of 30,000 people in Minnesota's scenic southeast corner, had been a progressive education pioneer from the earliest days of the Minnesota territory. It was the first town in Minnesota to organize graded schools and, when legislation authorizing a normal school system was approved in 1858, it was the first to come forward with the required $5,000 subscription fee (in fact, exceeding that sum by $2,000) to earn the right to develop the state's first such institution.

More than a century and a quarter later, that ongoing support for education had helped earn for the community inclusion in Minnesota's high-technology corridor. The distinction was due to the city's collection of higher education institutions, its advanced materials industries and its proximity to Rochester, Minn., and La Crosse, Wisc. Both communities are known for health care excellence, and Rochester is also the home of the IBM division that in 1990 won the national Malcolm Baldrige Quality Award. (Winona State's College of Nursing and Health Science, which enjoys a particularly strong reputation, not surprisingly has strong ties both to the Rochester-based Mayo Foundation, its clinic and hospitals, and the Gundersen Clinic and Lutheran Hospital in La Crosse.)

With the engineering program approved, planning began for the University's first new academic building in nearly two decades, a 158,000-square-foot facility to provide long overdue accommodations for health sciences as well as engineering. Again, community leaders initiated a strong lobbying effort that culminated in project funding in 1989.

The community also participated vigorously in the process that brought Winona State its 13th president. Deeply affected by the death in August 1988 of popular WSU President Thomas Stark, the community nonetheless was excited to find in Darrell Krueger someone who clearly articulated the need for enhanced educational quality, who had been on the cutting edge of the assessment movement, and who clearly stood for more than preserving the status quo.

These were, however, bittersweet times. As the community mustered support for engineering and its new home, a development occurred that did not represent good news: the College of Saint Teresa, a fixture on Winona's west side for more than seven decades, closed its doors at the conclusion of the 1988-89 academic year.

The decade-ending recession also was being felt – across the public sector, including deeply in education, and in many of the private sector establishments as well.

Several Winona industries, however, were quietly moving to world-class status and each – through crucial links with education – would play a significant role in the quality movement that has gripped the community during the early 1990s. Fastenal Company, a nuts-and-bolts-packaging firm saluted as one of the best small companies in the U.S., and electronics manufacturers DCM Tech and EMD Associates, winner of the Minnesota Quality Award and a Baldrige finalist in 1992, would be major players in the quality transformation.

A NEW PRESIDENT ARRIVES

This then was the scene in the spring of 1989, as Darrell Krueger walked on to the Winona State campus. Nominated for its presidency after 18 years as the vice president for academic affairs and dean of instruction at Northeast Missouri State University, he had stirred the interest of the Minnesota State University Board with his vision of how effectively to use what he called Winona State's special qualities: an outstandingly well-prepared faculty, an institution poised to make a lasting contribution to Minnesota and the nation, an enviable location, and clear and present opportunities that existed in (and because of) the community.

The Board, convinced that at least one of these "clear and present opportunities" was a potential pitfall, was sufficiently intrigued to make him the institution's 13th president. It did that over objections raised by a search committee concerned about his deep background in assessment, his expressions of concern over Winona State's wildly escalating enrollments and Minnesota's enrollment-driven funding formula, and a worry that his consuming interest in improving educational quality might not fit well with the University's traditional interest in access.

What has happened in the ensuing four years, however, has demonstrated emphatically that quality is a commodity that is both cherished and aggressively sought after, a commodity that is – at the same time – both highly importable and exportable and, most notably, a commodity that does create win-win outcomes in potentially difficult situations.

The impacts of that were being evidenced even before Krueger officially took office on July 1, 1989.

Because Winona State was the Minnesota State University System percentage leader in enrollment gains through the 1980s, its facilities were filled to and, in many cases, beyond capacity. The closing of the College of Saint Teresa seemed to offer an enviable solution – both for the University and the community. Winona State's center-city campus made major new construction problematic, both because of its location in a neighborhood of historically significant homes and because campus expansion removed properties from the tax rolls in a community locked between the Mississippi River and towering bluffs and unable to expand. For that reason, a Winona State takeover of the former college's facilities was widely advocated within the Winona State community and the community at large.

The Minnesota State University Board, however, failed to share the takeover enthusiasm, communicating – from the System Offices in St. Paul and during visits to the community to meet with campus and city officials – its concern over the developing plan. The Board, in fact, charged Krueger upon his appointment with finding an acceptable solution to the College of Saint Teresa issue without heavy University involvement.

On two extended visits to the campus he would lead in a matter of months, Krueger resided in Lourdes Hall on the College of Saint Teresa campus. The largest building on the campus (217,000 square feet), the 400-plus-bed residence hall constructed in the early 1920s had provided room and board to Winona State students for a number of years during which CST enrollments were declining.

An outspoken advocate of the importance of learning communities to student achievement, Krueger had been instrumental in creating residential colleges (living/learning environments) at Northeast Missouri State. There his theory was quickly proved, as achievement levels rose dramatically. Lourdes Hall, he realized, offered potential as the quintessential residential college, and he was determined to preserve it for his new institution.

VACATED CAMPUS OFFERS UNUSUAL OPPORTUNITIES

At the same time, his solitary tours of the campus revealed opportunities to meet dreams he had been unable to realize in Missouri. Northeast officials had authored – but never advanced – a plan to create a residential science and mathematics high school where an advanced curriculum could challenge exceptionally talented students. At CST, Krueger noted, Roger Bacon Hall, the former College's science center, offered an ideal instructional setting for this purpose. Twin 200-bed dormitories on the campus and nearby seemed ready-made for the residential component.

Additional facilities on the campus included the main administration building, a large building connected to it that had been devoted primarily to the performing arts, a 1960s-era library, a large residence hall used by the Sisters of St. Francis (the order that operated the college), and the campus centerpiece, a beautiful Northern Italian Romanesque chapel.

Krueger knew there must be outstanding and productive uses for those facilities as well, and in discussing his vision with campus and community leaders, he was urged repeatedly to visit with principals of the Hiawatha Education Foundation.

In its infancy, the Foundation was the creation of the five founders of Fastenal Company. Organized in the 1960s, Fastenal had gone public in 1987, the first stock issue providing its founders – four of whom are graduates of Cotter High School – with substantial wealth. In recognition of their good fortune and common heritage – and because of their concern that education was not effectively meeting new global challenges – they moved quickly to create and endow the Hiawatha Education Foundation. The Foundation's mission was to aid secondary education in general and Cotter High School in specific.

In the Foundation, Krueger found a community resource again ready to provide help.

The initial meeting was held on May 23, 1989, and Fastenal (and Hiawatha) President Bob Kierlin and Treasurer Steve Slaggie listened intently as Krueger talked about the critical need to improve education, the opportunities the CST campus offered, and why it was unlikely that Winona State could either achieve or afford full acquisition. The Fastenal/Hiawatha officials noted that when the CST closing was announced they had talked about it being a potentially excellent site for Cotter High School. Krueger agreed, noting the campus could also house a residential science and mathematics high school. As the meeting ended, Kierlin had one short question: "How can we help?"

"Why don't you buy the campus?" responded Krueger. "We would try to acquire Lourdes Hall, and Roger Bacon, Maria and Loretto Halls (the residence halls) could be gifted to the state for use as the residential high school, and there would be plenty of room for Cotter as well."

That evening – fewer than 12 hours after the breakfast meeting ended – Kierlin telephoned to say he had spent the day in discussions with College of Saint Teresa officials, that they had reached verbal agreement, and that the Foundation's attorneys expected to complete work on a formal purchase agreement the next day.

IDEAS BASED ON QUALITY SELL WELL – AND QUICKLY

Good ideas, ideas based on quality, sell well – and quickly.

The call signaled the beginning of communications with campus constituency group leaders and with selected community leaders, from which emerged changed priorities for the University, widespread community appreciation, and the beginning of Winona State's quality enhancement journey.

With plans for the College of Saint Teresa transformation underway, Winona State administrators and constituency group leaders, including the entire faculty association executive committee, spent a number of summertime hours together to read and explore contemporary literature on the state of education in the nation.

"A Nation at Risk," "Involvement in Learning" and "Integrity in the College Curriculum" were read and discussed, the final session focusing on a document, "The Seven Principles for Good Practice in Undergraduate Education," written by Dr. Zelda Gamson and Dr. Arthur Chickering following a gathering of noted educators at The Johnson Foundation's Wingspread Center in Racine, Wisc. The project was initiated in 1986 under the auspices of the American Association for Higher Education, the Education Commission of the States and The Johnson Foundation.

During that final session, Dr. Krueger noted that Northeast Missouri State's assessment efforts had crystallized following receipt of the special insert to The Wingspread Journal that included The Seven Principles. Until then, he noted, Northeast had generated reams of student outcomes data, but little was known about why progress had – or had not – occurred. The Seven Principles changed that, he noted, because suddenly it was easy to trace progress to areas where high levels of student-faculty interaction, student cooperation, active learning, prompt feedback and time on task were present, along with high expectations and respect for diverse talents and ways of learning.

The continuation of these discussions during the summer of 1989 overcame skepticism about yet another way to measure effectiveness and resulted in adoption of "The Seven Principles for Good Practice in Undergraduate Education" as a model for all areas of the University. Quality enhancement initiatives quickly involved everyone at Winona State, and news of the work spread rapidly.

As the academic year began, faculty worked together to produce as a first item an "Expectations" document. That work clearly articulated those things to which faculty, administration, staff and students are expected to dedicate themselves. That was linked to a model for analyzing indicators of effectiveness within the context of the learning environment at three levels (institutional, campus and students), the resources needed at each level and the desired outcomes. The model is significant because it establishes the context within which the outcomes were developed.

Those tasks complete, the University community began work on a long-range plan and the indicators of effectiveness by which its quality efforts would be measured.

Early work on the indicators was aided by Dr. Peter T. Ewell of the National Center for Higher Education Management Systems. Ewell helped to develop measures – most of them unobtrusive – to help in the evaluation of how effectively the institution is practicing The Seven Principles. Emphasizing that his work was intended to broadly guide the development of quality improvement efforts, Ewell noted the indicators were not intended to be applied judgmentally, narrowly or comparatively. They were intended to be, he said, as comprehensive as possible in providing a "menu for choice."

WSU QUALITY REVOLUTION GAINS MOMENTUM

With a multiple of initiatives now underway, what has become affectionately known as the Winona State University Quality Revolution was steadily gaining momentum.

The outstanding relationship that Winona State enjoys with the Rochester, Minn., division of IBM helped to complete the transition phase at the University. Winona State, which operates a center at Rochester, supplies the division with many employees and, as a result, IBM treats Winona State as one of its customers. Because of that, Winona State representatives are regularly invited to participate in IBM training sessions.

Through the Rochester division's first (unsuccessful) and second (this time successful) Baldrige Award applications, Dr. Krueger and others from Winona State had participated in training sessions based on Total Quality Management (TQM) or Continuous Quality Improvement (CQI) concepts. They found these concepts equally as useful to policymakers in education as to business, especially in academic support and student services areas. More and more, Krueger began to envision joining continuous improvement concepts with The Seven Principles as a way to dramatically improve educational quality. The Seven Principles now occupied his thoughts as those processes that improve the academic enterprise.

During a transformational leadership workshop, IBM officials talked about reaching the zenith of the growth curve in the existing paradigm and the need to shift paradigms if the firm was to increase its market share. Discussions at Winona State began to focus on the need for a new paradigm in education, a paradigm that would focus funding on results rather than input variables, such as enrollment and credit hours generated.

TQM's focus on process improvement and continuous inspection provided more help to the University's quality enhancement initiatives. While many assessment programs, for instance, represent inspection at the end of the educational process – too late to provide help or any sort of meaningful progress – the use of quality indicators shifts the focus to process and continuously monitors progress.

That focus on process improvement also helps to encourage teamwork and to drive fear out of an organization because systems – not individuals – are seen as the root cause of problems.

Also intriguing was the TQM tenet that higher quality need not result in higher costs because process review frequently results in ways to do things more effectively and with less rework. That was a particularly intriguing notion because Minnesota, like most states, was being impacted by the economic downturn and already sparse educational resources were shrinking.

With the resource issue in mind, University officials also began to look at what impact another CQI concept – cycle time – might have on education. An analysis by Dr. Douglas Sweetland, Winona State vice president for academic affairs and an economist, showed that reducing time to graduation for "traditional" baccalaureate students (now 5 1/2 to 6 years) by only one term could result in savings of millions of dollars.

As these items became popular topics of conversation on campus, the desire to both learn more and do more grew.

EMPLOYEE EDUCATION EFFORTS INTENSIFY

Employee education efforts intensified. More employees were involved in IBM training sessions, and the firm generously granted the University the right to conduct its own transformational leadership workshops following the IBM model.

Additional funds were reallocated to training, and attendance at national conferences and workshops was encouraged. Among those most favored were sessions dealing with assessment and continuous improvement. Funds also were

---

used to conduct workshops on campus, including a continuous improvement symposium that involved employees from all areas of the University.

As word of the efforts was more widely communicated, other actions occurred. A familiar face and voice at national conferences, Krueger's presentations shifted to the importance of creating new paradigms in education and there was widespread interest in the work Winona State was doing in the area of outcomes indicators. Others from Winona State also were sought after as presenters.

Minnesota State University System Chancellor Robert Carothers (now president of the University of Rhode Island and a frequent presenter on quality topics), impressed by happenings at Winona State, expanded the efforts throughout the System. The System's "Q-7: Quality on the Line" initiative resulted from the work of a Blue Ribbon Commission on Access and Quality. The goal of the 17-member commission, representing a broad cross-section of the people of Minnesota, was to advise the State University Board on the standards of educational quality needed to prepare its students and state for the challenges of the next century.

The Commission identified seven Indicators of Quality – student-centered and future-oriented – that represent what students graduating from state universities should know and be able to do in order to serve themselves, their families, their communities and their world into the next century. Central to success, the Commission said, are students who are prepared for college when they enter and who, upon graduation, have enhanced higher-order thinking skills, expanded their global understanding, multicultural perspective, scientific and quantitative literacy, and demonstrated their readiness for work and career and abilities to be good citizens who behave ethically.

These messages were carried to – and understood by – the

state's policymakers. No longer, said Carothers and Krueger, should educational resources be allocated solely on the basis of enrollment as measured by the credit hour. Student and institutional achievement had to be part of the funding equation, they maintained, to ensure the state's long-term good health.

The University of Minnesota, two years earlier through its "Commitment to Focus" program, had made a similar argument and was removed from the enrollment-driven formula.

Especially intriguing was Krueger's theory – used frequently in testimony before legislative committees and in private audiences with policymakers – that what is valued is what is measured and what is measured is what is funded. The state, he argued constantly, must expect more than enrollment for its educational dollar.

EDUCATIONAL FUNDING PRIORITIES RE-EXAMINED

Legislators agreed that educational funding priorities should be re-examined, and when the state's future funding task force was created by legislative mandate two years later, Krueger was named to the group by the Speaker of the House of Representatives and elected its chair at the organizational meeting. Although its work is not yet complete, recommendations for a base-plus-incentives (both components measured by indicators tied to quality enhancements) funding formula seem likely.

While the University sought initially to generate progress on its quality initiatives through self help, annually reallocating more than $1 million of its rapidly shrinking resources to these efforts, it also found other avenues of support – in the local community, from alumni and still others far removed from the campus.

With better-prepared students attracted to the University in ever-increasing numbers, available scholarship funds (no dollars that flow to the University through state appropriation can be used for scholarship purposes in the Minnesota State University System) were quickly exhausted. Efforts to improve that were embraced. Contributions to the Winona State Foundation and support provided to the University from the foundation, much of it to fund scholarship awards, multiplied by a factor of six between 1988 and 1993. Gifts of equipment and materials also escalated.

With the quality movement entrenched on the campus and growing, more formal outreach efforts to others in education began. Communications established in 1990 with The Johnson Foundation, custodian and distributor of The Seven Principles, resulted in a national conference at Wingspread in April of 1991.

The Foundation, Winona State, Ramapo College of New Jersey and Wake Forest University joined to sponsor at Wingspread, Racine, a gathering of representatives of colleges and universities using The Principles to guide educational improvement efforts.

During the three-day session, plans were made to produce two publications, the first a definitive work designed for educators on effective use of The Principles to guide the undergraduate experience, and the second for prospective students and their parents. Now ready for publication, the first volume is edited by Krueger, Dr. Robert Scott, Ramapo President, and Dr. David Brown, Wake Forest Provost. It includes a chapter on each Principle and cites numerous examples of effective practice. The second volume, currently being developed, focuses on things prospective students and their parents should examine and questions they should ask during the process of selecting an undergraduate institution.

A second Wingspread conference – co-sponsored by The Johnson Foundation, the American Association for Higher Education and Winona State – was held a year later and gathered together educators, business people and industrialists. The conference was designed to develop an architecture for supporting TQM and The Seven Principles in higher education – including identification of key educational processes – and to determine focused activities that will: 1) move the process forward, and 2) overcome present-day inhibitors to continuous improvement in education.

The action agenda developed at Wingspread in October 1992 is being carried forward on a number of national fronts. Dr. Arthur Chickering of George Mason University will focus on identification of core educational processes and benchmarking The Seven Principles, which he co-authored with Dr. Zelda Gamson. Krueger and fellow presidents Paul Thompson of Weber State and Dean Hubbard of Northwest Missouri State will gather together Baldrige Award criteria users to begin the process of benchmarking use of the criteria in higher education. Simultaneously, Dr. Ted Marchese, AAHE vice president, and Dr. Monica Manning, executive officer of The Nova Group, St. Paul, co-directors of the Academic Quality Consortium, will use a number of the items to guide development of consortial activities. Already established forums, such as AAHE's conference on Assessment and Continuous Quality Improvement and the Total Quality Symposium, will also be used to shepherd the agenda.

Between the two conferences, another significant development occurred for Winona State. In response to a proposal to create a Seven Principles National Resource Center on its campus, The Johnson Foundation conveyed custodianship of The Principles and their related institutional, faculty and student inventories – self-guides to effective practice – to the Winona State Foundation. The Center, soon to be the part of a much bigger endeavor, currently distributes the materials.

ADDITIONAL OUTREACH AND PARTNERSHIP

That larger endeavor represents additional outreach and partnership, this time within the local community but with a national ambition. In response to a proposal from the Winona State Foundation, a unique partnership has been created to plan The Center for Effective Teaching on the former Saint Teresa campus.

The Center will be created by Winona State, The Hiawatha Education Foundation, Saint Mary's College of Minnesota (a private, liberal-arts college headquartered in Winona) and Cotter High School. It will be designed to expand on the latest pedagogy and methodology, including The Seven Principles, and to create professional development models which can be implemented at The Center or at any school system or teacher education program in the country.

Now that Winona State has acquired Lourdes Hall, where its residential college concept was successfully implemented two years ago, the Center will be the unifying factor on a campus that clearly comprises an unequalled educational laboratory.

It will occupy the building that once served as a nuns' residence hall at the center of the campus, a building being completely restored through The Hiawatha Education Foundation's redirection of the dollars that Winona State paid to acquire Lourdes. In addition to The Center's office, the building will provide full conference facilities, including residential facilities for 36 people and a fully-equipped food service.

The Center's program will be able to utilize as laboratories the residential college (the only such facility at a public institution in the Upper Midwest), Cotter High School (which through the efforts of the Hiawatha Foundation is the most technologically advanced and equipped secondary school in the nation), two private residential academies for gifted students of high school age (one specializing in science and mathematics and one in international studies), and the Saint Mary's School of Education (which moves to quarters on the campus in the fall of 1993).

The residential academies became exclusively a private venture after plans for such a public institution advanced by a community task force chaired by Krueger were embraced by then Gov. Rudy Perpich and the Minnesota Legislature. When Perpich was unseated by Arne Carlson in 1990, priorities of the state administration changed and Winona was told such a school would be possible only if funding could be secured from private sources. With The Hiawatha Education Foundation moving rapidly to put the entire College of Saint Teresa campus to educational uses, Kierlin and his partners decided not to let a good idea flounder.

Cotter High School's move to the campus had been approved and Saint Teresa Hall, a large building that had housed CST administration and classrooms, and the attached Saint Cecelia Hall, were being remodeled for that purpose. The former library had been transformed into a health center and expanded to include gymnasium and indoor tennis facilities for use by campus occupants and the community at large. The Preparatory School for the Performing Arts had taken up residence on the campus, and negotiations were underway for the acquisition of Lourdes Hall by the Minnesota State University System and Winona State.

Hiawatha officials announced they would provide facilities and start-up funding for the academies, entered into a contract with Saint Mary's College of Minnesota for management of the private schools on the campus and told Winona State to proceed with plans for The Center for Effective Teaching, to be operated as a public-private partnership.

These quality enhancement initiatives in education had involved a number of community leaders who believed total quality or continuous improvement concepts could be the catalyst for progress. Their interest in learning more about the concepts as well as from each other led them quickly to others in Winona – business people and industrialists – who had quietly been involved with the movement in their enterprises.

CREATING A TOTAL QUALITY ENVIRONMENT

An informal discussion group (now known as the leadership forum), that included educators, representatives of government, business and industry, began getting together in May of 1991 with the common purpose of achieving progress through improved knowledge. At first, meetings were held monthly at Winona State. Discussion topics were developed, and information and knowledge were freely shared. As the group became more familiar with the world's leading quality disciples – Deming, Juran, Crosby, Feigenbaum and Ishikawa – and their theories (principally through the efforts of Winona State business administration professor Dr. Mary Gander and Winona Technical College Leadership for Transformation Instructor Tom Dukich, a former Deming associate), another Krueger idea – this one to transform Winona and Winona County into the nation's first total quality environment – began to take shape.

Moving that agenda forward, the group knew, was not going to be possible through once-a-month meetings or an informal structure. Dan Rukavina, who with his partner Dave Arnold had moved EMD/DCM to the position of recognized quality leadership in the state through the use of TQM concepts, suggested that a positive first step would be for the group to attend a four-day seminar in St. Louis: "Quality, Productivity and Competitive Position," featuring Deming. EMD/DCM also stepped forward with a grant to make certain that all members of the group could attend.

The fact that Winona was represented at the conference

by 35 people created widespread recognition of the community's total quality interests. Hearing Deming address the issue of the importance of improving systems caused the group to think about the community as a system made up of various parts and of the importance of creating a formal entity to pursue quality progress.

Upon their return home, the Winona Council for Quality was formally created, and a grant from the Southeast Minnesota Initiative Fund has allowed the group to employ a director, the only such position in Minnesota. Membership and activity has expanded dramatically. While the leadership forum still meets monthly, other Council groups meet weekly, and interaction is occurring with many community groups and organizations. In addition to completing specific tasks, such as a comprehensive survey of both public and private training activities being conducted in the community, Council members are active participants on a cultural diversity task force, formed to make certain the city is meeting the needs of a growing number of residents of other cultures, and on a steering committee that is developing a long-range plan for Winona. Still other members are working on total quality projects with United Way agencies and human services providers.

"The goal," says Council director Randy Shenkat, "is to involve everyone in the total quality effort. That is done most effectively when the Council works with and through organizations already in place. We are greatly encouraged by what is happening here – on all fronts."

BUSINESS-AS-USUAL VANISHES

Certainly the quest for enhanced quality has proved to be infectious. Business-as-usual has vanished, and the results are being felt.

At Winona State, for instance, the work that began in 1989 has manifested itself in a number of ways:

❖ A long-range plan has been completed and accepted by all constituencies.

❖ A new mission statement has been prepared and accepted.

❖ Indicators of educational effectiveness, prepared by the all-University Outcomes Processes and Indicator Committee, have been accepted and improved by the faculty.

❖ A thorough review of the general education curriculum has been completed by a faculty committee and submitted for review and comment.

[All of this work is based on The Seven Principles for Good Practice in Undergraduate Education.]

❖ Indicator development designed to quantitatively measure quality has led to the collection of baseline data for use in benchmarking.

❖ The University has helped pioneer in Minnesota, through a program developed by the Minnesota Council for Quality and the Minnesota Academic Excellence Foundation, an assessment of the compatibility – and adaptability – of Baldrige Award criteria to education in general and higher education in specific.

❖ A number of educational programs have been implemented to ensure that quality concepts are shared at all campus levels, including the IBM-developed "Transformational Leadership" workshop delivered to date to about one-half of all employees, "Connections" training for employees who deal with the public on a daily basis and the student workers' component known as "Partners."

❖ Many employee groups have completed continuous improvement classes taught by University faculty, including business office staff and 3 - 11 p.m. shift custodians, who now have developed a pilot project that allows them to determine schedules and areas of responsibility and to work without supervision.

❖ Reallocating resources to quality initiatives has created a Challenge Grant program, which encourages development of quality indicators within departments as well as inter-departmental cooperation, and a Student Research grant program that fosters exemplary student projects with a high level of faculty-advisor involvement, in addition to expanding the number of fully paid education leaves, summer research grants, and assistance to faculty members completing doctoral programs.

❖ An Educational Technology Center – funded through grants in excess of $400,000 for the purchase of interactive computer technology, laser discs and other forms of classroom instructional media – has been developed to teach teachers how to use technology-based teaching methods.

❖ To ensure student-faculty ratios remain small (currently 21 to 1) and that adequate course offerings exist, enrollment has been carefully managed, focusing both on the number of students admitted (a freshman class limit of 1,300) and their readiness for college (admissions standards have been adjusted upward three times in four years).

QUALITY EFFORTS DO MAKE A DIFFERENCE

Discussions about these initiatives inevitably lead to the question: "Do the efforts make a difference?"

University officials do not consider it coincidental that in 1993, while the number of students attracted to Minnesota institutions has declined sharply, Winona State on February 5 closed admissions after an increase of 48 percent in freshman applications, a 60-percent increase in honors admits and a new-entering class that will include more than 40 high school valedictorians, compared to two four years ago.

Darrell W. Krueger, president of Winona State University, is a nationally-recognized leader in the area of outcomes assessment. In 1991 and 1992, he convened conferences of national leaders in higher education to discuss "Total Quality Management and The Seven Principles: Improving Undergraduate Education."

Krueger came to Winona State University from Northeast Missouri State University in Kirksville, where he was vice president for academic affairs and dean of instruction since 1973. Prior to that, he served as assistant professor of political science at NMSU.

Krueger graduated Summa Cum Laude as co-valedictorian from Southern Utah State College with a bachelor of arts degree (1967) in political science and history. He earned a master's degree (1969) and a Ph.D. degree (1971) from the University of Arizona, Tucson. His areas of study focused on government, comparative politics, international relations and political theory.

While a graduate student, Krueger was elected to Phi Beta Kappa, was a Woodrow Wilson National Fellowship Foundation Dissertation Fellow, National Defense Education Act Title IV Fellow and received a Special University of Arizona Dissertation Fellowship.

President Krueger has been listed in *Who's Who in Society, Who's Who of Emerging Leaders in America, International Who's Who of Intellectuals, Who's Who in the Midwest* and *Men of Achievement.* He was an Outstanding Educator in America and received a Distinguished Leadership Award.

Gary W. Evans, who in 1987 joined the staff of Winona State University as director of development, has served for the past four years as the University's vice president of university relations and development.

During his time at Winona State, assets of the Winona State University Foundation have increased six-fold, annual gift income has multiplied by a factor of eight, and annual Foundation support of the University has quadrupled.

In addition to development, his areas of supervision include alumni affairs, public information services, government relations, publications and print shop.

He has been instrumental in helping Winona State plan and implement two conferences that brought together national leaders in higher education: "Improving Undergraduate Education: The Seven Principles in Action" and "Improving Undergraduate Education Through TQM and The Seven Principles for Good Practice." Both were held at The Johnson Foundation's Wingspread Conference Center, Racine, Wisconsin.

Evans, who attended Winona State University, joined the University staff after a 28-year newspaper career. He served as a reporter/editor/columnist for the Albert Lea (Minnesota) *Tribune*, *The Minneapolis Tribune* and *The Winona Daily News*.

He has been extremely active in Winona community affairs. In 1987, he received the Community Achievement Award from the Winona Area Chamber of Commerce and in 1990 was honored as the recipient of Community Memorial Hospital's Adith Miller Community Service Tribute award.

PART II:

CQI in the Classroom

TQM in the Teaching/Learning Process

Stanley J. Spanbauer

In today's educational environment, more than in any other preceding era, the only constant is change. Some schools can effectively manage change. They are continuously adapting their environment, strategies, systems and culture to survive and even prosper despite the trauma and shock waves created by change forces within and most often external to the institution. In those successful schools, there seem to be two primary strategies which come up time and again. The first is a systematic approach which fosters continual review of processes that relate directly to students. The second, and most important, is direct and active involvement by the teachers in decision making and management of the school.

In this chapter, I will especially focus on the empowerment of teachers, since their role is critical to the teaching/learning process at the heart of education. Before I do, I would like to spend some time discussing the components of Total Quality Management (TQM) – many of which are similar to those which have been exhibited in successful schools for decades. However, TQM is much more than managing change and coping with forces external to the school itself. It is a precise, comprehensive and cultural transformation driven and supported by strong organizational philosophy. It is a deliberate plan to innovate and excel at everything you do while continuously striving for improvement. These structural and cultural changes may require individuals to turn their backs on some of their oldest traditions.

The basic tenets of TQM, which appear to be successful in business and industry and are now being applied in a growing number of schools, are shown in Table 1, which depicts the components usually found in a TQM improvement model.

Table 1
TQM Implementation Model for Education

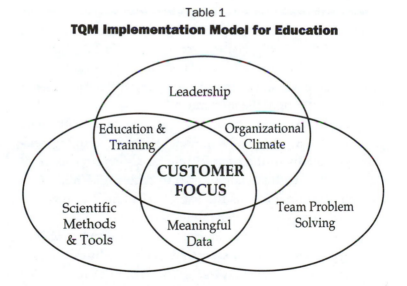

To begin with, a TQM environment requires attention to leadership which focuses on empowerment, enablement and shared decision making while coaching others to assume more responsibility. It calls, more or less, for a "hands off" approach to administration, with emphasis on facilitation rather than on directives.

TQM calls for a customer-focus approach – a specific process for identifying customers, gathering information from them and responding to their needs in order to meet and exceed expectations. Along with this customer focus, TQM promotes effective planning, using ideas from throughout the organization as well as from the outside. This internal and external information is brought together by utilizing a set of breakthrough planning tools. These tools will help develop a set of strategic directions which are consistent with the mission and purpose of the organization.

The TQM system calls for reliance on prevention of problems rather than inspection of end products by setting processes in place to ensure that preventative measures will be taken. This limits the chance of failure later on and leads to a decline of rework, especially in service departments. Rework, TQM experts contend, is up to 40 percent of all work. The idea is to ferret out waste and simplify and standardize processes in order to "get it right the first time."

TQM requires a problem-solving environment, with teams of individuals continually moving toward assuming self-managed status in their work units and departments. This environment, with attention given to problem identification and elimination, calls for the use of scientific methods and statistical approaches which fall under the umbrella of a concept called "process management." In this concept, problem-solving processes require a set of tools and procedures common to research-oriented faculty everywhere. In this investigative atmosphere, improved information systems produce concise, user-friendly reports which are made available to everyone in the organization who needs the data to make decisions.

Coupled with a comprehensive research design, this problem-solving approach systematically measures results and analyzes costs in ways not done before, especially in education. This "assessment" atmosphere calls for the definition of a set of "indicators of excellence," with measurement occurring routinely to see how well staff are doing in reaching those parameters. It tosses out the typical emphasis on a specific set of isolated outcomes; instead, it requires a comprehensive bank of assessment tools which encourage continuous improvement rather than on-going inspection and comparison with other departments or organizations.

What is being advocated is a new paradigm which touches every personnel level in the organization. In this paradigm shift, an ongoing education and training program is needed for all staff. The basic concepts of quality are taught, together with the tools and technologies needed, with the desired outcome being creative applications of TQM throughout the organization to better meet or exceed customers' needs. This professional development strategy is ongoing, because TQM provides a long-term, systematic, transformational method for reform, which is molded by those who deal with the customers on a regular basis.

APPLICATIONS IN THE CLASSROOM

Now, how does this all relate to education? How can these private-sector prescriptions be applied by faculty and staff? How will the empowerment of teachers improve the learning processes in schools?

To start with, this TQM thrust requires more than minor adjustments in curriculum and scheduling. It involves a shift in beliefs and attitudes about what is possible in education. It maps out a lifetime continuous improvement plan, rather than promoting "quick fix" approaches usually advocated by people on the outside. This plan unleashes the power of instructors in a renewal atmosphere of team involvement, wherein creativity flourishes.

TQM, applied appropriately, moves away from protection of turf and leads to a breakdown of departmental barriers, with common movement toward the mission, vision and purpose of the college. This change in the decision-making practice shifts focus away from crisis management to fact-based administration. TQM provides the framework which complements, rather than competes with, other models for educational reform. It is the umbrella under which school improvement strategies, such as accelerated learning, site-based management, teacher empowerment, outcome-based education, institutional effectiveness, community-based education and pupil-centered learning can re-empower education.

Let's look at the specific role of instructors in this new culture. Teachers remain at the heart of education. For education to be effective, every educational experience should shift the focus from less to more interaction between instructors and learners, with learners at the center of interaction. This interaction between students and teachers is central to the TQM environment. Teachers shift from their primary role as disseminators of information to a new role as facilitators of learning, using a variety of methods and tools. It should be noted that this facilitative role is being assumed by a large number of instructors already. It's really nothing new. What is new is the department faculty (team) involvement in the analysis and documentation of the assignment functions of each member, with the realization that instructors have different strengths and preferences. Some teachers are best as lecturers, others as discussion leaders, and others excel as team builders and conflict-resolution experts. Some are excellent curriculum designers, others are experts in using computers to teach, and some are best in management functions. Still others prefer to be researchers, counselors, advisors, coaches and facilitators.

In the TQM-based instructional environment, department faculty agree as a first step to spend the time necessary to conduct this sort of continual analysis; defining and documenting each person's competencies in order to establish the optimal teaching/learning environment. The trick is to take the functional information and apply it to the process of instruction and the sequence of courses which are offered by the department. In the end, there is a plan for the teaching/learning process which details and uses the strengths of each instructor as well as teacher aides and other department staff.

This may challenge the individual instructor in a single classroom system which is so common today, especially in our colleges and universities. It seeks to meet the needs of students through an optimal teaching/learning setting that features cooperation and teamwork by faculty. The result of all this is a plan for departmental instruction which captures the best of everything – computers, media, tools – with the instructional team in the center of it all. TQM experts, including Deming, Crosby and Juran, agree that this front-end planning is critical.

The other aspect of instructional planning which is essential in schools is curriculum design. Here's where compromise may be needed by faculty to adhere to the basic TQM principle of establishing measurable standards and focusing on mastery learning. This means that all learning objectives are written in measurable terms. TQM advocates argue that it is possible for instructors to define outcomes and intended competency levels. They contend that it doesn't matter the domain: cognitive, psycho-motor or affective – you can define expectations based on standards which have evolved from a variety of sources. Based on that assumption, a TQM curriculum design requirement is to write clear, measurable objectives which are coupled with teaching/learning activities that target mastery levels by students. No longer are students rated using only a few major examinations. A variety of assessment approaches are used with the goal being to eliminate surprise exam questions at the end of the term. Again, computers are useful tools in both documenting instructional materials and managing the assessment system defined by the faculty team.

This TQM approach requires teamwork and consensus-building activities, as well as a plan for staff education, training and facilitation. Most of all, TQM requires leadership competencies from deans, department chairs and faculty. This planning and problem-solving environment must be carefully nurtured by supportive management and support staff. While the process is costly, both in terms of the financial and the time investments which are needed to get things started on the path to continuous improvement, TQM planning tools and expertise are essential preliminary requirements. The investment will be worth it.

This planning feature is the first part of the Plan, Do, Check, Act (PDCA) cycle, which Shewhart developed in the 1930s and Deming and others teach today. It cannot be side-tracked or substituted for easier, quick-fix strategies that are doomed to failure. Other education levels must recognize that this investment is an essential part of it all, even though some other TQM components can be initiated at the same time. An attractive feature of TQM is the uniqueness of the strategies employed by different organizations. It seems that the best strategies include a school-wide model which provides for creative approaches by individual department faculty and staff. These evolve as the process of continuous improvement spreads and as education and training continues.

The next part in the PDCA cycle is the "Do" or implementation step. In the teaching/learning process, implementation takes place in the actual setting of the classroom or laboratory. This implementation system is typically outlined as instructional strategies or instructional activities. In TQM, these things are carefully documented, and it doesn't matter whether team approaches or single-instructor systems are used. Detail is necessary, with the understanding that diversion may be called for later in the actual instructional setting.

An analogy may help clarify the underlying concept of TQM in education. This compares the instructor with the corporate leader or the small business owner. Using this model, the teacher is looked upon as the leader who exhibits the same competencies which distinguish leadership from management. Teachers need skills in facilitation, coaching, empowerment and enablement. The teacher is viewed as the visionary, problem solver, and team developer. He or she uses the tools of process management and relies on good data gathered in the actual instructional setting.

This model of leadership in education is shown in Table 2. It encourages the managing of processes in the classroom while ensuring that all students, instructors and aides are working together in a problem-solving environment. It doesn't really matter if it is a single teacher with a group of 20 students or a team of instructors who are looking for ways to foster continuous improvement toward the optimization of learning.

The model in Table 2 shows the leader/customer relationship which is also central to TQM in education. The goal is to create an environment which uses the TQM principles, tools and techniques to foster learning, while teaching students the TQM competencies which are being used in the private sector. When this happens, we have reached the ultimate in TQM application in education.

The next phase of the PDCA cycle is the "Check," or research step. This calls for a careful assessment of what has happened using the TQM measurement tools common in business and industry. The same tests of validity and reliability taught in basic statistics/research courses are required in measurement approaches in a system called statistical process control (SPC).

Table 2

The Leadership Model in Education

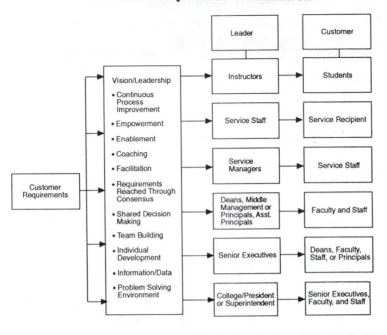

Leader ⟶ Managing processes (not things) and seeing that all (Faculty, Staff, Students) work together for the optimization of the Teaching/Learning System.

The use of a formal problem solving process and scientific methodology is at the crux of the TQM effort. At least initially, these improvement features require outside facilitation. Deans, department chairs, and other managers need training in statistical thinking, together with some type of organizational support to provide the necessary leadership in process improvement.

Given adequate knowledge and support, the teacher can use TQM in grading, teaching, classroom management and customer services. Basic tools, including flow charts, cause-and-effect diagrams, pareto charts, run charts and control charts, are available. The instructor may also examine other ways to gather input, including focus groups, suggestion systems and surveys. While the calculation and analysis of this data requires some basic skills of statistical process control, no elaborate training is required. The main premise is to use meaningful data and appropriate tools to see how well everything is working. Attention is focused on a comprehensive system with different types of input.

The "Check" phase provides enough information to assist the teacher in reaching a comfortable decision. The next step is to standardize the processes which have been used, or change some aspects of the process and continue to check it all out until the results are satisfactory. The goal is to have the environment and strategies cause optimum learning for students by using good data and TQM tools to check it all out.

APPLICATIONS AT FOX VALLEY TECHNICAL COLLEGE

There are many examples of TQM applications to the teaching/learning process at Fox Valley Technical College (FVTC). Because the College has been engaged in TQM since 1985, the faculty have been involved in several activities which are forerunners to this all. The institution-wide initiatives are as follows:

❖ Designing and implementing 56 hours of TQM training for 260 full- and part-time instructors who are involved in the 62 instructional programs of the college. This included 36 hours of training in TQM applications in the teaching/learning process.

❖ Organizing a new department responsible for the coordination of professional development programs and activities, with a full-time training director hired to coordinate the programs.

❖ Documenting on the computer a professional growth plan for each individual in the college including full- and part-time instructors.

❖ Establishing a Quality and Productivity Resource Center for use by faculty and staff of the college and for people from business and industry.

❖ Providing specialized training in conflict-resolution and consensus-reaching techniques for more than 50 faculty and staff who are available for facilitation activities with the instructional teams.

❖ Organizing and operating a comprehensive basic skills department with multiple individualized laboratories located throughout the district. Last year, over 8,000 students took at least one basic skills course to get ready for enrollment and improve success rates in the higher-level courses of the college.

❖ Developing a set of quality elements (indicators of excellence) in eight different segments of TQM at FVTC including a set for curriculum and instruction. These elements are agreed-upon standards for use in the teaching/learning process.

❖ Approving and implementing a $5 million advanced computer technology plan for the college, which includes upgrading the system for use by instructors in curriculum design, instruction and assessment.

❖ Establishing a set of agreed-upon TQM competencies for graduates, with a plan to integrate these competencies into the curriculum over a three-year period.

❖ Enacting a series of customer-satisfaction guarantees for both graduates of programs and employers who contract with the district or hire students after completing programs.

These district-wide initiatives have been important to the overall application of TQM in the classroom. As in most quality improvement efforts, the most significant impact happens at the point of contact of the individuals closest to the consumers or customers. In education, that point is at the teaching/ learning station. At Fox Valley Technical College, instructors apply TQM in several different ways. Some examples are as follows:

❖ An automated office system has been set up to provide multiple-entry instruction simultaneously in the same setting in which more than 30 courses are being taught to hundreds of students by a faculty/staff team.

❖ The flexographic printing department has become a leader in the United States for technical education in this field. This leadership comes through empowering faculty to operate as a self managing team. The December 1991 issue of *FLEXO* magazine, the publication of the industry's trade association, stated that "Fox Valley's purely flexographic curriculum is among the best in the country, if not the best at present."

❖ An electro-mechanical classroom/laboratory has been organized to provide instruction in three separate shifts, to students in 16 different courses, all being taught at the same time with several instructors working as a team.

❖ Marketing department instructors involve students in brainstorming sessions using computerized "team focus" software while forming self-managing marketing teams.

❖ Courses have been designed for printing and publishing students on quality concepts, the quality philosophy, the importance of the customer, SPC, problem identification, problem solving and the benefits of forming teams to deal with problems.

❖ Students chart their own progress in courses using the basic management tools of TQM.

❖ Students prepare project team records using forms designed by instructors with input from students, or by students with input from instructors.

❖ Technical training seminars, which serve customers in the flexographic printing industry from around the world, are provided. The content of these seminars was created through customer input. From ongoing customer evaluations, the seminars continuously evolve to meet customer needs.

❖ Sales instructors use a team-building module which has a set of TQM competencies related both to teams and measurement.

❖ Students in English classes use the Plan, Do, Check, Act problem-solving process in teamwork activities structured by faculty.

❖ Student teams collaborate in writing assignments in English, after setting up roles/ responsibilities (function-analysis charts) and ground rules to evaluate team and individual progress.

❖ Every educational program requires an advisory team (advisory committee) of people from the industry in order to maintain the quality of the program and keep it customer focused.

❖ An entire associate degree program, "Quality Improvement Specialist," was designed and implemented with all 13 core courses having continuous TQM applications related to classroom management, climate, grading, assignments, tools and techniques.

❖ Students in TQM courses use team building, problem solving, and basic tools while working on actual problems in the organization.

❖ Students complete a research assignment in the "Business Report Writing" courses, on "Empowering People by Implementing Teams" with a focus on increasing student productivity, quality and customer satisfaction.

❖ Nursing students define customers in medical settings and decide on strategies to meet and exceed expectations of those customers.

❖ Students in sales and writing courses work as teams and establish roles and responsibilities of team members, while setting requirements related to evaluation, attendance, participation, attitude and objectives.

❖ Instructors from several different departments teach various aspects of computer-integrated manufacturing using a college-wide network of computer-linked software, which was set up by the faculty.

❖ Accelerated learning techniques are piloted in a competency-based setting with special aesthetic features.

These are only a few of the examples of TQM applications in the classroom and laboratories of FVTC. Many others are being piloted across the campus as instructors engage in projects with their teams and the students they serve. Using the PDCA process, they are realizing the tremendous impact of TQM concepts, tools, and techniques in their classrooms. The guarantee of TQM competencies for graduates is being initiated, and the instructors are requiring additional support and assistance as they modify their courses and revise their curriculum.

As we know, instructor roles have usually been identified and critiqued based on amount of direct contact with students. Work loads and assignments have been calculated to come up with comparables such as student/teacher ratios or class sizes. As teachers assume new roles and as teams emerge in schools, further analysis of the role and function of teachers is needed. New measures related to TQM in the teaching/ learning process must be reviewed and tested.

These reform aspects of quality in the teaching/learning process must be assessed and driven by their impact on student learning. Traditional measures of quality, such as achievement tests, grade point averages and class sizes will need review; new assessment tools will have to be identified/piloted and checked before they are standardized. Faculty and staff must be involved in the identification of the criteria, and this new assessment system should be piloted in actual school settings.

There is no magic wand for creating quality in the classroom; however, many educators are beginning to recognize that the basic tenets of TQM merit their consideration. TQM is attractive because many of the concepts have been tested and used for years in successful schools. What's different about TQM is its application across all processes in schools; nothing is immune from the review which is essential for continuous process improvement. The strength of TQM lies in its methodology and strategy for unleashing the power within those who, in the past, were left to struggle on their own in an environment steeped in tradition and laden with bureaucracy. Instructors at FVTC, through their creative efforts, have formed 16 self-supporting businesses which provide additional finances for the college. This creativity builds rapport among the faculty and administration who together accept the risk and the recognition involved. It also fosters continued analysis of the various projects and systems in the college.

There is always room for improvement, even in schools which have a solid record of past success. A broad-based initiative such as TQM requires the unified attention of the entire top administration, with solid support by the Board of Trustees. This top-level commitment needs to be apparent to those on the firing line in schools – the instructors who, day in and day out, establish, implement, monitor, and standardize the processes related to learning. This power invested in instructors can change and revolutionize our schools. The vision and action which faculty can provide will shape our education of the future in ways never known before.

Stanley J. Spanbauer has had a long-standing commitment to education and efforts to stay on its leading edge. He has served as president of Fox Valley Technical School since 1982. Prior to that, he held a variety of teaching and administrative positions at the university and technical/community college levels. He also serves as executive director of the Quality Academy.

Spanbauer has been an innovator throughout his career, introducing to FVTC such concepts as competency-based education, open-entry/exit systems, flexible year-round education, broad-based computer literacy programs, automated office systems and computer-based education.

He spearheaded the College's movement in economic development initiatives by working with private sector groups to create one of the first technical research parks attached to a two-year college. This involvement in economic development led to the evolution of the quality improvement process at the College. Under his leadership, the College became the first public school in the country to adopt a Continuous Quality Improvement process, which encompasses all aspects of the system. Since its initiation, Spanbauer has worked with several educators as a teacher and consultant about quality, and most recently, he led a team which conducted workshops throughout Australia.

Spanbauer is a charter member and vice president of the newly-organized Continuous Quality Improvement Network for Technical/Community Colleges.

23

LEARN: The Student Quality Team Process for Improving Teaching and Learning

Kathryn H. Baugher

For years, there has been ongoing debate about the purpose and effectiveness of course evaluations in higher education. These evaluations are typically pencil-and-paper questionnaires administered by some proctor at the end of a course, often at the conclusion of the final examination. These questionnaires cover topics ranging from "fairness of grading" to "subject knowledge of the instructor." There remains a great deal of skepticism on the part of both instructors and students as to the ability or desire of students to "rate" such course characteristics.

As I continue to research alternative evaluation tools, I take the opportunity to gather feedback from many sources about end-of-course evaluations. While many students concede that end-of-course evaluations might be helpful at some colleges or universities, they are convinced these evaluations are useless at their own institution. Easily 80 percent of the students with whom I talk feel that there is no value to the evaluation whatsoever. I believe that students have a general impression that some great university out there has found an effective means of utilizing end-of-course evaluations; however, they are quick to add that their institution is not that one.

Another 10 percent of the students in this dialogue are genuinely frightened of these evaluations. Students who are honest on these often disguise their handwriting or avoid writing sentences altogether. They are concerned that a professor will know who made which comments and will retaliate in future courses. Students are also concerned that even though they believe "everyone in the class feels this way," only they will have the courage to write it down, and so the comment will be dismissed as the concern of one individual.

Some of the students represented in this group are fearful of what consequence a truthful response might bring to an instructor. One student recounts the following incident:

> Often new instructors are hired and asked to teach courses that are not in their area of expertise. Then when they receive a poor course evaluation, they are released. It's really not their fault that they had to teach outside their area and were punished for it. I've felt really bad when that happened and I knew our class had given the instructor a poor rating (Baugher, p. 58).

Discussion of these evaluations with administrators and instructors prove that these fears of students are not totally without justification. A former academic vice president relates the following:

> I am the one guilty of leading the faculty... in the development of a student evaluation program. This program was developed primarily for the improvement of instruction; however, with time, the academic deans started using student evaluations as an excuse mechanism for decisions to delay promotions, tenure

and salary increases. At that time, student evaluations no longer were helpful in the improvement of academic programs. In fact, from several studies...and from a discussion of this subject with academic administrators throughout the United States, I became convinced that the way we were using student evaluations...was a deterrent to the improvement of academic programs (Baugher, p. 59).

Instructors concur that administrators often use course evaluations randomly and to support their own purposes. They can recount many instances when course evaluations were used as excuses to delay or deny rewards, but can recall few instances when the evaluations were used in a positive manner.

Instructors also mention the time delay which is frequently a part of end-of-course evaluation systems. Receiving results varies from two to six months, typically. Instructors argue that this delay effectively eliminates the possibility of adapting the course for the immediately succeeding term. They also assert courses taught infrequently are even less likely to be positively affected by previous evaluations. Instructors, like their students, are frustrated in attempting to utilize these evaluations.

Students, instructors and administrators encourage the search for tools which provide feedback as a course progresses, allowing mid-course correction as necessary and allowing professors to adjust teaching styles and assignments to the distinct needs of a particular class. A growing body of work in this area is that of K. Patricia Cross and Thomas Angelo's classroom research. Many examples are developing, as instructors seek to find means of obtaining formative, on-going classroom assessment. Although there are many, many different tools for conducting classroom research, they are generally of short duration, administered and evaluated by the instructor, and helpful in determining where students stand in relationship to course content.

The LEARN team process is one form of classroom research. It differs slightly from the previously given description in that it utilizes a team of students to design, administer and evaluate feedback measures as well as implement suggestions. Its goal is the same as most classroom research; however, there is some variation in the focus of a LEARN team. Generally, classroom research appears to be designed to identify strengths and weaknesses or problem areas. The focus of the LEARN process is the improvement of the classroom teaching and learning process. This difference in focus is at the heart of the LEARN process – to help students and instructors begin to focus on constant improvement of processes, rather than on seeking out and solving problems.

TWO SIDES OF THE SAME COIN

By learning you will teach; by teaching you will learn.
– Latin proverb

To teach is to learn.
– Japanese proverb

The more the LEARN process is used, the more we discover that teaching and learning are indeed two sides of the same coin.

At Belmont University, I am involved with a team whose task is to envision the structure of Belmont as a system. To do this, the team has struggled with identifying the critical processes and the central or core process of the University. We are still grappling with all the implications and possible visual images of defining Belmont's core process as "Teaching/Learning." At one time or another, we have called the core process "Teaching, Learning," "Learning and Assessing Learning," and "Teaching/Learning," but the one thing to which we have agreed is that the core process at Belmont is a CO-dependent process between faculty and students which requires total commitment from all involved.

The co-dependent nature of Teaching/Learning has been a significant learning for me which has arisen somewhat unexpectedly from the implementation of LEARN. Combining a focus on process improvement (rather than problem solving) with the joint responsibility for this improvement on the part of both the student and the instructor moves thinking beyond "points of learning" (pictured in diagram 1) to "channels of learning" (pictured in diagram 2).

Diagram 1
Points of Learning

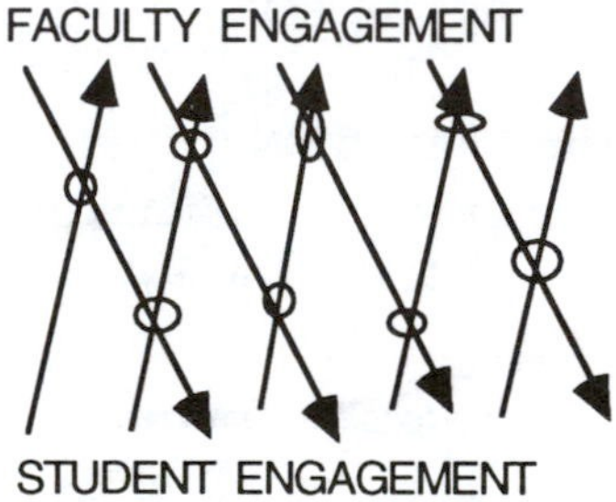

FACULTY ENGAGEMENT

STUDENT ENGAGEMENT

The circled areas represent "points of learning." These points are the intersection of faculty and student engagement. They are the points at which learning occurs. Occasionally, students will acquire knowledge through independent sources, but in the classroom, the primary source is at the point where student and faculty engage one another in mutual learning.

There are barriers to learning. Problems may also arise in the teaching process. Certainly there is room for improvement. The purpose of LEARN is to enlist students and faculty as a team, working together to remove barriers to learning and thus, to continually improve the teaching/learning process. The ultimate goal of the continual improvement of this process is to create not points of learning, but channels of learning; to have students and faculty engaged so often that the points simply flow together in a stream of learning:

Diagram 2
Channels of Learning

FACULTY ENGAGEMENT

STUDENT ENGAGEMENT

Channels of Learning occur only when barriers to learning are removed, and both instructor and student understand the needs of the other in the teaching/learning process. When a channel is opened, there is a sense that the learning which has occurred is beyond the simple addition of the two inputs, the learning is exponential.

How can students and instructors come together to see themselves as partners in a co-dependent process? How can they work together to understand the barriers to learning occurring in their classroom and in the University's system? How can they develop plans to remove these barriers and seek out continuous improvement in the teaching/learning process?

THE LEARN PROCESS

LEARN is a team process designed to assist students and instructors in working together to improve the classroom teaching and learning process. The quality team uses the LEARN acronym to work through a basic quality improvement model.

The steps are:

L Locate an opportunity for improvement
E Establish a team to work on the process
A Assess the current process
R Research root causes
N Nominate an improvement and enter the PDSA cycle

The team works through this process several times during the course of the class, identifying improvements and implementing suggestions.

SYNOPSIS OF THE PROCESS

An instructor determines that one or several of the courses he or she is teaching might be improved by using a LEARN team. This is the "L" phase. It is the buy-in phase for the instructor, the point in time when the decision is made to either investigate the possibility of course improvement through this model or, if that determination has already occurred, to further improve a course. The instructor should acquire copies of the LEARN manual for each member of the quality team (generally three to five copies per course).

During an early class session, the instructor should discuss the LEARN process briefly (five to 10 minutes) with the students and detail his reasons for attempting a LEARN team. The instructor may pass around one of the manuals if the students have an interest in previewing the materials. The method for obtaining team members should be discussed with the class. Generally, volunteers are used. Election by the class and appointment by the instructor are also possibilities. The means of selection should be determined by the anticipated task of the team.

Once the team has been selected, team roles should be assigned, and the manual should be reviewed so that team members are familiar with the tools and worksheets available to help them work through the process. Team selection and introduction are parts of the "E" phase. At this point, the team and instructor should evaluate their previous experience with LEARN and other continuous improvement processes in order to determine if there is a need for a facilitator. If so, someone with experience on the University campus should be contacted to meet with the team regularly or on an as-needed basis.

I will address this issue in greater detail in subsequent sections of this chapter, but it is of such significance, I feel I must address it here also. Most instructors (nine out of 10) believe that they should not be a member of the team, at least not the leader. However, this is an erroneous assumption; our experience with LEARN has proven that it is almost always detrimental to the team. Instructors believe that their presence might stifle or inhibit the team. This is simply not the case. Students need to see that an instructor is committed to this process by his or her own commitment of time and energy to its success. They feel empowered to make changes by the "owner" of the process. All of the great successes of student teams have occurred when the instructor was a contributing team member or leader. The teams who have faltered have done so due to lack of leadership.

The "A" phase – assess the current process – involves using the LEARN team as a focus group of the class. Using simple brainstorming techniques, the team identifies opportunities for improvement within the course. The team attempts to brainstorm all opportunities, making no attempt to exclude options they feel are beyond their scope. Once these opportunities are identified, the team surveys the class to determine which issues are most significant to the class. The team is looking for issues that present the greatest opportunity for improving learning in the class. The team is responsible for designing, administering and evaluating the survey. If the instructor is not a member of the team, he or she should be informed of these results.

Once the current process has been assessed and the team has identified the issues of greatest importance to the class, the "R" phase begins. The team uses a cause-and-effect diagram to research the causes of the barriers which have been uncovered or what might be used to cause some particular improvement. Again, the team utilizes a brainstorming mode in order to discover all the possible causes. The team may utilize a second cause-and-effect diagram to brainstorm possible solutions or courses of action.

With this data in hand, the "N" phase begins. The team must reach consensus on an improvement and undertake a pilot using the PDSA cycle. I have listed some improvements undertaken by LEARN teams at the end of this chapter. Recently, we began development of a method for LEARN teams to identify barriers to their classroom learning that are system problems across the University. For example, one LEARN team uncovered a problem with computer facilities. This problem is not unique to that single class. Some communication tool would allow this team to provide feedback to the University system and bring about an improvement for many students.

This basic synopsis provides a background of the substance of the LEARN process. The following section details some of the distinctives of LEARN.

WHAT THE LEARN TEAM DOES:

❖ **Acts as a quality team**, providing their own insights and suggestions, as well as designing and administering surveys to the class. This distinctive of the LEARN process enables it to be more effective than end-of-the-course evaluations or even teacher-administered questions and papers during the course because the students interpret their own answers with the instructor. The LEARN process seeks to go to root causes for course improvement rather than seeking out simple statements from students about their own individual difficulties.

❖ **Focuses on process improvement rather than problem solving**. This enables even the most competent, well-respected faculty member to use a LEARN team because the team is not looking for problems, they are looking for the barriers to learning within an individual course that might improve the learning for that particular set of students.

❖ **Implements its own improvements**, rather than merely dropping its suggestions in the lap of the instructor. This distinctive is one of the elements of the LEARN process that brings the sense of responsibility for one's own learning home to students. It is not simply the instructor who is responsible for the learning in the classroom. A wonderful synergistic blend of forces must be present for real learning. Students begin to accept their own part in this process as they seek to implement improvements. They also come to understand other barriers of the total University system that prohibit maximization of instruction.

WHAT THE LEARN TEAM DOES NOT DO:

❖ **Dictate course content to the instructor.** The LEARN team's responsibility is to design improvements in the teaching and learning process. Asking questions such as: What are the opportunities for improvement that exist in this course? What exists in the University system that prohibits the optimal teaching and learning experience in this course? It is the instructor's responsibility to know what needs to be taught in terms of content, and students expect research and preparation on the part of the instructor to stay current. Where the LEARN team is most helpful is in identifying barriers to learning and implementing improvements which result in improved learning on the part of the students.

❖ **Deal with individual student grievances.** There are

University procedures in place to deal with these issues. The purpose of the LEARN team is to uncover barriers to learning that exist because the process needs improvement. It is not the purpose of LEARN to champion the causes or concerns of individual students.

❖ **Equate improvement with responding to student whims.** One of the greatest concerns and criticisms I hear from instructors (and, believe it or not, students) is that this type of involvement from students in assessment is nothing short of selling out to the "customer is always right" mentality. That is an incorrect assumption about this process. Students and instructors must work together in order to improve the process. Only by working together can the areas of improvement be correctly identified. Remember, the focus of LEARN is a team approach to process improvement. Once the LEARN process has been in operation about half the term, students begin to dialogue about what are the serious issues that must be uncovered and addressed.

WHAT WE HAVE LEARNED BY USING LEARN

The pilot for LEARN was conducted during the summer term of 1992 at Samford University. The following fall semester, over 30 classes used the process at Samford and Belmont Universities. It is currently in use in over 50 courses in a variety of institutions. These attempts to use and refine the process have yielded the following issues, many of which are being designed or implemented at the present time:

1. It is very important, if not imperative, that the instructor be a member of the LEARN team. When it is possible, the instructor should serve as the team leader.

2. A communication mechanism should be available (whether a University tool or a part of LEARN) to provide feedback to the system from student quality teams. This feed-

back will prevent improvement from occurring in isolated areas which should occur system-wide. In other words, it allows our system to learn.

3. This system takes time outside of class to accomplish. There needs to be commitment to this process in order to persist through the entire process. We continue to look for ways to streamline the process and help take less time.

4. Students become very interested in continuing this program and spreading it to other classes. They also become interested in learning more about continuous improvement. It is now important to develop some means for providing education to students about Total Quality Management (TQM) and to develop a University-wide support structure for LEARN teams.

5. The current American educational system spends at least 12 years telling students that they can sit in class and the teacher will give them learning. They don't see the process as co-dependent at all. Being involved with a LEARN team really awakens this sense of responsibility for learning in students. They begin to distinguish their own preferences from barriers to learning.

6. No matter how simple the manual and process are to understand and follow, many instructors and teams lack the confidence to have a highly successful team. They need encouragement. It is important to develop some training materials to give teams the confidence they need to carry out their tasks.

As we continue to use and track the LEARN process, new opportunities for improvement will continue to surface. Students and instructors are being utilized to help address these issues, and to design more helpful tools and methods. Beginning in the fall of 1994, we plan to implement a pilot in a high-school setting. Additionally, we hope to have additional training materials developed for use with LEARN, and a pilot program for students to earn certification in continuous-improvement theory and techniques.

It's an exciting adventure in which to participate! I really believe that I am learning most of all.

Table 1
Improvements Undertaken by some LEARN teams

1. Obtaining enough left-handed desks for students.
2. Better organization of class material for improved retention.
3. Reassigning grade values to assignments to more accurately reflect the work required and the contribution of the assignment to learning.
4. Changing dates of tests/assignments to provide for better feedback to students.
5. Organizing study sessions and study groups.
6. Working with the computer center to provide training to lab assistants on all programs used by students within particular labs.
7. "Buddy" assignments for students to check with each other to improve class preparation and participation.

REFERENCE

Baugher, Kathryn H. "Student Quality Teams: Adapting Deming at Samford University." Peabody College of Vanderbilt University dissertation, 1992.

Kathryn H. Baugher was born and raised in Nashville, Tenn. She attended Samford University in Birmingham, Ala., where she earned the B.S. degree in education, graduating cum laude. She subsequently attended Southwestern Baptist Theological Seminary in Fort Worth, Texas. She completed the master of arts degree in 1984 and was selected the President's Merit Scholar in religious education.

In 1984, Baugher began work at Samford University in the Office of Admissions. She began work on the Ed. D. at Peabody College of Vanderbilt University in 1989 while continuing to work at Samford. Samford's movement into quality improvement provided a topic with the assistance of Dr. John Harris, assistant to the provost for assessment and quality improvement, noted expert in assessment and quality improvement for education.

At the center of Baugher's dissertation was the development and piloting of the LEARN process and manual. The focus of LEARN is the improvement of the teaching and learning process by using a student quality team in the classroom. Baugher continues to improve the process through its use at Samford and Belmont Universities.

Baugher joined the Belmont University staff as dean of admissions in February 1993. Her work includes adapting Continuous Quality Improvement (CQI) techniques in many areas of admissions and University administration. She also pursues research and improvement of the LEARN process and other applications of CQI to the classroom.

The Empowering Educator: A CQI Approach to Classroom Leadership

Gary M. Shulman
David L. Luechauer

Organizations are like circus elephants to the extent that they both learn through conditioning. Young elephants learn to stay in place from trainers who shackle them with heavy chains connected to deeply-embedded stakes. Older elephants never try to get away, even though they have the strength to remove the stake and gain their freedom. Their early conditioning limits their movements with only a small metal bracelet around their foot that, astonishingly, is attached to nothing. Like powerful elephants, many organizations (educational and industrial) are bound by early and possibly obsolete conditioned limitations. "We've always done it this way" is as constraining to an organization's and individual's progress as the unattached chain around the elephant's foot (Belasco, 1990).

Contemporary managers can no longer act as dictators,

cops or task masters. The traditional bureaucratic culture that for many generations emphasized the planning, organizing, directing and controlling functions is becoming obsolete. It is being replaced by a Continuous Quality Improvement (CQI) culture that focuses on leading, empowering, assessing and partnering (Schmidt & Finnigan, 1992). Many authors suggest that this alternative approach to management enhances variables critical to organizational performance and will better enable those firms that can break free of traditional managerial restraints to survive in an increasingly competitive global environment. They also believe that empowered managers who are capable of empowering those around them by creating an atmosphere that promotes trust, teamwork, autonomy, process improvement and the ability to cope with change will become the new prototypes (Atchinson, 1991; Block, 1987; Louis, 1986; Neilsen, 1986). It is not surprising that Corning's CEO, Jamie Houghton said, "If you really believe in quality, empower your people" (Dumaine, 1990).

Traditional pedagogies are not compatible with the quality practices and needs of evolving contemporary industry (c.f. Dumaine, 1990; Stewart, 1991). In fact, many corporations are suggesting that our products – students – lack necessary skills and competencies required of the modern workforce. As one human resource manager told us, the cost of training the college graduates we have hired recently in both rudimentary and functional skills has almost caught up with the cost of sending them to school in the first place ... one of these expenses has got to go. Comments like this serve as a warning sign that a significant segment of customers is not happy. Therefore, if we adopt the customer focus (e.g., Peters & Austin, 1985) so many value, then we must change the industrial equivalent of the production process (the pedagogy).

Our changing role as educators and suppliers to organizational employers creates conditions that encourage students to make demands on themselves and not to be dependent on us (Belenky, et al., 1986; Glasser, 1990; McKeachie, 1986). Individual independence, initiative and creativity are highly valued in competitive markets. Yet, these qualities are not typically being nurtured in the traditional educational system that rewards compliance and conformity. We believe that the payoff for traditional dependency is that if we act on someone else's choice and it does not work out well, it is not our fault. But blaming others while remaining shackled to obsolete practices offers little real consolation to the poorly performing individual or organization. Therefore, the need to change paradigms is as great in educational organizations as it is in business or governmental organizations.

It is unfortunate that, like their managerial counterparts, many educators have yet to figure out how to manage the classroom environment so that students are intrinsically motivated to perform high-quality work. As a result, many students voice the same concerns raised by their counterparts in industry. For example, Macher (1988) found that most workers today love their trade or profession but hate their jobs. If you listen as we did in a recent series of interviews with 40 juniors and seniors, you will often hear students complain that they love their majors but hate their classes. They talk openly about: a) the lack of support, attention or guidance they receive from educators; b) the gap between their course work and relevant applications to the world in which they live or are preparing to enter; c) the few opportunities they have to participate in class; and, d) how classes seem structured in ways that over-emphasize grades at the expense of learning. In fact, regarding their college experience, we found that most students could only recall having taken one or two classes in which they felt actively involved and excited about learning. As a general rule, educator-student cooperation and student involvement in the teaching-learning process is rare.

Current thinking in organizational behavior points to the need and effectiveness of empowerment in organizations. Block (1987) believes that a cycle of traditional bureaucratic control "unintentionally encourages people to maintain what they have, to be cautious and dependent." The bureaucratic cycle has four characteristic elements: a) the use of patriarchal contracts; b) the creation of myopic self-interest; c) the use of manipulative tactics; and, d) the perpetuation of a dependence mentality. Block contends that while this cycle "has the advantage of clarity [it] pays the price of not allowing people to take responsibility." Further, the cycle: a) creates its own resistance; b) denies self-expression; c) reinforces the belief that success is outside the person's control; d) promotes approval seeking; e) makes people say what they don't mean; and, f) fosters the use of negative political behavior. Thus, "operating in a bureaucratic [cycle] increases the tendency to experience ourselves as vulnerable, losing control, and somewhat helpless." Although this was intended to describe an industrial philosophy, it directly parallels the prevailing traditional philosophy operating in many classes. Many educators still approach their classes in the bureaucratic way by over-emphasizing lesson plans, hierarchical class structures, directing student behavior and controlling reward or punishment mechanisms. We believe that bureaucratic practices in education generate detrimental consequences similar to those in other types of bureaucratic organizations. Moreover, the public and private sectors are becoming less tolerant of poorly-performing organizations that remain bound to obsolete traditions and practices.

An empowerment paradigm can provide a mechanism to break the chains of the past. It can be characterized by four elements: a) the use of "psychological" contracts; b) the creation of enlightened self-interest; c) the use of authentic tactics; and, d) the development of autonomy. Block devotes considerable effort to indicating how these elements act as antidotes for industrial bureaucracy. The practices he describes are as applicable to the teaching-learning process as they are to industry. Examples include: educators calling and viewing themselves as facilitators rather than instructors, calling students learning partners in an effort to reduce the hierarchical role relationship, creating a vision for the class, conducting attitude surveys during the term rather than at the end of the term only, encouraging participation and free expression, being flexible in setting assignment due dates, being more supportive and less judgmental, being more open with information (e.g., stating how they intend to assess assignments), and being available to students.

To survive in modern organizations (corporate or educational), students must learn how to become both empowered themselves and how to empower others in order to contribute to desirable quality outcomes. This is a necessary, but insufficient, requirement for adopting a Continuous Quality Improvement approach. We suggest that traditional bureaucratic pedagogies, to which many educators are accustomed, neither teach nor develop skills essential for implementing quality systems. Furthermore, the use of bureaucratic pedagogies limits student involvement in the teaching-learning process and decreases student commitment and motivation to perform high-quality work. In place of the traditional bureaucratic paradigm, we propose and encourage educators to adopt an empowering style and to implement a CQI-based approach. We believe this approach serves to create challenging and stimulating classes that increase student feelings of ownership, self-efficacy and motivation. This allows them to own their learning of the concepts explored in class and encourages a substantial majority of them to perform high-quality work. It is precisely these qualities that are required by their future employers. Unfortunately, they are not being developed within the traditional educational paradigm. Therefore, we describe the methods educators may use to model the behavior of empowering managers and to create empowered students.

Industrial organizations are experiencing a significant paradigm shift in how they are managing for quality and survival. We argue that similar environmental forces that impact educational organizations require an equally significant paradigm shift in how quality teaching-learning takes place (Schlecty, 1990). Therefore, we introduce our quality learning model and describe some methods and materials that are based on it.

QUALITY LEARNING MODEL

The fundamental value in common for educational and industrial organizations is continuous improvement of relevant processes and outcomes. Like their industrial counterparts, educators must shift away from bureaucratic control of the learning process toward a paradigm based on cooperation, trust and mutual sharing of control (Glasser, 1990; Louis, 1986; McKeachie, 1986). Figure 1 is inspired by the Continuous Quality Improvement model used by the Champion International Corporation, a paper products organization (Shulman, Douglas & Schultz, 1993). It is recognized that the industrial approach to CQI has been presented in depth elsewhere (c.f. Schmidt & Finnigan, 1992); therefore, the ensuing brief remarks will be limited to discussing how the CQI approach has been adapted to education.

Quality learning and continuous improvement are the desired values represented by the innermost circle in the center of the model and the area beyond the perimeter of the outermost circle, respectively. Continuous improvement applies to all aspects of what an individual or organization does and therefore is represented without any boundaries because it is related to everything else. Quality learning, on the other hand, although an abstract concept, is comparatively more limited in

Figure 1

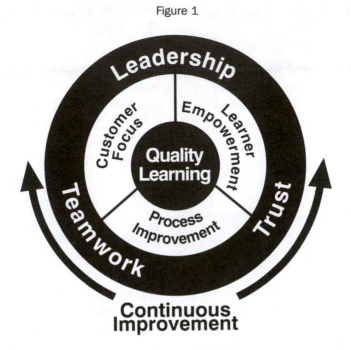

application and meaning. To join these two values and achieve the benefits of a synergistic outcome, the empowering educator must create an environment where core (middle circle) and foundation (outer circle) conditions are favorable.

Favorable core conditions are produced by a strong customer focus, the acquisition of process-improvement skills, and creating empowered learners. Learning does not exist in a vacuum. The empowering educator must identify and prioritize the direct and indirect stakeholders or customers of the learning enterprise. This provides the long-term view that guides what is to be taught by considering for whom it is being taught (e.g., students, graduate or professional schools, employers, parents.). Process-improvement skills are used to detect and remove common causes of variation in order to improve learning capability. Learner empowerment is the process of aligning student goals for the class with faculty goals (see Figure 2). Alignment does not mean forcing the student to want what the educator wants. Rather, it is a process of sharing control and enabling learners to become involved, self-sufficient, committed and intrinsically motivated (Luechauer & Shulman, 1992a,b; Shulman & Luechauer, 1991; Shulman, Douglas & Schultz, 1993). Notice that both vectors representing typical divergent faculty and student goals move toward each other and combine to create a synergistic learning outcome. All three elements are important. For present purposes, however, we will emphasize the empowerment concept. Later, we suggest some specific techniques for creating empowerment.

Figure 2

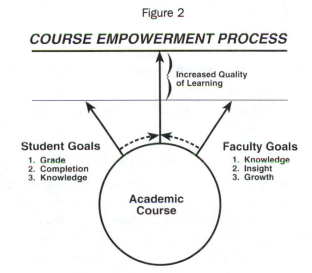

COURSE EMPOWERMENT PROCESS

Increased Quality
of Learning

Student Goals
1. Grade
2. Completion
3. Knowledge

Faculty Goals
1. Knowledge
2. Insight
3. Growth

**Academic
Course**

Favorable foundation conditions are made through the interplay of educator leadership, mutual educator-student trust, and teamwork or partnering among students and between the educator and students. Each of these elements is necessary but not sufficient to achieve high-quality learning outcomes. For example, it is clear that there cannot be effective leadership or teamwork without the foundation of a trusting relationship. Empowering leaders or educators enables people to take personal responsibility and ownership for the tasks they perform. This enables learners to meet their needs for power, significance, autonomy and true camaraderie (e.g., Macher, 1988).

Educators cannot force students to do quality work because no one can really make anyone do anything (Glasser, 1990). Except for good grades, there are few extrinsic rewards available that students find meaningful. For educators that do not teach in need-satisfying ways, the temptation is to rely on bureaucratic methods to make students learn. To this point, Block (1987) has observed, "The power of an [educator] is asymmetrical. It is easier to use authority to tighten up, shrink and make [students] more cautious than it is to use power to open up, expand and make [students] more courageous and motivated to learn." People cannot be motivated from the outside, because our motivation comes from within ourselves. Those who bemoan that students are not motivated are sometimes really admitting that they do not know how to convince students to work.

The foundation of CQI supports strengthening an individual's belief in his or her sense of personal effectiveness (Conger & Kanungo, 1988). As an enabling process, it changes the internal beliefs of people. It implies raising students' convictions in their own effectiveness (learning) rather than raising their hopes for favorable performance outcomes (grades). The challenge for educators is to make the connection between course assignments and high-quality, meaningful work abundantly clear to students. According to Deming (1982), the empowering manager should spend time and energy figuring out how to run the system so that employees will see that it is to their benefit to do quality work. Similarly, empowering educators strive to develop a system that promotes student commitment to performing high-quality work.

Glasser (1990) asserts that real power comes from students' perceptions of the educators as competent to do the job, which is to show and model what is to be done and to create a good environment in which to work. Empowering educators use collaborative problem solving and cogent communication.

There are five guidelines for implementation:

1. The educator discusses with the students the quality of the work to be done and the time needed to do it so that they have a chance to offer input.

2. The educator makes quality expectations clear so that the students know the evaluation standards.

3. The students are continually asked for their input as to what they believe may be a better way to demonstrate quality performance.

4. The educator asks the students to assess their own work for quality. The educator has communicated what quality means and accepts that students know how to produce high-quality work. Consequently, student input is considered in the evaluation process.

5. The educator is a facilitator because everything possible is done to provide students with the best learning conditions as well as a supportive, collaborative and non-coercive atmosphere in which to perform (Glasser, 1990).

The parallel to CQI approaches in industry is startling and self-evident.

LEARNING METHODS AND MATERIALS

This section presents selected techniques that might be helpful in applying the quality learning model. Empowerment and CQI in both management and education is a philosophy as well as a practice. Philosophically, the move to an empowerment-based paradigm is rooted in trust, in the belief that students want more from a class than a grade, and in the idea that if given a chance, both students and educators can rise to the level of responsibility required by implementing such a paradigm. Operationally, the list of techniques educators might employ to empower students is limited only by creativity and contextual appropriateness. The key is to fashion an open, creative, team environment in which both educators and students understand the vision (e.g., empowerment, continuous quality improvement) and are motivated to contribute to its success (c.f. Walton, 1990).

"The admonition to go forth and empower your [students] is as frustrating as it is compelling" (Zemke, 1988). As Block states, "There is nothing more difficult in the creation of an entrepreneurial cycle than to ask people to let go of [their] historical, popular and well-reinforced [attitudes and behaviors]." The empowerment and CQI approach asks both educators and students to let go of tradition and break free of the self-imposed limitations shackling us to the past like the adult circus elephant.

There are infinite ways to operationalize the empowerment and CQI-based approaches and defeat the dysfunctions associated with a traditional bureaucratic orientation to the teaching-learning process. To stimulate your creativity to this end, we offer examples of class materials we have found useful. In describing the materials, we refer to the conditions promoting quality learning in Figure 1 that we believe are present. Using the model in Figure 1 as a springboard, you can devise materials customized to your disciplinary needs.

Model Empowerment Syllabus

The initial step by the empowering educator to create a quality-driven class is the articulation of a vision of greatness. This vision describes a commitment to a preferred future. The assumption is that this vision is desirable for all concerned. Creating this vision is the prerequisite act of leadership (Block,

1987); it is the foundation condition in the quality learning model (Figure 1). Educators can articulate the essential class vision through the syllabus. Exhibit A shows how we use the syllabus to communicate our vision and introduce the concepts of empowerment and CQI to students.

Student Reaction To Syllabus Activity

The goal of this assignment is to facilitate students' internalization of the principles of empowerment and ultimately CQI. Exhibit B sets an important precedent by soliciting student reaction to the syllabus. It guarantees that students read the vision statement (syllabus) carefully and thoughtfully. Moreover, the responses help the facilitator gauge initial attitudes and aid in planning future class communications. This information exchange is essential to the alignment process whereby the educator's vision and the student's goals are negotiated to some degree and blended into a **shared** vision. Kouzes and Posner (1987) note that effective leaders inspire a shared vision. Engaging in the alignment process early in the term promotes the foundation conditions of teamwork and trust (between the educator and students).

We note that alignment is a mutual responsibility. Therefore, an additional strategy we have employed is not only to ask our students what makes them feel powerless, but to also request that they generate their own ideas on how to overcome these barriers (c.f. Conger, 1989; Walton, 1990). Sometimes their ideas work. Sometimes they do not. However, the important point is that the students feel they played a role in the process that leads to increased commitment and acceptance of the vision (Block, 1987; Conger & Kanungo, 1988; Conger 1989). However, "An [empowered] educator is not another student; the role carries an authority based on cooperation not subordination" (Belenky, et al., 1986, p. 227). Of course, educators can identify barriers and suggest means for eliminating them.

Generating Your Class Requirements

The premise of this assignment is that students will be more committed to performing quality work on projects that they find meaningful and relevant. By creating a collaborative climate where students have the opportunity to shape the nature of their work, it is assumed that they will take psychological ownership of the assignments that they create. Exhibit C provides a mechanism for the creation of groups to work on salient issues like their industrial counterparts' self-managed work teams. This is clearly analogous to the premise underlying many process action teams created in companies following quality improvement approaches.

This activity reinforces the foundation conditions of teamwork and trust, as well as the core condition of learner empowerment. Students work on salient issues in groups and must make decisions acceptable to other student team members as well as to the facilitator. The activity builds trust because now the syllabus words are being translated into action. It also promotes the core condition of learner empowerment as students take psychological ownership of the outcomes of a course they helped devise.

For many educators, the ideas espoused here may seem radical. They may fear that students simply cannot be trusted to assume the level of responsibility this approach requires. These are the same concerns managers often raise regarding their employees. Nonetheless, we should remember that Peters & Austin (1985) and many others have found that workers set more stringent control and quality standards when they are generated from the bottom up, not dictated from the top down. Furthermore, these ideas are based on the belief that if companies such as Saturn, Square D, Honda of America, Johnsonville Sausage, Quad Graphics and others can trust 18-22 year olds on the shop floor to measure their own performance, design their own systems, tinker with multi-million-dollar machinery, and hire or fire employees, surely educators can allow and promote greater levels of student involvement in the teaching-learning process.

Participation Performance Assessment Guidelines

Once students become aware of what we mean by quality, we ask them to think about quality as it applies to class performance. Exhibit D reinforces the idea that ultimately the student must take responsibility for his or her actions. The first step in taking responsibility is to assess their behavior. We are trying to reduce the student's dependence on the educators for rewards (grades) and have the student develop the ability to reward himself or herself. The students also realize that they have the opportunity to influence the facilitator's evaluation of their performance. By doing this, we believe, as does Glasser (1990), that we are encouraging students to judge the quality of their lives. The underlying assumption is that the success or failure of our lives is largely dependent on our willingness to evaluate the quality of our performance. Students can then resolve to improve it if they find it deficient.

This activity reinforces the foundation condition of trust, and core conditions of learner empowerment and process improvement. Students are typically amazed that they are trusted to make self-assessments. We find that they rise to the occasion once there is alignment between educator and student goals. Students also take ownership for their class behavior because they are involved in the assessment process. Because they monitor their own behavior regularly, students can see when they need to work on process improvements to effect changes in their learning.

Educator Readiness for CQI

Exhibit E differs fundamentally from the other documents because it is intended for use by educators only and not

---

their students. It is an open-ended activity for assessing whether conditions are conducive to building a quality-driven classroom based on the empowerment paradigm. Commitment to the principles must be unwavering in order to avoid derailment by potential restraining forces in the implementation phase. This activity focuses on several foundation and core conditions but deals primarily with leadership.

Empowerment is not for everyone (Block, 1987; Peters & Austin, 1985; Conger, 1989). In his preface, Block observes, "You may feel very strongly that a [bureaucratic pedagogy] is . . . a living example of your own deepest beliefs . . . that it operates very efficiently and achieves your goals . . . that [student] gratification should be postponed and [your class] is not a place for self-expression . . . that [being a student] holds no promise for meaning or great satisfaction."

Empowerment is not for educators who believe their students do not possess the requisite skills, experience, desire, or knowledge to take control and responsibility for their own learning. Nor is empowerment for educators who feel insecure. As Kanter (1979) writes, "Only [educators] who feel secure in their own power outward . . . can see empowering [students] as a gain rather than a loss."

In contrast to the traditional bureaucratic attitude, empowering educators accept McClelland's (1975) admonition that, ". . . If [educators] want to have far-reaching influence, they must make their [students] feel powerful and able to accomplish things on their own" (p. 263). Further, they believe that their influence and effectiveness increases to the extent that power is shared in the teaching-learning process. Empowering educators also believe that the student is just as important as the instructor in the learning process. That is, they believe students learn best when they are actively involved not when they are passive recipients of the instructor's pearls of wisdom (Golin, 1990). As a result, empowering educators value and use pedagogies that emphasize active learning rather than passive reception (Golin, 1990; McKeachie, 1986). They realize learning only occurs in the mind of the student (c.f. Belenky, Clinchy, Goldberger & Tarule, 1986). Therefore, they believe that their role is not to disseminate information, but rather to create conditions that foster the readiness, willingness and ability of students to formulate their own knowledge (c.f. Belenky, et al., 1986; McKeachie, 1986). They strive to connect with their students and they seek to know how their students are experiencing the material (Belenky, et al., 1986). Empowering educators value emotion in the learning process and encourage self-expression both in and out of class (c.f. Block, 1987). They trust students and do not demand that the student must endeavor to earn their trust. Rather, they begin with this trust and treat their students accordingly from the outset of class. Finally, empowering educators believe that, "While the captain may choose direction, the engine room drives the ship" (Block, 1987). They realize that while they can go to great lengths to state their intentions, give directions, and generate rewards or sanctions, the critical choices (e.g., whether to study, participate, attend, value the topic, etc.) are made by their students. Therefore, empowering educators ultimately value, believe it is possible, and strive to create a learning environment where the desire to learn comes from factors inside not outside the student.

CONCLUSION

We believe empowered educators are leaders that create conditions promoting a quality-driven class environment that supports student learning. This chapter showed how the empowerment concept has guided us in creating conditions that encourage students to make quality learning demands on themselves (Belenky, et al., 1986; Glasser, 1990; McKeachie, 1986). It is predicated on removing fear from the learning environment and does not rely on coercion or dependence on extrinsic factors such as grades or threats for motivation (Deming, 1982; Walton, 1990). We believe that shifting paradigms from the traditional culture to empowerment and CQI in the classroom is imperative for preparing students to better adapt to rapid changes taking place in industrial, political, and social organizations.

Hopefully, the discussion of empowerment and our CQI class materials will stimulate you to consider exciting new ways to conduct your class. We hope the chapter challenges, stimulates constructive controversy, and generates inspiration for greater application of these concepts.

Exhibit A
Model Empowerment Syllabus

Facilitator:
Office:
Phone:
Office Hours:
Textbooks:

Class Philosophy

Modern managers and educators cannot act as dictators, cops or task masters. To be effective, corporate or educational leaders must create an atmosphere of trust that promotes the continuous improvement of system processes and outcomes. Therefore, our class focus will be on improving the quality of both personal and organizational systems. Moreover, our class values personal responsibility, autonomy, continuous learning, and the ability to change. By becoming both empowered people and people capable of empowering those around us, we will learn how to make a difference by improving processes that contribute to quality outcomes.

Empowerment is the process of enabling people to take personal responsibility and ownership of the tasks they perform. The concept of empowerment will serve as the foundation on which this class is built, the thread that unifies the topics we explore, and the skill we will strive to develop throughout the semester. Much of what we do in this class will be designed to help you understand and experience the concept of empowerment. I believe that the internalization of empowerment philosophy and mastery of empowerment practices will contribute to your personal development and improve the quality of our learning.

This class requires hard work, courage, the ability to tolerate ambiguity and the sincere desire to learn, experiment, and take risks. The class may be frustrating for the grade conscious, the lazy, the uninspired, those who need structure imposed by others, or those who crave the security and dependence of a traditionally-run class. In short, if you can find the thrill to "thriving on chaos" and are willing to "dig deep within yourself," you will enjoy the challenge of this course.

Mission

To create a challenging and stimulating class that increases the students' feelings of ownership, self-efficacy and motivation so that they can *own* their learning of the concepts we explore. (To boldly go where few have gone before!)

Together, as learning partners, we will strive to create a climate that demands and rewards:

1) Preparation, understanding, critical review, integration, application, and extension of the concepts we explore

2) Both the student learning partner and facilitator for adding value to the class by going beyond routine compliance with the parameters of their roles

3) Trust and academic rigor so we may abandon a typical class format and engage in teamwork, experiential learning activities, in-depth topical discussions, self/peer assessment, etc.

Objectives

The goal of the course is to help learning partners become knowledgeable and effective _____ *(fill in what is relevant to your discipline; e.g., managers, communicators, professionals, sociologists, human beings, etc.).* Thus, the course will deal with applied as well as theoretical and research issues. Learning objectives for the course include the ability to *(include the traditional learning objectives relevant to your course):*

1) Analyze _____ *(insert discipline specific material)*

2) Critically read and integrate research in the field

3) Ask thoughtful questions

4) Demonstrate empowerment behaviors

5) Implement continuous improvement strategies

Operational Goals

To help achieve the philosophy, mission, and objectives of this class, the following operational goals have been developed. Each of us is expected to:

1) Attend each class

2) Take ownership and responsibility for the conduct of this class

3) Be prepared (e.g., read and prepare to discuss material prior to class)

4) Contribute to discussion/activities in a substantive and thoughtful manner

5) Review (think about material after class and provide comments when necessary to facilitator or student partners)

Format

This class will differ substantially from most classes in the University. **Ownership and control of the class and learning are the partner's responsibility. My role is simply to facilitate this process.** Class sessions will consist of a mix of lecturettes, discussions, experiential learning activities, etc. You will be asked to read a great deal. However, class time will largely be spent exploring a finite amount of material in depth. Nonetheless, your complete **preparation and active participation** in all aspects of the class is necessary and will be expected.

Course Requirements and Grading

To promote your sense of ownership in our class, your team (four to six learning partners) will generate most of the course requirements except for those pertaining to class participation and the final exam. University policy requires a final exam. Its format and weight, however, is negotiable.

Participation. Adapting a method developed by the facilitator, you will be responsible for assessing your level of contribution to this class on a weekly basis. You will begin this process by the third week of class. Your team will determine the percentage this contributes to your final grade.

Assignments. Your team is responsible for generating the remaining requirements, corresponding percentages used for determining your final grade, and outcome criteria that can be used to assess performance levels. The document you produce will be added to this syllabus and act as our "learning performance" contract. Information on the process you are to follow to generate the requirements will be forthcoming. While I will be extremely flexible in allowing you to design your own requirements, there are three thoughts you should keep in mind:

1) **I will not allow the academic integrity of the class to be compromised.** I expect you to develop requirements appropriate for this level course and which have the capability of distinguishing among different levels of performance.

2) **I view grades as indicators of performance, not learning.** Thus, final grades will be based not only on compliance with and completion of class requirements, but also on the extent to which you demonstrate that you add value to the class.

3) **I will share the responsibility of assessment with you.** I view the giving and receiving of constructive feedback as an essential skill.

Grading Philosophy. My operating premise is that grades are the focus of considerable misplaced attention and are of secondary importance. All too often students tie their grades to personal and outsiders' assessments of their self-worth, value and esteem. This thinking is misguided! Students in this class must resist the temptation to assume that grades offer any indication of their identity, effort, learning, etc. Nevertheless, grades are a requirement of this University and the facilitator has the responsibility of assigning you a final grade at the end of the term. Therefore, assessments will be generated for the tasks required in this class and they will be used, in part, to determine your final grade. Assessments are based on the extent to which performances meet your expectations, facilitator expectations, and other learning partner expectations. Average performance is doing what is expected and performing at the level of those around you.

Contingency Provision

The facilitator reserves the right to modify the provisions outlined in this and subsequent documents if a need arises. Any changes, however, will be announced and will strive to meet the criteria of equity and fair treatment for the partners.

Points of Clarification

Ultimately, my desire is to align my vision of a learning-focused, stimulating and rigorous class with your goals. The following may help us achieve alignment:

1) We are in this together. While I want you to feel free to express yourself and learn in your own way, our goal is to achieve the vision and mission outlined earlier. Thus, you are encouraged to remember that I am giving you a significant stake in the class rather than turning it completely over to you.

2) My primary role is to create a vision for what a class can be like, and then work to see that conditions are created both in and out of the classroom that facilitate the attainment of my vision. My role is not to police you or "make you learn."

3) The trust and empowerment I give you significantly increases the work, level of maturity, and responsibility expected of you!

4) I do not transmit knowledge. I simply try to help create the conditions that make you ready, willing, and able to create your own distinct knowledge of the topics we explore.

5) Learning is an internal and person-specific phenomenon. There is little way for me to assess "how much you learned." Grades will assess how you performed, not what you learned.

6) I don't give grades. You will earn all of them yourself. You will participate in assessing yourself. This does not mean you can be easy on yourself or peers. A high grade is reachable, but not an automatic entitlement.

7) Emotional investment is a necessary part of learning. I accept that you may leave class on occasion with strong positive, negative or mixed feelings.

8) We are learning partners; therefore, we share the responsibility of making the class a positive experience.

9) Committing ourselves to continuous improvement makes each of us capable of "achieving greatness." We must develop our

abilities by setting high aspirations or goals and then dedicating ourselves to working toward their realization.

10) I will try my best to get to know you and be available to help you achieve your vision of quality learning. You may initiate interaction at any time. However, do not assume that just because I like you as a person that it will prevent me from objectively and rigorously evaluating your performance or make up for deficient performance. Remember that having fun is compatible with high-quality standards and performance expectations.

Exhibit B
Student Reaction To Syllabus Activity

Overview
In this class, the syllabus expresses the philosophical foundation that will guide the facilitator's contribution to the course. It serves as the basis for the facilitator's half of the psychological contract we will share this semester. It is important that you make an informed and deliberate decision about becoming an active, contributing class member. Therefore, a thorough understanding and thoughtful reaction to the syllabus is a requirement for this class.

Directions
1) You are to generate brief yet **thoughtful and insightful typed** responses to each of the questions below. Your responses should offer honest (even critical) personal reactions to the material and processes it suggests.

2) Your responses are **due at the beginning of our next class** session and will serve as the basis for our discussion/activity.

Warning
1) Partners (students) who do not comply with the directions and deadline may be dropped from the class by the facilitator.

2) Superficial responses are subject to a re-write.

Questions
1) What do the philosophy and mission statements mean to you? How do you feel about them?

2) What specifically will you have to do to contribute to the

---

attainment of the course objectives and goals?

3) How do you feel about the facilitator's approach to grading?

4) How do you feel about the "points of clarification" section? Which point do you like the most? Why? Which point do you like the least? Why?

5) Briefly describe the rights and responsibilities of you and the facilitator in this class. Are you "cut out" to be a learning partner? Why do you think so?

6) What do you think is the single greatest barrier to achieving the mission of this class? Suggest how the facilitator might overcome this barrier?

7) List any questions, concerns or comments you have for the facilitator?

Exhibit C
Generating Your Class Requirements

As noted on your syllabus, your team will be determining the other requirements used to measure your performance in this class. You must be thorough in this activity. Your goal is to create requirements that each of you will find to be both fun and challenging to complete. In the final analysis, you are the ones who will be responsible for doing the work. Therefore, try to be patient, creative, and to take this activity seriously.

The assignments you create will be acceptable if they contribute to our achieving the philosophy, mission and objectives of this class and are commensurate with the workload expectations of a (*fill in*)-level class.

Students often struggle with this assignment. So to help get you thinking, consider some requirements used by previous classes:

Annotated bibliographies	Personal action plans
Book report/analysis	Personal closure statements
Case studies	Reading-related quizzes
Contemporary-issue presentation	Professional periodical review
Create simulation	Research project/study
Create an employee manual	Class-related video production
Employee interviews	Lead topical discussion
Groups run class for a day	"System" observation
Manager interviews	Theory/model development
Movie analysis	Topical critiques/extensions

Out-of-class study groups	Topical reaction papers
Performing skits/plays	Charity fund raiser
Review of literature paper	Quizzes over readings

These are just suggestions – **you may pick from this list, modify ideas on this list, or generate your own activities.** Some of the more abstract ideas will be explained. Feel free but **not compelled** to pick any of these. Many teams have opted to make some of these individual projects. Remember that none of the projects substitutes for a final exam. The nature of the final exam will be discussed in class.

You must also develop a "non-participation and non-pre-paredness" policy which notes the action(s) to be taken in the event that someone shows up for class or team meetings either not prepared or not willing to play an active role. The best policies are those in which both the partners and the facilitator share responsibility for administration. Do not make any provisions which allow any number of absences or days for not preparing or participating. There are no legitimate reasons for being absent, unprepared or unwilling to participate. You are either in class ready, willing and able to participate and learn, or you are not. The reason for your lack of preparation, attendance or participation is a moot point! (If you don't show up or perform on your "real" job, you don't get paid). State your policy in observable and measurable specific behavioral terms (number of minutes late, number of missed deadlines, number of absences, etc.).

Generating Requirements Directions

The main purpose in this activity is for you to create assignments that you will enjoy doing and serve to meet our quality, ownership, preparation and participation objectives.

You will be placed into groups of four to six partners. Meeting outside of class, your team must prepare a document that details the requirements you want to propose. This will be due on a date that will be announced by the facilitator.

Your document must specifically state the nature of the assignments, when they are to be completed, how they are to be evaluated, what percentage of your final grade they will account for, etc. Be prepared to meet on more than one occasion as a team. A representative will be appointed by the team to type the final draft of your document and present it to the facilitator.

Provided that the document is complete and acceptable to the parties involved, it will serve as the remainder of our learning performance contract. To the extent that the document is incomplete, you will continue through the process until a mutuall- acceptable document is created.

Points To Ponder

1) **The facilitator has noted over the years that this can be a very time-consuming and frustrating experience for partners.** Your results and ultimate satisfaction depend on a number of factors: a) the time you devote to this activity, b) your willingness to assume the necessary risk/responsibility, c) your ability to trade a grade/requirement-filling focus to a learning orientation, and d) limited facilitator involvement. To this last point (d), the facilitator will let you "stew" in chaos, anguish and ambiguity until **you** are ready to put closure on this activity. Going through this process will prepare you for the real challenges you will face professionally when you are out of school in the future.

2) Your natural inclination, given the lack of ownership you have been given in the learning process over the years, will be to rush through this process. Avoid the temptation to merely "go through the motions," because you will have to live with the consequences of your actions for the entire semester. If you take this seriously, you will learn more about yourself and the processes of socialization and empowerment than you ever dreamed possible. **Be creative.** This is your chance to do what you want with this class. You are powerful – now try to be remarkable!

3) You will be asked to take part in the assessment of the requirements you select so keep this in mind when deciding what you want to do.

Exhibit D

Participation Performance Assessment Guidelines

Directions: For the duration of the semester, your contribution to class will be recorded via either self-assessment, peer assessment and/or facilitator assessment. The three suggested areas which will serve as the focus for evaluation are: 1) your contribution during experiential activities, 2) your contribution during class discussions, and 3) the extent to which you display knowledge of the assigned readings. A rating for the focal areas based on the following scale is to be generated for each class. Please note, every possible attitude/behavior which would warrant the following ratings cannot be listed.

As a result, these are "general" guidelines designed to capture the essence of the rating. Bring your performance log to class every day.

N/A = NOT APPLICABLE (i.e. we did not engage in that focal area). This rating doesn't apply to the reading area which can be rated, regardless of format.

0 = INSIGNIFICANT CONTRIBUTION. Characterized by a failure to display interest or make relevant comments. Listened, but not intently. Did not utilize reading material when making comments [for the reading area].

1 = MARGINAL CONTRIBUTION. Characterized by minor involvement that added little to the process. Knowledge of the readings could be inferred, but was not directly linked or stated.

2 = EXPECTED CONTRIBUTION. Characterized by meaningful involvement that added to the process. Lived up to the expectations of peers and the facilitator for how a member of our class should act. Showed willingness, preparation, ability and understanding during the activity or discussion. Comments or questions were clearly linked to readings.

3 = SUBSTANTIAL CONTRIBUTION. Characterized by meaningful involvement that added to the process. In some documentable way or another performance exceeded that which would be expected by peers and the facilitator. Offered provocative and relevant comments or questions.

4 = EXCEPTIONAL (WOW!) CONTRIBUTION. Characterized by being an outstanding participant in that area. Far exceeded expectations. Peers and the facilitator learned a great deal, gained insights, were emotionally affected or inspired.

Notes: 1) Contribution does not refer only to "comments" – good questions, providing the class with needed direction, providing constructive feedback to partners, clarifying points, or generally improving the climate of class may be considered in the performance assessment. 2) You don't have to be exceptional every day to get an acceptable final score (we will take a "long-term" view). 3) Perceptual differences in ratings between the student and facilitator will be resolved in a conference.

Educator Readiness for CQI

To assess your commitment to adopting a CQI approach to becoming an empowering educator, you may wish to reflect on these questions:

1. What are my motives for considering a new teaching-learning approach?

2. What is there about the teaching-learning process that most excites me? Can I achieve desirable outcomes without a "CQI" or empowerment approach?

3. Do I feel comfortable viewing my students as partners? As customers?

4. Do I truly believe that the processes of teaching and learning can be continuously improved in my class?

5. How comfortable do I feel releasing authority and power to students?

6. How well do I handle ambiguity and uncertainty?

7. What am I willing to risk or give up to build a "quality-driven" class environment?

8. How comfortable will I feel "advocating" quality or empowerment to my students and colleagues?

9. How have I dealt with long-term commitments to change in the past?

10. How comfortable will I be in a learning role? Do I mind being seen by others as a learner?

11. Am I willing to change my style of teaching, if necessary, to make the CQI and empowerment approach work?

Inevitably, you will discover potential forces restraining efforts to implement the empowering educator philosophy or practices. Devise methods for removing these possible barriers in advance of any attempted implementation. If these barriers seem like insurmountable obstacles, you are probably not ready to commit to changing your teaching-learning system. Resolve to review these questions again periodically when you or conditions may have changed.

REFERENCES

Atchinson, T. "The Employment Relationship: Un-tied or Re-tied?" Academy of Management Executive, 1991, 5(4), 52-62.

Belasco, J. *Teaching the Elephant to Dance: Empowering Change in Your Organization.* New York: Crown Publishers, 1990.

Belenky, M., Clinchy, B., Goldberger, N. and Tarule, J. *Women's Ways of Knowing: The Development of Self, Voice, and Mind.* New York: Basic Books, 1986.

Berlew, D. "Managing Human Energy: Pushing Versus Pulling." In S. Srivastva (ed.), *Executive Power.* San Fransisco: Jossey-Bass, 1986.

Block, P. *The Empowered Manager: Positive Political Skills at Work.* San Francisco: Jossey-Bass, 1987.

Conger, J. "Leadership: The Art of Empowering Others." *Academy of Management Executive,* 1989, 3, 17-24.

Conger, J. and Kanungo, R. "The Empowerment Process: Integrating Theory and Practice." *Academy of Management Review,* 1988, 13, 471-482.

Deming, W.E. *Out of the Crisis.* Cambridge, Mass.: MIT, Center for Advanced Engineering Study, 1982.

Dumain, B. "Who Needs a Boss?" *Fortune,* May 1990, 2(12), 52-60.

Glasser, W. *The Quality School: Managing Students Without Coercion.* New York: Harper & Row, 1990.

Golin, S. "Four Arguments for Peer Collaboration and Student Interviewing: The Master Educators Program." *AAHE Bulletin,* Dec. 1990, 121-124.

Kanter, R. "Power Failure in Management Circuits." *Harvard Business Review,* 1979, 57(4), 65-75.

Kouzes, J. and Posner, B. *The Leadership Challenge: How to Get Extraordinary Things Done in Organizations.* San Francisco: Jossey-Bass, 1987.

Louis, M. "Putting Executive Action in Context: An Alternative View of Powers." In S. Srivastva (ed.), *Executive Power.* San Fransisco: Jossey-Bass, 1986, 111-131.

Luechauer, D. and Shulman G. "Moving from Bureaucracy to Empowerment: Shifting Paradigms to Practie What We Preach in Class." In T. Head & T. Keaveny (eds.), *Conference Proceedings.* St. Charles, Ill.: Midwest Academy of Management, 1992, 09-115a.

Luechauer, D. and Shulman, F. "Practicing What We Teach." *At Work: Stories of Tomorrow's Workplace,* 1992, 1(2), 17-18b.

Macher, K. "Empowerment and the Bureaucracy." *Training and Development Journal,* 1988, 42, 41-45.

McClelland, D. *Power: The Inner Experience.* New York: Irvington, 1975.

McKeachie, W. *Teaching Tips: A Guidebook for the Beginning College Teacher* (8th ed.). Tortonto: D.C. Heath, 1986.

Neilsen, E. "Empowerment Strategies: Balancing Authority and Responsibility." In S. Srivastva (ed.), *Executive Power*. San Fransisco: Jossey-Bass, 1986, 78-110.

Peters, T. and Austin, N. *A Passion for Excellence*. New York: Random House, 1985.

Pickett, W. "Quality Management in a Hostile Enviornment or What's a Nice College Like You Doing With a Management Philosophy Like That." Paper presented at the American Association for Higher Education annual convention, Chicago, Ill., 1992.

Schlecty, P. *Schools for the Twenty First Century: Leadership Imperative for Educational Reform*. San Fransciso: Jossey-Bass, 1990.

Schmidet, W. and Finnegan, J. *The Race Without a Finish Line: America's Quest for Total Quality*. San Fransciso: Jossey-Bass, 1992.

Schulman, G., Douglas, J., and Schultz, S. "The Job Empowerment Instrument: A Replication." In T. Head & R. Katerberg (eds.), *Conference Proceedings*. Indianapolis: Midwest Academy of Management, 1993, 322-328.

Stewart, T. "GE Keeps Those Ideas Coming." *Fortune*, Aug. 12, 1991, 120, 41-49.

Thomas, K. and Velthouse, B. "Cognitive Elements of Empowerment: An 'Interpretive' Model of Intrinsic Task Motivation." *Academy of Management Review*, 1990, 15, 666-681.

Walton, M. *Deming Management at Work*. New York: Putnam, 1990.

Zemke, R. "Empowerment: Helping People Take Charge." Training: *The Magazine of Human Resource Development*, 1988, 25, 63-64.

David L. Luechauer is an assistant professor in the Management Department at Butler University. He received his doctoral degree from the University of Cincinnati with specialities in organizational behavior, group dynamics and social psychology.

Luechauer has received recognition for his publication and teaching efforts from professional organizations and universities. He has also served as a management consultant to both profit and non-profit organizations across the United States. Luechauer's research, consulting, and teaching interests include: empowerment, group dynamics, team building, change management, leadership, and organizational culture. Currently, he is preparing a book (with Gary Shulman) that explains how the values and practices of empowerment can be used to facilitate learning in educational and organizational settings.

Gary M. Shulman is currently an associate professor and director of graduate studies for the speech communication program at Miami University in Oxford, Ohio. He received his doctoral degree from Purdue University with specialties in organizational and interpersonal communication. He completed his undergraduate education in business at Hunter College, C.U.N.Y.

Shulman has received recognition for his publication and teaching efforts from numerous professional associations and universities.

Shulman's research interests include the use of empowerment values and practices in industrial and educational organizations, preparing for and coping with organizational change, and developing a quality improvement orientation. Currently he is part of a team working on adapting continuous quality improvement philosophy and techniques to public education.

25

Constancy of Purpose: Ability-based Education and Assessment-As-Learning

William McEachern
Kathleen O'Brien

Over the past 20 years, the faculty and academic staff of Alverno College have drawn upon the principles of ability-based education and assessment to continuously improve teaching and learning processes across the College. More recently, Alverno established a Quality Council to explore how Continuous Quality Improvement (CQI) principles might be applied in an organizational environment already committed to continuous improvement of teaching and learning. As a result, we have discovered points of connection between CQI and the principles underlying ability-based education that includes Assessment-As-Learning. In this chapter, we will examine these principles as a reflection of Continuous Quality Improvement principles applied to the teaching and learning process and draw some conclusions regarding the congruence between them.

ALVERNO'S MISSION AND CONSTANCY OF PURPOSE

Alverno's philosophy of education and quality principles are captured in a recently-refined mission statement that gives expression to the underlying principles of outcome-oriented, ability-based education and assessment that have been, in Deming's language, our way of assuring "constancy of purpose" since the early 1970s.

Alverno exists to promote the personal and professional development of women. This defines both our long-term aim and our daily pursuits. To accomplish our mission, we must work constantly in four areas:

❖ **Creating a community of learning.** The common purpose that gathers everyone at Alverno is the pursuit of knowledge and the development of students' abilities.

❖ **Creating a curriculum.** A curriculum is the way students learn. Learning at Alverno is rooted in the liberal arts and the Catholic tradition. We organize learning to develop students' abilities, accommodate the diverse needs of women and keep Alverno affordable for women of varied economic circumstances.

❖ **Creating ties to the community.** To prepare students for their professions and for the responsibilities of citizenship, Alverno builds relationships benefiting students with business, industry and community institutions.

❖ **Creating relationships with higher education.** Faculty and staff welcome from other educators constructive criticism of their teaching, scholarship and research. In this way, we hold ourselves responsible for a continuing contribution to the advancement of undergraduate education.

This mission finds expression in an educational philosophy focused on developing each learner in an outcome-oriented curriculum that uses performance assessment as a means to improve learning-in-process, and in academic structures that support faculty and staff in constantly improving the central process of our educational mission: teaching and learning. It is the unrelenting focus on everything connected with teaching and learning as a process that accounts for the "constancy of purpose" that often leads others to view Alverno as an educational institution embodying the principles of CQI.

We do not use the language of CQI when discussing these processes, because the quality principles have been integral to our curriculum for many years and have become business-as-usual (Spanbauer, 1992). We have found many of the principles and practices associated with quality initiatives congruent with our own educational principles and practices, particularly our theory and practice of assessment. In a sense, CQI principles and practice help validate what we have found as valuable in ability-based education that includes Assessment-As-Learning. This congruence is also significant, we believe, because it demonstrates that there are other routes to quality that have been developed and tested in higher education and that do not rely on importing the tools and methods of CQI developed in business and industry. As we explore this congruence, we will set forth a brief history of the Alverno educational model, the role of our faculty in this particular context and the way we structure our work together to improve the learning of our students.

DEVELOPMENT OF THE ALVERNO LEARNING PROCESS

Alverno faculty planned a new curriculum in the early 1970s, focusing on how a college education should prepare students to learn for life. As they planned this curriculum, the faculty held on to a number of educational values that guided their work: that learning should be active and become self-sustaining; that students should be involved in learning; that faculty should aim at individual development of students and the realization of human potential; that self assessment is both a means and end of learning; that knowledge is enhanced when applied; that achievement of competence can be assessed (Mentkowski and Loacker, 1985; Loacker, Cromwell and O'Brien, 1986). In 1973, the faculty expressed these values in a curriculum that continues to help unify our educational efforts and in which all students demonstrate eight major abilities within their disciplines or professional areas in order to graduate. These abilities include communication, analysis, problem solving, valuing in a decision-making context, social interaction, global perspective taking, effective citizenship and aesthetic response (Alverno Faculty, 1992). Rather than take for granted that these eight abilities would be developed across the usual general education and disciplinary courses, the faculty restructured the curriculum, making the mastery and demonstration of these abilities a requirement of graduation.

The educational values that guided the faculty in developing and continually refining the curriculum have their counterparts when looked at from a student perspective.

The curriculum:

❖ **Paces student learning.** Instead of focusing on general education (the eight abilities) or major outcomes only at several critical points in the learner's academic career, such as at graduation, the abilities are developed gradually and continuously. Beginning levels of the eight abilities are introduced across a wide selection of first- and second-semester courses, then more complex abilities are integrated into third- and fourth-semester courses. In the student's advanced level-work in the major or support areas, the focus is on advanced-level abilities.

❖ **Provides the opportunity for both breadth and specialization.** Students develop and demonstrate their abilities in multiple contexts that encompass different discipline areas as well as different courses. As students move into their advanced-level work in their major and support areas, they develop more sophisticated ways to use those abilities that are integral to the outcomes of their disciplines.

❖ **Requires learning and development across the curriculum.** It is not enough for students to develop and demonstrate an ability in a particular course where the primary learning occurs. Students are constantly challenged to draw upon and apply their abilities in new and more complex situations. Consequently, students are regularly called upon to make oral presentations, examine their own and others' values, and work effectively as team members so that they reinforce and refine the abilities they have previously learned.

❖ **Requires recurrent demonstrations of student performance in a variety of contexts.** Students are challenged to demonstrate writing, reading, speaking, thinking critically, interacting in a group and involvement in one-on-one interactions in the kinds of work situations or life roles that most often necessitate these abilities.

❖ **Integrates learning and assessment.** Assessment is at its most powerful when it moves beyond evaluation to learning. In the spirit of its etymological definition "to sit down beside," assessment is a process involving the continuous improvement of the student's learning by providing developmental feedback that influences future learning goals. In this way, assessment places in the hands of the student the means to become an autonomous, independent, self-directed learner.

❖ **Provides opportunities for both internal and external assessment.** Student performance is evaluated within the context of individual courses as well as in integrated, comprehensive assessments outside any particular course. In this way, students are challenged to transfer their learning into situations that extend beyond the classroom and any individual learning experience. These assessments are also opportunities for students to receive feedback from volunteer assessors, professionals and business people from the community, who bring their professional experience to the assessment of student performance.

FACULTY ROLE

The teaching and learning model that emerged from the principles and educational values described above is embodied in a faculty who share common educational goals, work collaboratively and take responsibility for continuously improving our theory and practice. Faculty at Alverno see themselves as responsible for managing the learning process both within their classroom and across the College.

Recently, the faculty have been engaged in discussions on the nature of teaching and the domains that underlie the work we do as teachers (Riordan, 1993). A fundamental assumption underlying these discussions is that teaching extends beyond what we do in the classroom. Consequently, to develop and improve the teaching/learning process, we must break open what we mean by teaching and the scholarship involved in developing as teachers. In his work with the Alverno faculty, Riordan (1993) has identified six domains or processes that make up the teaching enterprise: disciplines as frameworks for student learning; student learning styles and needs; assessment of student learning; curriculum coherence for student learning; collaborative inquiry; and pedagogical strategies. It is the work faculty do to improve the processes inherent in each of these domains that we believe enhances the quality of undergraduate education at our institution. The articulation of these domains and our systematic inquiry into each is in a sense our strategic plan for improving the educational process at the College.

Our emphasis on the continuous improvement of teaching and learning also finds expression in faculty-developed criteria for academic rank. These criteria focus on four areas of faculty responsibility: teaching effectiveness, responsible work within the institution, scholarly activity, and community service. The criteria for associate professor in Table 1 illustrate the multiple roles faculty exhibit, their responsibility for the curriculum, and to show how "constancy of purpose" is integrated into peer review and the College's reward system.

Table 1
CRITERIA FOR ASSOCIATE PROFESSOR

Teaches Effectively
❖ Integrates disciplinary/professional learning with teaching experience to shape teaching practice
❖ Applies developmental frameworks and learning theory to teaching practice
❖ Organizes learning experience to allow for flexibility in responding to students
❖ Engages in dialogue about teaching in the higher education community

Works Responsibly in the College Community
❖ Provides leadership in developing curriculum and teaching effectiveness
❖ Develops institutional role through significant contributions
❖ Creates strategies to enhance effective collaboration in the institution
❖ Pursues opportunities to improve the quality of teaching and learning across the institution

Develops Scholarship
❖ Holds terminal degree
❖ Pursues specialized research that integrates disciplinary area and teaching
❖ Applies specialized scholarly research to improvement of teaching and curriculum development in the institution
❖ Makes contributions to broader professional community

Serves the Wider Community

❖ Renders distinctive service to the wider community

[Taken from "The Alverno Educator's Handbook" (1992 rev.), Chapter 7, p.4.]

In addition, recognizing that teaching effectiveness is itself a developmental process, the faculty differentiated the criteria by rank. To illustrate this point, the criteria for teaching effectiveness at the other ranks are in Table 2.

Table 2
CRITERIA FOR RANK: Teaching Effectiveness

Beginning Assistant Professor

❖ Develops understanding of ability-based curriculum and assessment
❖ Teaches for appropriate abilities in disciplinary context
❖ Provides direction, clarity and structure for students
❖ Provides timely and helpful feedback
❖ Is available to and respectful of students
❖ Communicates enthusiasm for one's discipline

Experienced Assistant Professor

❖ Creates learning experiences and assessments that reflect integration of discipline and generic abilities
❖ Organizes learning experiences that assist students to achieve outcomes
❖ Provides feedback directed toward specific abilities and individual needs
❖ Responds to students in a variety of settings with sensitivity to background and learning style
❖ Generates student enthusiasm for learning
❖ Refines teaching practice based on self-assessment and feedback

Associate Professor

❖ Integrates disciplinary and professional learning with teaching experience to shape teaching practice
❖ Applies developmental frameworks and learning theory to teaching practice

- ❖ Organizes learning experiences to allow for flexibility in responding to students
- ❖ Engages in dialogue about teaching in higher education community

Professor
- ❖ Expands scope of scholarship to include new areas, other disciplines to inform student-centered teaching practice
- ❖ Takes leadership in developing materials, presentations to address significant curriculum concerns
- ❖ Influences professional dialogue about teaching scholarship in higher education community

[Taken from "The Alverno Educator's Handbook," Chapter 7, pp. 1-6.]

ORGANIZATIONAL STRUCTURE AND CQI

Academic Departments

The emphasis on the continuous improvement of the teaching and learning process is supported by a College organizational structure that provides time and resources for self-directed faculty work teams to focus on curriculum design and improvement. For example, faculty hold joint appointments in discipline and ability departments; a biology faculty member, for instance, holds an appointment in the Natural Science Division but may also be a member of the Problem Solving Competence Department. Every Friday afternoon during the semester is set aside for meetings of one or the other of these departments.

Alverno makes extensive use of teams to deal with academic and curricular issues (discipline division meetings, ability department meetings, standing and ad hoc committees) and promotes consensus and participatory decision making. In academic departments, decision making is decentralized, with departments setting their own goals and establishing their own priorities within the broad context of the Alverno mission. Curriculum and teaching decisions are in the hands of the faculty through their work in both discipline and ability departments as well as College-wide committees. The faculty and staff closest to the tasks are the ones who have the responsibility for improving them, whether those tasks be advising, curriculum design and revision, or other academic matters. In the spirit of CQI, resolving problems and pursuing opportunities for improvement are joined at the level closest to the student.

In sum, the institutional culture, rank criteria, academic decision-making approaches and reward structures emphasize the central role of teaching and learning and the need to continuously improve our practice.

Assessment and Organizational Structure

As mentioned earlier, in the process of defining the eight abilities and restructuring the curriculum and their own courses, faculty realized that students were more likely to develop as autonomous learners if they were actively engaged in testing these abilities individually and directly (Mentkowski and Loacker, 1985). The faculty subsequently designed an institution-wide measurement system to assess each student's progress in developing the abilities, a system we refer to as Assessment-As-Learning (Alverno College Faculty, 1985). This system provides diagnostic feedback to each learner and certifies that each student had achieved the eight abilities and the outcomes of her major. In 1976, the College also established an Office of Research and Evaluation to evaluate the quality, effectiveness and validity of the curriculum, to establish the validity of college-learned abilities for lifelong learning and to inform theory and practice in student learning and development (Mentkowski and Doherty, 1984). This office, in collaboration with the Assessment Council (a body comprised of faculty representing the eight ability areas and the disciplines), are the primary organizational structures charged with quality assurance of the assessment process. For a more extended explanation of assessment, see the reference "Assessment at Alverno College" (1985).

KEY FEATURES OF ASSESSMENT-AS-LEARNING IN RELATION TO CQI

Assessment as practiced at Alverno is a multidimensional **process** of judging the individual in action **on the basis of explicit outcomes and public criteria.** This definition of assessment reflects two important aspects of Assessment-As-Learning in relation to Continous Quality Improvement: it is a process, and it involves judgments based on data. Assessment-As-Learning involves the following points:

❖ **Samples of behavior:** Observing knowledge in use rather than observing "the right answer" on a test provides a more meaningful indicator of a student's true ability. The focus here is not on inspection but rather on improvement. Assessment principles move us beyond testing for the acquisition of knowledge to assessment as a means of observing knowledge in action and providing developmental feedback to students. In the spirit of Deming, "quality comes not from inspection, but from the improvement of the process" (Deming, 1982, p.22).

❖ **Performance of ability representing an expected learning outcome:** The Alverno faculty have developed a coherent framework for learning that integrates and relates college-wide outcomes (the eight general education abilities), discipline outcomes (expressed in the outcomes for each major and support area), course outcomes (identified in individual course syllabi) and assessment outcomes (stated in relationship to each assessment the student experiences). These outcomes represent a set of statements of what students can do with what they know and are developed out of what contemporary life requires and the faculty's experience with students. They are benchmarks that learners can use to measure their own development. If teaching is seen not just as the transmission of information from the teacher to the learner but a partnership that results in the creation of knowledge-in-action in the student, then students are active partners in the learning process, "producers" of the expected outcomes. This version of the teaching-learning process provides an interesting illustration of what Juran calls "The Triple Role" (Juran, 1992, p. 23). According to Juran, any individual involved in a process can be viewed as a customer, processor and supplier. Given the focus on outcomes just described, the student, often perceived as the "customer" is now the "supplier" of his or her "product" (learning).

❖ **Expert judgment based on explicit criteria:** Judgment itself is a process of using criteria as standards to evaluate the learner's demonstration of knowledge-in-action. Alverno recognized early on that norm-referenced approaches or grading on a curve would not be appropriate approaches to evaluating students, partly because learning (and for that matter, most human endeavors) is inherently a communal process, and because a single score or rank does not capture the uniqueness or quality in student performance. This approach echoes Deming's concern that in the business world, performance standards too often focus on the ability to meet quotas or numerical goals rather than quality (Deming, 1982). Managerial-use quantitative performance standards only ensures that employees meet daily quotas in terms of numbers, not quality. Using explicit criteria, on the other hand, provides the learner with a clearer picture of what is expected and what quality performance is. Also, using traditional letter grades tends to result in the sort of student to student competition that does not foster learning. (See William Gartner's article on using Deming's approach in a business class for an interesting case study on the impact of letter grades and criteria in the classroom.)

❖ **Feedback related to abilities:** Feedback is both an event – a time for the assessor "to sit down beside" the student – and a process identifying how the student's performance meets the criteria – how the performance reflects the student's individual strengths and weaknesses, and what the direction of future learning ought to be. Feedback focuses on behavior – the data of the assessment process. It is based on observations and the inferences that can be made from these observations.

❖ **Self-assessment as an end as well as a means to life-long learning:** Self-assessment is itself a process beginning with the ability to make accurate self-observations of performance, moving to the habit of questioning the meaning of those observations and making accurate self-judgments using performance criteria, and ending with goals for ongoing development and improvement. Along with feedback, self-assessment is a primary means for empowering the learner to become a self-directed, life-long learner.

The model introduced at the beginning of this chapter also provides the framework for a design process that focuses on the continuous improvement of our assessments. For many years, Alverno faculty have used the heuristic set out below, in a manner similar to the process Deming called the Shewart Cycle, which later became known as the Deming Cycle (or Plan-Do-Check-Act Cycle). This heuristic provides an assessment design and improvement process whereby faculty:

❖ Identify learning outcomes
❖ Generate broad criteria for performance evaluation
❖ Design an assessment instrument or process
❖ Refine broad criteria
❖ Determine who will judge the performance
❖ Determine a feedback process
❖ Evaluate the instrument or process

Alverno Assessment Design Process

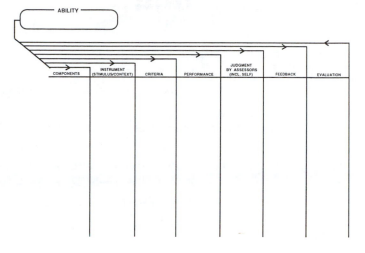

In sum, outcomes provide a direction for learning, ensure the continuity of the curriculum, provide accountability, and serve as integrating vehicles. The ability-based educational model that includes Assessment-As-Learning, provides both learner and faculty member with the primary means by which learning is made public and accessible in ways that enable both educator and student to plan for improvement.

Conclusions Regarding the Congruence Between Assessment-As-Learning and Continuous Quality Improvement Principles

As we reflected on our practice as educators over the past 20-odd years, our work on continuous improvement of administrative processes through the Alverno College Quality Council, and the national dialogue concerning the application of CQI principles in education, we became increasingly aware of those points of connection between the ability-based, Assessment-As-Learning model and CQI principles. In conclusion, we can summarize and make explicit those points of connection as they have been developed in this chapter and as we see them at this point in our continuous improvement journey. They are:

❖ Constancy of purpose

❖ Customer focus/Focus on student learning

❖ Reduce variation/Enhance curricular coherence

❖ Participative decision-making processes/Collaborative inquiry

❖ Commitment to continous personal and professional development

❖ Data-based problem solving/Measurement against explicit, meaningful standards

❖ Commitment to continous improvement

Constancy of purpose. For CQI to work, there must be a constancy of purpose, an unrelenting focus on doing the right things and doing things right. Alverno's constancy of purpose finds expression in the institutional mission statement, values, and beliefs with which this chapter began. Alverno's Assessment-As-Learning principles also share a recognition with CQI principles of the need for a common language within an organization to promote and support its "constancy of purpose." While CQI provides a language that focuses attention on the customer, on continous improvement, and on the processes that can be improved, Alverno's language focuses students and faculty on the unique needs of the learner, on student performance and development, and on teaching and learning as a process. Over the years, Alverno has created a college environment and organizational structures that support this "constancy of purpose" while at the same time creating our own language to share this experience.

Customer focus/focus on student learning. Organizations that practice CQI principles make external and internal customers the focus of everything they do. Similarly, an ability-based, Assessment-As-Learning curricular model shifts the focus from teacher, faculty and the discipline to the learner, the learning community and learning outcomes. It is the student-as-learner who is the unrelentingly focus of everything we do.

Reduce variation as much as possible/Enhance curricular coherence. Deming clearly asserts management's responsibility for designing and maintaining systems that improve quality by reducing variation and letting employees do their jobs. The Alverno counterpart to this is total faculty responsibility for and engagement in designing and continually refining an outcome-oriented curriculum that provides a coherent framework for the learner. Alverno faculty did this first by restructuring the curriculum to make the mastery and demonstration of abilities a requirement for graduation. The faculty continue to take responsibility for refining our curricular "system" by comparing general education and major/support area outcomes to what contemporary life requires, researching whether the curriculum prepares students for life after graduation, and systematically refining our assessment processes. It is this collaborative inquiry and shared ownership of the curriculum that makes possible the constancy of purpose and a coherent educational framework.

Participative decision-making processes/Collaborative inquiry. Employees empowered to solve problems at appropriate organizational levels is a key feature of CQI approaches. In our experience, the overall quality of an ability-based, Assessment-As-Learning curriculum is maintained and improved when faculty collaborate continuously. This collaboration is accomplished through joint faculty appointments in discipline and ability departments, cross-College problem-solving teams that include both faculty and academic staff, an organizational communication and work style that promotes collaboration and collaborative problem solving, and an institutional research model that focuses on shared ownership and responsibility for the curriculum and its ongoing improvement. These elements have helped Alverno create a culture that embodies open decision-making processes and shared ownership and responsibility. Equally important is the fact that explicit outcomes and public criteria assist students to develop the ability to accurately assess their own performance and develop as autonomous learners, thereby taking responsibility for their own learning and development.

Commitment to continuous personal and professional development. Recognizing that people are an organization's greatest asset, Alverno shares with CQI principles a commitment to the ongoing development of its faculty and staff. In both cases, a commitment to personal and professional development provides the solid foundation on which the organization itself grows and develops. It is the means of ensuring that central principles, whether related to teaching and learning or continuous improvement, are understood and correctly applied. Toward this end, Alverno has, over the years, developed a well-defined in-service program for new and continuing faculty and staff that consists of new faculty and staff orientations, workshops, and College-wide institutes that bring all faculty and staff together three times a year. These activities focus on critical and emerging issues related to teaching and learning, strategies for improved effectiveness in all matters related to the development of our students, and the communication of information related to institutional goals and progress toward them.

Data-based problem solving/Measurement against explicit, meaningful standards. Judgments regarding student performance in an Assessment-As-Learning environment, share with process improvement decisions in a CQI environment, the need for data as the basis for action. The ability-based curriculum and principles of assessment that focus teaching and learning across Alverno ensure that faculty make judgments regarding student performance based on data. Through the use of explicit outcomes and student performance criteria, their common understanding of the abilities that are at the heart of the curriculum, and their discipline expertise faculty are able to describe in specific behavioral terms the accomplishments of their students. This principle extends beyond the classroom to the measurement of faculty effectiveness through the use of the rank criteria previously set forth in this chapter. These criteria ensure that faculty effectiveness is itself described in specific behavioral terms.

COMMITMENT TO CONTINUOUS IMPROVEMENT

The corollary to process improvement in Assessment-As-Learning is the belief that learning does not stop at graduation and that it is indeed a life-long process. Consequently, the undergraduate experience should provide the student with those tools, skills and strategies needed to be a self-directed life-long learner. This is the ultimate goal of ability-based education and Assessment-As-Learning as described in this chapter.

REFERENCES

Alverno College Faculty. *Assessment at Alverno College* (rev.ed.) Milwaukee, Wisc.: Alverno Productions, 1985.

Alverno College Faculty. *Liberal Leaning at Alverno College* (rev. ed.). Milwaukee, Wisc.: Alverno Productions, 1992.

Alverno Educator's Handbook. "Chapter Seven: Rank and Promotion," 1-6, 1986, 1992 (rev.).

Deming, W. E. *Quality, Productivity, and Competitive Position.* Cambridge, MA: MIT Center for Advanced Engineering Study, 1982.

Gartner, W..B. "Dr. Deming Comes to Class," *Journal of Managment Education,* May 1993, *17*,(2), 143-158.

Juran, J. M. *Juran on Quality by Design.* New York: Free Press, 1992.

Loacker, G., Cromwell, L. and O'Brien, K. "Assessment in Higher Education:

To Serve the Learner." In C. Adelman (ed.), *Assessment in Higher Education: Issues and Context*. Report no. OR 86-303. Washington, D.C.: U.S. Department of Education, 1986.

Mentkowski, M. and Doherty, A. *Careering After College: Establishing the Validity of Abilities Learned in College for Later Careering and Professional Performance*. (Final report to the National Institute of Education: Overview and Summary) (rev.ed.). Milwaukee, Wisc.: Alverno Productions. (ERIC Document Reproduction Service No. ED 238 556), 1984.

Mentkowski, M. and Loacker, G. "Assessing and Validating the Outcomes of College." In P. Ewell (ed.), Assessing Educational Outcomes. *New Directions for Institutional Research*. San Francisco: Jossey-Bass, 1985.

Riordan, T. *Beyond the Debate: The Nature of Teaching*. Milwaukee, Wisc.: Alverno Productions, 1993.

Spanbauer, J. *A Quality System for Education*. Milwaukee, Wisc.: ASQC Press, 1992, 170.

William McEachern is an associate professor of business and management at Alverno College and current dean of the Business School. A graduate of the University of Toronto, he has worked in public accounting in Canada and the United States. At Alverno, he has been active in the design and implementation of the college's developmental assessment methods to evaluate student outcomes. He has also recruited and trained bank officers as assessors for an innovative and integrated assessment  of business majors. His teaching interests include accounting, finance, and small business management.

McEachern is a member of the Milwaukee Section of the American Society for Quality Control; the Milwaukee: First in Quality Education Committee; the Alverno College Quality Council and is advisor to the college's ASQC student chapter.

Kathleen O'Brien is the academic dean at Alverno College. In 1976, she established the Business and Management Division and chaired it until August 1991. She holds an M.B.A. from Vanderbilt University and a Ph.D. in management from the Graduate School of Business, University of Wisconsin-Madison. Since 1976, she has been involved in designing and implementing an outcome-oriented business degree program that relies heavily on assessments to chart the development of its students. She has also served as a consultant to a number of colleges and universities on ability-based education and assessment. She assisted in the design of an ability-based executive M.B.A. program for Nijenrode School of Business in the Netherlands and also taught in that program's summer session for five years.

She has done research on the validity of the outcomes of the business major as related to those abilities which characterize successful managers. Recently, she has studied the development of self-assessment ability and methods that can increase the accuracy of these self-appraisals.

26

Total Quality Management: A Class That "Walks Its Talk"

Merlin J. Ricklefs

Each year, the University of Minnesota-Duluth appoints a 3M McKnight Distinguished Visiting Professor in Industrial Engineering from the academic or corporate/industrial world. The goal of the 3M McKnight Visiting Professorship is "to provide a base of outstanding expertise that enhances technology development resulting in regional economic development." Responsibilities include developing and teaching a class, engaging with local organization and industry workers to strengthen their ties with the University, and presenting public lectures and keynote speeches within the region.

It was my privilege to be selected by the University for this professorship during the 1991-92 year. I drew upon my 31 years of experience with IBM, primarily in management positions which were associated with the development of midrange computer systems and later as the IBM-Rochester Site

Quality Manager, where I held a leadership role in winning the 1990 Malcolm Baldrige National Quality Award for the site.

I chose to develop a class in Total Quality Management (TQM) as part of the professorship. My role and responsibilities were also expanded to include coaching and advising the administration, faculty and staff on how to adapt the concepts and principles of TQM into the academic and business life of the University.

Following is a brief description of that experience and the program in TQM which I developed and delivered to the University. This program owes much of its success to the enthusiastic support, ideas and participation of the faculty, administration and staff of UMD.

The class, titled Total Quality Management, was presented to undergraduate students in both engineering and business, as well as graduate students enrolled in M.B.A. and Ph.D. programs. In addition, we opened the class to the community. The response was so positive that we scheduled a completely separate session as an Executive Development Class for people from the city of Duluth, the University and the surrounding area. They represented University leaders, company presidents, technical specialists focused on quality, and others interested in learning and understanding TQM concepts and principles.

The program went beyond teaching TQM in the classroom. The course presentation methods were deliberately constructed to demonstrate the concepts I was teaching. In addition, the students were actively engaged in developing stronger links between the classroom and local technology-based industries and between the classroom and the University administration. A summary of the content within the TQM course is listed in Figure 1 on the following page.

The class had a set of **objectives**. These objectives were discussed in some detail to help set student expectations.

Figure 1

Total Quality Management Class Content

Lecture/Discussion
- ❖ Introduction and class overview
- ❖ Today's changing economic environment
- ❖ Basic principles and concepts
- ❖ Malcolm Baldrige National Quality Award...the process
- ❖ Leveraging the MBNQA for self-assessment
- ❖ Characteristics of leading companies (MBNQA winners)
- ❖ Philosophy and teachings of leading experts
- ❖ Strategy for customer-focused quality improvement
- ❖ Initiatives for people development and empowerment
  - – education
  - – survey techniques
  - – management as a role model
- ❖ Initiatives for quality as a primary business strategy
  - – strategic planning and requirements
  - – customer involvement
  - – process management
  - – defect elimination
  - – cycle time reduction
  - – measurements
  - – benchmarking
- ❖ International perspective
- ❖ How to get started

Special Project
- ❖ Provide a realistic environment for learning
- ❖ Partner teams with local industries and the University
- ❖ Coach the teams to perform a business assessment based on the Baldrige criteria
  - –strengths
  - – areas for improvement
  - – recommended actions for improvement

Course Objectives

Upon the successful completion of this course, it is expected you will:

1) Understand the fundamental concepts and principles of a Total Quality Management System.

2) Understand how to define and implement a quality improvement strategy in all areas of an organization.

3) Learn how to apply the Malcolm Baldrige criteria to a total business self assessment.

The term **Total Quality Management** is frequently shortened to TQM. Each person has his or her own definition for the acronym and often thinks of it as a program – a program that has a beginning, some special activities, an end and then goes away. However, I believe that Total Quality Management will be with us for a long time. It is not a program. It is a different way to think and a different way to act. It is a way of life. I offer a very simple definition of Total Quality Management: **"a system of management that integrates a continuous focus on improvement into all facets of all areas of an organization."** Improvement is "customer-focused" improvement. If you wish to use "leadership" instead of "management," that is excellent. Good management is good leadership. My point is that quality improvement must be as pervasive and all inclusive as possible.

Two years ago I had the opportunity to work with the University of New Mexico in delivering a National Television University symposium. Dr. Joseph Mullins, the Director of Manufacturing Engineering, said that by the end of the century, there will be two types of manufacturing industries within the United States. There will be those that implement Total Quality Management effectively and there will be those that disappear. I don't know if there is a direct parallel to education, but I think it is worth pondering.

Next, I believe it is important that we have a common

understanding of the definition of quality. Juran discusses the big "Q" and the little "q" of quality. I have found it helpful to describe this in the following way. Defect-free products and services are really the traditional little "q" of quality. In today's global environment, this is no longer a significant differentiating characteristic. It is an expected minimum requirement. The big "Q" of quality requires excellence in all areas of the business production and service processes. It requires excellence from our suppliers as well as our customers and an understanding that there are both internal as well as external customers and suppliers.

Each individual within an organization provides a **deliverable** (i.e. makes a contribution); each provides that deliverable to somebody. That somebody who receives the deliverable, by definition, is a **customer**. Each individual is dependent upon somebody or something in order to accomplish his or her task successfully. That dependency, by definition, is a **supplier**. All elements of the product and service are included within the big "Q" definition of quality. That includes price, function, schedule, performance, marketing, delivery, sales and support. There is no virtue in delivering a defect-free product or service that is too late for the customer to use. There is no virtue in delivering a defect-free product or service on time that is too expensive for the customer to buy. There is no virtue in delivering a defect-free product or service on time that the customer can afford but which does not have the function the customer really wants and needs. All of those things must be part of the quality equation.

In addition, customers want to do business with organizations that are going to remain stable and healthy suppliers. You buy a pair of shoes. You like the service and you like the shoes. You would go back to the same store and buy the same brand again in the future. You buy a car, a washing machine, health care; as a satisfied customer you would like to do repeat business with a stable and healthy supplier. To me, that brings profit, revenue and financial responsibility directly into the quality equation and makes them part of the quality definition. I believe that is particularly true in education. People want to have their degree from an institution that's going to be there over time. An institution that grows in reputation and stature will cause degrees past and present to grow in value.

This definition of quality considers the entire customer relationship and is measured by customer satisfaction. The corollary is that a **defect**, by definition, is any deviation from 100 percent customer satisfaction. If it's admissions, the registrar, the person behind the information desk, the professor in the classroom, the chancellor or the president who has defects or flaws in what he or she is doing, it is a defect to the total customer relationship – a defect in the big "Q" of quality.

Why focus on quality? Survival, and more importantly, prosperity are dependent on quality. I felt it was important that my class understand a simple principle of economics. The environment has changed. After World War II, this nation was the only industrialized nation in the world that survived with its industries intact. We were in a surplus-demand and limited-supply environment. In that situation, the reward went to those organizations who were able to supply in quantity. Quality was not necessarily an important issue. Regardless of quality, the need was so great, there was someone somewhere who would buy, leading us to develop some very bad habits. That is no longer the situation. Today, we are in an environment where there are many who can produce as well as we can, in the volumes we can, with higher levels of quality. We are in an environment where there is a surplus supply and a limited demand. Rosabeth Moss Kanter summarized it very well in the *Harvard Business Review* when she stated, "The power is shifting from the people who sell to the people who buy. The reason for that is they have more choices, they can get it from anywhere, and there are more companies, more organizations, competing for their attention." The most successful will be those who can deliver with quality in the big "Q" sense. I believe this principle of supply and demand applies to universities also.

Among the results that can be realized from implementing a quality improvement program are increased productivity and lower cost. Increased productivity can be derived from doing things right the first time. However, doing things right the first time is only half of a quality improvement initiative. Defining the right things to do is equally important. From an industrial point of view, there's no virtue in building the world's most efficient warehouse if you didn't need the warehouse to start with. In a parallel way, there may be no virtue in improving the teaching methods within a classroom where the class content may no longer have relevance in society or to future employers. There is little virtue in optimizing educational processes that are not important to implementing the mission and goals of the university.

Creating a vision and developing a sense of purpose for an organization is fundamental to leading and motivating the members of that organization. The Total Quality Management class had its own **vision**. The students were taken through a special exercise during the first session to obtain buy-in to this vision. The vision was, **"Participation in this class will make a difference in the professional life of each student and the business direction of each of the participating organizations."**

To complete the special projects identified in Figure 1, the class was divided into teams. The undergraduate teams each worked with an industry in the community, and the graduate team worked with the University itself. During our first team meeting with the participating organizations, I reviewed the class vision statement. The message communicated to the president of the company/chancellor of the university was that we as a student team had a vision. That vision is, we would like to come back within one or two years and have you say, "Our morale is improved, our customer satisfaction is up, we've gained market share, our profit and revenue is improved. And you know, it was that group of students who were here one or two years ago that really got us thinking about how we were managing our organization. That was the beginning of our turnaround." So, looking the president in the eye I asked, "Do you buy that vision?" What do you think he said? "Sure!" What a great way to get started.

In addition to discussing vision at the first class session, we discussed **principles for academic excellence.**

Principles for Academic Excellence:

❖ There is a measurable difference between enthusiastic support and passive participation (academically reflected in grades).

❖ Content is a better judge of contribution than volume.

❖ Understanding is increased through student discussions and sharing of work (guideline...ask to review from others only that which you are prepared to share of your own).

❖ Attendance by itself accomplishes little except to use natural resources – space, food, and energy.

❖ Learning and contributing can be fun.

Also, the class was presented a statement of the **anticipated student (customer) interest profile**. In this particular situation, when I was the professor standing in front of the class, they, in my mind, were my **customers.**

Anticipated Student (Customer) Interest Profile:

Upper-level or graduate students in the College of Science and Engineering and the School of Business and Economics:

❖ Interested in strengthening their technical and management leadership skills
❖ See a need for quality improvement

❖ Concerned about America's ability to compete in today's global economic environment

❖ Desire knowledge of the Malcolm Baldrige process and elements of a Total Quality Management system as it applies to technology management, technology development and business

Community leaders, business leaders, faculty and administration:

❖ Aware of the global competitive challenge and recognize the need to improve.

❖ Hold some expectation that incorporating the principles of a total quality management system into their organization will help.

❖ Possess a limited knowledge of the Baldrige process but have an interest in learning more.

❖ Overall have a desire (approaching commitment) to improve customer satisfaction (everyone has customers), improve profits, and enhance competitiveness.

After discussing the student interest profile, I made it clear that if the students did not see themselves within this interest profile, then they were probably in the wrong class. If that were the case, we should discuss it because that's the customer to whom I was planning to deliver.

In addition, I identified a set of **Critical Success Factors** – characteristics for how the students needed to perform in this particular class if they were going to be successful.

Critical Success Factors:
Ability to:

❖ Define complex problems
❖ Think creatively and critically
❖ Work in groups or teams
❖ Evaluate evidence (work with imperfect data under imperfect circumstances)
❖ Identify solutions

❖ Make decisions (draw conclusions, make recommendations)
❖ Communicate effectively to a variety of audiences

We came back to these critical success factors many times
as the students were doing their special projects. We especially
focused on working as a team on real-world problems with
imperfect data under imperfect circumstances.

We also had a set of **key processes**. Associated with those
key processes were a set of **measurements**. The primary purpose for introducing the concept of key processes and measurements into the classroom was to introduce quality improvement terminology into a real-life academic environment. The
first key process was **reading assignments**. The text and other
reference material selected for the class was the following:

❖ *Total Quality* by Ernst and Young
❖ *Malcolm Baldrige Award Winning Quality* by Mark Gra-
ham Brown
❖ Malcolm Baldrige National Quality Award Criteria
❖ A three-ring binder of current literature and important
reference material

Ernst and Young wrote their book for the busy executive
who only had time to read one book. It reads well and is
structured to form a handy reference. Chapter one is particularly informative and direct.

Brown's book helps interpret every "Area to Address"
within the Baldrige criteria. It explains what the examiners are
looking for and also what one would expect to see implemented
in an organization that has a good quality improvement system.

The Baldrige Award Criteria provides, in addition to the
criteria items, a well-written, concise guide for implementing
a quality improvement system.

The three-ring binder contained recent articles from leading business publications, abstracts of each Baldrige winner and summaries of leading quality experts.

The second key process was **prepare three questions** on the assigned homework prior to each class. The students were to pursue the answer to these questions during the class. The questions were handed in and they became a small part of their overall course grade. This idea came from Professor Bob Bratlin, who invited me to be a guest lecturer for his M.B.A. class at the University of St. Thomas in St. Paul. He told me very little about the class ahead of time. As I put up my first introductory overhead, I received a barrage of questions. I finally got through that overhead, went to the next, and received the same audience response. I had two hours worth of material and only used six to eight overheads. This class took me through my entire presentation strictly on interactive dialogue. Afterwards, I questioned Professor Bratlin. "This was the most dynamic audience I've ever been in front of. What did you do to these folks?" "Well," he said, "I make them write three questions before they come in. They hand them in, and it's a small part of their grade." I said, "That's a good idea; I'm going to implement it." I offer it as a suggestion. It is a tool that has worked very effectively for me in a variety of situations.

I took it one step further. I had each of the students, on a simple form, circle 1 through 5, indicating how well the class answered their questions. This provided me some ongoing feedback on how well the class performed that day. The emphasis is on how well the class answered their questions, not how well I, the professor, answered their questions. Teaching and learning in the classroom is a cooperative effort.

The third key process was **executive briefings**. During my years of experience managing professional people, I was often saddened by the inability of some very capable technical contributors who could not effectively communicate their achievements, and therefore could not make as much of a difference as they would like. One of the principles this class learned was that there is a lot more virtue in content and clarity than in volume. For the executive briefings, the students were given a large volume of material, which they were assigned to condense into one page. They were instructed to communicate the most information in the least amount of time and space. They were to assume that I was their division president, at least two levels removed from them, and they had to write to me, on one page, the essence of what they learned from this package of material. There was a tutorial on how to write an executive briefing early in the quarter, a statement of purpose for each executive briefing assignment, and a scoring guideline which described how the briefings would be graded. As an example, one assignment required that the two-page abstracts published by the Malcolm Baldrige National Quality Award Foundation for all Baldrige winners be consolidated to one page. The statement of purpose was "describe the characteristics most winners have in common." Small typing, squeezing out to the borders, etc., were off limits. It had to be a one-page, legitimate executive briefing. The students were also advised to realistically plan on three drafts to get to a final version. One student came to me after the first exercise and said, "Wow. I put four hours into this. This is hard work." I smiled and said, "That's exactly the way it's supposed to be. What did you learn?" The student acknowledged she had learned a lot.

The fourth key process was the **special project**. As I indicated, undergraduate teams (four) of both business and engineering students, each worked with industries in the area. The graduate students worked as a single team with the university itself. The undergraduate students did an assessment based on the Baldrige criteria Category 1.0 (Leadership) and Category 7.0 (Customer Satisfaction). The graduate students (to add rigor to their program) did their assessment of the University based on all seven categories of the Baldrige criteria.

These are:

Category 1.0	Leadership
Category 2.0	Information and Analysis
Category 3.0	Strategic Quality Planning
Category 4.0	Human Resources
Category 5.0	Management of Process Quality
Category 6.0	Results
Category 7.0	Customer Satisfaction

These projects were challenging pieces of work for a one-quarter class. The students were amazed and pleased how much they were able to learn about a complex organization in a short period of time.

The first step for the special project was for each student to rewrite their assigned section of the Baldrige criteria into layman's language. Next, each team submitted their questions to their respective organization. The organization then wrote a response to each question, which was really a description of how they did things in their organization. The results of this first cycle were off the mark. The students did not write the questions as astutely as they could have, and the companies did not respond as astutely as they could have. This was part of the learning experience and was anticipated.

A second cycle was built into the schedule for the students to rewrite the questions, go back to their organization, and obtain additional information. Following that series of steps, they identified the strengths and weaknesses of the organization, which we discussed as opportunities (areas) for improvement. Building on that information, they developed a set of recommendations. The final exam for the class was to present to the president/chancellor of the organization 1) a formal written report, and 2) a stand-up presentation summarizing strengths, opportunities for improvement and their recommendations.

This provided a very professional real-world experience for the students. For the undergraduate students, it meant standing in front of the president and the entire senior management team, telling them what they were doing right, where they had room for improvement and thoughtfully presenting a set of recommendations for how they could improve. One company president immediately offered the students a job to help implement their recommendations. This was exciting feedback for that team of students.

The approach in forming the teams was very simple. First it was "engineering students, raise your hands and count off; business students, raise your hands and count off. All the one's are a team, two's are a team, etc." Although this did not accommodate other student characteristics or interests, it did establish a balance of engineering and business students on each team, which satisfied one of my most important criteria. The graduate students were formed into their own separate team.

Next, the teams were organized by having the members each select a **team operational responsibility** and a **specific technical responsibility**. These responsibilities were structured to provide each member a leadership role in which they were dependent upon each other's cooperation in order to complete his or her task. In addition, each member developed a unique expertise and performed a unique function. Collectively, the team could become much stronger and more capable faster than any of the individuals alone.

This approach seeks to combine the strengths of the individual initiative with the strengths of teamwork. It promotes a balance between the innovation and motivation, derived from the individual, with the breadth, depth and collective judgment that can come from teamwork.

In addition to the delegation of responsibility and authority for individual roles, it also provides for delegation of accountability to each individual for the success of the group as a whole. It is very apparent to all team members whenever one fails to execute his or her leadership role effectively or fails to provide critical support when needed. This individual accountability is important in both the real-world and in the classroom.

The **team operational responsibilities** were defined as:

❖ Team leader to assure effective and efficient team meetings

❖ Team leader interface and interview strategy team leader to summarize the company/university background and current business position for assessment consensus on strengths and areas for improvement

❖ Team leader for consensus on final recommendations

❖ Team leader for final report and presentation (if the other team leaders do their job well, this task is easy)

The **specific technical responsibilities** were individually assigned "Areas to Address" from the Baldrige criteria.

By participating in the above special project and other classroom processes, the students developed an understanding for how the Baldrige criteria can be used for learning the concepts and principles of a quality improvement system, how to apply it as an assessment tool, and how to use what they learned to develop and implement a customer-focused quality improvement strategy.

The customer-focused approach to quality improvement requires a major focus on people development and empowerment and on integrating quality as a primary strategy into the leadership of an organization. The strategy can be summarized for teaching purposes into a fish-bone diagram like that shown in Figure 2. The goal should be adapted to the particular organization, but should include the concept of becoming the

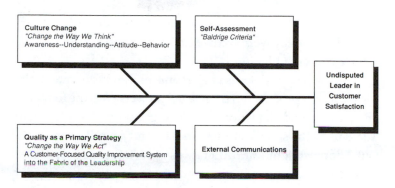

Figure 2
Quality Improvement Strategy

Culture Change
"Change the Way We Think"
Awareness--Understanding--Attitude--Behavior

Self-Assessment
"Baldrige Criteria"

Undisputed Leader in Customer Satisfaction

Quality as a Primary Strategy
"Change the Way We Act"
A Customer-Focused Quality Improvement System into the Fabric of the Leadership

External Communications

undisputed leader in customer satisfaction. The Baldrige process is an excellent assessment tool for defining where an organization is on its quality journey and how far it has yet to go.

The culture change focuses on **"changing the way we think"** and can be divided into four stages:

❖ **Awareness:** some problems exist and you learn what they are

❖ **Understanding:** you can do something about them

❖ **Attitude**: you want to do something about them

❖ **Behavior:** you develop the skills to be able to do something different tomorrow than you were able to do yesterday so you can produce the results we are looking for.

Quality, as a primary strategy, focuses on **"changing the way we act"** and stresses driving a customer-focused quality improvement system into the fabric of the leadership for an organization.

External communications merely highlight the fact that

---

organizations that are progressing well on their quality journey tend to be externally visible because they communicate effectively.

Some of the most important initiatives required to implement this strategy were studied in the class and are listed in the course content in Figure 1.

So far I have discussed elements of the class content, the class roll-out process and the special projects with the four area institutions and the University. The Executive Development Class used the same lecture materials and a similar class roll-out. The most significant differences were: 1) the special projects were focused on conducting an assessment of the particular organization the students happened to represent, and 2) I volunteered to speak to the president and senior management team of the students in the class where there was an interest. This was significant in helping the students transfer the knowledge they learned in class back to their companies and to the University.

Another important aspect of the program was my linkage with the director of Instructional Development Services (IDS) for the university. IDS is responsible for stimulating faculty development by helping faculty improve in their teaching skills. The director's regular attendance in the TQM class accomplished two goals: 1) I benefited from the advice, coaching and one-on-one feedback; 2) the IDS Director learned about customer-focused quality improvement. Some of those concepts and principles are being integrated into the IDS faculty development program and are being deployed across the University. We also surveyed the students extensively to learn how different students (engineering vs. business and undergraduate vs. graduate vs. executive development) responded to the same instructor, teaching methods and materials.

I would like to conclude by describing how the University evaluated the recommendations for improvement from the graduate students' special project. Their seven-category assessment of the University included approximately 250 recommendations. To prioritize these recommendations, we defined a process which asked the 21 senior administrators to rank in order of l) importance to the success of the University and 2) effort required to take actions that would make a noticeable improvement. This approach identified the most important recommendations that were the easiest to implement as the highest priority. This simple technique helped the University identify where to start.

For Americans, the process of continuous improvement does not fit as naturally into our culture as it does to some others. A recent study by the American Quality Foundation concluded, "America's culture is still basically an adolescent culture. It is characterized by irrepressible optimism, wild enthusiasm and high energy. It is emotional and volatile, impaired by high hopes and lofty visions, countered by bouts of depression and self-criticism. It places great faith in the magic of technology to achieve impossible dreams. It is always restless and impatient to change, never knowing quite what it is or might be . . . improvement for Americans is personal . . . improvement means never being satisfied with who or what we are. "

It is important to understand this cultural characteristic of Americans. As we proceed to develop educational programs and implement continuous improvement strategies, this knowledge may help us understand why implementation may be more difficult than anticipated. Also, we should take advantage of the American strengths to innovate, take risks and make break-through changes in those situations where we conclude that continuous improvement may never allow us to achieve the goals we ultimately want to achieve. In those cases we may want to completely eliminate the existing process and "re-engineer" or define a new process. This is a bold step and requires visionary leadership. There are times when "break-through" thinking is proper, and there are times when continuous improvement is the most constructive course. Leadership must decide which course of action is the right one to pursue.

Response to the overall program, the class and the special project was very positive. Representative comments from survey feedback are included in Figure 3.

The overall message delivered to the class and to the participating organizations was, "Winning is a continuous, relentless pursuit of not only satisfied customers, meeting their needs and wants, but exceeding their expectations and achieving delighted customers. In the ultimate sense, we want to achieve successful customers. Successful customers realize new opportunities, and through these new opportunities, they will grow and experience new challenges. We hope they will come back to us for additional solutions. For the University, that may mean alumni personally returning to graduate school; hiring new graduates; engaging in joint ventures; proudly recommending attendance to their children, employees, and friends; and ultimately sharing their fame and fortune.

Figure 3

Closing the Loop for Continuous Improvement:
A Summary of Survey Feedback
Strengths and Opportunities for Improvement

Students

❖ "The content of the course was very important and the method of learning was very appropriate."

❖ "I was excited to go to class. I enjoyed participating in groups and group activities. This was a tremendous learning experience."

❖ "... too much for a three-credit course."

❖ "Change the class to allow more time."

Participating Faculty

❖ "Learned a lot for the time spent."

❖ "A positive experience working with motivated students from different disciplines learning to work together."

❖ "The scope of the graduate student project may have been too large."

Participating Companies

❖ "The course had a unique approach that benefited both ourselves and the students."

❖ "It was a good self-analysis."

❖ "It gave us exposure to a great tool for planning a quality strategy."

❖ "The questions could be better tailored to a small size company."

University as a Participant

❖ "There was a surprising amount of correct info about the University."

❖ "A great learning tool – we now have a base from which to demonstrate progress."

❖ "Would have liked greater University attendance." (final report)

Merlin J. Ricklefs is co-founder and president of Quality Associates International, a firm that focuses on adapting the concepts and principles of customer-focused quality improvement to higher education and technology-based research and manufacturing companies. He was the 1991-92 3M McKnight Distinguished Visiting Professor in Industrial Engineering and Professor in the Graduate School of Business at the University of Minnesota-Duluth. While at the University, he devel-

oped a program that integrates Total Quality Management into the curriculum content, classroom teaching processes, University administration and University linkages with area industries.

Ricklefs was previously the IBM-Rochester site quality manager, where he had a leadership role in winning the 1990 Malcolm Baldrige National Quality Award. During his 31 years with IBM, he held several management positions in the development of mid-range computer systems, including IBM corporate program director of storage products and manager of business and systems evaluation.

Ricklefs is a frequent conference presenter and workshop leader. He has recently led studies and participated in national conferences devoted to linking TQM to university teaching principles, strategic workforce development issues and small business assessment processes. He has demonstrated the ability to achieve measurable results in a wide range of unstructured, complex, multi-discipline environments. He has B.S. and M.S. degrees in engineering from Iowa State University, and is a graduate of IBM's management of technology program. He is a senior member of The American Society of Quality Control and a 1992 Minnesota Quality Award examiner.

27

CQI: A Model for Reform Based on Assessment-As-Learning and TQM

Ralph Mullin
George Wilson
Michael Grelle

A department head decided to purchase a bulletin board for her office which cost $26.45. Petty cash could not be used for anything over $25, so she had to submit a formal purchase order. The purchase order required five signatures. To save time, she decided to hand carry the purchase order around campus and get the signatures herself. When she came to the last office to get the fifth signature, she was frustrated to find eight people before her in line. She finally got into the office and complained rather forcefully about having to stand in line so long. The next day, five chairs were put in the hall outside the office.

Too often we become so accustomed to doing things a particular way that we are unable to step back far enough to scrutinize the whole process. Fundamental change is seriously impeded by tunnel vision brought on by seven of the most dangerous words in the English language – "We have always done it that way." Changes tend to be made within the existing system rather than change to the system itself. Thomas Kuhn (1970), explains this phenomenon in his description of a paradigm. When a paradigm has been in place for an extended period of time, its principles and assumptions become culturally ingrained. They create boundaries which direct and confine our thinking, although we are not conscious of their influence. Hegel (1954) describes this blindness of the familiar as, "The obvious is unknowable." Whitehead (1925) similarly suggests, "It requires a very unusual mind to undertake the analysis of the obvious."

When observation and data seem to conflict with expectations, the immediate reaction is to cite errors in data collection and interpretation or to seek solutions within existing limits. Kuhn refers to inconsistencies in observation, compared to the expectations of accepted theory, as anomalies. He states that a change or shift to a new paradigm is preceded by a period of increasingly frequent anomalies which eventually force explicit recognition, articulation and examination of the principles and assumptions of the existing paradigm.

As is obvious to the general public, to business, to government and to some educators, the current educational system is producing too many anomalies. What is not yet obvious is that changes that result in substantive, lasting improvement in the quality of student learning will require a shift to a new paradigm.

Deming, the father of the total quality movement, has repeatedly stated that individuals generally want to do their best. Deming (1986) suggests that 85 percent of quality problems arise from system error, while only 15 percent arise from individual error. He concludes that focusing resources on system improvement is far more effective than focusing on individual improvement. Peter Senge (1990) suggests organizational change efforts generally fail because they do not approach the problem using systems thinking. The implication for higher education is that innovations within the current system will continue to produce marginal results, compared to the same resources focused on system reform.

An alternative model is needed that addresses the following questions: What should determine student competence? What should students be learning in school? What should drive the curriculum and other means? What experiences do students need to optimize learning? What is the role of assessment?

The time has come for higher education to stop "putting more chairs in the hall." It is also time to explicitly evaluate the merits of higher education's paradigm and core process. Faculty must lead this effort. Until the assumptions and principles underlying the current course-credit completion model are brought into conscious awareness and carefully examined, until alternative models are developed from more logical sets of assumptions, and until alternative models are actively tested, reform efforts will continue to produce, at best, minimal improvements in student learning. One such alternative is the Continuous Process Improvement (CPI) model being developed at Central Missouri State University (Central). This chapter describes CPI, contrasts it with the course-credit model, reviews Central's experience in implementing the paradigm shift and summarizes lessons learned from practice.

The authors' general premise is that education is in the early stages of a paradigm shift and that educators and the public will increasingly experience anomalies, i.e., failures in the current paradigm, until the paradigm for higher education, the course-credit completion model, is replaced.

THE CPI CONCEPTUAL FRAMEWORK

Central's CPI model builds on the 10 Assessment-As-

Learning (AAL) assumptions originally developed by Alverno College (Exhibit 1). The principles of Total Quality Management (TQM), which are highly complementary with AAL, provide additional underpinning for the CPI model and provide functional terminology for communicating the CPI model to employers. Basic AAL assumptions and TQM principles applied in the CPI model are summarized in Exhibits 1 and 2, respectively. This section describes the major elements that comprise the CPI model: the organizational mission, the core process criterion, and the core process design. The CPI paradigm shift is then described in terms of fundamental changes in the framework of higher education.

Organizational Mission

The TQM literature emphasizes that organizational change begins with re-envisioning the mission. This critical examination begins the process of paradigm shift. Without this examination, nothing that follows will work. The mission must clearly define a singular, simple, focused purpose for the organization's existence. The mission provides the basis for designing and validating the core process. Creating a clear, singular focus for a complex organization sounds deceptively simple. It is not.

The process of collaboratively re-envisioning and consensually agreeing on the organizational mission is as important as the mission statement itself. The mission sets the stage for rethinking strategies and methods, while the process provides an evolutionary means for participants to take ownership in a singular mission and the implicit set of values it represents.

The first assumption of AAL embraced in Central's CPI model is that student learning is the University's mission and primary purpose. As the TQM literature suggests, such an organizational mission will provide direction and motivation only if it is individually and collectively valued. Faculty must own both the process and the product of re-envisioning the mission. If faculty, staff and administration consensually value a singular mission, and that mission is student learning, then the CPI model is relevant. This is a necessary condition for successful implementation of CPI.

Core Process Criterion

The University's core process is the system by which the mission, student learning, is accomplished. The utility of the core process lies in its ability to produce outcomes consistent with the mission. In the CPI model, the faculty of each major program specify the criteria for the core process in terms of a comprehensive set of performance-based student abilities or "general outcomes." General outcomes involve complex abilities which integrate knowledge, skills and attitudes (KSAs). These general outcomes define the desired "ends" of the core process and focus all learning activities and methods. This core process criterion is consistent with Exhibit 1, Assumption #2, "Education goes beyond knowing to being able to do what one knows."

Faculty take ownership through the consensual process of defining the general outcomes. Articulating the outcomes and making them public allows other important constituents (employers, graduate schools, etc.) to participate in outcomes validation and to share ownership (Exhibit 1, Assumption #9). The set of general outcomes becomes the end of the educational system and the criterion for measuring the effectiveness of the core process.

Core Process Design

The classroom is the basic vehicle for student learning. The CPI design for classroom learning, established on principles of AAL, involves faculty and students. Faculty: (1) define performance-based student abilities to be learned and demonstrated in the course, (2) write criteria which specify the expected characteristics and quality of performance for each ability, (3) observe student performance based on the stated abilities and specific criteria, (4) assess student performance based on expert judgment, and (5) provide developmental feedback to the student against the specific criteria. Students: (6) process the feedback cognitively, and (7) repeat the performance. The CPI design of the core process is depicted in Figure 1. This learning process is supported by most cognitive and behavioral learning theory, and by substantial empirical evidence (Bandura, 1977, Luthans & Kreitner, 1985).

Figure 1
CPI Core Process Design

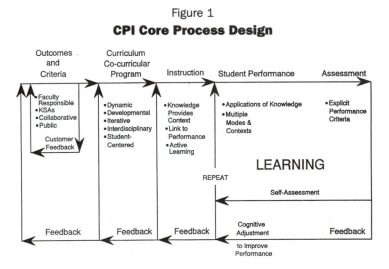

In the CPI model, students acquire complex abilities developmentally when they "make an action out of knowledge" based on specific performance criteria, receive feedback based on expert judgment, and cognitively adjust to improve their subsequent performance (Exhibit 1, Assumption #6). Students learn from repeated opportunities to practice desired abilities in various situations and contexts. These multiple experiences facilitate the retention of knowledge and the transfer of abilities to new situations at higher levels of generalization (Exhibit 1, Assumption #5).

Observation and assessment of student performances is not a series of discrete milestones, but a continuous and integral part of the CPI core process design (Exhibit 1, Assumption #4). Assessment produces feedback as a part of a continuous improvement process for each individual student. Because general outcomes involve multidimensional, complex abilities, students must perform and be assessed in a variety of modes and contexts (Exhibit 1, Assumption #5).

In the CPI model, courses and sets of courses (curriculum) are the means that provide a structure for student learning. Each course is developed as an element in a coherent curriculum, structured so that students acquire complex abilities developmentally across courses. Although feedback from student performances guides student learning, it also provides information for continuous review and improvement of courses and curriculum (Exhibit 1, Assumption #9). Creation, maintenance and improvement of a coherent curriculum is iterative, continuous and dynamic (Exhibit 1, Assumption #8). Curriculum management depends on faculty investment in a community of learning and judgment (Exhibit 1, Assumption #7).

CPI Paradigm Shift

Degree requirements drive student and faculty action in the learning process. In the traditional course-credit model, degree requirements are stated exclusively in terms of required courses. The set of required courses serves as the criterion for the core process, as the organizing principle for structuring the major program and as the end of the educational process. Since the course-credit criterion provides no systematic mechanism to coordinate and integrate student learning developmentally across the curriculum, courses typically evolve as discrete packets of content knowledge. Neither faculty nor students have the means or the impetus to transfer or generalize knowledge and skills from one course to another.

The CPI model shifts the measure of student competency and the organizing principle for the degree program from the completion of courses to the demonstration of performance-based abilities. In the CPI model, the required curriculum becomes a means for systematic, developmental student learning while performance-based student abilities are its ends. Changing the role of curriculum from ends to means is subtle but profound. It is a paradigm shift which compels at least eight fundamental, systemic changes in program design and pedagogy.

First, the CPI description of the major in terms of ability-based performances provides a **common organizational principle** for faculty and student action. Individual courses are unified around performance-based abilities that describe the major program, such that complex communication, interpersonal, thinking, valuing and technical skills are learned developmentally across a variety of context and content specific courses.

Second, the CPI public articulation of the performance-based abilities allows **involvement** of all "customers and suppliers" in designing the learning process. All interested constituencies, including students, alumni, employers and other faculty can review and assess outcomes for relevancy and importance. They provide the means for developing relationships with elementary and secondary educators (suppliers).

Third, the CPI emphasis for student learning shifts from the recollection of **content knowledge** to the demonstration of performance-based abilities. This demonstration requires each student to integrate KSAs. This shift in emphasis enhances the value of "content knowledge," by promoting learning at a higher level of understanding. The preeminence of student performance is consistent with the AAL Assumption #2, that "education goes beyond knowing to being able to do what one knows."

Fourth, the CPI focus on student abilities forces systematic consideration of the developmental nature of the learning process. **Curriculum**, as the "means," must be designed to foster student progress from basic to more advanced proficiency levels, and to engender student learning of complex abilities as a developmental process. CPI recognizes that many alternative learning paths may develop the desired student abilities. Empowered with the knowledge of the expected outcomes, students can take additional responsibility and initiative for their own intellectual development.

Fifth, CPI allows **co-curricular learning** activities to directly complement formal course work. Leadership of organizations, internships, developmental seminars, work experience and other campus activities provide valuable learning opportunities which contribute to the development of desired student abilities. Instructors may help students to identify appropriate co-curricular learning opportunities related to student performance expectations and individual student abilities.

Sixth, CPI makes **assessment** an integral, continuous part of the learning process, instead of inspection and a grade at the end. Assessment is a continuous process, not a series of discrete steps. Expert judgment based on the observation of student performances provides feedback for performance improvement. Students learn to regard assessment of performances in terms of constructive opportunity for improvement, rather than as a mechanism to determine a grade.

Seventh, and most importantly, CPI unifies the curriculum around performance-based student abilities to enjoin a constructive change in classroom **teaching methods**. Instead of learning exclusively "about" the content knowledge related to a discrete course, students must learn to apply, assess and reflect on content knowledge in a variety of contexts. By understanding the performance-based abilities expected of them, students are better able to recognize how skills and knowledge are to be transferred and developed across courses. The public statement of these abilities provides an explicit road map to guide individual student learning, thereby increasing both the opportunity and motivation to learn.

Eighth, CPI **feedback**, although primarily used for individual student development, is also useful for improvement of courses and curriculum. Over time, the observation of student performances provides information about the relationship between student performances and curriculum to assess the efficacy of the core process.

These eight fundamental differences are summarized in Exhibit 3, which presents a comparison between CPI and the course-credit model. These differences constitute a paradigm shift, requiring major changes in the organizational culture.

CENTRAL'S IMPLEMENTATION EXPERIENCE

Central's experience with assessment and quality improvement is divided into three stages and time periods: (1) preliminary stage, 1985-1988, (2) model discovery and development, 1988-1991, and (3) the CPI/FIPSE Project, 1991-1994.

Preliminary Stage

In 1985, Central's Faculty Senate responded to calls by state government and administration for greater institutional accountability by establishing an assessment policy and committee in 1985. During the same period, the University established the following: (1) assessment of math and writing skills of entering freshmen for placement guidance prior to enrollment, (2) a writing-across-the-curriculum program, (3) assessment of the English department's writing program, and (4) further development of Central's Educational Development Center.

The Assessment Committee spent much time and effort responding to departmental requests for examples of assessment and tests. Increasingly, committee members were frustrated by: (1) requests for a test to assess a major program for which faculty could not clearly define the outcomes to be assessed, (2) the lack of congruence between the content of standardized tests and content being taught (content and construct validity), and (3) the lack of usefulness of test results either to improve student learning or to evaluate programs. Over and over again, members raised the same questions: "What is it that we should be measuring? Why? And to what end?" This increasing frustration served to clarify the needs: (1) explicit definition of the purpose and ends of assessment, (2) the expected outcomes of student learning, and (3) a comprehensive assessment model to explain the complex learning and measurement process. In the fall of 1987, the committee began an intentional search for a model and funded the first phase of an experimentation program.

Model Discovery, June 1988-June 1991

This three-year phase was characterized by: (1) discovery of a sound model, (2) faculty exposure, understanding and acceptance, (3) experimentation with alternative assessment methods, (4) discovery that the principles of TQM and Assessment-As-Learning (AAL) are highly congruent, (5) recognition that a fundamental cultural change was evolving which would require multiple transformation phases, and (6) design and development of goals, strategies. and an implementation program.

The search for a sound model to guide reform ended in June 1988 at the American Association for Higher Education (AAHE) Third Annual Assessment Conference, where Alverno College's Assessment-As-Learning model was discovered. Focusing on student learning resolved purpose or mission. Understanding assessment as an integral element in the learning process itself, coupled with Alverno's logically sound set of assumptions, provided a clear conceptual basis for a model.

Although a few faculty received the model positively, most simply did not grasp the profound implications of the assumptions and completeness of the model (Exhibit 1). Bursting paradigms and changing organizational culture, involving basic assumptions, values, behaviors and relationships, would be difficult, gradual and time-consuming. Recognizing this need, the Faculty Senate Assessment Committee made faculty exposure to assessment experiences a priority. Over 50 faculty participated in a variety of assessment conferences in the next two years. Members of the Assessment Committee became committed to the assumptions of assessment as learning by attending a number of assessment conferences where Alverno was represented, generally by Dr. Georgine Loacker. By fall 1989, the Committee framed a set of principles defining assessment at Central, and sponsored two important on-campus conferences: a series of seven meetings conducted by Peter Ewell, involving over 200 faculty, and a three-day Assessment-As-Learning workshop conducted by a team of four faculty from Alverno with 125 faculty participating. Over 40 selected faculty, representing four colleges and 17 disciplines, received intensive training at the week-long Alverno workshops in 1989, 1990 and 1991.

An experimentation program was planned to determine what might be learned from a traditional standardized test and whether skill development might be integrated with content knowledge learning to increase both. The experimentation used two sets of measures developed by the American Assembly of Collegiate Schools of Business (AACSB). Both sets were developed to measure a clearly defined and specified set of outcomes generated by AACSB's Outcomes Measurement Project (1987). The first set measured a common body of

knowledge to which students are expected to be exposed in most business schools' core curriculum. This instrument was a traditional multiple-choice test of recognition. While this set required some reasoning and calculation, it basically tested content recall. The second set was intended to measure the **skills** and **personal characteristics** commonly agreed to be required for success in business (Gordon & Howell, 1959; Porter & McKibben, 1989). This latter set used assessment-center exercises evaluated by trained assessors at Development Dimension International (DDI), a pioneer in the assessment center method in industry and developers of the measures for AACSB.

The purpose of the experimentation program was to learn more about testing versus **performance-based assessment**, and the **usefulness** of each for both student learning and program evaluation. The results of the knowledge test yielded no useful comparative data in that the standard error was greater than the difference in means from comparable schools. In other words, on average, our students were no better or worse than those at other business schools in the sample, which provided no data which was useful for either program evaluation or student learning.

The performance-based assessments were used in three phases: (1) a one-group pre-/post- design with 35 students in 1988, (2) a Solomon four-design test with 276 students in 1990, and (3) application of assessment methods in 17 different courses in four colleges during the 1990-91 school year. As an example of how the faculty educational effort interacted with the experimental program, faculty who taught the 17 courses in Phase III were the evaluation team for the Phase II research. The evaluation team committed to attend the five-day Alverno workshop, teach a course using AAL methods (Phase III), and later mentor other faculty in Phase IV (CPI/FIPSE project).

The results of the two field experiments using the assessment battery evaluated by DDI are reported in *Managerial Skills: Explorations in Transferring Practical Knowledge*, Sage Publications, 1991. The empirical results were highly supportive and conveyed that our approach to assessment and reform was scholarly and rigorous.

Early in 1990, continuing discussions between a dean, several faculty, and executives of major firms led to the realization of the striking conceptual similarities between TQM and Assessment-As-Learning. This discovery enriched thinking about how to implement the Central model and how to communicate to employers effectively. By early fall 1990, we were prepared to frame how we might implement a model of AAL and TQM at Central. A strategy was developed beginning with reform in the academic major, starting with the 10 (of 34) departments most open to reform. Each successive year, as faculty experienced success, the number of departments involved was to increase. A future three-year phase (1994-97) might include general education and other departments. To proceed at a faster pace might increase the risk of faculty failing to develop ownership. The policy of volunteer participation – that interested departments ask for a solid consensus of their faculty, after full discussion of the required commitment, before deciding to join the project – was emphasized repeatedly.

A preliminary proposal was drafted and submitted to FIPSE, forcing participants to think through the goals, plans, programs and resources needed. In January 1991, FIPSE invited a final proposal, compelling development of details on the design, goals and a program of implementation. While a project team of faculty had been organized, decisions could not be made on many of the goals without actually gaining commitments from all faculty in participating departments. A draft proposal was sent to all 34 departments inviting them to consider participation. Preliminary meetings with department chairs were followed by meetings with the entire faculty of departments showing interest. Faculty were asked to read the preliminary proposal in advance to better understand specific commitments. Ten departments (12 academic majors) with balanced representation from the four colleges (three majors from each college) volunteered. The 10 department chairs helped develop materials to include as exhibits with our final proposal. A team of the project director, co-director and CPI team advisor did the final editing. This broad involvement of faculty, an essential TQM principle, was a key to success.

The CPI/FIPSE Project, 1991-1994

From March to September 1991, planning proceeded on the assumption the FIPSE grant would be approved. We discussed with our president and provost how we might continue to implement the model without FIPSE funds (with only Central's $50,000 direct-matching funds), at a sharply reduced pace. End-of-the-fiscal-year funds enabled a new high of 26 faculty to attend Alverno's workshop in June and to buy supplies. When final notice of the award from FIPSE was received in September, 16 hours of initial training for faculty in the 10 participating departments had already been conducted. Before FIPSE approval, most of Central's matching money had been committed for training and release time for the 12 departmental project coordinators. The project was launched. The 14 departments, 19 programs and 200 faculty, including second-year additions (1992-93), are shown in Table 1. The goals of this three-year phase (1991-94) are shown in Exhibit 4. A summary of the nine program components or tasks to implement our goals are shown in Exhibit 5.

The first year's achievements included faculty training, outcomes definition and validation and curricular evaluation. Assessment-As-Learning in the classroom, comprehensive assessment and curricular change are year two (1992-93) emphases (Exhibit 6). New initiatives in year two (1992-93) in-

Table 1
Participants and Contact Person

COLLEGE	DEPARTMENT	FACULTY	PROGRAM	STUDENTS	COORDINATOR	PHONE NUMBER
Business & Economics	Economics & Finance	10	Economics	35	Mark Karscig, D-310C	816-543-4817
		6	Finance	170	Jose' Mercado, D-301B	816-543-8650
	Graduate Programs (COBE)	(10) 4	MBA[1]	180	Harry Poynter, D-108C	816-543-8571
	Internship & Co-op Ed.	1	Internship[1]	70	Bill Garber, D-102E	816-543-4632
	Management	12	Management	500	Janet Winter, D-400C	816-543-8568
Education & Human Services	Curriculum and Instruction	11	Secondary Education	900	Wayne Williams, LOV 302A	816-543-8701
		10	Elementary Education[1]	1100	Carol Mihalevich, LOV 209	816-543-8731
	Special Services	4	Recreation & Tourism[1]	150	Bob Slana, LOV 201B	816-543-8932
	Speech Pathology & Audiology	8	Speech Pathology	175	Marilynn Schmidt, MAR 137	816-543-4916
	Physical Education	12	Physical Education	180	Joyce Bailey, MAR 102	816-543-4172
Arts & Sciences	Chemistry & Physics	7	Chemistry	40	Mike Powers, WCM 415	816-543-8727
	Communication	14	Journalism	110	Carol Mills, MAR 136F	816-543-4609
		7	Organizational Communication	95	Joe Mazza, MAR 136L	816-543-8583
	English	37	English B.S.Ed	55	Allen Ramsey, MAR 336M	816-543-8705
	Mathematics & Computer Science	(23) 9	Math[1]	189	Larry Cammack	816-543-8865
Applied Science & Technology	Electronics Technology	9	Electronics Technology[1]	150	Clarke Homoly, TRG 318H	816-543-4980
	Human Environmental Sciences	(7) 4	Hotel and Restaurant Admin.	150	Sandra Dessenko, G-232	816-543-8737
	Manufacturing & Construction	17	Manufacturing[1]	100	Lyman Hannah, COT 101	816-543-8593
	Nursing		Construction[1]			
		17	Nursing	195	Julie Clawson, SHC 117	816-543-8305
	TOTAL FACULTY	**199**	**TOTAL STUDENTS**	**4869**		

Grelle, Michael, Psychology, LOV 112-B, 543-4208
Mullin, Ralph, Management, D-401E, 543-4818
Wilson, George, Economics & Finance, D-212C, 543-8597

[1] First Year 1992-93

14 Departments
19 Majors
20 Programs

clude expanding the project by: (1) adding seven new programs, (2) decentralizing by greater involvement of the college deans who now meet with their CPI chairs and departmental project coordinators monthly, (3) initiating CPI/TQM training and planning with the president's cabinet and administrative departments, (4) developing a preferred supplier program beginning with a one-day workshop with high school principals and teachers, (5) faculty participation in industry TQM training programs, and (6) further development of customer relations guided by a Quality Advisory Team from TQM companies.

LESSONS

What has been learned from Central's experience that might be of value to others beginning the process?

Paradigm. The first order of business is to challenge the fundamental way higher education approaches its mission. Reform programs need to explicitly recognize the need for revolutionary and systemic change in the educational process. Simply overlaying TQM principles over a flawed existing structure will not produce lasting change in organizational culture and behavior. The power of a theoretically-sound model of the learning process is a necessary condition for reform.

Core process. TQM companies have learned this is essential. Clear definition of mission and the related core process provides meaning and focus to everything else, and is the fundamental control mechanism that directs and motivates people and functions in complex social systems. For Central, the mission is learning and the student learning process is the focus for all university functions.

Principles. The assumptions of AAL and principles of TQM provide invaluable guidance. However, principles only instruct practice and must meet the three "I" test to be effective – interpretation, integration (simultaneous application) and implementation. For example, "focus on customer" must be interpreted and understood in a comprehensive way as meaning anyone whom you serve, who uses or benefits from the value of your effort. If one narrowly interprets this principle to simply identify the student or the employer as the customer, the principle has lost its power to explain and guide. Failures were invariably a result of not attending to all relevant principles simultaneously. TQM is not simplistic; it is complex and requires systematic application (integration). Quality results are still dependent on quality implementation. TQM is not a magic formula. Careful focus on implementing the details is still necessary.

Leadership. Some articles on TQM stress top-down leadership as a first and necessary condition. Others, particularly in education, suggest that bottom-up leadership is the key. It takes both, and one must understand the different roles and timing. In higher education, the starting point is with faculty. The power motivating change must come from faculty who value learning, teaching and service enough to want to improve.

Again from experience, it may be advantageous for faculty leaders **not** to be protected or of high status with the administration. Faculty leaders will be most respected by other faculty if they are viewed as independent and internally motivated. Motives and values are main factors when asking people to transcend their self interests by taking risks and doing the hard work of reform.

Top-down leadership must empower faculty to lead, encourage innovation, and provide funding and freedom to experiment. Central's leadership did not officially sanction the model early on, but allowed faculty to develop support. Faculty were attracted because they believed in the logic of the model, not because of official sanction. Leaders must be patient in order to allow enough time for faculty to take ownership voluntarily. The people who will make quality improvement succeed or fail must be involved and empowered in making design and measurement decisions.

Involvement. Balancing representation among our four colleges was important, and incorporated from the beginning.

Focus. We learned from Alverno to fund hot spots of energy, concentrating time and money on those who are most committed and producing results. Also, no energy should be expended on those who refuse to be open to logical argument while keeping open to change.

Patience. Torbert (1992) suggests one of three reasons TQM fails is because it requires "multiple transformation phases over a decade of time." Planning must be done in terms of decades. Reform leaders must emphasize there is no quick fix. Cultural change, involving everyone in an institution, will demand patience and transcending leadership.

Money. Seed money, in this case from FIPSE and Central, may be necessary to overcome inertia, get new processes going, and flexibly fund hot spots of energy. External funds also strengthen credibility.

Training. The need for training is constant and eternal. At each progressive stage, more and more skills and knowledge are needed.

CONCLUSION

A paradigm shift is starting in higher education. Institutions on the leading edge will gain an advantage – just as in business. The Continuous Process Improvement model is one viable alternative guide for reform. At least four reasons exist to draw from CPI as a guide to reform.

First, the CPI model strikes at the heart of the serious flaws in the obsolete course-credit completion model. Since this paradigm powerfully influences all curricular and pedagogical decisions, a precondition for **fundamental reform** is to draw it into consciousness and examine it. The CPI model does this.

Second, the CPI model focuses on **system** versus individual improvement where Deming (1960) insists 85 percent of improvement potential exists.

Third, the CPI model as an alternative paradigm forces the educational process to be responsive to the ever-changing needs of society because it requires explicit definition of **student performance outcomes** as defined by both internal and external customers (faculty, students, alumni, employers, etc.). These outcomes provide an effective means for coordination and control of the complex and interactive educational process. Extensive in-class and comprehensive assessment of student demonstration of these outcomes provide the measurement data for continuous learning and improvement – a fundamental assumption of Assessment-As-Learning and a TQM principle. The course-credit model provides no comparable mechanism to drive continuous improvement.

Fourth, Central's CPI project, initiated and developed by faculty, is demonstrating that faculty will provide **leadership** for substantive improvement. The model assures, once accepted by faculty, their full interactive involvement. With faculty leadership and involvement, real reform that reaches into the classroom and affects student learning will happen, resulting in long-term change.

A comprehensive state university of 12,000 students from mid-America has limited credibility; however, if Central's implementation continues to be effective, the CPI model will add evidence to Alverno's 25 years of experience that outcomes-driven, performance-based, assessment-integrative, student-focused learning is significantly more effective than the flawed course-credit model. The next step is to have a large research-oriented public or private university demonstrate and test a similar model.

Exhibit 1

Assessment-As-Learning Assumptions

Student Learning and Assessment

1. Student learning is a primary purpose of an educational institution.

2. Education goes beyond knowing to being able to do what one knows.

3. Learning must be active and collaborative.

4. Assessment is integral to learning.

5. Abilities must be developed and assessed in multiple modes and contexts.

6. Performance assessment – with explicit criteria, feedback and self assessment – is an effective strategy for ability-based, student-centered education.

Curricular Coherence and Development

7. A coherent curriculum calls for faculty investment in a community of learning and judgment.

8. The process of implementation and institutionalization of a curriculum is as important as the curriculum; the process is dynamic, iterative and continuous.

9. Educators are responsible for making learning more available by articulating outcomes and making them public.

10. Responsibility for education involves assessing student outcomes, documenting inputs and relating student performance over time to the curriculum.

From the Consortium of Teaching, Learning and Assessment, funded by W.K. Kellogg Foundation, including Alverno College, Bloomfield Hills Model High School, Central Missouri State University, Clayton State College, Gallaudet University, Macomb Community College, Purdue University School of Pharmacy, South Division High School, Township High School District #214, University of Wisconsin Medical School, and the University of New Mexico School of Medicine.

Exhibit 2
Key Principles of TQM

TQM is a set of management principles and core values. While each of the founders of TQM (Deming, Juran, Crosby) define their essentials differently, there are common themes which can be distilled into a set of principles. We focus on four: l) Customer Focus; 2) Commitment to Continuous Process Improvement; 3) Involvement; and 4) Systems Thinking.

1. Customer Focus: Customer satisfaction is the criterion for quality. Just as the value of a gift is defined by the receiver, quality is defined by the customer. Defining customer satisfaction is the beginning, the end, continuous. Everyone in the system must identify and develop a working relationship with their customers. External customers are the receivers of your system's product or service. Internal customers are within the system, e.g., students, the instructor next in line who is dependent on what the student learns in your class. Internal customers are important in defining, assessing and improving the process. Everyone should identify, define, measure and meet the criteria for satisfaction of their customers. This begins when people make a deliberate effort to identify their internal and external customers. It matures when all customer-supplier relationships are well-defined partnerships.

2. Commitment to Continuous Process Improvement: Everything is a process. TQM focuses on how each process can be improved. Continuous improvement assumes well-defined objectives, criteria and measurement (assessment). This requires a deep personal and shared commitment to quality (excellence) which transcends other personal and short-term concerns; thus, the commitment is by nature enduring and strategic. This correctly implies the necessity of a fundamental cultural change in many organizations.

3. Total Involvement: Involvement goes beyond many earlier participatory management notions. It means more than encouraging cooperation, sharing responsibility, participation in some decision making, and working in teams. Involvement is facilitated by providing quality education and training initiatives which allow employees to learn and use skills which go beyond current job task requirements in order to redesign work processes. Involvement may be the key to simplifying processes. Involvement assumes everyone is a valued and competent partner who believes in and acts on the ideal of quality.

4. System Thinking: TQM asserts 85 percent of total error is "common cause variation" or "system error;" only 15 percent results from individual performance. TQM is fundamentally different (paradigm shift) from traditional management which may be inordinately concerned with individual performance.

Exhibit 3
Eight Fundamental Differences

CPI Model	**Course-Credit Model**
1. Common Organizational Principle: Explicitly defined performance-based student abilities are the organizing principles for curriculum and pedagogy. The comprehensive set of general outcomes require students to integrate knowledge, skills, and attitudes and unify the curriculum.	1. Required courses are the basis for organizing the degree program. Individual courses evolve as discrete packets of knowledge because no set of comprehensive student learning goals exists.
2. Involvement: General outcomes are determined and validated by faculty, students, alumni, employers and others. Participation of all constituencies provides clear direction for improvement and continuous feedback. General outcomes provide a basis for active collaboration with high schools (suppliers).	2. No mechanism systematically provides information and feedback from various constituencies.
3. Content Knowledge: Content knowledge provides the context for all learning. Students learn by making an action out of knowledge. Content knowledge must be demonstrated.	3. Content knowledge is the primary focus of individual courses. It is seldom developed in the context of general abilities, demonstrated in an active performance context or transferred outside the individual course.
4. Curriculum: Curriculum provides the "means" for student learning. Curriculum is unified by outcomes, creating a developmentally sequenced, logically coordinated program of courses. Curriculum changes in response to feedback and other information.	4. Curriculum is the "end" as well as the "means" for the learning process. There is no unifying principle or systematic process to create a connection between and across courses. Individual courses are structured by individual faculty with little outside interaction.
5. Co-Curricular Learning: Co-curricular learning complements classroom learning. Outcomes provide connection between courses and cocurricular activities. Activities provide means for performance knowledge and skill practice.	5. Out-of-class activities are generally regarded as competitive with classroom work. Skill development in co-curricular activities is independent of course end degree requirements.
6. Assessment: Emphasis is on performance-based assessment relative to explicitly stated outcomes. Assessment is an integral part of the learning process. Assessments are developmentally connected and carefully sequenced throughout the program. Both internal (in-class) and external (out-of-class) assessments are used.	6. Instructors typically "inspect" quality at end of the learning process. Assessment has little impact on individual student development because feedback is limited, easily ignored and often viewed by students as irrelevant. "Objective," non-performance-based measures are often used. Assessment is used to determine grades.
7. Teaching Methods: Assessment-As-Learning teaching methods demand student involvement. Students learn "to do" rather than "about" the course material. Practice is essential to learning and retention. Students must think, judge, decide, act and create. Students and faculty are often co-learners, and effective learning experiences include group learning, peer tutoring and collaborating with others. Students self assess and peer assess against established criteria.	7. Professors lecture. Students listen, take notes and read the course text. Examinations focus on recall of information. Feedback to students is typically limited to examination scores and cursory comments. Feedback is seldom used as a basis for student development. Students are inclined to be passive rather than active learners.
8. Feedback: Feedback from assessments identifies strengths and weaknesses. Students learn self-assessment skills. Information obtained from assessments is used for improvements.	8. Little feedback is produced for either student performance improvement or curriculum improvement. No systematic mechanism provides for effective use of feedback that is produced.

Exhibit 4: CPI/FIPSE Project, 1991-94
Outcomes

1. A new Continuous Process Improvement model for design, development and implementation of curricular, pedagogical, program and institutional reform. The model will be driven by the principles of Alverno's Assessment As Learning (AAL) and Total Quality Management (TQM) and will focus on student learning as the core process.

2. General student outcomes and exit-level capabilities for Central's general education program and program-specific outcomes for 19 majors.

3. A cohesive, integrated (course content and general outcomes), outcomes-driven, and assessable curriculum for 19 major programs in four colleges; a continuous system of evaluation (curricular matrix) based on feedback from student performance; and a method and structure to continuously modify curriculum.

4. A capability to do a program of in-course and comprehensive assessments and to have prepared and have in use learning exercises for in-course and instruments and procedures for comprehensive assessment of students' demonstration of outcomes.

5. A demonstrated set of outcomes-focused, performance-based teaching methods and materials which integrate assessment with knowledge and skill development and provide systematic feedback to students, for improving performance, and teacher for modifying classroom exercises and techniques.

6. A renewed and enhanced faculty (200) who have: (a) collaborated within and across disciplines to identify student outcomes and criteria; (b) evaluated and modified curriculum and developed new teaching and assessment methods; (c) articulated both general and program-specific student outcomes to students, faculty, staff, and external stakeholders; (d) demonstrated competence in assessor skills; and, (e) have become better teachers, capable of mentoring the remaining faculty (300).

7. An extensive nonacademic student services staff experienced in systematically providing opportunities for students to enhance abilities learned in the classroom – specifically, a co-curricular program which officially documents the student's nonacademic involvement and helps the student apply the principles of self-assessment to general intellectual skills.

8. Students (5000) who have completed a student orientation course to prepare students for the outcomes-based learning system, and can: 1) demonstrate ability to articulate expected outcomes; 2) demonstrate competence on a set of ability and knowledge outcomes; 3) provide potential employers assessment-center-type validations of ability levels; 4) meet the demands made of them by professional schools, graduate schools, and the private and public sectors.

Exhibit 5: CPI/FIPSE Project, 1991-94

Program Components

1. Faculty and professional staff **training** (40 hours) in the Assessment As Learning approach and the Continuous Process Improvement model.

2. Definition of general and program-specific **outcomes** – knowledge, skills and attitudes (KSAs).

3. Validation of the general outcomes by senior students, graduates and employers.

4. Evaluation of curriculum, integration of course outcomes and development of a **curriculum matrix.**

5. Course preparation and development of course-specific learning exercises and assessments.

6. Development of **co-curricular** outcomes and assessment processes.

7. Development of a **student orientation course** or module.

8. Comprehensive **assessor training** for selected faculty (two per department, 20 total).

9. Development of criteria and design of **comprehensive assessments**, methods, instruments and procedures to assess student performance on general outcomes (to be implemented in the fall of 1992).

Exhibit 6: CPI/FIPSE Project, 1991-94

Program Emphases In Second Year

1. **In-class Application (Pedagogy):** Faculty will develop course-specific outcomes from the curriculum matrix to implement systematic in-class learning and assessment of the general outcomes; outcomes-focused, performance-based methods using feedback from student performance assessments will be used as a basis for improving instruction and evaluating curricular effectiveness.

2. **Comprehensive Assessment:** Develop assessment instruments and procedures to measure student achievement of explicit outcomes at entry to and exit from the major.

3. **Curricular Change:** Implement changes suggested by the curriculum matrix, and continuously evaluate and modify curriculum based on feedback from student assessment.

4. **Student Orientation:** Prepare students for the outcomes-based learning system.

5. **Co-Curricular:** The co-curricular transcript program will provide students opportunities to diagnose, practice, and develop targeted ability outcomes in their out-of-class experiences.

6. **Faculty Training:** Expand faculty training to include a) four CPI forums, b) basic training in outcomes and criteria writing for new faculty/departments, and c) industry TQM training for 12 selected faculty.

7. **Student Outcomes:** Continue to refine and validate student outcomes with customers.

8. **Impact:** Present and publish project experiences and the model.

REFERENCES

Baudura, A. *Social Learning Theory*. Englewood Cliffs, N.J.: Prentice-Hall, 1977.

Cappelli, P. "Workplace: Assessing Performance to Improve the Fit," *Change*, Nov./Dec., 1992.

Deming, W. E. *Out of the Crisis*. Cambridge, Mass.: MIT, Center for Advanced Engineering Study, 1986.

Gordon, R. A. and Howell, J.E. *Higher Education for Business*. New York: Garland, 1959.

Hegel, G. W. *The Philosophy of Hegel*. New York: Modern Library, 1954.

Kuhn, T. S. *The Structure of Scientific Revolutions*. Chicago, Ill.: The University of Chicago Press, 1970.

Luthans, F. and Kreitner, R. *Organizational Behavior Modification and Beyond: An Operant and Social Learning Approach*. Glenview, Ill.: Scott, Foresman and Company, 1985.

Porter, L. W. and McKibben L. E. *Management Education & Development*. New York: McGraw-Hill, 1989.

Senge, P. *The Fifth Discipline: The Art & Practice of Learning Organization*. New York: Doubleday, 1990.

Torbert, W. R. "The True Challenge of Generating Continual Quality Improvement," *Journal of Management Inquiry*, 1992, 4.

Whitehead, A. N. *Science and the Modern World. Lowell Lectures, 1925*. New York: The MacMillan Company, 1925.

Ralph F. Mullin, George W. Wilson, and Michael J. Grelle have worked as a team for six years to design and implement a model for continuous assessment of explicitly defined student outcomes to improve the quality of student learning at Central Missouri State University. The last two of these six years have been devoted to what is called the CPI/FIPSE project described in the chapter – CPI is an acronym for Continuous Process Improvement, FIPSE is for Fund for the Improvement of Postsecondary Education. While these three faculty work as a team, they do play different roles. Mullin is the spiritual leader concerned with planning, finance and external relations. Grelle is the "good guy" concerned with internal relations, training, evaluation. Wilson is the logician, writer and humorist. All three are devoted teachers.

Ralph Mullin is director of the CPI/ FIPSE project. He has served six years on Central's Assessment Committee, and he has served continuously on the College of Business & Economics Assessment Committee. Mullin is currently an associate professor of management at Central. He has 23 years of management experience in the private sector prior to his Ph.D. in 1987. Working with his dean, Paul Shaffer, he served as principal investigator of the Assessment-As-Learning Research Project, 1988-1990.

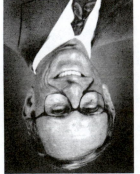

George Wilson was one of four faculty to first represent his college at Alverno's five-day workshop on Assessment-As-Learning. He is professor of economics and assistant to the dean, College of Business and Economics. Wilson has served as chair of his department and as president of the University Faculty Senate. He is respected as an economist and as a wise counsel throughout the Central campus. He is currently serving his college as coordinator of the AACSB accreditation self study.

Mike Grelle is co-director of the CPI/ FIPSE project. He also has served six years on Central's Assessment Committee (two as chair), in addition to chairing his college and department's assessment committee. Grelle, working with Mullin and Shaffer, was an investigator of the Assessment-As-Learning Research Project, 1988-1990. Grelle, a professor of psychology, has won numerous teaching awards and is considered by students and faculty to be one of the best teachers at Central.

Index

ORDER FORM

Continuous Quality Improvement

Name _____

Mailing Address _____

City _____ State _____ ZIP _____

No. copies of CQI book _____ x $22.95 = $ _____

Add $3.00 per copy* for postage $ _____

Missouri residents add 5.725% sales tax $ _____

Total enclosed $ _____

Make check or money order payable to **Prescott Publishing** and mail along with this form to:

Prescott Publishing Co.
P.O. Box 713
Maryville, MO 64468

☐ Please charge my MasterCard / VISA account

Card # _____

Expiration Date _____

Credit card holders may order toll-free by calling 1-800-528-5197

*Additional copies to same shipping address are $1.00 each.